Embodied Modernities

Embodied Modernities
Corporeality, Representation, and Chinese Cultures

Edited by
Fran Martin and Larissa Heinrich

University of Hawai'i Press
Honolulu

© 2006 University of Hawaiʻi Press
All rights reserved
Printed in the United States of America
11 10 09 08 07 06   6 5 4 3 2 1

Library of Congress Cataloging-in-Publication Data
Embodied modernities : corporeality, representation, and Chinese cultures / edited by Fran Martin and Larissa Heinrich.
p. cm.
Includes bibliographical references and index.
ISBN-13: 978-0-8248-2963-6 (hardcover : alk. paper)
ISBN-10: 0-8248-2963-8 (hardcover : alk. paper)
1. Body, Human—Social aspects—China. 2. Body, Human—Social aspects—Asia. 3. Sex role—China. 4. Sex role—Asia. 5. Body, Human, in popular culture. 6. Body, Human, in motion pictures. 7. China—Social life and customs. 8. Asia—Social life and customs. I. Martin, Fran, 1971- II. Heinrich, Larissa.
GT497.C6E43 2006
306.4—dc22
2006000828

University of Hawaiʻi Press books are printed on acid-free paper and meet the guidelines for permanence and durability of the Council on Library Resources.

Designed by University of Hawaiʻi Press production staff
Printed by The Maple-Vail Book Manufacturing Group

Contents

vii   *Notes and Acknowledgments*

I. Thresholds of Modernity

CHAPTER 1 / Larissa Heinrich and Fran Martin
3   Introduction to Part I

CHAPTER 2 / Angela Zito
21   Bound to Be Represented: Theorizing/Fetishizing Footbinding

CHAPTER 3 / Cuncun Wu and Mark Stevenson
42   Male Love Lost: The Fate of Male Same-Sex Prostitution in Beijing in the Late Nineteenth and Early Twentieth Centuries

CHAPTER 4 / Maram Epstein
60   Rewriting Sexual Ideals in *Yesou puyan*

CHAPTER 5 / John Zou
79   Cross-Dressed Nation: Mei Lanfang and the Clothing of Modern Chinese Men

CHAPTER 6 / Tze-lan D. Sang
98   The Transgender Body in Wang Dulu's *Crouching Tiger, Hidden Dragon*

II. Contemporary Embodiments

CHAPTER 7 / Larissa Heinrich and Fran Martin
115   Introduction to Part II

POST-MAO PEOPLE'S REPUBLIC OF CHINA

CHAPTER 8 / Larissa Heinrich
126   Souvenirs of the Organ Trade: The Diasporic Body in Contemporary Chinese Literature and Art

CHAPTER 9 / Louise Edwards
146 Sport, Fashion, and Beauty: New Incarnations of the Female Politician in Contemporary China

CHAPTER 10 / Jami Proctor-Xu
162 Sites of Transformation: The Body and Ruins in Zhang Yang's *Shower*

CONTEMPORARY TAIWAN

CHAPTER 11 / Fran Martin
177 Stigmatic Bodies: The Corporeal Qiu Miaojin

CHAPTER 12 / Teri Silvio
195 Informationalized Affect: The Body in Taiwanese Digital Video Puppetry and COSplay

TRANSNATIONAL INCORPORATIONS IN HONG KONG CINEMA

CHAPTER 13 / Chris Berry
218 Stellar Transit: Bruce Lee's Body or Chinese Masculinity in a Transnational Frame

CHAPTER 14 / Olivia Khoo
235 Love in Ruins: Spectral Bodies in Wong Kar-wai's *In the Mood for Love*

253 *Bibliography*
277 *Filmography*
279 *Contributors*
283 *Index*

Notes and Acknowledgments

THIS BOOK USES the Hanyu Pinyin system of romanization for Mandarin Chinese words, names, and phrases—except in cases where a different conventional or preferred spelling exists, as is often the case in Taiwan with personal names, place names, and other proper names.

All English translations from Chinese material are by chapter authors unless otherwise specified.

Special thanks to Sabdha Charlton and Maya Kriem, who compiled the aggregate bibliography, and to Alison Huber, who compiled the index. Thanks, too, to Pamela Kelley at the University of Hawai'i Press for her unflagging support throughout the lengthy process of this book's production.

PART I
Thresholds of Modernity

CHAPTER 1

Introduction to Part I

LARISSA HEINRICH and FRAN MARTIN

WHILE PREPARING THIS anthology we were struck by an item of entertainment news that seemed aptly to encapsulate some of the cultural and intellectual coincidences that inspired the present volume: the phenomenon of film director Ang Lee dressing up as the Incredible Hulk during production of his movie *Hulk*. Shortly after the film was released in 2002, an interview with the prolific director revealed that partway through production, Lee grew concerned about the characterization of the title character, which was to be almost fully computer animated rather than played by a body-builder as it had been in the earlier television series called "The Incredible Hulk." The cutting-edge techniques used to animate the enormous green muscle-bound figure of the Hulk called for the use of a motion-sensor suit—a sort of full-body prosthetic that translates the wearer's movements into digital data that animators can then transform into animated graphics. But the director worried that the animators might be unaccustomed to animating human body forms, commenting that they still needed "some realistic reference to begin with. Then there's attitude, too, the body performance, the body language."[1] Frustrated when an actor proved inadequate to the task, Lee—who trained as an actor prior to commencing his directing career—decided to don the motion-sensor suit himself. Lee wore the cumbersome suit for six to eight hours a day over a period of nine months, working tirelessly to create a physical performance and body language that would satisfy his exacting vision of the creature's characterization.

Lee's donning of the motion-sensor suit could not have happened at any other historical juncture; it marks a paradigmatically early-twenty-first century moment. Not only was the technology new, but it enabled the performance of a notably late-modern model of identity and the body. Lee framed his desire to wear the suit by appealing to the idea of an authentic corporeal humanity: He hoped that inserting his own flesh-and-blood frame into the prosthetic suit would lend an aura of reality to the digital code representing the Hulk on screen. But paradoxically, Lee's effort underscores the highly syncretic, volatile character of bodies and identities today. As a diasporic Taiwanese-born director—hailed as a "national treasure" by Taiwan's government for winning glory in the international arena—Lee-as-Hulk performs a kind of national and ethnic cross-dressing by creating a body-language for an archetype of white Americana.[2]

The hypermasculine muscularity of the Hulk marks this as a highly gendered national and ethnic identity. Further, the character is encumbered by numerous cultural references: for example, the myth of Hercules and the Freudian themes that self-consciously inform Lee's direction of the plot—the relationship between Bruce Banner and his father in Lee's film is fraught, and Lee admits to using the film to explore his relationship with his own father.[3] The muscularity of the title character even carries specific historical and cultural resonances when we consider the Taiwanese body activating it. One might recall, for instance, that the Greco-European concept of musculature itself was largely without cognate in Chinese anatomical learning before the nineteenth century.[4] Equally, as the 2008 Olympics draw near and propaganda about China's desire to demonstrate its strength on the international stage intensifies, we might reflect on the long and uncomfortable history of racist western representations of China as the (weak and effeminate) "sick man of Asia." Called upon to secure a core of human authenticity at the heart of the digital Hulk, Lee's body in fact tends to undermine, rather than bolster, one's faith in the organic body as guarantor of authentic humanity or cultural identity. A Taiwanese director inhabits the digital spectacle of hypermuscular Americanism for a global film audience—the national, ethnic, and ontological status of the resultant body-image on screen is uniquely difficult to determine, but in spite of Lee's hopes it does little to restore belief in the human body as guarantor of unproblematic realness and presence. Hidden beneath layers of hi-tech costume and digital code, Ang Lee was, in short, performing "Hulk drag."

As we prepared this manuscript, Lee's Hulk drag struck us as highly suggestive in at least two ways. First, with its melding of muscle with machine and digital monster image with solid human flesh, the incident raises questions about both the conceptualization and the representation of human bodies in the hypertechnological, hypermediated world of late modernity. Second, the multiple national and ethnic crossings enacted in the Taiwan-born director's performance of the American pop-culture myth for a global audience raises questions about the increasingly complex, mobile, and multiple meanings of "Chineseness" in light of intensifying cultural globalization. These two sets of complexly interrelated questions concerning contemporary body representations and modern "Chineseness" provide the impetus behind this book's project.

Embodied Modernities, then, presents a critical treatment of corporeality and representation in Chinese contexts in the light of recent transformations in culture, technology, and body scholarship. Collectively, the essays gathered here offer a wide-ranging exploration of what embodiment means in the context of increasingly fractal understandings of Chinese identity. The central focus of the essays is body representation, as distinct from—though in some cases also incorporating—ethnographic accounts of lived body cultures. We have chosen to focus on body representations not because we think that material experiences of embodiment are reducible to textuality, but because, as the extant social sciences research on lived body cultures in modern China attests, ethnographies of quotidian bodily practices are clearly crucial to approaching a full understanding of what bodies mean in Chinese contexts. However, rather than conceiving of body representations and body practices as two discrete realms, we assume that to a large degree, publicly available representations of bodies shape lived experiences of bodies. Hence, as the chapters that follow demonstrate, by examining such representations in modern Chinese public cultures—be they popular fiction, film, print journalism, contemporary art, or digital video serials—we are able to view the structures of body knowledge that, to a large extent, *produce* the very bodies that modern social subjects experience in everyday life.

In recent years, scholarship on embodiment, Chinese identity, and modernity has undergone a series of radical shifts, leading to new and complex understandings of each term, as we discuss in detail below. The thirteen essays collected here bring these questions into suggestive proximity. Facilitating new dialogues between the history of science, modern literary studies, diaspora studies, cultural anthropology, and contemporary Chinese film and popular cultural studies, the volume directs critical attention to the question of the body between the late nineteenth and early twenty-first centuries across the People's Republic of China, Taiwan, Hong Kong, and Chinese diasporic cultures worldwide.

Studies on Pre-1949 Chinese Body Cultures

One might say that there are as many ways to approach the study of the body as there are disciplines: What constitutes "body studies" spans anthropology, art history, religion, philosophy, literary studies, and other disciplines across the humanities and social sciences. Body studies that focus on China span an equally broad spectrum.[5] A foundational discipline that offers early examples of these prior to 1949 is the history of Chinese science, and its subset medicine, epitomized in the scholarly legacy of Joseph Needham's encyclopedic research on science and technology in China. Now-classic studies by medical historians like Paul Unschuld, Manfred Porkert, and Nathan Sivin all provide comprehensive philological explorations of Chinese medical approaches to explaining the body and its systems from the perspective of medical history, while tackling the challenging problem of how to translate central ideas and terminology between the Chinese and western Hippocratic approaches. How to explain descriptors for the body within a system that did not prioritize dissection-based anatomical learning? How to translate and explain Chinese body-related terms such as *qi, xue,* and *xin* that have no practical cognate in modern western medical and anatomical traditions?[6] In looking for the material body and its textual traces, these works introduce key Chinese medical understandings of the body in the premodern period.

Scholarship on Chinese medical history and the history of science post-Foucault, meanwhile, has advanced the idea that corporeality, including the expression of disease, is shaped in a fundamental sense by cultural practice. Charlotte Furth's work on childbirth, "the growing body," and blood in Chinese medicine, as well as her more recent monograph, *A Flourishing Yin,* approach Chinese expressions of corporeality as the product of traditional understandings of the body and health in medical, philosophical, and folk traditions.[7] Yi-Li Wu's work on classical Chinese gynecology, as well as her research into translations of Western-style gynecological anatomy in the late nineteenth century, likewise evaluates Chinese medicine and medical understandings of the body not according to how they measure against western models, but on their own terms.[8] Taking us up to the late Qing and Republican periods, Hiroko Sakamoto traces important connections between social constructions of nationalism and conceptualizations of the human body in the opening decades of the twentieth century, while relatedly, Ruth Rogaski's new study, *Hygienic Modernity,* shows how concepts of "hygiene" *(weisheng)* introduced in this period and associated with "modernity" entailed not only ideas about human bodies but also ideas about race, scientific knowledge, and national sovereignty.[9] Finally, in *The Expressiveness of the Body and the Divergence of Greek and Chinese Medicine,* Shigehisa Kuriyama compares and contrasts key conceptual lineages in western and Chinese anatomical traditions, treating them as equals and focusing not on questions of translation or "lack" of certain conventions or practices from one or the other tradition so much as a practical understanding of the distinctive ways in which these two systems conceived of and accounted for the workings of the human body.

Besides explorations of medical understandings of the body in premodern and pre-Communist China, key studies that situate understandings of the body within broader religious, philosophical, and ideological discourses also form an important background to this book. Two exemplary models of this are

Kristof Schipper's *The Taoist Body*, and Catherine Despeux's *Taoïsme et corps humain*, which analyze understandings of corporeality in classical religious and philosophical tracts, exploring understandings of the body as a microcosm not of scientific principles but of Taoist philosophy. Though not focused exclusively on the body *per se*, Patricia Berger's *Empire of Emptiness*, on Buddhist art and political authority in the Qing, and Richard Vinograd's *Boundaries of the Self* follow a comparable method in outlining the connections between Buddhist and other religious belief systems and images of the human body in Qing dynasty China. Along similar lines, Mark Elvin's "Tales of *Shen* and *Xin*" has become something of a touchstone in the field of Chinese body studies for the model it proposes of a distinctively Chinese conceptualization of subject ("heart-mind," *xin*) and body ("body-self," *shen*) persisting from dynastic through Maoist times. Angela Zito's study of Grand Sacrifice, *Of Body and Brush*, meanwhile, reveals complex relations between ritual *(li)*, the representation of the Emperor's body, and the production of subjectivity. All of these examples move decidedly away from the idea of regarding "the Chinese body" as a universally decodable object toward understanding the body as a changeable construct subject to the contingencies of culture and history.

Perhaps the most significant point of departure for this volume, though, is Angela Zito and Tani Barlow's 1994 edited collection, *Body, Subject, and Power in China*, which crystallizes very concretely many of the methodological developments in contemporary Chinese body scholarship discussed above. Zito and Barlow's volume engages with what were then newly emerging topics in Chinese body scholarship, including the nature versus culture paradigm, differential cultural constructions of bodies, and the gendering of bodies as a social process. The volume's individual chapters reflect in a direct way the initial impact of post-structuralist critical theories on Chinese body studies.[10] They are marked by their collective approach to bodies not as transparent, stable objects of analysis, but rather as variable knowledge formations constructed through historically specific regimes of discourse and social discipline.[11] It is in this sense that *Body, Subject, and Power* provides the methodological point of departure for the present volume.

Tani Barlow's essay in that volume, "Theorizing Woman: *Funü, Guojia, Jiating*," models especially clearly the broad conceptual framework and the historicist methodology that we have presumed as central in preparing this volume. Adopting a groundbreaking approach, Barlow's essay traced a Foucauldian-style genealogy of Chinese concepts of femininity between the late imperial and the Maoist eras through attention to the three historically specific sociolinguistic categories. These are the kin-inflected *funü* (kinswoman) of the Qing, the modern, western-inflected *nüxing* (woman) of the

Republican period, and finally the collectivist *funü* (socialist woman) of China under Mao, which is instantiated most directly in the discourse of the state-run All-China Women's Federation. Provocatively, Barlow argued that since social subjectivity is staged within language, and since available categories for understanding gender vary historically, one cannot appeal to "Chinese women" as a transhistorical presence, but can only attend to the different ways in which femininity has been constructed in distinct historical periods. Thus, for example, it would be nonsensical to speak of "Chinese women" *per se* in the premodern period, when no overarching category of "women" existed, and female subject-positions were defined solely as kin-positions (mother, daughter, wife) within the patrilinear family. Similarly, the modern mainland Chinese term *funü* relates less to the premodern representations of femininity in China than to other categories installed as part of socialist modernization — categories like "worker" *(gongren),* "youth" *(qingnian)* and "proletariat" *(wuchanjieji).*[12] This Foucauldian approach to categories of social subjecthood has profoundly influenced much recent work in studies of Chinese corporeality and centrally informs the project of this book. Along with Barlow, Sang, and other contemporary scholars of gender and sexuality in modern Chinese contexts, we assume from the outset that modern categories of personhood are just that — *modern.*[13] Categories like woman *(nüxing/nüren),* man *(nanxing/nanren),* homosexual *(tongxing'ai/tongxinglian)* and heterosexual *(yixing'ai/yixinglian)* trace their genesis back to the indigenization of Japanese and western sexology and gender concepts during the Republican period and constitute distinctively *new* ways of conceptualizing bodies, selves, desires, and kinship. As the chapters in Part I by Wu and Stevenson, Sang, and Epstein in particular demonstrate — once again following Foucault — it is imperative to distinguish conceptually between modern-style individual sexual and gender *identities* and premodern regimes of gendered, kinship, and sexual *behavior.*[14] Thus, the focus of many of our chapters on representations of gendered and sexual bodies is not intended to provide an account, for example, of something like "women's/homosexual/transgendered bodies throughout Chinese history." Rather, this focus bespeaks our interest in exploring the historically variable ways in which gendered and sexual bodies have come to *mean* over the past one hundred and twenty years, across diverse Chinese societies.

If *Body, Subject, and Power in China* reflected the initial impact of contemporary critical theory on Chinese body scholarship, then taken as a whole, this volume demonstrates the further development of post-structuralist methodologies in this field. Thematically, unlike Zito and Barlow's volume, it focuses solely on the modern period, defined loosely around the twentieth century — indeed, as we discuss below, the idea of Chinese modernities is a guiding rubric for the book as a whole. As well as bringing together new work on representations of embodiment in late-nineteenth-century and Republican-era "thresholds of modernity," the collection also brings into focus recent developments in late-modern Chinese body representation over the decade since *Body, Subject*'s publication. From the premodern bodies of the *xianggong* catamite and the hypermasculine hero of the popular novel *Yesou puyan* through to the globally mobile, late-modern star bodies of Bruce Lee and Maggie Cheung and the violently fragmented bodies of contemporary mainland Chinese experimental art, the bodies discussed in this volume are approached as the effects of historically specific regimes of representation and power. From the perspective of the late-modern moment at which this volume has been written, modern Chinese bodies seem anything but self-explanatory and historically constant; instead, they appear to be the unpredictable effects of radically contingent, ceaselessly transforming constellations of cultural knowledge and practice.

Republican Culture as an Alternative Modernity

If a primary aim of this book is to rethink Chinese body politics in the light of recent developments in both body scholarship and body cultures, this general project is focused more finely through attention to the idea of Chinese modernities, especially in light of recent scholarship on alternative modernities. In this sense, the book's project is twofold: It seeks both to rethink Chinese bodies by approaching them as an aspect of Chinese modernities and to offer a fresh view of those sets of experience through the lens of changing representations of bodies. The point of reference for our approach to Chinese modernities is an influential strand of scholarship on non-western modernities that has emerged from studies of postcolonial societies and cultures and globalization over the past ten years. Writing variously on "alternative," "other" or "hybrid" modernities, scholars including Arjun Appadurai, Aihwa Ong, Lisa Rofel, Dilip Parameshwar Gaonkar, and Lydia Liu have contributed to a fundamental reorientation of the very notion.[15] Collectively, this work demonstrates that modernity, a state of culture once presumed to be both inherently western (based on the European Enlightenment values of humanism, scientific rationality, and social progress) and potentially universal, is in practice "not one but many," not (only) western but also manifest in distinct syncretic formations across the diverse non-western sites of colonial and postcolonial encounters.[16] Such an approach leads away from the once-assumed opposition between a modern west and a non- or premodern non-west, and toward renewed attempts, in Ong's words, "to consider how non-western societies themselves make modernities after their own fashion, in the remaking of rationality, capitalism and the nation in ways that borrow from but also transform western universalizing forms."[17] To Ong's list of the elements of western modernity that emerge, re-made, from these local sites, we would add the modern body. Like rationality, capitalism, and the nation, this body in its Chinese incarnations is also a product of modern times; its modernity is mapped in a newly acquired scientific tracery of nerves, blood vessels, and musculature as much as in its novel metaphoric potential to signify at different times both universal humanity and the painful emergence of a modern Chinese nation.[18] Indeed, in a strong sense the body, understood as a series of constantly transforming concepts and practices in cultural and historical context, can be interpreted as symptomatic of Chinese modernities.

Over recent years, the cultural history of Chinese modernity in the Republican period, between the founding of the Republic of China in 1911 and the Communist revolution and founding of the People's Republic of China in 1949, has become the focus of a rapidly expanding field of inquiry. As Wen-hsin Yeh observes, this trend can be attributed both to the relatively recent access researchers have gained to archives housing materials pertaining to this period in the People's Republic, and to a broad shift in scholarship toward a focus on the micro-level of everyday cultural practice rather than the top-down effects of large-scale institutional structures.[19] Shu-mei Shih identifies a further reason why the Republican period may have attracted such intense interest.[20] Shih highlights the cultural and historical parallels between the 1920s–1930s and the 1980s–1990s by pointing out mainland Chinese intellectuals' engagement and subsequent re-engagement with western modernity and modernism, first in the context of China's semi-colonization by European and Japanese powers, and half a century later in the context of post-Mao cultural internationalization. In this account, a hybrid formation of Chinese modernity emerged in the Republican period from China's ambivalent engagement with modern metropolitan Western and Japanese cultures, interrupted, as it were, by Communist nationalism between 1949 and 1979. This pattern would reassemble in a new but related form in the China of the "New Era."[21]

Following from our interest in probing further historical questions raised by Shih and others about the unpredictable cultural continuities and discontinuities between these two key moments of contemporary Chinese history, the essays included here fall into two sections, the first addressing the Republican period and the second the contemporary.[22] Many of the chapters in the first part of this book (especially Zito, Wu and Stevenson, and Epstein) are interested in how Republican Chinese body representations reveal current excitements and anxieties about China's cultural engagement with the west, a theme of transnational cultural flow and the hybrid character of Chinese modernities that returns strongly in almost all of the essays in the book's second section.²³ By sketching out these broad cultural linkages, *Embodied Modernities* aims to contribute to the growing body of work exploring the genealogy of present-day Chinese experience.²⁴

While Shih's book on Chinese literary modernism, *The Lure of the Modern*, proposes the city and the nation as the two critical thematic foci for discussions of Chinese modernity and modernism, we propose that consideration of body representations offers an equally illuminating rubric through which to approach Chinese modernities. First, since the body is experientially central to individual, quotidian experiences of modernity, representations of the body across a wide range of texts reveal a series of broader themes that are central to the broader cultural experience of modernity. Second, like the city and the nation, the body has been subject to particularly rapid and thorough-going reconceptualizations over the past century, hence changes in how bodies have been represented in this period reveal key cultural transformations that have accompanied the processes of modernization. These include the translation of scientific discourses on anatomy, medicine, gender, and sexuality; the implementation of a Maoist vision of the collective body of Chinese socialism; and the articulation of transforming discourses on the modern Chinese nation and cultural identity allegorized as body representations (for example, the notorious "sick man of Asia" in the early twentieth century, or the spectacularly anticolonial figure of the late-twentieth-century Hong Kong action star, Bruce Lee). In all of these, body representations can be seen not merely as random instances of Chinese cultural production, but as in fact exemplary of some of the central preoccupations of modern Chinese cultures. In other words, between the late nineteenth and the early twenty-first centuries, the cultural modernities of mainland China, Taiwan, Hong Kong, and the Chinese diaspora have to a significant degree been figured in and through representations of human bodies.

A key text in the new wave of Republican Chinese modernity studies is Leo Ou-fan Lee's study of 1930s and 1940s Shanghai.²⁵ As Yeh has observed, a central significance of Lee's study lies in his methodological departure from previous studies on the May Fourth period by focusing on popular commodity culture rather than the elite realm of philosophical discourse—further to this, we might add that Lee's approach also marks a shift from the methodologies of Cold War-era area studies to a focus on cultural history and urban imaginaries, an approach that has more in common with contemporary cultural studies.²⁶ Shifting attention from elite literature and the high culture of Republican Chinese modernism, Lee looks to the everyday culture embodied in commercial graphic art, popular film, fiction, periodicals and pictorial journals, fashion, and the popular imaginary to construct his account of the Republican "Shanghai modern."[27] This volume echoes Lee's move away from the presumption that elite intellectual culture provides the key to understanding modern Chinese complexities.[28] The authors of the chapters in Part I discuss popular fiction and theater, and the focus on popular cultural forms and popular responses to other cultural forms continues through Part II. Looking to martial arts fiction rather than May Fourth classics, or to the cross-dressing of popular entertainer Mei Lanfang rather than the agonized national body inscribed by Lu Xun produces a very distinct view of the experiences and meanings of Chinese modernities—a view we think is more broadly representative because it engages seriously with mass-cultural forms and popular readings.

If one of the aims of this volume is to contribute to the study of modern popular cultural forms and experiences that have frequently been sidelined by the scholarly privileging of elite culture, this attention is also echoed in other aspects of the volume's thematics. We proposed above that Chinese modernities are already, by definition, "other" to the presumptive centrality and universality of Euro-American modernity. What interest us more specifically in this volume are the margins of that margin: works and experiences that have been considered peripheral to the mainstream of modern Chinese cultures. The volume addresses these margins in two major ways. First, many of the chapters focus on representations and experiences of "othered" bodies and subjects, especially gender nonnormative persons (female masculinities and male femininities), women, and youth cultures. Second, many of the chapters in Part II take up a geocultural focus on areas other than the Chinese mainland—Taiwan, Hong Kong, and the worldwide Chinese diaspora. These areas have sometimes been considered the geocultural peripheries of a China whose presumptive focus tends to fall on the mainland (this question is discussed further below and in the Introduction to Part II). Our desire to focus so strongly on marginalized aspects of modern Chinese cultures is undergirded by the conviction that, in a fundamental sense, centers are always defined by their structuring and dependent relation to their peripheries. According to that logic, Chinese modernity as a grand narrative, whenever and wherever this narrative is appealed to, is necessarily defined as much by its excluded "others"— those subordinated subjects who cannot easily be counted within its scope— as by those forms of culture and subjectivity that it privileges.[29] By turning critical attention to what has often been left out of dominant histories of modern Chinese social life, this volume is particularly interested in nonnormative formations of gender and sexuality (addressed in detail by Wu and Stevenson, Zou, Sang, Martin, and Berry). Given the centrality of gender and sexual ideologies to the dominant modern imaginaries, we feel that analyzing these marginalized formations reveals just as much about the structuring anxieties and suppressed histories of currently dominant gender and sexual regimes as it does about the subjects that these chapters most directly address.[30] Our approach here might be called "peripheralist": It aims to illuminate the contours of dominant gendered and sexual formations through attention to those ways of being that, through the workings of cultural history, have been excluded from serious scholarly consideration.

Arranged in two approximately chronological sections, the chapters in this volume trace a historical trajectory from the initial indigenization of modern European understandings of the body around the turn of the nineteenth century to more recent developments in the ways bodies are understood and represented. The contributors to Part I read traces of that modern body's traffic both in the aspirations of local modernist intellectuals, specifically in public debates over the abolition of footbinding and male prostitution, and in western conceptualizations of disease, gender, and the nation that crop up in Republican-era literary and theatrical cultures. In Part II we encounter late-modern texts that wrestle with the specter of the global organ trade, hotly contested ideologies of gender and sexuality, the violence of urban hyper-development, diasporic cross-cultural encounters, Taiwanese digital video fan practices, and the transnational projections of Hong Kong cinema. As a whole, then, the book demonstrates how changing trends in the public representation of both privileged and marginalized bodies encode many of the broader preoccupations of modern Chinese cultures. Nation-building, sex and gender, health and illness, medical science, state politics, changing cities, and transcultural interactions are seen afresh through attention to the multiform modern and late-modern body-texts in which these concepts and processes leave their traces. This focus on changing representations of bodies thus presents an alternative, and, we feel, a productive way of approaching Chinese modernities.

Dispersing Chineseness

As observed above, this volume thinks through the margins of Chinese modernities by focusing on what were once considered the geopolitical peripheries of "Chineseness." The book includes work on all four of the areas that make up what has been variously referred to as "greater China" and "transnational China" — the People's Republic of China on the mainland, Taiwan, Hong Kong, and the worldwide Chinese diaspora.[31] But our intention in including chapters on all of these areas is emphatically not to imply that all of them can be unproblematically subsumed within a greater whole called "China," nor that these disparate areas are culturally united through some shared cultural essence. In distinction to Tu Wei-ming's famous defense of the diasporic periphery as the emergent center of a reconfigured and organic "cultural China," this collection suggests precisely a *dispersion* of China and Chineseness in the contemporary world, such that no transparent, unitary, or final meaning can be attached to those terms.[32] Rather than the irresistible centripetal force that "China" is often presumed to exert—not least in the aggressive political centrism and territorial expansionism of the People's Republic today—the idea of Chineseness that emerges from this collection is instead a centrifugal one, underscoring its actual fragmentation, both geocultural and conceptual.[33] In this, our approach is aligned with those of other scholars engaged in mapping the shifting, plural, and internally discontinuous meanings of Chinese identity today.[34] There do exist, of course, certain historical threads linking the discrepant modernities of the People's Republic of China, Taiwan, Hong Kong, and Chinese diasporic cultures. Indeed, as we outline below, a central project in several of the essays collected here is to track the strands of influence linking body representations at distinct historical moments and geographic sites that remain, in Xiaobing Tang's phrase, "absorbed in the same maelstrom of [Chinese] modernity."[35] However, equally as important as these historical linkages are the countless ways in which the sites analyzed differ from each other. The examples discussed in the chapters of this book do not add up to any complete or sum entity that one might designate "the modern Chinese body." Rather, they reveal the impossibility of reaching such a neat conclusion, foregrounding instead the multiplicity and heterogeneity of modern Chinese body representations. Given all this, a note on our use of the term "Chinese" is in order. In the pages that follow, this adjective is not used to imply an equation of all of the different nouns it qualifies. More simply, it is used to designate texts and practices that are either written, performed, or experienced in a Chinese language, or have primary investments in exploring the multiple significances and effects of the idea of "Chineseness" in the modern period.[36]

The Essays: Part I

The essays collected in the first part of this volume, "Thresholds of Modernity," share a common concern with mapping the chaotic transition between premodern and modern regimes of subjecthood and corporeality. The section title draws from Angela Zito's discussion of the negative representation of footbinding in the late nineteenth century, which, she proposes, positions its abolition as a symbolic threshold marking modernity's nether limit. As the section title implies, all these essays focus on body cultures in the late nineteenth and early twentieth centuries, not only for the intrinsic historical interest of the primary material, but for the new light this analysis sheds on emergent regimes of body knowledge that would remain influential throughout the modern era. Framing representations of footbinding as the ground for a series of cultural encounters—both discursive and actual—between China and the west, Zito's essay compares discussions of footbinding at three distinct historical and cultural moments. These are the anti-footbinding discourse of late-nineteenth-century missionary women in China, critiques of footbinding by western radical feminists in the late twentieth century, and discussions of Chinese women's bodies in present-day international and postcolonial feminisms. Zito traces a common thread linking all of these seemingly unrelated critiques: the tendency for each to press "footbinding" into service in a strictly *fetishistic* way. That is, Zito proposes that for the past one hundred and twenty years, the reified image of the Chinese woman's bound foot has consistently enabled cultural critics to displace onto a convenient "other" contradictions and anxieties that more properly pertain to the immediate cultural and historical contexts of the critics themselves.

Zito's essay deploys a cross-historical methodology that is taken up elsewhere in this book. Rather than proposing a direct causal relation between the distinct moments under discussion, this approach sketches a more indirect historical logic. Sharing something in common with Foucauldian genealogy, it is a way of writing "histories of the present."[37] This methodology is also employed in the chapters by Heinrich (contrasting Lu Xun's turn-of-the-century anatomical imaginary with body representations in contemporary Chinese art and literature), Martin (juxtaposing Taiwanese lesbian author Qiu Miaojin's late-1980s writing with Yu Dafu's 1932 description of a monstrous female homosexual), and Berry (who finds in Bruce Lee's star body a transfiguration of the classical *wu* ideal of martial masculinity). This approach should be carefully distinguished from a transhistorical approach, which would disregard historical specificity to propose that cultural phenomena persist, unchanging, through time eternal. In contrast, the cross-historical approach emphasizes change as much as linkages. It appeals to the past heuristically and interestedly, as a means of shedding light on particular aspects of the present.

Dealing, like Zito, with the transition between imperial conceptualizations of corporeality and modern body regimes, Wu and Stevenson's essay investigates the shifting meanings of the low-class, effeminate, rigorously cultivated catamite body of the feminine-role *(dan)* actor in Beijing opera—known socially as the *xianggong*—in the opening decades of the twentieth century. The authors argue that with China's cultural modernization, the once-common figure of the *xianggong* was effectively erased from history; it was omitted from both the emergent sexological discourse of homosexuality as *tongxing'ai,* and from new official histories of Chinese national theater. In discussing the decline of the *xianggong*, Wu and Stevenson touch on a theme common to several of the essays in the first part of the volume: the response of Republican Chinese intellectuals to the crisis of the semi-colonial Chinese nation and the attendant vexing issue of national modernization framed as westernization. In this context, the authors argue that cultural panic over male prostitution in Republican Beijing led to the disappearance of the *xianggong*'s social role, and it was sparked not by any direct intervention by western powers, but instead by a new sensitivity on the part of Chinese intellectuals and officials to a perceived western gaze. This represents an important complication of the influential proposal that sexual modernization in China equates straightforwardly to sexual westernization and the consequent suppression of an indigenous premodern Chinese "tolerance" for sex between men.[38] Instead of a clear-cut opposition between western sexual modernity and Chinese sexual tradition, Wu and Stevenson argue that the suppression of the *xianggong* role in early twentieth-century Beijing entails a more complex scenario. They contend that as part of the nation-building project, Chinese intellectuals sought to transform local body cultures in a self-policing response to the perception of a censorious—yet in large part *imagined*—western gaze. Such a formulation underscores the agency of local intellectuals in shaping modern Chinese body cultures. At the same time it also challenges the notion, implicit in some of the extant scholarship, that sexual modernity in China resulted from ideologies of western sexual-scientific modernity somehow imposing themselves, autonomous and unmediated, upon premodern Chinese subjects.[39]

Maram Epstein's chapter, too, touches on the relation between body representations and the difficult emergence of the modern Chinese nation. Identifying a tendency in the extant scholarship to assume that modern Chinese representations of masculine bodies in crisis are always simply allegories for the crisis of the emergent nation, Epstein argues that this view needs to be tempered by an understanding of the historical roots of the "male marginality complex" in late imperial popular fiction. Engaging with a 1929 redaction of the eighteenth-century novel *Yesou puyan* (A Rustic's Words of Exposure), Epstein finds in the novel's protagonist, Wen Suchen, a wishful resolution of the tension between individual autonomy and the Confucian ritual imperative—a tension that she argues already fractures imperial-era Chinese masculinity well before the crisis of the modern nation. Epstein draws a contrast between the 1929 redaction of *Yesou puyan* and the eighteenth century original, observing that the Republican edition shows a relative wane of emphasis on the question of Chinese–foreign relations and a correspondingly increased interest in masculinity and sexuality. Epstein discerns in the Republican redaction a new association of sex with pleasure rather than reproductive duty, a new anchoring of masculine and feminine genders in sexed bodies, an increased importance of the body to masculine identity, and—resonating with Wu and Stevenson's discussion—a new tendency to frame sexual relations between men as deviant behavior. Epstein thus positions the 1929 redaction of *Yesou puyan* as a kind of barometer of changing conceptualizations of sexed and gendered bodies in China in this period. Her observations are congruent with those made by other contributors to this section, who also find modern, scientific, European ideas of the body blending with older local understandings of social status and ritual role to produce fundamentally syncretic modern understandings of body and self. We might call this messy, incomplete transition from ritual-based understandings of the self-as-social-role to models that incorporate elements of European body-science the *corporealization* of the modern Chinese social subject.

Picking up a thread from Wu and Stevenson, John Zou's essay about the star body of *dan* actor Mei Lanfang also addresses the corporealization of modern Chinese masculinity. He argues that by theatrically foregrounding the incongruity between man's body and woman's clothing, Mei Lanfang's celebrity cross-dressing paradoxically contributes to the emergence of a modern notion of essential maleness, or what Zou calls the notion of the "unclothed and essentially male body." As Zou points out, this emergent gender-essentialism at the level of the body stands in sharp distinction to the imperial encoding of the social and political identity of the masculine subject in and through his clothing. Given Mei's perverse reinforcement of the rising ideology of masculinity as above all a bodily state, Zou provocatively proposes that the cross-dressed yet symbolically unclothed Mei can be understood as an embodiment of Republican Chinese modernity itself.

While several of the earlier chapters underscore Republican-era intellectuals' indigenization of elements of western scientism and the consequent corporealization of the modern Chinese social subject, Tze-lan D. Sang draws attention to the incompleteness of this project by focusing on popular culture in Wang Dulu's serialized martial arts novels of the early 1940s. Sang proposes that the transgender or "intersexual" body of Yu Jiaolong, the hard-fighting hero/ine of Wang's novel *Crouching Tiger, Hidden Dragon*, bespeaks the survival of a late imperial popular taste for representations of female masculinity; this survival contrasts with the heteronormative and essentialist constructions of gendered bodies advocated by a modernizing elite. Sang argues that the literary figure of Yu Jiaolong provokes the reader's desire for a "gender-queer body," making Wang's text more radical, from the viewpoint of contemporary queer and transgender theory, than Ang Lee's 2000 film adaptation, which

Sang suggests actually suppresses Yu Jiaolong's transgender status. Thus although, like Zou, Sang focuses on a popular-culture figure that embodies transgender erotic appeal, her conclusion about Yu Jiaolong's radical potential provides an interesting counterpoint to Zou's proposal that Mei Lanfang's cross-dressing in fact *reinforced* the modern understanding of sex and gender as immanent within bodies. Sang frames Yu Jiaolong's heroic, transgendered body as the trace of an alternative, popular understanding of sex, gender, and bodies that persisted stubbornly alongside, yet counter to, twentieth-century discourses of gender essentialism. As several authors explore in Part II, however, the normative force of gender as a binary, corporeal structure that appeared to gain in strength as the twentieth century progressed would emerge as a key focus for critique by sexual and gendered "others" at century's end.

Notes

1. See Alsetter, "Trailer Park."
2. See for example Kao, "Fame"; Government Information Office, "Republic."
3. See for example Anthony, "The Long and Shirt of it."
4. Kuriyama, *Expressiveness of the Body*.
5. On premodern Chinese body cultures see, for example, Kristofer Schipper's, Jean Lévi's, and Catherine Despeux's studies of the Daoist body in classical texts and religious cultures. Schipper, *Taoist Body*; Lévi, "Body"; and Despeux, *Taoïsme*. In art history, John Hay's explorations of Chinese art and calligraphy demonstrate how western understandings of the body in art—for example traditions of the nude—depended on presuppositions that were not pertinent to the Chinese canon, thereby calling into question a battery of assumptions about the body and representation that western scholars brought with them to their analyses of Chinese art. Hay, "Body Invisible" and "Human Body." In comparative philosophy, Wu Kuang-ming's *On Chinese Body Thinking* proposes a qualitative distinction between western abstract thinking and what Wu styles Chinese "body thinking" in pre-Han Chinese philosophy.
6. See also Sivin, "State, Cosmos, and Body." At the time of this writing, Sivin has also compiled an impressive and ever-expanding web-based archive of general studies of the body: http://ccat.sas.upenn.edu/~nsivin/bib414.html.
7. Furth, "Blood, Body and Gender"; Furth, "Concepts of Pregnancy"; and Furth, "From Birth to Birth."
8. Wu Yi-Li, "Ghost Fetuses, False Pregnancies."
9. Sakamoto, *The Myth of Nationalism*.
10. This conceptual shift in Chinese body studies over the past decade has reflected a broader series of transformations in conceptualizing bodies in humanities scholarship over recent years. One of the most influential areas of work in this regard has been feminist philosophy. With the impact of Foucault's historicizing approach to modern sexuality, as well as post-structuralism's critique of essentialism more generally, feminist philosophers since

the mid-1980s including Donna Haraway, Judith Butler, Elizabeth Grosz, Moira Gatens and many others have mounted a radical critique of naturalist epistemologies of sex, gender, and the body. See, for example, Haraway, "Manifesto for Cyborgs"; Haraway, *Simians;* Haraway, *Modest Witness;* Butler, *Gender Trouble;* Butler, *Bodies That Matter;* Grosz, *Volatile Bodies;* and Gatens, *Imaginary Bodies.* See also Claudia Springer's study on conceptualizing embodiment in the electronic age in *Electronic Eros.*

11. A Foucaldian approach to the construction of the subject through discourse and social discipline is especially evident in the contributions by Anagnost, "Politicized Body"; and Barlow, "Theorizing Woman." For a collection of recent essays on the history of medicine in modern China and Taiwan informed by similarly historicist, constructionist approaches, see Li Shang-jen, ed., *Medicine, Imperialism and Modernity.*

12. Barlow, "Theorizing Woman," 254.

13. Sang, *Emerging,* 275–276.

14. Foucault, *History of Sexuality Volume 1.*

15. See, for example, Appadurai, *Modernity;* Ong, "Anthropology"; Ong, *Flexible Citizenship,* chap. 1; Nonini and Ong, *Ungrounded Empires;* Rofel, *Other Modernities;* and Gaonkar, *Alternative Modernities,* especially Gaonkar, "On Alternative Modernities." See also Lydia Liu's study of the transcultural invention of the modern idea of "China" through the "clash of empires" between the British Empire and the Qing dynasty in the late nineteenth century. Liu, *The Clash of Empires.*

16. Gaonkar, "On Alternative Modernities," 23.

17. Ong, "Anthropology," 64.

18. See the important strand of work theorising the entanglements between gendered bodies and the project of the modern Chinese nation and Chinese modernity itself, especially as represented in Republican era fiction. For example, Liu, "Female Body"; Yue, "Modern Chinese Fiction"; the essays collected in Barlow, *Gender Politics;* and Zito (this volume).

19. Yeh, "Introduction," 1.

20. Shu-mei Shih, *Lure,* vii–xiii, 377.

21. Note David Der-wei Wang's proposal that latterly repressed, indigenous forms of Chinese nonrealist literary modernity were already emerging by the time significant cultural hybridization with European and Japanese forms got underway in the May Fourth period, and that these "repressed modernities" return in the alternative literary modernisms of late-twentieth-century mainland China, Taiwan, Hong Kong, and the Chinese diaspora. Wang, *Splendor.* Contrast also Shu-mei Shih's bracketing-off socialist modernity both with Xiaobing Tang's view of romantic-revolutionary heroism as a *central* aspect of the dialectic of Chinese modernity and with Xiaobin Yang's observation of the Enlightenment-style teleological view of national history that is common to both Republican and Maoist modernities. Note also Yang's observation of the related critiques of such modernist totalism found both in certain examples of May Fourth fiction and again in the "postmodern" avant-garde fiction of the 1980s. Tang, *Chinese Modern;* Yang, *Chinese Postmodern.*

22. Sang's periodization is similar in *Emerging Lesbian;* see note 21 above on Wang's and Yang's linking of early and late-twentieth-century literary modernisms.

23. Chow, *Woman and Chinese Modernity,* 27.

24. Foucault, *Discipline and Punish,* 30–31.

25. Lee, *Shanghai Modern*.

26. Yeh, "Introduction," 5–7; cf. Dirlik and Zhang, "Introduction," 11–15.

27. See also Xiaobing Tang's focus on representations of quotidian culture as central to the dialectic of modernity in *Chinese Modern*.

28. Although Yeh's collection includes Lee's essay "The cultural construction of modernity in urban Shanghai," Yeh still characterizes the subject of *Becoming Chinese* as "middle-class elites" (p. 26); and indeed most of the chapters deal with this class fraction, for example in their collective attention to publishers, advertisers, merchants, entrepreneurs, urban consumers, middle-class urban women's redemptive societies, government and politicians, educators, students, and elite authors and intellectuals.

29. Cf. Anbin Shi, *Comparative Approach*, 1–17.

30. Cf. Rofel, *Other Modernities*, 19–21.

31. Ong, "Anthropology."

32. Tu, "Cultural China."

33. Cf. Hsu's proposal of the centripetal, expansionist, and centrist force of modern transnational Chinese culture in "A Reflection on Marginality."

34. See, for example, Ien Ang, *Not Speaking Chinese;* Chow, "Chineseness"; Chun, "Fuck Chineseness"; Shi, *Comparative Approach;* and Dirlik and Zhang, "Introduction."

35. Tang, *Chinese Modern*, 347.

36. On this point we dissent from Xiaobing Tang's suggestion of a conceptually *unitary* pan-Chinese modernity and modernism based on the Chinese language in *Chinese Modern* (pp. 345–347). Unlike Tang with his dream of an ultimately singular—if also diverse—modern *Zhongwen wenxue* (Chinese literature), the current volume seeks more to pluralize than to unify our understandings of the various Chinese modernities.

37. Foucault, *Discipline and Punish*, 30–31.

38. See, for example, Hinsch, *Passions;* Chou, *Houzhimin tongzhi*.

39. For an excellent critique of this simplistic argument on sexual modernization as passive westernization, see Sang, *Emerging Lesbian*, 99–126.

CHAPTER 2

Bound to Be Represented
Theorizing/Fetishizing Footbinding

ANGELA ZITO

> A specimen of a Chinese foot, the account of which I have the honor to lay before the Royal Society, was removed from the dead body of a female found floating in the river at Canton.... Without entering into an inquiry whether this curious dissection and, as we should esteem it, hideous deformity, of the Chinese female foot, had its origin in Oriental jealousy, or was the result of an unnatural taste in beauty, I shall content myself with describing the remarkable deviations from original structure it everywhere represents.
> —B. B. Cooper, letter of March 5, 1829

"The Body in Pieces"

As Dr. Cooper, surgeon at St. Guy's Hospital, London, isolates the bound foot, he presents us with a fine example of the medicalized excision of the body into its parts.[1] And just as this fragment of the bound-foot body was cut off from physical integration, Cooper likewise disconnects the body itself from its social life-world. His only references to that life-world are "Oriental jealousy" and "unnatural taste."[2]

Fifty years later, Mary Porter Gamewell, an American missionary in China from 1871–1906, founded one of the first girls' schools that refused admission to the footbound. She faced great opposition from her own community, who thought the custom so entrenched that she would fail and that to concede after the point would be regarded everywhere as a surrender of Christian conscience to heathen principle; and that would be to wound the body of Christ in a vital part.[3]

What part, we might ask? Its heart? Its head? Its feet? In this case, the Christian critics reduce to "heathen principle" the social milieu that produced footbinding as an index of feminine value and direct our attention, willy-nilly, to another body-in-parts, that of the Christ.

FIGURE 2.1. Henry Fuseli, *Artist Overwhelmed by the Grandeur of Antique Ruins* (1778–1779), © 2003 Kunsthaus Zürich. All rights reserved. Used with permission.

What links these two examples of nineteenth-century treatments of footbinding? Both easily reduce and dismiss living context, while the body itself appears in pieces. To better understand this rhetoric, we turn to a third example of footly fragmentation: the famous drawing by Henry Fuseli, *Artist Overwhelmed by the Grandeur of Antique Ruins* (1778–1779, Fig. 2.1). Art historian Linda Nochlin has brilliantly analyzed the painting of a distraught artist draped over a gigantic stone sculptured foot, calling it emblematic of "the fragment as a metaphor for modernity." The artist is

> by comparison with the fragmented grandeur of the past, lacking. His little feet, almost feminine in their daintiness, seem hardly capable of bearing his weight. The artist is not merely overwhelmed but is in mourning, mourning a terrible loss, a state of felicity and totality which must now be inevitably displaced into the past or the future: nostalgia or utopia are the alternatives offered.[4]

Fuseli's fragment of the stone foot signals nostalgia. Nochlin describes how, ten years later, that trope was drastically changed by the French Revolution, the "transformative event that ushered in the modern period, which constituted the fragment as a positive rather than a negative trope."[5] Here Nochlin alludes to modernity's endless appetite for the new, as it actually or imaginatively destroys the old. After all, a revolution celebrates ruin; taking things apart is its modus operandi.

The early and ongoing fascination of westerners for the fragment of the bound foot, its fetishization, is thus a positively modern phenomenon. That fetishization occurs in a scene of progressive modern dis-integration of the body. Yet is the body not, for sensory creatures, the very primordium that undergirds experience? Both imputations of primordial Utopian plenitude and its modern fragmentation are grounded in scientific ideas of the body's materiality as simply another aspect of Nature. Dr. Cooper's last statement becomes a pun: the "remarkable deviations from original structure it *everywhere* represents" points not only to a foot damaged "everywhere," as in "completely destroyed," but one understood as such "everywhere" around the world because all people share the "original structure." This body of biology provides an ever-firmer basis for community, with everybody's Other body, the "rock bottom of universality, the hard core of nature, the backdrop of any history."[6] Yet are issues of intercultural corporeality so easily handled? How can the same terrain that grounds our principled sameness also provide ground for specific ethnic identity? And what about that pesky purveyor of difference, Nature's Other, "Culture"?

For the past twenty years, scholars in the human sciences have been meticulously excavating and animating a sense of embodied life from the "bedrock" of nature into which it had been sunk. To be sure one can study the body as an object. But human beings do not live their lives only as objects. They live distanced from that "nature" by various frames and codes. People experience the world through their bodies in social practice: diet, sex and gender mores, the physical environment, both built and nonbuilt, rhythms of household life and intimate relationships, communal ritual, work, art. Here we find human life organized, often at psychic and social remove, through embodied subjectification.[7] In short, people become simultaneously objects and subjects, and embodied practices allow us to glimpse that elusive process. Yet the project of accounting for totality continues to elude us, for totalities can never be thoroughly and finally analyzed, but only engaged repeatedly in history as various ideological projects that motivate us as theorists. Footbinding in China provides an excellent example of "embodied subjectification." Young girls were slowly "invited" to take up the subject position (to act and speak in the role) of sexually mature women through the painful process of deforming their feet in binding cloths. Their embodied subjectification has been approached by numerous critics, whose theories for how it could be ended provide a fascinating array of "ideologically motivated projects."

Footbinding has remained such a powerful marker for the Otherness of nonmodern Chinese bodily practice that its *actual demise* has produced retrospectively one threshold for modernity itself in China.[8] Here I will attempt to theorize this "marker" and its meaning for us today as various moments of its "fetishization." The essay thus deals less with the social production of the bound foot in China itself (for that, see essays by Blake, Turner, and Ko) and more with accounting closely for the manner in which we have received news of it, and with how it continues to engage us as empowered, theorizing subjects.[9] I am drawing explicit attention to *theories that are particularly modern*—similarities between the productive preoccupations of colonialist missionaries and merchants with the Chinese bound foot, the postcolonialist usefulness of footbinding as a western feminist fetish, and recent moments in the intercultural analysis of corporeality. It is my contention that footbinding (and its demise *as imagined*) not only marks corporeal modernity in China, but remains also a powerful marker of thresholds of feminist theorizing and displacement.

Fetishizing as Theory

> It is in these "disavowals" and "perspectives of flight" whose possibility is opened in the clash of incommensurable difference that the fetish might be identified as the site of both the formation and the revelation of ideology and value-consciousness.
> William Pietz, "Problem of the Fetish"[10]

Insisting that much engagement with footbinding by Europeans and Americans has been conducted through fetishization may sound oddly dismissive. William Pietz assists in defending this point with his perspective upon the fetish as mode of categorization in cross-cultural terrain. He brilliantly enlarges the fetish as a theoretical object beyond pejorative psychoanalytic reduction by historicizing it when he draws attention to its invention by the Portuguese to describe the objects venerated by peoples of west Africa in the sixteenth century. The term derives from the Portuguese *fetico,* meaning "ignorant magical practices," a term derived in turn from the Latin *facticius,* "to make."[11] By the eighteenth century, "fetishisme" meant primitive religion; by mid-nineteenth century, Marx had borrowed this usage from Hegel to poke fun at the bourgeoisie's worship of commodities; only at the turn of the twentieth century did Freud narrow the term to its now-usual associations with masculine castration fear.[12]

Pietz's complex reformulation contextualizes the current, prevalent psychoanalytic usage of fetishization that links it to pathology, drawing out its implications for material cultural investigation. As he says:

> Nineteenth century economic, sociological anthropological, and psychological discourses about the fetish constantly stress the idea of certain material objects as the loci of fixed structures of the inscription, displacement, reversal and overestimation of value.[13]

As such, he makes a de facto case for the fetish as modern in the terms that Nochlin has noted: a strategy for dealing with the precious, useful fragments of occluded, ungraspable, socially lived wholes. It is materiality in modern motion, crisscrossing social domains.

Leaning upon and moving outward from Pietz, I will use fetishization in a few specific ways. First, grounded in the trope of synecdoche, fetishization requires the abstraction of one part to stand for a much more complex whole, even as it occludes that whole (as the glove stands for the experience of the beloved and Unconscious desire; as the commodity stands for the process of the creation of surplus; as the bound foot stands for imagined Chinese barbarity). Second, from the psychoanalytic angle, fetishization also draws our attention to the process of displacing and rechanneling energetic investment and the gain of knowledge: While dealing with the world, it produces the subject in its engagement with that world. Third, the fetish functions as a veiled marker of alterity, allowing that which is invisible (too complex, too painful) to be made visible, while preserving the innocence of its own process. The fetish allows us to explain what is strange, while marking and preserving its irredeemable alienness. Fourth, the fetish returns our attention to corporeal materiality, to the subjection of the human body "as the material locus of action and desire to the influence of certain material objects" and as a site for the work of cultural practice.[14] Fifth, fetishization engages feminism through the fetish's close relationship to the materiality of the body and its ability to link the social and the personal. Thus, "fetishization" has been taken up by feminist thinkers who reread Freud's scene of male castration as, literally, a drama.[15]

> Feminist essentialism is resisted through fetishism's implicit challenge to a stable phallic referent . . . fetishism conceived as a mock performance of phallic women vested with preposterous props and veils springs gender codes loose from the moorings of biological essentialism.[16]

Here Emily Apter is not recommending a naïve project of de-reification that would allow "seeing through" to a whole new truth. For her and for me, fetishization could also name for us one strategy of dealing with reification. In this view, theory is a kind of selective "remembering" that makes visible parts of the necessary process of reification at the heart of culture making. Like the fetishist, the feminist theorist risks mistaking her chosen part for the whole of the object of analysis. She also must remember that, even as she uses these valuable theoretical tools to analyze our world, she is a modern subject, shaped by the same discourses that produce the tools.

"Woman's Work For Woman"

> A Christian woman should have a Christian foot.
> Rev. Mr. Talmadge, *Records of the General Conference of the Protestant Missionaries*, 1879[17]

From a modern feminist point of view, both westerners and Chinese who opposed footbinding seem often to have missed the point.[18] From the beginnings of the final critique of footbinding in the late nineteenth century, reformers often slighted the fact that these were *female* bodies in pain (the substitution of the body of Christ for the body of the footbound woman was not unusual).[19] People were horrified because helpless *children* were being maimed.[20] Chinese non-Christian elite male reformers reasoned that strong *citizens* were needed in service to the nation. When European women did discuss the pain of footbinding, they often did so in interestingly indirect ways. The specifically female nature of this pain was consistently highlighted only in the late twentieth century, during Second Wave feminism.[21]

Yet this moment of retheorization ended other stories and performed a kind of displacement into silence. A taboo of sorts has lain upon analysis of footbinding as a social process of engendering, one that has been broken only in the past few years. The question this section attempts to answer is: what did the nineteenth-century Christian white women crusading against footbinding accomplish, both socially and personally? In other words, how could their work on the foot be considered "fetishization" in the terms I have outlined here?

Two "General Conferences of the Protestant Missionaries" were held at Shanghai, one in 1877 and one in 1890. From their proceedings we can see a shift in perceptions of Chinese embodied life. The proceedings published in 1879 are greatly preoccupied with issues of ritual and especially bowing in ancestral veneration: Was it idolatrous, and what to do about it?[22] But after 1880 there seems to have been increasing attention paid to footbinding at the field level, as a problem conjoining issues of hygiene and salvation according to the new "social gospel" that sought to address the needs of "whole men and women."[23] By the General Conference of 1890, Rev. Noyes, still vociferous in his disgust with ancestor worship, also condemns worship of Confucius, reverence for lettered paper, bowing to officials, polygamy, and breaking the Sabbath. For those critiques he finds scriptural support, but despite the fact that the Bible does not address them explicitly, he also attacks opium smoking and footbinding, calling the latter "inhuman, refined cruelty."[24]

The treaty port world of China was an all-male preserve until the nineteenth century, when wives and unmarried women missionaries arrived. But even then, foreigners rarely met Chinese wives or single female servants. So the absent "Chinese Woman" became the object of desire, an absence to be conjured as a possible missing link in the divine plan for conversion. People steeped in the Victorian cult of domesticity doubted that the work of public salvation could be successfully undertaken without support from the private realm of the family.[25] And only women could breach Chinese family walls to penetrate the very ground of everyday life. There they could proselytize heathen mothers, reaching them because they shared fundamental concerns and attributes as women.

Yet the gendered division of labor reflected how the soul remained more important, and women whose writings on footbinding were included in the General Conference proceedings embraced their place within the masculine missionary hierarchy.[26] Men held preaching for the soul to be their particular preserve, while women organized bodies in schools, ran hospitals, and modeled the example of good Christian wives. Christian discovery of Chinese bodies attached to souls marked those bodies as terrain for civilizing labors, and missionaries were summoned to abolish footbinding. The same conference proceedings that contemplated the divide between the body and soul, called upon women to bridge that gap. Within this cultural framework, footbinding *naturally* became a woman's issue. Given such public attention to womanly commonalities of experience and affect, it is all the more startling that, when they wrote about footbinding, they so often deflected discussion away from what many feminists today would count as the main issue—violence done to women's bodies because they are women.

Anti-footbinding activist Mrs. Archibald Little was an independent-minded novelist of feminist leanings. She lived mainly in the southwest area of Szechuan for twenty years at the turn of the century after her rather late marriage to a shipping magnate.[27] She founded the Natural Feet Society in 1895, along with nine other western women of different nationalities. Although it was a nondenominational effort to secularize anti-footbinding work, it came into being under the aegis of the Shanghai Mission.[28]

On the question of pain, Mrs. Little notes:

> The Chinese as a nation are curiously callous to suffering in either themselves or others, not taking pleasure in the infliction of it, as is the case with other highly strung natures, but strangely indifferent to it.[29]

How then does she discuss the curious pain of footbinding, which she knows exists, but only as the pain of people who don't suffer? Alicia Little was not at all indifferent herself—she simply approached the specific issues around pain indirectly through three strategies.

One method was to mediate it through the pain of another Other, in this case the Italian Catholic nuns of Hankow who bound their students' feet:

> The bandages were only tightened once a week. The children were of course exempted from all lessons on those days. And the Italian sister who had to be present suffered so much from witnessing the little girls suffering that she had to be continually changed. No Italian female being able to endure the pain of it week after week.[30]

Secondly, in the absence of Chinese testimony (they are "curiously callous" = silent in Mrs. Little's view) she presented expert witnesses to the physiological damage of footbinding through doctors' testimony. In Mrs. Little's memoir, physicians from Shanghai, Nanjing, and Chongking discuss the loss of toes, whole feet, and lives to footbinding.[31] Little speaks of footbinding pain quite often by detouring through imported voices (mostly male—and although one of Little's physicians was a woman, the medical discourse remained profoundly masculinist).

Finally, and perhaps most often, Little was most direct and eloquent on the issue of pain when she discussed the victims as children:

> That expression of helpless rage and agony and hate in the poor little wizened child's face is more than I can ever hope to forget, and would alone spur me on to redoubled efforts to do away with a custom, that has been more than so many children can endure, and that must have saturated so many childish souls with bitterness, before they passed away from a world made impossible for them.[32]

What did this rhetoric serve to produce for her and other anti-footbinding European activists?

Homi Bhabha holds ambivalence to be key in how the stereotype functioned in colonial discourse as fetishization. The ambivalence of the stereotype, fixed yet in constant need of reiteration, "turns on the *recognition and disavowal* of racial/cultural/historical difference."[33] He notes how it acts as a "non-repressive form of knowledge that allows for the possibility of embracing two contradictory beliefs."[34] Although he concentrates upon race, Bhabha's connection of subjectivities within ideological formations via fetishization is also useful in understanding gender stereotyping, class anxieties, and the "work" of attention to footbinding. The latter functioned personally for its nineteenth-century discussants by enabling them to displace attention from such painful issues as physical disgust, suffering inappropriate to one's class station, and anxiety about geographic and social displacement. Little's equivocal disgust for Chinese women's bodies and the distanced recognition of Chinese women's pain seems to have allowed her to displace her own ambivalence, first around class, and secondly around gender.

The issue of class for Europeans and Americans living outside their countries in the nineteenth century was complex. Both men and women found many opportunities to better their standing by emigrating or serving abroad.[35] The call to philanthropy and moral reform was also an important way in which women "bettered" themselves—by helping "inferiors."[36] Little stood within a tradition of public service that was "top down" in its bestowal of benevolence. Although she carefully pointed out that footbinding was *not* a mark of status, that all classes suffered equally, she was especially appalled at its manifestation among the upper classes and seems to have felt not only anxiety at having to save their social inferiors, but also a certain amount of consternation that *rich* women could be so abused.[37]

Mrs. Little could not make up her mind: she had much respect for Chinese women's modesty, even in prostitution,[38] but betrayed disgust and impatience at their bodies and bodily presentation:

> Only their deformed feet and faces are seen . . . even the hands are concealed in their large sleeves. . . . Their faces at parties are often so rouged as to look like masks. . . . There is no single feature in the face that we could call pretty, and in accordance with etiquette the face is entirely devoid of expression. I have never been able to find anything pretty about a Chinese female except her hands and arms. . . . Doubtless her feet and legs would be pretty too if left alone. Now her *poor* legs are like two sticks.[39]

One of Mrs. Little's favorite adjectives throughout her memoirs is "poor," a good bourgeois term of condescending pity that seems to conflate economic want with painful physical circumstance, even though the women who are described by the term are members of the elite.

The Pain that Engenders

> Not only did little feet become the most important factor in women's sexuality: without a "three-inch Golden Lotus" a woman was not able to become a woman.
>
> Gao Hongxing, *Chanzu shi*[40]

Legends of the origins of footbinding are quite telling. There is the empress with oddly small feet who "bound them with fillets, affecting to make that pass for beauty which was really a deformity."[41] Some say the empress was a fox spirit who had to disguise her furry paws by binding them; others that she was clubfooted and hounded the emperor to force all girls to bind their feet.[42] The idea for the custom may have been brought in a Buddhist tale of a beautiful woman who had the feet of a deer that left mysterious lotus flower prints (symbol of the Buddha's enlightenment). These legends all show a deformity turned to advantage: how a child born female, a condition construed as a terrible social and moral disadvantage, successfully becomes a person called feminine.

Historians fix the beginnings of footbinding during the Song period (960–1279), a time of expanding urbanization and leisure and the onset of a decline in the status and privileges of women.[43] It does seem to have originated at court and spread through imitation.[44] Footbinding reached its apogee, both in terms of class and region, in the seventeenth and eighteenth centuries. When the Manchus from the northeast conquered the Han Chinese in the mid-seventeenth century, they tried, repeatedly and unsuccessfully, to ban footbinding by edict (1638, 1644, 1645, 1660).[45] By 1668, the useless decrees were rescinded for the kingdom as a whole, and only Manchu women were forbidden to bind.[46] Binding was more common in the north than the south, and it took decades of activist work after the founding of the Republic in 1911 for the practice to cease completely.[47] Choosing not to bind a daughter's feet, or to unbind one's own, were decisions first made in the upper classes and only later among laboring women. Women were often reluctant to unbind, for relinquishing their lotuses involved considerable pain: physical, social, and psychological. Considering the number of women subjected to (and by) this process, remarkably few died.[48]

The dissemination of the social gospel that gave substance to the cliché "cleanliness is next to godliness" grew up in the wake of a general medicalization of life in Europe and the United States. But I think this attention to the signs of "difference-as-deficit" borne in the (dirty) body was also stimulated by the new biologized racism that swept the British empire in the late nineteenth century.[49] By that time Europeans and Americans felt certain that humans were, in their deepest identities, *biologically* raced and gendered in ways that could be scientifically demonstrated.[50] The Chinese, however, did not share these discursive plots.[51] In the nineteenth century when missionaries were confronting footbinding, Chinese bodies were lived within a cosmology of transforming resonances and were thought to be formed of a complex network of energized matter known as *qi*.[52] In Chinese medicine (even today), the body's systems are organized as functional multiplicities, not as subsets of "organs."[53] Health is based in constant and patterned change and circulation, not fixity or stability. People did not consist of divinely endowed or biologically fixed human nature. Instead they are materializations of dynamically contingent positions both in space and in social hierarchy.

The construction of gender was a social performance of this general devotion to patterned circulation and transformation, sharing with medicine the logic of yin/yang. Tani Barlow discusses gender in this light:

> What appear as "gender" are yin/yang differentiated positions: not two anatomical "sexes," but a profusion of relational, bound, unequal dyads, each signifying difference and positioning difference analogically.[54]

These "performances" of gendered positions were accomplished especially within the systematic scripts for social activity called *li* (usually translated as "ritual"). Footbinding, likewise, both marked and produced the ever-shifting world of hierarchical relationships that comprised Chinese sociocorporeal life. By binding a girl's feet, the contact of cloth (either silk or cotton) and skin exemplified in its grueling daily regime the exercise and effects of agency in a world of interpenetrating strata and layers of embodiment. One widespread body-imaginary in the late imperial period depicted the body as layers of energetic, circulating *qi*, extending outward through its enfolding clothing.[55] Thus Ko points out that footbinding was a ritual of civility akin to clothing the body.[56] Within this body-imaginary, it functioned as a mark of genteel (feminine) civility, signifying gender difference in ways quite opaque to Europeans.

The organs that were the object of fixation for European gender distinction (the penis, the womb, the breasts) lacked a similar discursive weight and reality in China. Instead, and as a pronounced marker of gender distinction, Chinese women engaged in a process of continual physical transformation, molding a visible part of the body (which was then, of course, wrapped in shoes almost never removed in the sight of another). Feet were held in common with men, so this somatic gender distinction, rather than being "discovered" in nature, was created through culture, through a process of cosmetic manipulation.

How must encountering this process have affected non-Chinese women who believed implicitly that gender distinctions rested naturally in original endowments of genitalia and breasts? Big-footed missionary women, especially unmarried, literate, professional ones, were *not thought of as women by the Chinese.* This lack of recognition of gender on both sides led to a "profound confusion of sexual stereotypes . . . western women found Chinese men unmanly and Chinese men found western women unwomanly."[57] Yet we have noted that the missionaries' feminine identity within their home "cult of domesticity" was crucial to their missionary work and sense of self.

One can imagine this contradiction as a troubling liberation, allowing them to discuss footbinding as torture, but not gendered torture. For if western women admitted bound feet as gender markers, rather than scars of barbarity, they would have been admitting the existence of a kind of femininity quite different from their own, admitting that they were not, in local terms, women. Here lies another reason why footbinding, as painful oppression, may have often been displaced by nineteenth-century women from gender to age or citizenship. They could object to pain inflicted upon children, upon human beings, but not upon women *as women.*

As the anti-footbinding movement spread, Mrs. Little grew more and more delighted with the willingness of Chinese women to attend meetings and to speak out; she herself "began to forget that anyone had ever laughed at her."[58] In her memoir, even at this point, however, she extensively incorporates a Chinese male voice into her anti-footbinding campaign. The "Suifu Appeal," the first document of its kind to circulate in thousands of copies, contains two arguments against footbinding put forward by Mr. Chou, a literatus. The arguments are both internally and externally oriented: First, he mentions an earlier (seventeenth-century) edict banning footbinding that has been ignored; he calls this a crime against the dynasty. Second, he says:

> The present is no time of peace. Foreign women have natural feet; they are daring and can defend themselves; whilst Chinese females have bound feet and can barely bear the weight of their clothes. . . . Of England, France, Germany, America, only the Chinese voluntarily incur suffering and injury.[59]

With the Suifu Appeal the discourse on footbinding shifted. Nineteenth-century western women's articulating the pain of footbinding at a distance, as not *merely* a gendered discourse, allowed Chinese intellectuals to incorporate anti-footbinding into the nationalist discourse. Anti-footbinding would now move from a focus, however indirect, on women's bodily pain to become, in the hands of male reformers, a fetish for the Chinese nation as crippled. As Pietz explains the term fetish, footbinding was now reified, historical, territorialized, personalized; it was also an obstacle to nationhood.[60] In the early twentieth century, a second discursive context thus overtook and absorbed footbinding. The physical pain of Chinese women was abstracted and revalued as the pain of the national body.[61] The footbound woman became a fetish for the Chinese only when it summarized and made visible the problems of colonial oppression, as a "femininization" of China, one that necessitated the naming and alienating of something called "tradition."

What is gained and lost in this historical shift? In the long term, the connection of woman = victim = struggling nation set up the burial of the "woman question" under nationalist concerns in postmonarchical and postrevolutionary China. The shift also bequeathed to late twentieth-century feminists a tendency to reverse the equation to read backwards: third world = victim = woman.[62]

Footbinding still wields great influence as a feminist fetish in the sense I have used that term here. In the seventies both Andrea Dworkin and Mary Daly wrote influential texts on footbinding that were emblematic of the "cultural feminist" turn within radical feminism. Alice Echols notes that cultural feminists reject earlier radical questioning of gender distinctions in favor of recuperating an essential femininity upon which women could unite.[63] But the idea of Universal Sisterhood breaks down quickly when confronted with differences of race, class, or cultural experience.

Mary Daly's influential *Gyn/ecology* on violence against women describes such practices as reenactments of murder of the goddess. Audre Lorde's letter to Daly, reprinted in the *Sister Outsider* anthology, lays out an eloquent criticism of Daly's book: Women of color have no goddesses but instead appear only as quintessential victims in the later chapters on Suttee *(sati)*, footbinding, and African genital mutilation.[64] Lorde accuses Daly of racism, but how does this racism play out? Stating that there are no non-European goddesses is tantamount to saying that non-European women have no history, that is, no sense of a past narrative upon which to build rational future choices. This disregard for "the historical" goes beyond heady abandonment of dusty academic convention (Daly gives good footnote) to have real moral consequences for her text. She intermixes past practices that have ceased, like footbinding, witch burning, and Nazi medicine with other practices that continue unabated today.

With no discussion of how the now-defunct practices were overcome through the active contention of their victims, we miss an opportunity to learn about resistance. Daly's "snapshot" of human female misery provides a deeply felt call to arms that disempowers the very people she hopes to enlist by depriving them of historical lessons. She does this equally well for Chinese, American, and European women. But as non-Europeans, Chinese women are doubly deprived of both their own history of resistance and any "matriarchal" history upon which Daly might base resistance to patriarchy today.

This failure of cultural feminists to historicize is a famous weakness. Dworkin likewise fails to contextualize footbinding. In her book *Woman Hating* she devotes a chapter to "Gynocide: Chinese Footbinding."[65] She is particularly sensitive to the damage done to the mother-daughter relationship when the mother takes on the role of patriarchal enforcer and binds the daughter's feet. But she completely neglects the Chinese context of the practice—in her treatment we are in the realm of "all cultures, then and now."[66] Thus we never understand how this particular physical pain serves as both focus and veil for the pain of impending separation when the daughter must marry into another family, usually into another town or village, and is, in any case, identified as a temporary member of her natal family from birth. In the institutional context of strict virilocal marriage, one must be careful not to overly romanticize the mother-daughter bond.

Why has the problem of bound feet lingered in a way that engages our voyeuristic indignation? What does it make visible? What does it hide? How does it enable those who invoke it?

Daly and Dworkin both seem to rely upon a version of the Universal Body of nature and medicine with which we opened this essay—what women have in common, all over the world, is their bionature. The problem remains today; however, there are no more feet to unbind. The numbing foreclosure effect of *Woman Hating* and *Gyn/ecology*'s doomsday forever-victim shows up in any classroom where one tries to teach about Chinese women. It empowers no one to spring into action in the world.

On the other hand, Christian women of the nineteenth century who lived in China were both personally and publicly empowered by their fetishization of footbinding. Their anti-footbinding agitation may have only borne fruit when the cause was taken up by Chinese men with a nationalist agenda; nonetheless, their contribution to ending footbinding was quite real, even if its indirect benefit to national liberation and the end of missionizing had ironic consequences for them as they were forced to leave China.

In once sense, however, footbinding does serve cultural feminism in ways similar to its colonial function for nineteenth-century Christian reformers:

it empowers by providing others to save. In crusading against footbinding, Christian women could displace "more direct self-referential feminism" away from themselves—where it surely would have caused trouble at home—onto a Chinese cause.[67] Their inability to confront the problematic of their own status nonetheless empowered them as agents of capitalist, imperialist empire and progress. Cultural feminists, by blaming women's oppression solely upon patriarchally motivated bodily violations like footbinding, can disengage from the necessity to confront the material legacy of imperialist capitalism—they can ignore racism and poverty—and empower themselves as feminists of a certain sort. Radical cultural feminists like Daly and Dworkin are part of the larger failure of first-world white feminists to account clearly for the fact that the oppression of "women" is not (and has not historically been) based solely on sexed gender difference from men, nor is it solely perpetrated by men. Racism, colonialism and neocolonialism, class-based exploitation, homophobia, and religious intolerance form a complex web that hampers all women in varying degrees.[68] These issues present one itch that feminist practice has been scratching for at least twenty years, and I would like to announce that we can stop. However, recent work in "international feminism" harbors within it many of the same contradictions that can be found in these early texts.[69]

Tani Barlow's work on "International Feminism in a Global Frame" treats it as an ideological formation that operates to make contradictions under global capital disappear, rather than simply an innocent project of the ethically correct. She describes how international feminism succeeds in naturalizing the scene in many ways: first, as a type of "internationalist" discourse, this feminism "reinforces, legitimizes and naturalizes" the very nations it is supposed to be superceding.[70] Secondly, it "presumes most women's work and reproductive obligations bring us into routine proximity to nature" and "assumes an anatomically fixed category."[71] Third, through ecofeminism, it offers nature itself as something that contains geopolitics and national politics, where "national questions are male and natural matters are female." In the Chinese case, the issue that has replaced footbinding as the current horror is female infanticide.

How do such moves by scholars of "international feminism" repeat earlier patterns of fetishization in feminist engagement and theoretical practice? Briefly, the ingredients for the fetish are here: There is the concentration upon the female body, the reduction of that body to its injuries and what that reduction occludes—class, race, economic, political, and religious tribulation; there is also what the reduction enables: the working through of issues of feminist import at home (i.e., violence in the family) through discussion of "others."

There is also the equally important question of why the body itself—and especially the bodies of women—remains such a significant site for the simultaneous production of senses of self, collectivity, and alterity.

Telling Painful Secrets

> And meanwhile I understand that each of the western theories can only work as a mirror or metaphor for the one-thousand-year-old mystery of the Chinese male erotic fixation. And the reflections from the mirror are as fragmentary and partial as the fetishistic gaze itself.
> Wang Ping, *Aching for Beauty*[72]

The work of Wang Ping, poet and scholar, shares, and yet deforms in specific ways, some of the assumptions and outcomes outlined here. Her book, *Aching for Beauty: Footbinding in China,* opens with a flurry of discussion linking the bound foot back to its body, but the body Wang conjures is precisely the biobody of sex and death.[73] Explicit in her desire to reclaim her female ancestors and break the taboo of silence around their pain, Wang's work presents rich examples of fetishization as a theoretical turn, albeit in a postcolonial and post-structuralist vein. For Wang, the stubbornly engaging and glacially transforming trope of fetishizing the body of the Other Woman becomes the site of reclamation. I will return, in my discussion of her work, to the four usages of the fetish outlined above.

First, *Aching for Beauty* engages footbinding as cultural practice, an outcome of expressly erotic violence so transforming that it turned Chinese women's bodies into mediating, hybrid objects. Reminding the men who encountered them of beasts, vegetables and objects for collection, these feet incited riots of poetic language: "Violence renders the feet sacred."[74] Wang turns our attention fully upon this fetish as "the material locus of action and desire."[75] Second, she abstracts footbinding as the summarizing part of Chinese women's lives, and it soon ramifies metonymically to touch upon "the context of their everyday lives and work environment, of their social economic and linguistic backgrounds,"[76] the part that provides perspective upon the whole.

Third, and what sets her apart from second-wave feminists, is her wish to speak openly of footbinding as "something that can generate" feminine sexuality and women's agency. She recognizes its power in preparation for marriage and in articulating women's hierarchies, and thinks of it as a form of secret, female knowledge, "the place of honor, identity and livelihood for many women."[77] She reads the textual silence around footbinding as "an oral culture exclusive to women who passed it from body to body, mouth to mouth, handiwork to handiwork . . . their writing/handiwork/speech allow them to . . . redefine and reconstruct their fetishized bodies as a whole."[78] In my view, Wang herself fetishizes footbinding, but in order to displace and transform painful moments of destruction into something of utility, even beauty.

Fourth, Wang spends the first half of the book exploring in horrific detail the connections between footbinding and death and violence, reaching a crescendo in her comparison of it with the gory execution practice of the thousand cuts.[79] Only after footbinding has been firmly established as the marker of the alterity of China past do we move onto explaining and redeeming its otherness. Its redemption lies, for Wang, in its creation of a kind of hybrid and androgynous body that mediated sex and gender difference, "producing the body of an immortal or a god."[80] How does this project enable Wang Ping in terms of self-creation? She ends her book quoting a gender-bending stanza from Eve Ensler's *Vagina Monologues* where leather jackets, silk stockings, tuxedos and pink boas blend as vaginal fashions, and adds:

> What contemporary American women imagine or practice had already been translated into reality in China a thousand years ago. For a millennium, Chinese women bound their feet (their symbolic vaginas) and dressed them in all manners (binding, covering, piercing) and styles (transvestites, animals, plants, objects) just as twentieth-century Americans imagine in their vagina monologues. Across time, space and culture, the currents of eastern and western female imaginations have finally merged.[81]

Though Wang means to end the book on a gendered note, competition between east/west racialized knowledge creeps in. What we really have is another hybrid transformation: one achieved through her use of theories that bend and reshape her narratives of footbinding. The success of the final merging of eastern and western female imaginations rests upon Wang's ability, as a Chinese diasporic writer, to achieve a distanced domestication of the horror of the bound foot.

Coda

In my discussion of colonial(ist) writings on footbinding and pain we see something of the complex process that lies behind the historical artifact that some feminists would call "Footbinding as Female Torture." I suggest that the gap between the narrative of the (painful) process and the (contrived) sign of the accomplishment of its end is analogous to the distance traversed between "coloniality" and "postcoloniality." Current uses of footbinding illustrate the temptation to engage in a constant and early foreclosure, but one that seems to be, paradoxically, built into the process of making/writing history itself.

Bound feet literally disappear as a problem for Chinese women whose limitations now take on other, less striking forms. Bound feet reappear as a trope for white feminists like Mary Daly and Andrea Dworkin. Colonialism ostensibly disappears after independence as the colonizer departs. But of course, the history never goes away. Current debates over postcoloniality as a phase, or postcolonialism as a discourse, readily allow us to reconjure the colonial in a contained fashion, as "postcolonial" contains "colonial."

If we view it optimistically, perhaps "postcolonialism" operates fetishistically in a fashion analogous to the way footbinding operated for missionaries: domesticating the difficult and bringing it near. Like a very long handle with a hook on the end, postcoloniality as discursive fetish device can allow different people to get a grip on the colonial past and drag it onto the shores of perceptibility.

So fetishism can be seen as a process bound up with colonialism, capitalism and modernism. I find it directly relevant for critical cross-cultural work on women and gender because it seems to tell by displacement (in true fetishistic fashion) the story of the consolidation of a European bourgeois subjectivity. That subjectivity required a literal racial Other, took the form of a neutral liberal subject to earn alienated wages through the production of commodities, and created forms of gender distinction that reified lived bodies into medical symptoms of inferiority.

In this essay I have tried to move beyond fetish as merely perverse to extend Pietz's and Bhabha's more Foulcauldian ideas of the fetish as a discursive enabler, productive in the sense that ideology is productive of subject positions. Thus I suggest that we might also find new possibilities in postcolonial theory's slippery relations of containment that both enable and erase. Perhaps it contains the "colonial" as only a *seemingly* abandoned object and allows us to think in two times at once, seeing the past in the present. In intercultural work we must learn to cope with our fetishizations—they are bound to be represented.

Notes

My thanks to Tani Barlow, John Calagione, Philip Corrigan, Judith Farquhar, Antonia Finnane, Jay Geller, Harry Harootunian, Gail Hershatter, James Hevia, Dorothy Ko, Keith McMahon, Daniel Nugent, Lisa Rofel, Timea Szell, Maggie Sales, Judith Weisenfeld, Meg McLagan and members of the Human Rights Working Group at the Center for Religion and Media, NYU, who commented on earlier versions and other work on footbinding.

Epigraph. Cooper, *Chinese Repository.*
1. The title of this section is from Nochlin, *Body in Pieces.*
2. Cooper, *Chinese Repository.*
3. Tuttle, *Mary Porter Gamewell,* 66; Little, *Intimate China,* 99.
4. Nochlin, *Body in Pieces,* 8.
5. Ibid.
6. Latour, *War of the Worlds,* 13.
7. See Asad, *Genealogies of Religion.*
8. See Ko, "Bondage in Time," 200.
9. Blake, "Footbinding"; Turner, "Locating Footbinding"; and Ko "Body as Attire."
10. Pietz, "Problem of the Fetish," 12.
11. Ibid., 5.
12. Freud, "Fetishism."
13. Pietz, "Problem of the Fetish," 9.
14. Ibid., 10.
15. Freud, "Fetishism." See also McClintock, "Angel of Progress" and *Imperial Leather,* chaps. 2–4.
16. Apter, "Introduction," 4–5.
17. *Records of the General Conference of the Protestant Missionaries of China Held at Shanghai, May 10–24, 1877.*
18. The title of this section is the name of a Presbyterian missionary journal.
19. Ropp, *Dissent,* 120–151.
20. Chen Roshui (1280) provides an extremely early example of this line of critique. Levy, *Chinese Footbinding,* 65.
21. See Daly, *Gyn/ecology;* Dworkin, *Woman Hating.*
22. See Zito, "Secularizing Pain of Footbinding."
23. Hunter, *Gospel of Gentility,* 9.
24. *Records of the General Conference of the Protestant Missionaries of China Held at Shanghai, May 7–20, 1890,* 607; see also Rev. Ohlinger, 604–605 in the same work.
25. See Hunter, *Gospel of Gentility,* 128–173; McClintock, *Imperial Leather,* 258–295.
26. Mrs. T. P. Crawford advises that women need not worry about producing books. *Records of the General Conference of the Protestant Missionaries of China Held at Shanghai, May 10–24, 1877,* 151. Miss Mary Laurence: "We do not want to raise the cry of women's rights, nor in any degree countenance the Chinese error that in our honorable country women have the upper hand because the British scepter has for so many prosperous years been swayed by a woman's hand" (ibid., p. 469).
27. Alicia Helen Neva Bewick, in the convention of the times, signed her books as "Mrs. Archibald Little" after her marriage. Elizabeth Croll presents a very sympathetic portrait of her in *Wise Daughters,* 23–62.
28. Drucker, "Influence," 189; Little, *Intimate China,* 102.
29. Little, *Intimate China,* 93.
30. Ibid., 96. By 1898, the school's girls were no longer binding their feet.
31. Ibid., 96–98.
32. Little, *Blue Gown,* 289.
33. Fanon cited in Bhabha, "Other Question," 23.

34. Bhabha, "Other Question," 32.
35. Callaway, "Dressing"; Ware, *Beyond the Pale*, 127.
36. Ware, *Beyond the Pale*, 128.
37. On class differences see *Records of the General Conference of the Protestant Missionaries of China Held at Shanghai, May 10–24, 1877*, 133, 137. As her anti-footbinding movement grew, Mrs. Little happily pointed out that "Best of all, Chinese ladies of distinction [were] coming forward to found a school for girls of the upper classes." *Intimate China*, 163.
38. Little, *Intimate China*, 116.
39. Ibid., 125, emphasis added.
40. Gao Hongxing, *Chanzu shi*, 2.
41. Du Haide cited in Levy, *Chinese Footbinding*, 37.
42. Levy, *Chinese Footbinding*, 37.
43. See Gao, *Chanzu shi*, 17–18; Ebrey, *Confucianism*, 220–221.
44. Fairbank and Reischauer, *China*, 42–43; Eastman, *Family*, 22–23. Both sources are popular textbooks.
45. Gao, *Chanzu shi*, 25–26.
46. Ibid., 24. Ko has noted astutely how footbinding was further emphasized as a sign of Han patriotism and civility in the face of barbaric conquest. Ko, *Teachers*.
47. See Turner, "Locating Footbinding," 456.
48. Levy, *Chinese Footbinding*. In Chinese see Jia, *Zhongguo funü chanzu kao*; Yao, *Caifei Lu*; and Gao, *Chanzu shi*.
49. Ware, *Beyond the Pale*; Hall, "Missionary Stories."
50. Laqueur, *Making Sex*; Schiebinger, *Nature's Body*; Young, *White Mythologies*.
51. The essays in Zito and Barlow, *Body, Subject and Power in China*, suggest that, in the absence of scientific biologism, Chinese bodies and subjectivities were organized along other discursive lines. See also the essays on China in Kasulis et al., *Self as Body*, 149–294. Cole offers a provocative discussion of Buddhist organization of gendered bodies. Cole, *Mothers and Sons*.
52. Zito, "Silk and Skin."
53. Kaptchuk, *Web*; Farquhar, *Knowing Practice*; Porkert, *Chinese Medicine*.
54. Barlow, "Theorizing Woman," 259. See also Furth, *Flourishing Yin*.
55. Hay "Body Invisible"; Zito, "Silk and Skin."
56. Ko, "Body as Attire."
57. Hunter, *Gospel of Gentility*, 204; Gao, *Chanzu shi*, 2.
58. Little, *Intimate China*, 156.
59. Ibid., 160–162.
60. See Ko, "Body as Attire."
61. Little, *Intimate China*, 155–162; Little, *Blue Gown*, 253–304; and Drucker "Influence of Western Women," 194.
62. Mohanty et al., *Third World Women*.
63. See Echols, *New Feminism*.
64. Lorde, *Sister Outsider*.
65. Dworkin, *Woman Hating*.
66. Ibid., 120.
67. Hunter, *Gospel of Gentility*, 87–88.

68. See Mohanty, *Third World Women,* especially essays by Mohanty, Chow, Russo, and Johnson-Odim.

69. In discussions on "international feminism" that follow, I am indebted to Tani Barlow for sharing with me her unpublished work on "Teaching International Feminism."

70. She quotes Malkki, "Citizens of Humanity."

71. Barlow, "Teaching International Feminism."

72. Wang, *Aching for Beauty,* 101.

73. Wang cites George Hershey's sociobiological work on the function of secondary sex characteristics in sexual selection and Bataille on the flesh as the implacable Other of rationality. Wang, *Aching for Beauty,* 14, 48.

74. Wang, *Aching for Beauty,* 4.

75. Pietz, "Fetish," 10.

76. Wang, *Aching for Beauty,* 146.

77. Ibid., 6–9, 19, 53; quote from introduction, xi.

78. Ibid., 145–146.

79. Ibid., 137–142.

80. Ibid., 4.

81. Ibid., 233.

CHAPTER 3

Male Love Lost
The Fate of Male Same-Sex Prostitution in Beijing in the Late Nineteenth and Early Twentieth Centuries

CUNCUN WU and MARK STEVENSON

Introduction: Modernity or Westernization?

In Ba Jin's novel *Jia* (The Family, completed in 1931) there is a passage where the novel's young hero Juehui struggles inwardly over his relationship with his paternal grandfather. The grandfather is a solid, conservative representative of the generation that came to be identified with the closing years of the Qing dynasty, and in Juehui's mind, with everything old and moribund. He is a distant and greatly feared figure, and his grandson is fully aware of the absolute power he holds over their wealthy and influential family. In order to break the bonds of his grandfather's authority Juehui lists in his mind a number of his grandfather's "crimes" of which he has become more clearly aware. He has discovered in his grandmother's and grandfather's collected writings a number of poems that were exchanged with courtesans *(jiaoshu)* as well as copies of the poems the courtesans wrote in reply. Those were crimes committed before his grandfather turned thirty, so he might be excused, but in fact things got worse:

> Even these days Grandfather would every so often visit those male actors who played the young female roles *(xiaodan)*, and once Grandfather and Fourth Uncle even brought a well-known *dan* actor home and had him make up and pose for photographs. He had in fact witnessed, with his own eyes, the *dan* actor doing his hair and powdering his face in the family's parlor. Such happenings were nothing unusual in the seat of provincial government. Not that long ago there were several old diehard supporters of the Confucian Society, themselves committed to nothing less than "devoting the remaining years to the protection of the Way," who made a great fuss over their publication in the newspaper of an "Actor Popu-

larity Chart," selecting a certain actor of "young lady" roles as their champion. This was all supposed to be rather debonair.[1]

Beyond this the grandfather had disgraced himself in Juehui's mind by purchasing a concubine, and worst of all, he opposed the progress represented by the student movement that was his grandson's greatest passion. In fact, the old man would have preferred it if young people had not attended the new-style schools at all.

In an essay based on the afterword he prepared for the 1956 English edition of his novel, Ba Jin makes it clear that *Jia* drew upon the experiences of his own family in Chengdu, and that Grandfather was based on his own grandfather as well as other kinsmen of the same generation. He is also scathing in his views on the Chinese family as an institution, describing it as a cage that young Chinese should escape at any cost.[2]

Ba Jin and his grandfather did not just belong to two separate generations, they straddled two different worlds. No matter what our attitudes or views might be toward the historical evolution of China in the twentieth century, there is little doubt that in many Chinese people's minds "modernity" is a word equated with westernization. In the late nineteenth and early twentieth century, already defeated by western technology and military power, Chinese intellectuals began to question the value of their own culture, and to wonder if there might be found within it a fundamental flaw. Employing the "advanced" culture of the west as a measure, leading intellectuals in China began to examine their tradition much as a doctor might examine a patient in search of a diagnosis, in this case searching for an error in ways of thought or a deviation in moral fiber.[3]

Western influence on Chinese social life is especially apparent in the events of the first two decades of the twentieth century. Changes such as shifting from polygamy to monogamy, abandoning the imperial examination system in favor of European and British university degrees, opening up of education and public life to young women, and the gradual rejection of footbinding are all inextricably linked with ideas of progress introduced from the west. Each of these transformations was clearly believed to be a movement from the backward toward the advanced, from the conservative and old fashioned toward the modern, the innovative, and the open-minded. It is no surprise that most of the items in this list are included among the grievances twenty-seven-year-old Ba Jin assembled against the grandfathers of China as he remembers them from the early 1920s.[4]

Ba Jin describes Grandfather as having been a *mingshi,* a man of status, a learned gentleman of independent means, an aesthete; while the famed twentieth-century writer would become a *zuojia* (author), an emerging occupation that would later be counted among what were known as *zhishifenzi* (intellectuals, those members of society whose contribution was knowledge). The title *mingshi* exemplifies the status-based system of identity that was a perennial feature of the social landscape of imperial China. The word's first component, *ming* (name, fame), signified the recognition a person was accorded by others, and the second component, *shi* (scholar), had its origins in the hierarchy of the ancient Four Estates of civil servants *(shi),* farmers, craftsmen, and merchants. With the fall of the empire in 1911 the edifice that supported the old status system also collapsed. By the time Ba Jin had become a *zuojia* the *mingshi* were considered so moribund that the term had come to carry a strong flavor of contempt.⁵

In the passage translated above Ba Jin also refers to the female role *dan* actors in contemptuous tones, and since this is not necessarily a simple reflection of the author's own views, we might conclude that he felt this attitude reflected the values of young people at the time. Throughout Chinese history actors had belonged to the ranks of the *jianmin*, the "low people," along with prostitutes, singing girls, barbers, and servants, so such contempt was only to be expected; however, in the final century of the Qing dynasty many *dan* actors rose to prominence in a star system initially associated with the opera theaters *(liyuan)* of Beijing. While such actors were unable to escape their "low" status they did find themselves being fêted and doted upon by men from the highest ranks of China's social elite, the gentry (including *mingshi* like Grandfather).

What kind of relationship did Grandfather have with *dan* actors? There seems to have been no doubt in Ba Jin's mind that *dan* were to be lumped together with courtesans and concubines, that is to say, with relationships that did not meet the standards of the new generation's sexual morality. Courtesans and concubines continued to be available to elite men, in one form or another, throughout the Republican period. During the same period the *dan* actors of Beijing continued to perform their stage roles, and some even enjoyed fame and status like never before, but the system of theater-based prostitution quickly came under moral and legal scrutiny.

It is our aim in this chapter to identify some of the cultural changes that shaped the decline of theater-based male same-sex prostitution in Beijing in the early decades of the twentieth century. As the clumsiness of some of our word strings reveals, this is not an aspect of early twentieth-century Chinese history that is easy to "translate." This is not because of any obscurity (beyond what one might expect) within the Chinese source materials, but because same-sex desire in the source materials and same-sex desire in the language of contemporary scholarship belong to very different discursive and epistemological realms. As some of our footnotes also indicate, same-sex desire is an area of inquiry where there continues to be a considerable amount of debate, in Chinese history and elsewhere.[6] Our analysis here, for example, is based on quite a different understanding of premodern expressions of homoeroticism than that recently advanced by Sophie Volpp, who argues for a rhetorical reading of references to homoerotic behavior. Instead, we see a strong connection between homoerotic writing and the erotic life of the literati elite, and in turn see both as forming part of an influential fashion or sensibility. Rather than focus upon the debate around premodern homoeroticism,[7] we are particularly interested to foreground the aesthetic and affective dimensions of morality expressed in early twentieth-century concern over theater-based prostitution in Beijing, as well as the relationship of such concerns to a new-found sensitivity under a perceived foreign gaze. Thus, like Maram Epstein in her contribution to this volume, we wish to emphasize premodern themes as they were transformed in the early part of the twentieth century.

Xianggong: Shaping Homoerotic Desire

In terms of the broad sweep of Chinese history Juehui's attitudes are not unusual, but nor is Grandfather's behavior. Juehui's assessment of his grandfather's indulgences is in line with the orthodox Confucian morality set out in *jiaxun* (principles of family conduct); yet Grandfather would have understood that romantic liaisons with courtesans often signaled a sense of style among the literati elite. Nor does there appear to have been any evidence of a general moral stigma attached to same-sex desire, so long as it was expressed in ways that did not transgress specific boundaries of status and propriety.[8] Indeed, from the late Ming dynasty (c.1550–1644) until the fall of the Qing dynasty (1644–1911) relationships between upper class men and boy entertainers were fashionable. By the end of the Qing dynasty the opera theaters of Beijing supported a thriving nightlife where such liaisons were openly celebrated.[9] This close association of the Qing dynasty theater world with male same-sex prostitution was not recognized for most of the twentieth century, and many who have written on the theater have somehow been "blind" to the connection, or have consciously turned a blind eye, or even attempted to cover up or explain away the facts.[10] Colin Mackerras' work on the Beijing theater is a notable early exception,[11] but the importance of these links is still only rarely acknowledged. From the second half of the eighteenth century onwards, homoerotic sensibilities were to have a direct and profound influence on the shaping of Beijing opera style, at the same time shaping a system of male prostitution associated with the world of theater but becoming increasingly independent of theatrical performance.

From the mid-Qing until the early years of the twentieth century the term that came to be most widely used to refer to the catamites associated with opera troupes was *xianggong* (literally "gentleman"). The term denoted quite specifically the boy-actors who cross-dressed for young female *(dan)* roles on the public stages of Beijing *and* who were available as catamites. Without exception *xianggong* came either from utterly destitute families (in which case they had been sold, usually on contract), or they were born into the profession through descent within an acting family.

The training for all roles in Beijing opera was rigorous and physically demanding, an aspect of the tradition made known in the west through the Chen Kaige film *Farewell My Concubine*. The *xianggong*'s dual identity as actor and catamite meant that his training combined elements from both professions. The *biji* (miscellany) penned by Qing literati contain numerous and rich references to the selection and training of *dan*. In particular they were interested in the problem of how these boys were trained to perform their dual role. In the theater troupes certain instructors specialized in directing the training of boys to both act and to satisfy the men who came to enjoy the theater.

In line with the predominant aesthetic in Qing Beijing, effeminate, pale, and delicate looking boys became the first choice for *dan* training. Immediately after their arrival in a troupe, young boys were generally forced to affect a weak, feminine manner and maintain a light complexion. Several miscellanies compiled by aficionados remark that the methods and skills for training *dan* in Beijing were different from those used in other provinces. It is claimed that the training in Beijing was far more involved, with more care taken to nurture the tender, elegant, and spontaneous manner required of *dan* in the capital.

> In Beijing when the actors train their own students the elegant steps and seductive gaits are carefully executed; the turn of the head and the flashing of eyes are extremely refined. There may be some who are elegant and some common, but overall each frown or smile is something beyond the ordinary. . . . In Suzhou actors are only skilled in singing arias; their speech, expression, and appearance are completely undeveloped, and so they don't inspire attachment *(ai)*.[12]

Beyond the physical transformations achieved by dieting and exercise, the feminization of *dan* included training in deportment and imitation. A feminized appearance and air were the central means by which *dan* captured the attention of their audience (and received invitations to the dinner parties that followed the performances). The performance of young female roles *(dan)* by boy-actors soon became so formalized in the theaters of Beijing that the term *dan* came to refer to the actors themselves, both on stage and off.[13]

Audiences also contributed to the aura of feminization through their own discourse of connoisseurship. This interest found literary form from the Qianlong period (1736–1796) onwards in the shape of "flower guides" *(huapu)*, adapted from earlier booklets appraising famous prostitutes, and the *dan* became known as "flowers" *(hua)*. One of the central concerns of the *huapu* was to identify exactly which feminine traits each *dan* displayed, both on and off stage. The fashion for feminine boy-actors also meant that the authors of the *huapu* might exaggerate the *dan*'s feminine qualities or at least downplay any signs of masculinity. The highest praise for *dan/xianggong* always spoke of their unique femininity, and the slightest feminine air, once exaggerated in the heart of a besotted aficionado, could suddenly bring a boy some fame as a minor celebrity.

Venues and the Spatial Encoding of Same-sex Desire

Theaters, restaurants and "private residences" *(siyu)* were the main venues where the paths of the literati and the *xianggong* crossed, and these were the three dominant *public* arenas in Qing dynasty Beijing where the literati came together in search of leisure, sociality, and entertainment.

Theaters

Women were prohibited by government statute from entering theaters, and so theater audiences were made up of men from all levels of society in Beijing. While all the men in the audience shared an interest in the boy-actors, only the wealthy or influential vied for seats where the boys could be viewed to advantage. Indeed theaters in the late-Qing capital seem to have been venues for male homoerotic indulgence as much as for enjoying dramatic performance. A popular folksong from the Jiaqing reign period (1796–1821) describes a wealthy member of the audience:

> Sitting with his knees crossed
> The day's program is brought on a red card.
> A pair of boy-actors, white as jade, one left, one right,
> The eyes of the whole audience wander from the stage.[14]

The *dan* was the primary attraction.[15] The tremendous prosperity of the theater in Beijing during the Qing was not firstly a matter of dramatic sensibility (not at least in the usual sense), rather it was based on the admiration of boy-actors, a homoerotic sensibility closely associated with the display of personal status.[16] This trend can also be traced in the theater criticism of the day, where the majority of works focus on the *dan* to the exclusion of other roles. From reading contemporary commentators on the theater it becomes clear that appreciation of *dan* was based on their appearance *(se)*, with artistic and technical ability relegated to secondary importance. In *Pinhua baojian* (The Precious Mirror of Ranked Flowers), an important homoerotic novel from the middle of the Qing dynasty, the romantic literatus Tian Chunhang openly asserts:

> What matters to me is the person, not the play. When a play is elegant and the actors are average, it is less interesting than when the actors are elegant and the play is average. . . . The appearance of actors is more important to me than acting ability. The script, plot, and roles are immaterial; for me there is only the charm *(zise)* of the actor.[17]

Descriptions of theater architecture show in their terminology an association between the homoerotic atmosphere in Beijing theaters and the display of power. In the following passage from his miscellany *Jintai canleiji* (Record of the Golden Stage's Unwept Tears), Zhang Jiliang describes the division of theater space:

> All theaters have upstairs stalls. The balcony stalls have tables, which are known as "seats of the officials" *(guanzuo)*. The official seats to the right are called "stage entry" *(shangchangmen)* and the official seats to the left are called "stage exit" *(xiachangmen)*. Those hankering after *dan* are known as *dou*, and they compete for the stalls close to the stage exit. . . . The ticket for an official seat with a table is seven times the cost of a ticket for a casual seat. There is room at each table for two *dou*, with vacant seats for when the *dan* drop by to pay their respects.[18]

Perhaps the most powerful evocation of the eroticization of theater space is from another popular song from the Jiaqing reign period:

> There is no place as thrilling as the upstairs stalls,
> Those *dou* fellows look like they've money to spend.
> A single smile from behind the curtain and
> They won't begrudge the thousand paid for the best table.[19]

In his miscellany collection *Xuannan lingmeng lu* (A Record of Fragmented Dreams from South of Xuanwu Gate) the dilettante Shen Taimou

(1864–1924, nickname Nanye) describes the world of theater as he recalls it from his youth:

> The little boy-actors *(chuling)* from the Three Celebrations, Four Happinesses, and Spring Stage troupes usually take part in three sessions, after which they stand around stage right and stage left and look up toward the balcony. If they notice any familiar guests they rush upstairs to sit with them. Usually there may only be two or three guests in the party, while the boy-actors attending them could number twenty to thirty. The other theatergoers are unable to hide their envy; some even display a certain amount of jealousy, while the party let everyone see how pleased they are. In fact, such parties are not interested in the theater, and before the second last act is over they head off to a restaurant with their favorites.[20]

The recreations that followed required the company of *dan*, and once the flirtation at the theater was concluded the next venue for the *dou* and the *dan* was the restaurant.

Restaurants

The restaurants served as "middlemen" between the theaters and the *dou*. A man of high status who took his friends to one of the more prestigious restaurants was expected to "order" *xianggong* to keep his party company. Usually one actor was ordered for each member of the party. The actors provided by restaurants for their patrons were all from opera troupes in the near vicinity.

When serving *dou* at a restaurant *dan* were not only expected to sing arias, they were also expected to display a certain amount of physical affection. A number of Qing literati miscellanies reveal that some restaurants of the time even included secret rooms fitted with beds and quilts. The existence of secret rooms in restaurants may not have been widely known, and they appear not to have been a universal or even common service. Another locale was far more private and comfortable.

Private Residences

The term *siyu* (private residence) in Qing dynasty Beijing was originally a polite expression referring to a person's private home address. In the world of theater, however, it came to refer to the private residences of a master trainer *(shifu)*, and more specifically, to the larger residences that included apartments for the more popular *dan* in his troupe. The *dan* residents in such compounds (usually numbering two or three) were provided richly appointed apartments where they could receive admirers.[21]

At the end of the nineteenth century the *siyu* of Beijing were an openly recognized and well-recorded feature of the city. *Siyu* operated as exclusive nightclubs and were identified by lanterns and signboards:

> They each have a signboard above their gate, the letters bordered with gold proclaiming "The House of So-and-So," or displaying the actors' names. Inside the main gate the house is lit by an entrance lantern. As the sun disappears they set up stands of candles. The lamps of these places have an opening from which the light escapes, and can thus be told apart from the lamps of the whorehouses. As you pass by there is no need [for you] to inquire, with one look you will understand there are beautiful boys *(shuzi)* inside.[22]

Clearly the *siyu* were not simply the private residences of master trainers, but doubled as pleasure houses.

Male Love Lost: The Decline of *Siyu* in the Early Twentieth Century

From the beginning of the twentieth century there is some evidence that the *siyu* "pleasure houses" were already witnessing a decline. In 1909 Lanling Youhuansheng described the state of the *siyu* at the time:

> The pleasure houses of the *xianggu* are long renowned,
> Yet as the times change all is transformed.
> Take a look yourself in Cherry Lane,
> Now there are no bright lanterns to be found.[23]

The author adds in a note, "In the old days the pleasure houses of the *xianggu* [an alternative rendering of *xianggong*] all had bright lanterns hung at the gate. Cherry Lane was the busiest spot, but there is not a single house operating there now. And at Han Clan Pool and Shaanxi Lane they are [now] as few as the morning stars."[24]

Yet the *siyu* could not have declined to the point where the whole subculture was about to collapse, for two years after the above note appeared Tian Jiyun, one of the most famous *dan* in Beijing opera from the generation just prior to Mei Lanfang, began a campaign to close down what he referred to as the "private residence system" *(siyuzhi)*. Our evidence for this comes from the research of Pan Guangdan:

> [Tian] Jiyun considered the *siyu* system to be the most serious degradation of the theater, and in 1911 he planned to petition the emperor to institute a pro-

hibition. However, powerful interests in the *siyu* system stopped him before he could proceed with the formalities. A censor [employed in the imperial court] accepted [their] bribes and slandered him for "secretly consorting with revolutionary groups and insulting feudal officials in the performance of new opera," and he was incarcerated for one hundred days. With the promulgation of the Republic he continued his campaign, requesting that the new government outlaw the *siyu*, and eventually he succeeded. Later he also suggested that female actors should not be allowed to double as prostitutes, and was again successful.[25]

From the language of a police news bulletin issued on April 20, 1912, it is clear the new administration was ready to listen to Tian's concerns. There was also a new vocabulary through which to express the police department's own aims:

> Regarding the prohibition promulgated by the Outer City Police Headquarters: It has become clear that several houses in Han Clan Pool and Wailang Camp have been using opera as a means of luring young boys from decent families, then dressing them up and training them to sing. Initially this was only a form of cultural gathering, but over time it has become a den of all manner of foulness. Over the generations this has become a peculiar feature of the Beijing cultural landscape, sullying the nation's reputation and attracting the derision of foreign nations. To be referred to as "the likeness of a woman" *(xianggu)* is completely contrary to human nature *(rendao)*. Let it be known that in the reform of society the theater has a contribution to make, and taking up a career in acting does not disqualify one from inclusion in the citizenry. However, if one finds it necessary to entice others as a living and imitate the ways of prostitutes, one's dignity is utterly reduced. At the present time the Republic is in its infancy and there is an opportunity for something new to appear in place of stubborn and disgusting customs. This department has been given the responsibility for the reinstatement of decent ways of life and the protection of human rights. Thus we absolutely refuse to tolerate any example of such infamous behavior within the limits of the national capital. For the above reasons we now institute this prohibition and all are advised to desist from previous errors, find a respectable occupation, respect their human dignity, and join in creating an upright citizenry. If, following this prohibition, there are some who continue to traffic in young boys and open private residences, the law is in place and this police headquarters will show no leniency.[26]

Much of the "official" language in this passage reflects the entry of western legal and social values into Chinese administrative discourse, both in terms of its vocabulary and the ideas and structures that went with them. However, while the words and ideas are adopted from foreign forms of discourse they are also reinterpreted through the moral sensibility of a society that is still thoroughly Confucian, despite the demise of the imperial system of government. Words like police *(xunjing)*, citizenry *(guomin)*, dignity *(renge)*, and human rights *(renquan)* did not exist in the Chinese language until the late decades of the nineteenth century and only came into general use after the promulgation of the Republic. On the other hand, there is nothing at all new about issuing a prohibition on prostitution (male or female); such edicts were continually promulgated during the Qing dynasty. What stands out in this document is the concern with the way the behavior of "citizens" might attract the "derision of foreign nations" *(yixiao waibang)*, in this case a form of behavior (and here the emphasis is clearly on visible and public *prostitution*) that in the past might have offended heaven or morality.

Three weeks after the issuing of the police bulletin in April 1912 the local news-sheet *Beijing zhengzong aiguo bao* (Beijing True Patriotism News) included an editorial where western custom and precedent are cited directly as an argument for changing Chinese attitudes to the world of theater:

> We Chinese have always treated the words performer *(you)* and prostitute *(chang)* as if they were one and the same. In fact, performers are performers and prostitutes are prostitutes. In future we should consider them separately.
>
> During the era of imperial examinations the status of performers was held in the lowest regard. There was no awareness of the contribution dramatic and musical performance can make to the advancement of social morality *(shidao renxin)*. In western nations actors and singers are fêted by society and have rights under the governments of the day. Those who tread the boards should not be regarded with the derision they receive from Chinese people.[27]

Regardless of the "real" situation of actors in the west, what is significant is this author's conviction that the centuries-old association in Chinese culture of performers with prostitution should be brought to an end. His argument, like others of the time, required the introduction of two new elements: 1) a comparable civilization providing an exemplary alternative, that is, "the west"; and 2) a vision of social progress. Two not unrelated discourses are brought together in the mobilization of a linear temporality that came to describe "a dichotomous, discontinuous, and oppositional vision of tradition (as Chinese and particular) versus modernity (as Western and universal)."[28] The author does not appear to be interested in the nexus between the theater world, prostitution, and men of high social standing. His analysis, emanating as it does from the brush of a member of the educated elite, may instead be taken as further evidence of a change of opinion among the educated and fashionable.

In 1918, after an extended period of study in the United States at Cornell and Columbia universities, Hu Shi (1891–1962), one of the central figures of the New Culture and May Fourth movements, returned home to advance his push for the adoption of the vernacular *baihua* as the medium for educated discourse. From his letters to *Xin qingnian* (New Youth), ostensibly addressing literary reform, it is clear that Hu Shi saw himself as addressing a much broader agenda of cultural reform:

> *Pinhua baojian* is the *Rulin waishi* [The Scholars, a satirical exposé] of the Qianlong (1736–1796) and Jiaqing (1796–1821) periods in Beijing. It is of enormous historical importance. Those with little insight regard it as an obscene book *[yinshu]* simply because it describes the vogue for male homoerotic attraction *[nanse]*,[29] not knowing that its historical importance is in its blindness to the fact that male homoerotic attraction should be despised, just in the same way that *Niehai hua* [Flower in a Sea of Sin] and *Guanchang xianxingji* [Officialdom Unmasked] are also blind to the fact that indulging in whores and concubines were despicable things.[30]

The following year another letter from Hu Shi appeared in *Xin qingnian*, in which he included the following reiteration of his earlier comments:

> From the perspective of westerners [the hero of] *Shuihuzhuan* [The Water Margin], Wu Song, would be damned as "inhuman." Zhang Qiugu, [the hero] from the novel *Jiuweigui* [The Nine-Tailed Turtle], from your and my perspective should be damned as a filthy lecher. This is in the same spirit as my comment in the previous letter that *Pinhua baojian* is blind to the evils of male homoerotic attraction.[31]

One does not need to be *au fait* with Hu's intertextual references to sense the strength of his disapproval. Yet at the same time it is important to point out that *Pinhua baojian*, the novel he so condemns, is not obscene in the sense of a work that concerns itself with intimate physical details, but is rather a novel that "works out the relationship of sublime love step by step within its own appropriation of the theme of *qing* [feeling, passion] and the idealization of the feminine [embodied in the *dan*]."[32] Hu Shi is more worried about the possibility of same-sex desire being expressed in the act of *reading* than in its description within the text itself, for the novel celebrates same-sex desire without the slightest hint of "shame." Hu, on the other hand, has learned that "homosexuality" should be condemned for no other reason than it is evil, *tout court*. And the letter continues with a more general condemnation of Chinese sexual culture as a whole:

> I would never be able to agree with the comments made by yourself and Mr. Chen Duxiu in relation to *Jin ping mei*. In my view the so-called "love" *[qing'ai]* between men and women among the Chinese today is still limited to animalistic carnal lust. On the one hand, we must today do everything we can to reject books like *Jin ping mei,* and on the other hand we must apply ourselves to the translation of cultivated stories of love [from the western tradition]. In fifty years, it may be that we can succeed in changing current [sexual] attitudes.[33]

The changes had already begun, and they were not limited to members of the young educated elite; actors themselves also sensed a change in the cultural climate.[34] In 1916, in his miscellany *Liyuan jiahua* (Anecdotes from the Theater World), Wang Mengsheng comments on developments in the early twentieth century:

> I have heard that they had arranged to strike [against the *siyu* system], planning to support themselves exclusively by their [acting] ability, desisting completely from serving others with their beauty. It is such a wonderful thing, that they are able to step onto the path of virtue.[35]

The conjunction of actors and a "path of virtue" is unprecedented in Chinese cultural history, and this account actually implies that the problem of moral weakness lay with the boys. In the end, the evidence suggests, it was *dan* who stood up against the *siyu* system, divesting themselves of their *xianggong* identities. The actions of *dan* like Tian Jiyun, together with the new concern of the government for China's international moral standing, succeeded in closing down the *siyu*. In addition to the change in moral climate, other pressures would also have contributed to the decline of theater-based prostitution. The end of the examination system, for example, meant that there would be no further generations of literati—the theaters' largest and most important client base.[36]

It is perhaps no mere coincidence that the brothels of Beijing, from which the status-conscious literati had for over three hundred years turned away in favor of boy-entertainers, enjoyed an increase in business during the transition from the Qing dynasty to the Republic.[37] In his miscellany *Chunming menglu* (Dream Record of the Capital) the literatus He Gangde (1855–1935), who had served as a senior official in both the Qing and the Republican governments, comments on the change in entertainment fashion from the final years of the empire to the first years of the republic in Beijing:

> [Formerly,] for government officials in the capital, liaisons with actors or [female] prostitutes contravened regulations. Furthermore, while it was possible to overlook liaisons with actors, liaisons with prostitutes brought considerable disgrace. The brothels were concentrated within eight major lanes in the vicinity of Qianmen. The lanes in that area were dank and squalid. Any self-respecting person would naturally avoid the place. . . . Later the private residences *(xiachu,* an alternative expression for *siyu)* gradually disappeared, while the brothel doors were busier than ever. No one made much of visiting a brothel. Such was the influence of change in this [latest] era.[38]

He Gangde published his recollections in 1922. Seven years earlier Wang Mengsheng had made similar observations on the state of prostitution in the capital:

> In recent years the capital has become crowded with "flower groves." Influential and powerful men frequent them boldly as if there was no tomorrow. As for [the boy prostitutes], even without the reform it is unlikely they would have had any visitors.[39]

It is clear in the above passages that the authors are describing changes that took place from the last years of the Qing dynasty and which they witnessed continue through the first and second decades of the twentieth century. Xiaomingxiong's *History of Homosexuality in China (Zhongguo tongxing'ai shilu, xiuding ben)* arrives at a similar conclusion, arguing that the entry of the Eight Power Allied Forces into Beijing in 1900 precipitated the rapid decline of the city's elite homoerotic subculture. The evidence we have accumulated so far also agrees with his identification of at least one reason for the decline, in his words, that "the male mode *(nanfeng)* was not well suited to western custom."[40] The change came about not by direct interference from foreign troops or police forces, but through a growing consciousness that the practices surrounding male prostitution and the theater were perceived as ugly. The foreign gaze brought China's cultural elite into contact with an entirely new and different regime of proscription and morality. As the last generation of China's imperial elite were being introduced to the world of the *siyu* they must also have been increasingly conscious of the threat the incursion of values from outside their world presented to the continued evocation of *nanse* in the stage performances of the *dan*.

The passage from Ba Jin with which we opened suggests that eventually many would have sensed the message via their "grandsons," a new generation with very different ideas about love. We might also wonder why the literary location of this struggle needed to be separated by a generation and could not take place between adjacent generations, between father and son. Is it perhaps because that may have required a different kind of struggle, where sons who had also been "blind to the evils of male homoerotic attraction" were forced to confront their "sins"?

Conclusion

In the material we have been able to survey to date there were few voices willing to openly advocate for the continuation of the *siyu* system. There are nostalgic voices, and there are hints that at least before the end of the empire there were those who were able to remain active behind the scenes. Then there are voices of moral indignation, most of which make reference to the west as the source of a new moral standard. China's young intellectual elite were entering a period of busy discussion about love and sexuality, but the new discourse on same-sex love *(tongxing'ai)* initiated by the translation of western medical and psychological texts would not include references to *nanse* or *dan*. The emphasis was instead on the discursive regulation of new and emerging forms of sexuality. Indeed, as Tze-lan Sang has pointed out, "It was above all the incorporation of female same-sex relations that distinguished the new discursive domain from the late imperial discursive domain, marking it as modern."[41] The introduction of a dichotomy between the normal and the deviant in modern medical discourse developed in the 1920s was accompanied by a "modern" and "scientific" symmetry of male and female *tongxing'ai*.

We might wonder, what happened to the *dan* and *xianggong*? It is a strange irony that in the 1930s, not long after the *xianggong* had disappeared, at least one *dan* was being "hailed as a triumph of cultural exchange" after a six-month tour across the United States.[42] In fact, already by the 1920s Mei Lan-fang (1894–1961) had negotiated the spaces between discourses of modernity, sexuality, and cultural identity to "become the most renowned celebrity in all of China." In concluding his 1999 article reviewing Mei's career and role in the "recod[ing of] Peking opera into the genre representative of Chinese national culture" Joshua Goldstein makes two very interesting observations. Firstly, Mei's stage image became a spectacle within a spectacle, the Chinese media watched American audiences and critics watching Mei, "turning the western gaze into a spectacle itself." Secondly, Mei's innovations and "success at becoming an icon of Chinese national culture . . . enabled the forgetting of his historical contextuality. Instead of becoming a symbol of the complex struggle with colonial modernity fought by an entire generation of Republican-era actors and artists, Mei has instead become an icon used by cultural conservatives to symbolize a dehistoricized Chinese cultural essence."[43] Part of that decontextualization involved the disappearance of the *xianggong*, who neither made it into the discourse developing around *tongxing'ai* and homosexuality between the 1920s and 1940s, nor into the history of China's national theater. We can often be left with the impression that they did not make it into the twentieth century at all.

Notes

1. Ba Jin, *Jia*, 73. The passage describing Juehui's struggle may be found on pages 72–77.
2. Ba Jin, "He duzhe tan *Jia*," 478–486.
3. The idea of China being the "sick man of Asia" was promoted by the Japanese at the end of the nineteenth century, and by the early twentieth century it had found its way into the work of several reform-minded writers. For a discussion of how this idea was translated graphically in works of medical art, see Heinrich, "Handmaids."
4. Ba Jin, "He duzhe tan *Jia*," 480. Ba Jin says that the novel is based on the experience of his own family between 1920 and 1921.
5. The reputation of the *mingshi*-type literatus had been suffering a steady decline from at least the first half of the eighteenth century, their hypocrisy supplying the inspiration for Wu Jingzi's satire *Rulin waishi* [The Scholars]. This state of affairs may even have led to the emergence of a new word, *damingshi*, to describe truly talented members of the literati.
6. A useful essay on some of the conceptual problems in translating concepts of same-sex sexuality, both cross-culturally and historically, is Rupp, "Toward a Global History of Same-Sex Sexuality." An excellent discussion of the difficulties presented by Republican China can be found in Sang, *Emerging Lesbian*, 99–126. For references on theoretical disagreements, see also note 7 below.
7. See Volpp, "Classifying Lust"; Volpp, "Literary Circulation." For a detailed critique of the first article, and an argument for identifying a homoerotic fashion developing throughout this period, see Stevenson and Wu, "Quilts."
8. Vitiello, "Dragon's Whim," 341–373, 364–365ff.
9. Wu Cuncun, *Ming-Qing shehui xing'ai fengqi*, 114–226; Wu Cuncun, *Homoerotic Sensibilities*. For an analysis from a legal history perspective, see Sommer, "Penetrated Male." There is by no means agreement within contemporary scholarship over the existence of a fashion, nor on its significance. For a rhetorical analysis that challenges the identification of a homoerotic fashion in late imperial China, see Volpp, "Classifying Lust."
10. Such tendencies may be found in both Chinese writing and works by western scholars. See, for example, Qi, *Xiban*, 42; van Gulik, *Erotic Colour Prints*, part 3, poem 4.
11. Mackerras, *Peking Opera*.
12. Luomo'an, *"Huaifang ji,"* 594.

13. When not performing on stage *dan* actors wore traditional male attire.

14. Anonymous, *Dumen zhuzhici*, 1173.

15. Senior male roles *(laosheng)* did see an increase from the middle of the nineteenth century; however, this can be seen as a return to some "balance" in role types, and by this time the *off-stage* role of the *dan* was well established. See Mackerras, *Peking Opera*, 189-191; Wu Cuncun, *Homoerotic Sensibilities*, 116-158.

16. Roger Darrobers in *Opéra de Pékin* (pp. 350-364) notes this tendency, as well as a desire in the literati to see *dan* take up many of their own interests, such as calligraphy and painting. See also Mackerras, *Peking Opera*, 189.

17. Chen Sen, *Pinhua baojian*, 61, 184. For recent discussion of this work see Starr, "Shifting Boundaries"; McMahon, "Sublime Love." Both of these articles argue for an understanding of the *dan* as a *feminine* object of male desire within a highly socialized gender system.

18. Zhang Jiliang, *Jintai canlei ji*, 249. For a general description of the layout of the theater, stage and seating see Mackerras, *Peking Opera*, 201-204, where a diagram of a *xiyuan* is also available (p. 202, fig. 7).

19. Desuoting, *Caozhu yichuan*, 1172.

20. Shen Taimou, *Xuannan lingmeng lu*, 809.

21. Usage of this term can sometimes be confusing, because the literati admirers often write as if the *siyu* belonged to the *dan* themselves. Yet there is no doubt that all concerned were well aware of the true state of ownership.

22. Yilansheng, *Cemao yutan*, 603-604.

23. Youhuansheng, *Jinghua bai'er zhuzhici*, 294. The same poem and note is also found in Zhang Cixi, *Beiping liyuan zhuzhi ci huibian*, 1179.

24. Youhuansheng, *Jinghua bai'er zhuzhici*, 294.

25. Pan Guangdan, *Zhongguo lingren xueyuan zhi yanjiu*, 238-239.

26. Zhang Cixi, *Yanguilai yi suibi*, 1243. Darrobers is quite silent on this fear of derision from the west, but does mention a new concern on the part of the police with indecency in *Opéra de Pékin* (p. 445). Bret Hinsch raises the arrival of the west in his introduction and epilogue in *Passons*. Critical of Hinsch's "simplistic and naive interpretation . . . attributing social prejudice and official hostility towards homosexuals in twentieth-century China to an 'importation of western intolerance,' " Frank Dikötter discusses later influences of western discourses on homosexuality in *Sex, Culture and Modernity in China* (pp. 138-145). This criticism of Hinsch is somewhat unfair, since most of the primary sources Dikötter cites are from the Republican period (1911-1949), predominantly the 1930s, and are not related to the late nineteenth and early twentieth century problems identified by Hinsch nor, for that matter, the period under discussion here.

27. Xiafu, *Youchang bu yi xiangti binglun*.

28. Shu-mei Shih, *Lure*, 50.

29. Hu Shi had been absent from China for seven years at the time of writing this letter and his usage indicates that his understanding of *nanse* has been influenced by the use of "homosexuality" in English. In the imperial period *nüse* refers to women who (potentially) arouse erotic interest, or the *quality* of potential arousal that they embody. A similar range of meanings applies to *nanse* (sometimes translated as male love) where a male embodies potential to arouse. In both cases there is an observer (another connotation of *se* is

color) observing the observed, and it is also understood that the observer is male and the observed is young (regardless of the age of the observer).

30. Hu Shi, "Letter to Qian Xuantong." The authors of the last two novels mentioned are Zeng Pu (1872–1935) and Li Boyuan (1876–1906).

31. Hu Shi, "Lun xiaoshuo ji baihua yunwen," 75. See also Sang, *Emerging Lesbian*, 3–5.

32. McMahon, "Sublime Love," 72–73.

33. Hu Shi, "Lun xiaoshuo ji baihua yunwen," 76. Here Hu is addressing the editor of *Xin qingnian*, Chen Duxiu, as well as Qian Xuantong.

34. For evidence of shifts in attitudes toward same-sex attraction and cultural experiment in popular literature, see Maram Epstein (this volume).

35. Wang Mengsheng, *Liyuan jiahua*, 143–144.

36. The question of women attending the theater in the twentieth century is an important one, but it also raises some incredible complexities. While women attending the theaters was a fairly late development (they were excluded by law, right up until 1911), women from elite families were continuously exposed to the theater through performances in their homes, and many were just as taken with the *dan* as their male relatives. Their later admission into the world of Beijing theater culture may have even contributed to the fanning of *dan* stardom (there is considerable evidence of this, although their attitudes toward the *siyu* system may have been another matter entirely). We are not sure how to deal with all of this in the present essay, and would prefer to address it separately in the near future.

37. The key terms here are "literati" and "Beijing." The "steady growth of a commercial sex market" revealed in the legal evidence analyzed by Matthew Sommer relates only to men of commoner status. Sommer, *Sex*, 220–221, 258.

38. He, *Chunming menglu*, 105–106.

39. Wang Mengsheng, *Liyuan jiahua*, 144.

40. Xiaomingxiong, *Zhongguo tongxing'ai shilu*, 355.

41. Sang, *Emerging Lesbian*, 126.

42. Goldstein, "Mei Lanfang," 377. See also John Zou's essay (this volume).

43. Goldstein, "Mei Lanfang," 414, 415.

CHAPTER 4

Rewriting Sexual Ideals in *Yesou puyan*

MARAM EPSTEIN

IN 1929 A MINOR literary event took place in semi-colonial Shanghai. The small press, *Hao qingnian shudian* (Good Youth Publishing House), published a revised and abridged Qing literati novel under the title *Yuanzhu guben Yesou puyan* (Original, Old-style Rustic's Words of Exposure). Sales of the hundred-chapter abridgement were good enough that the press brought out six print runs during the four years between 1929 and 1933.[1] This essay attempts to explain the popularity of this handsome but poorly edited Republican-era abridgement of a marginal eighteenth-century novel called *Yesou puyan* (A Rustic's Words of Exposure, hereafter *YSPY*); this work had been largely forgotten for over a century after its composition until two versions were published in the 1880s.[2] When I began working on the novel, I had assumed that the sudden late nineteenth-century interest in it was due to its exuberant vision of China's centrality to the world. By the end of the 154-chapter novel, the entire known world has been brought under Chinese political and cultural domination: In Japan, Buddhist temples, formerly the site of esoteric sexual rites, are converted into Confucian academies, and in Europe the royalty adopt Chinese script, Confucian marriage practices, and a curriculum based on the Four Books and Five Classics. Embassies from Islamic countries and Southeast Asia arrive in Beijing to join in the birthday celebrations of the hero's mother. However, a comparative reading of the Republican abridgement has forced me to reject my initial assumption that readerly interest in *YSPY* lay in its narrative about Chinese cultural supremacy, since the abridgement cuts out almost all references to foreign nations or peoples. As I argue below, the redactors of this version used their revised text to model modern gender and sexual roles.

Indeed, many of the critical responses to this otherwise orthodox novel have pointed to its unusual use of sexualized details.[3] In 1935 the scholar Han Lü was the first to suggest that the literatus author Xia Jingqu (1705–1787) was slightly unbalanced;[4] in 1975 Hou Jian went one step further and dismissed the novel as the product of a deranged mind. As Hou Jian wrote in "The Perverse Psychology of *Yesou puyan*," the protagonist Wen Suchen's exaggerated reverence for his mother in conjunction with the frequent descriptions of aberrant sexuality and scatological details suggest that the author was psychologically unsound and suffered from an Oedipal complex.[5] More recently, based on the descriptions of tender intimacies between the protagonist and several of his six wives, which lead to his great fertility, Keith McMahon has argued that the novel provides a model for a proper, healthy Confucian sexuality.[6] Below, I compare the constructions of masculinity and sexuality in the two versions of *YSPY* to trace the changing ideals of masculinity from the late imperial to the Republican periods. In so doing, I hope to counter the tendency of scholarship on gender and sexuality in twentieth-century China to separate the modern from its late-imperial roots.

YSPY is exceptional for its creation of an unquestionably masculine and potent Confucian hero. The hypermasculine protagonist, Wen Suchen, seems an inversion of the flawed, weak, and frequently emasculated male characters so common in other literati novels. Wen Suchen is a Confucian superhero who combines the ideals of the literati *wen* and martial *wu* traditions. Not only does he master the Confucian disciplines of philosophy, poetry, medicine, dream divination, mathematics, archery, rhetoric, and warfare, Suchen defeats a large network of rebels who are using black magic to overthrow the Chinese emperor and reestablishes and reinvigorates Confucian rule. In contrast to other eighteenth-century protagonists for whom fertility is a source of concern, Suchen fathers twenty-four sons with his six wives and has over five hundred descendents by the end of the novel. In fact, Suchen is the embodiment of yang potency, as the following episodes illustrate. At one point Suchen cures the Stone Maiden who suffers from an excess of yin that has retarded her proper physical development, making her body unusually cold and pallid and her vagina impenetrable (hence the name of her condition); she has never menstruated, and her breasts are smaller than his. When the two are forced to share a bed, the yang energy from Suchen's body gradually "steams" her and sensations slowly arise in her numb body. The cure is not complete, however, until Suchen masturbates her and she begins to menstruate (97.1115). Her later fertility (she gives birth to twenty-eight sons after she marries someone else) seems as much a reflection of Suchen's potency as her own fecundity. An even more amazing demonstration of the power of Suchen's yang-identified body is the episode where he brings a corpse back to life by wrapping the body in straw and urinating on it (85.974).[7]

This anomalous characterization of a youthful, muscular, sexually potent and active male protagonist was the perfect answer to May Fourth appeals for a modern male Chinese subject; yet *YSPY* failed to influence other writers or move out of the margins of Chinese literary history. In contrast, the character Su Feiya, named after Sofia Perovskaia (1854–1881), immediately captured the modernist revolutionary imagination when her story was popularized in the 1902 *Dong'Ou nühaojie* (The Heroine from Eastern Europe). While it is impossible to account for why the fantasies of a positive and empowered masculinity in both versions of *YSPY* were unable to compete with dominant late-imperial and Republican-era representations of masculinity under siege, it is important to understand the deep native roots of the "crisis" of masculinity first articulated in the midst of intense interest in modernization and westernization during the May Fourth movement of the 1920s.[8] Precisely because the treatment of masculinity in *YSPY* is so exaggerated, the late-imperial and Republican versions of the novel throw into relief disjunctures and continuities in the cultural meanings projected onto masculinity, sex, and the body.

Masculinity and Its Meanings: Conflicts between Autonomy and Ritual

As Kam Louie has suggested, there is no one definition of, or model for, Chinese masculinity. In his recent study, Louie plots Chinese paradigms of masculinity along a continuum spanning the scholar ideal, which he categorizes as *wen*, the civil or mental, and the military ideal, or *wu*, the physical or martial. Based largely on twentieth-century sources, Louie argues that these modes of masculinity are based on interconnected biological and cultural vectors that preclude women and non-Chinese races.[9] He identifies several qualities as defining Chinese notions of masculinity: self-direction or autonomy; self-control, particularly in terms of sexual desire; loyalty to a homosocial code of ethics of either righteousness *(yi)* or loyalty *(zhong)*; and the trumping of physical strength by intellectual and aesthetic accomplishments.[10] Although I agree with Louie that traditional Chinese ideals of masculinity are spread along a martial-literati continuum, my readings of traditional ritual, fictional, and medical texts have led me to argue that biology was not foundational to traditional views of gender.[11] Gender and even the materiality of the body were informed by yin-yang symbolism. Although a complex system of complementary and analogical terms separated masculine from feminine, no absolute boundaries distinguished the two. Attempts to essentialize gender were a project of twentieth-century modernization and should not be read back into the premodern period. Unlike the European west, where the Judeo-Christian tradition established a hegemonic discourse reiterated in medical texts and legal codes that essentialized gender and assigned divinely mandated meanings to the sexed body, there were a variety of simultaneously circulating discourses in late-imperial China which conceptualized the relationship between sex, gender, and the body in different ways. Legal and medical discussions of naturally occurring sex changes accepted corporeal fluidity as consistent with the transformations of yin and yang; as Charlotte Furth has argued, these physical transformations did not threaten the "natural" order so long as the person was in the end properly stationed in the social order.[12]

In fiction, narrative interest in sexed bodies was less concerned with detailing specific sexual attributes or establishing gender norms than exploring the subject's ability to resist or conform to orthodox norms.[13] Differing from sexual handbooks that associate yang with a male body and yin with a female body, Cheng-Zhu Neo-Confucian rhetoric equates yang with regulatory orthodoxy and yin with a transgressive potential. In *YSPY*, yin-yang symbolism inflects the gendering of characters so that virtuous women in the novel take on masculine qualities while male characters who resist orthodoxy assume certain yin feminizing traits.[14]

The qualities that Louie uses to define Chinese masculinity stress the autonomous and bounded nature of the masculine subject. These masculine attributes do not take into account that in the premodern period personal virtue was based upon mastery of ritual protocol *(li)*. The five relationships upon which the Confucian social order was built—ruler-minister, parent-child, husband-wife, older sibling-younger sibling, and friend—generally privileged adult men and placed them in a yang-identified position of superiority to those around them. However, the need for an adult male to subordinate himself to his parents and political superiors meant that all socially engaged men necessarily adopted subordinate yin roles that limited their autonomy.[15] The frequency with which male protagonists are cast as orphans, outlaws or recluses in late-imperial fiction seems to reflect a desire to achieve independence from social hierarchies. Even Baoyu, the central male character in *Dream of the Red Chamber*, a novel that depicts life within a large multistem elite family, is effectively and artificially relieved of filial obligations after he moves into the sensuous garden world for which the novel is famed. In contrast, his father, who is both a mature and loyal servant of the state and a filial son, is pointedly ineffective in both roles. In chapter 33, a strong rebuke from his elderly mother reduces Jia Zheng to a state of cowering abjection in the scene where he attempts to discipline Baoyu, his own son, for indiscretions that had offended family and state mores.[16] The duty for a socially engaged adult male to subordinate himself to the frequently arbitrary demands of a parent or corrupt political bureaucracy made it impossible for men to create a truly coherent and empowered masculine identity.

Virtuous Masculinity: Filial Piety, Sex, and Self-Control

The character of Wen Suchen, the central protagonist of *Yesou puyan*, can be read as an attempt by the author Xia Jingqu to resolve the paradox of orthodox masculinity—the conflicting desires to achieve both autonomy and virtue. Suchen bridges *wen* and *wu* ideals and exemplifies political and filial loyalty. Suchen's task is simplified because his mother, Lady Shui, displaces the emperor as the symbolic center of the Chinese state. By the end of the novel, the entire empire, and indeed the world, has joined Suchen and the imperial family in elevating Lady Shui to the focus of a state cult. Foreign delegations arrive to pay homage and celebrate Chinese cultural dominance on the occasions of her seventieth and hundredth birthdays (chaps. 138 and 144). The novel concludes with a dream vision in which Lady Shui joins the assembly of the Confucian matriarchs and Suchen becomes one of the Confucian sages (chap. 154). Lady Shui's symbolic importance derives from the novel's construction of filial piety as the definitive expression of Confucian values; Suchen's dedication to his mother never brings him into conflict with the state.

For both *wen* and *wu* character types, one of the most important demonstrations of proper masculine virtue is resistance to sexual desire.[17] Although men were expected to do what was necessary to ensure continuation of the patriline, in traditional narratives a male character's virtue was demonstrated through his sexual self-control.[18] Although Suchen's characterization also incorporates aspects of a romantic *fengliu* lover derived from the scholar type, his virtue is repeatedly tested and he repeatedly proves his virtue by rejecting sexual pleasure.[19] The first test of Suchen's sexual virtue occurs early in the novel when a couple whom Suchen had rescued attempt to show their gratitude by presenting him with their beautiful younger sister, a genius at mathematics, as a concubine. Knowing Suchen will refuse the girl, they first get him drunk and send the girl Xuangu naked into his bed. When Xuangu lies next to him, the yang energy *(yang qi)* emanating from his body "steams" her so that her entire body gets hot and her heart beats out of control. He rolls over in his sleep and inserts a leg between her thighs.

> Xuangu's spring desires were aroused; how could she sleep with her skin touching Suchen? Suchen's thigh was sandwiched between her thighs, and even though a sheet separated them, the heat *(reqi)* (from his body) had already penetrated her "bud" and started it itching and despite herself the fire of passion *(yuhuo)* had been aroused. Instantly, her face reddened and her ears burned, and her heart was pounding. Unable to control herself, she had no choice but to grasp Suchen's

shoulders and bury her head in his chest and try to swallow her suffering. (7.75–76)

Significantly, it is Xuangu who feels sexual arousal; moreover, the stages of her arousal are a purely physical response to the hot yang energy emanating from his body. Suchen is oblivious to her arousal. Her presence soon wakes him up and he calls out in alarm and then wraps himself tightly in a blanket for protection. Suchen only agrees to take her as a concubine after she convinces him that her chastity has been compromised (7.76). The two spend several more intimate nights together tracing arcs and geometric theorems on each other's bodies, but Suchen insists that they need to receive his mother's permission before consummating the relationship. On another occasion when they share a bed, it becomes clear that Xuangu does not entirely understand her physical response to him; wanting nothing more than to have her and Suchen's bodies melt into one, she wonders why she never felt this way when sharing a bed with her sister-in-law. Suchen responds with a philosophical monologue on the nature of "the pleasures between a man and a woman" *(nannü zhi le)* and the distinction between sexual and emotional passions *(yu* and *qing)*. Xuangu learns from him how to control her bodily desires and concludes that the physical act of sex (literally "clouds and rain") is as unnecessary to pleasure as painting legs on a snake (8.93).

Unlike Xuangu, Suchen seems untouched by physical desires. Even after his mother and primary wife make the arrangements for Suchen to take several new concubines, Suchen needs to be forced to leave his mother's chambers. Suchen argues that he should observe proper hierarchy by spending the night with his primary wife; he only joins his new concubines after his wife angrily forces him to leave her room (49.574). Suchen twice more defers legitimate sexual passion in order to fulfill his filial obligations to be with his mother (57.656, 58.661). Although he shares nonsexual intimate moments with various of his concubines before they marry, conjugal love and sexuality are public arrangements that countenance no individual or private desires. Suchen's regimen of having intercourse with each wife once each month leads to his phenomenal levels of fertility (88.1012). Sexual pleasure falls a distant second to duty.

YSPY incorporates two opposing modes of sexual behavior. Proper sexual contact, as exemplified by Suchen, is hygienic and yang-based: it derives from self-restraint and promotes health and fertility.[20] In contrast, lack of sexual control on the part of either male or female characters is associated with a yin threat to the normative order.[21] For example, in order to cure the Chenghua

Emperor's illness, which has arisen from "being too unbridled in his intimacy with women, resulting in an increase of yin and the decline of yang," Suchen recommends that the emperor boost his yang energy by avoiding the women's quarters, eating a simple diet of rice gruel, and sleeping sandwiched between two robust boys (87.1001).

In *YSPY* threats to the normative Confucian order are sexualized. And even though hundreds of women are kidnapped and turned into the sexual slaves of the anti-imperial forces, the main narrative focus is Suchen's sexual vulnerability. When attacked, Suchen's first defense is self-control. In one such scene, Suchen is awakened by a beautiful woman. She pins him down with one hand and with her other reaches into his pants, strokes his penis *(yangwu)* and squeezes his testicles. Suchen realizes she is a *yaksha*, a female monster, and reaches for his dagger while hardening his testicles so they are like steel pellets. The *yaksha* then attacks him with her enormously long and sharp tongue. Suchen kills her by yanking out her tongue by the roots (65.738). Two chapters later, Suchen is kidnapped and held hostage by a eunuch who hopes to obtain his semen, a pure yang substance, to produce an elixir. Suchen is drugged and bound; the only part of his body that is not immobilized is his penis. Each woman in the eunuch's harem attempts to arouse him in a fantastic sex show.[22] Suchen realizes that he is in serious danger *(weiji)* and struggles to find a way to escape (68.775). Although the women finally succeed in inducing Suchen to have an erection, he ultimately defeats them by meditating and concentrating his yang essence in his marrow so that it will not be lost through ejaculation (68.777).

In keeping with the yang-identified values of the novel, the aesthetic frame of *YSPY* is shifted toward the masculine, inverting the feminized conventions of the scholar-beauty novel, a dominant genre of eighteenth-century fiction.[23] Scholar-beauty novels are typically structured around a plot in which a beautiful and talented scholar marries an equally beautiful and talented wife (or wives). Suchen and his six wives move into a lush garden; but in place of the self-expressive and sensual arts of poetry, painting, and drama, the usual preoccupations of scholar-beauty romances, the family stages a display of Confucian regimentation (chaps. 57–63). Fearing that they might be corrupted by living in such a sumptuous environment, Lady Shui arranges detailed schedules so that each family member divides his or her day between study and household responsibilities (60.683). The most striking transformation of the literati garden trope is the substitution of contests of martial arts and learned debate in place of the more usual poetry competitions (chap. 60). In Xia Jingqu's masculinist fantasy, masculine self-discipline is a moral quality to which men and women alike should aspire. Although only Suchen, a man, can embody the full regulative and generative power of yang, it is in the end through his self-control and filial piety that his masculine authority achieves its full potential.

Sexually and ritually, Suchen is the antithesis of Ximen Qing of the late-Ming novel *The Golden Lotus (Jin ping mei)*. Ximen Qing, who also has six wives, has no parents and no interest in limiting his sexual conquests. He beds dozens of women and a handful of pages before he dies of sexual exhaustion in chapter 79. Zhang Zhupo, the great Qing commentator to the novel, attributed Ximen Qing's destructive behavior to a failure of filial piety.[24] Moreover, despite his numerous sexual partners, he has great difficulty producing a male heir. Motivating Ximen Qing are the dual goals of sexual pleasure and power through domination; it is crucial to the semiotics of the novel that his political and economic powers peak in chapter 50 precisely when he obtains an aphrodisiac that enhances his sexual performance.[25] Although both Suchen and Ximen Qing are depicted as more powerful than the male characters who surround them, both fall victim to attacks of sexual vampirism. Suchen manages to survive by dint of self-control; Ximen Qing succumbs in his final sexual battle with his concubine Pan Jinlian.

Although Ximen Qing provides the model of debauched male behavior for late-imperial readers, certain aspects of his characterization prefigure qualities that became positively associated with masculinity in the Republican edition of *YSPY*. Among these are the linking of masculinity to sexual potency, physical superiority to women (rather than sexual self-control), and autonomy from parental control and other prescribed ritual obligations. A final similarity between the pornographic *Jin ping mei* and the Republican rewriting of *YSPY* is the promotion of sex as a means to physical and emotional pleasure rather than as linked to fertility and health.

Revising *YSPY* for a Republican Readership

Although the plot closely follows the original text, the abridged Republican-era version of *YSPY* reconfigures the relationship between gender, body, and sex. In this version, the major characters' behaviors conform to the essentialized gender norms being introduced to urban China in the popular press. The symbolic meanings associated with gender, particularly the idealization of masculine behaviors associated with yang ritual order, disappear from the abridgment. Furthermore, the range of meanings associated with sex becomes much narrower; the revision reduces the hygienic functions of the protagonist's sexed body while highlighting the sexual organs as a site of physical pleasure. In keeping with this sex-positive outlook, certain graphic depictions of sexual arousal are preserved in the abridged text while the many scenes depicting sexual vampirism are removed. The role given to the mother, Lady Wang, is minimized and trivialized; she no longer anchors the novel's moral vision. (Characters have different names in the abridgement: Suchen is given the Ming loyalist name Zhu Ming [Residing in the Ming], and Lady Shui is renamed Lady Wang.) Zhu Ming is given a degree of autonomy from his mother unthinkable for Suchen. These changes suggest that the editor(s) were attempting to modernize the novel's treatment of gender, sex, and family.

Astonishingly, given that the *Original, Old-style Yesou puyan* was published between 1929 and 1933, none of the episodes from the original novel that illustrate China's international military and cultural superiority were retained. Although one would think that the increasing aggressiveness of Japanese imperialism and Shanghai's semi-colonial status would have piqued readers' interest in the episodes narrating the sinification of Europe and colonization of Japan, the content of the abridgement is remarkably uninterested in China's national identity. The abridged text truncates the original narrative at chapter 100 (almost all references to non-Chinese peoples occur after chapter 100 in the original). Several brief references to invasions by Japanese pirates, which occur before chapter 100, are kept in the abridgement, but are not elaborated. While the abridgement does insert a handful of brief anti-Manchu or Chinese nationalist passages, they are so infrequent that they cannot be said to create a powerful nationalist agenda in the 1300-page novel.[26]

National concerns are overshadowed by sexual politics. In both versions of the novel, the mention of Japanese pirates is immediately overshadowed by a series of episodes linked by the theme of aberrant sexuality. Once the invasion by pirates is shown to be an empty rumor, an official describes a local Fujianese temple festival that celebrates male-male love.[27] Ten thousand people come to celebrate a "cash-hole" festival *(qianyan hui)*, but thirty thousand people gather the next day to celebrate the "bumhole" festival *(piyan hui)* dedicated to the god Xia Dehai.[28] Suchen/Zhu Ming comments that he had heard southerners were keen on the "southern mode" *(nanfeng)*, but that he had never heard of a bumhole festival (66.750; 64:191).[29] The abridgement repeats, verbatim, the punning description of how the yamens, schools, businesses, and even brothels empty out for the festival.

> Since southerners *(minren)* take the dry [land] and not the water route, none of the courtesans would have johns unless they all dressed like young men, sealed their front gates, and opened the back entrance to entertain their guests. It's for this reason that the courtesans celebrate the god's birthday. (66.750; 64:191)

The new official expresses his indignation that the degenerate local customs have forced him to pay his young servant extra to stay out of his bed and then insists he would like to behead everyone in the province to eradicate these aberrant practices (66.751; 64:194). However, despite the official's disgust, the descriptions of the temple celebration are much less negative than the many other descriptions of deviant sex found in the original text. Those examples of predatory heterosexual behavior have much more serious political and ethical implications than the male same-sex festival.

The light-hearted descriptions of the celebration of male love are consistent with other late-imperial fictional works that tend to view male-male sex as a source of humor rather than a threat.[30] Prior to the importation of western discourses on homosexuality, China did not have a well-defined rhetoric that condemned male same-sex practices as more degenerate or threatening than other forms of nonprocreative sex. Despite the lack of a modernized vocabulary to refer to male-male sexuality in the Republican text, the fact that all passages containing derogatory references to male same-sex practices are retained while other sexual passages are abbreviated or cut suggests the redactors of the abridged YSPY had a heightened interest in male same-sex eroticism as a deviant sexual and social practice.[31] This pejorative view explains why the cure for the emperor's yin excess that involves sandwiching him in bed between two young men (chap. 87) was removed from the Republican text.

The range of meanings associated with sexuality is narrowed in the modern text. Sexual contact in the abridged YSPY is heterosexual, is driven by a desire for pleasure, and serves to empower men rather than reveal their vulnerability. Even though Zhu Ming's male body continues to have extraordinary healing powers, he does not effect cures through mimicking sex. As in the original, Zhu Ming brings a corpse back to life by urinating on him (78:145) and cures the Stone Maiden of her sexual immaturity by warming her body when they share a bed; however, the sexualized details of this scene are omitted (89:68–69).

Perhaps the most significant change in the Republican text is that sex is no longer used to test Suchen/Zhu Ming. For example, the *yaksha*'s attack on him is no longer directed toward his sexual organs: Zhu Ming realizes that the beautiful woman who is pinning him down must be a monster, so he kills her (62:166). He at no point feels danger when he is drugged and bound by the eunuch and his harem. The women, some with their "snow-white breasts exposed, intentionally trying to excite him," surround Zhu Ming who is acutely embarrassed by their sex show (*fengliu zhen*), but "does not fear at all" (66:216–217). Within this context in which heterosexual sex no longer threatens the integrity of the male body, the lengthy and sometimes graphically violent references to male-male sex take on a heightened importance as the primary representation of degenerate sex.

Another marked shift in the treatment of sex in the abridged *YSPY* is its increased association with pleasure rather than with the themes of self-control or fertility. Although the Republican text cuts many less sexually graphic details in scenes of sexual vampirism, it retains most of the details of the stages of Xuangu's sexual arousal when she climbs in bed with Zhu Ming (7:95) and retains verbatim the lengthy discussion between her and Zhu Ming about the difference between love *(qing)* and physical desire *(yu)* (9:117–118). Fertility is no longer the primary goal of marital intimacy; in fact, the lengthy description of how Lady Shui organizes Suchen's domestic and sexual schedules is completely absent from the abridgement. Added, however, are several passages, such as the following, that illustrate the centrality of sexual pleasure to the health of a marriage. As narrated, Zhu Ming visits the rooms of his wives each day according to schedule

> and carries out one session of "public business." With lips and bodies clinging, he wants to give pleasure to all his forty-eight thousand pores. One pore in particular was the focus of his pleasure. (62:162)

Equally striking is the way the very last paragraph of the novel adds a new sexual dimension to the narrative in place of the original Confucian dream vision. This interpolated scene allows the readers to eavesdrop on the wedding night of Zhu Ming and his new concubine Biyu who is consumed by desire for him. This abrupt ending, which serves as a culmination of Zhu Ming's unsuccessful battles to save China, suggests that sanctioned sexual conquest has become the reward and perhaps even proof of male heroism. Consistent with the original text is that sexual desire and arousal are focalized through the women, while Zhu Ming voices restraint. In each case, he insists on waiting until the ritually appropriate moment to consummate the relationship.

As sex becomes increasingly linked to pleasure rather than duty and self-control in the Republican text, the narrative emphasis shifts to Zhu Ming's relationships with his wives rather than with his mother. The excision of the larger-than-life mother figure allows for the creation of a more nuclear family and more intimate emotional bonds between husband and wives in place of marital relationships based on duty that is mediated through the mother. Lady Wang is no longer at the center of the novel's larger moral vision, nor for that matter of Zhu Ming's familial or affective life. Accordingly, Zhu Ming's most important domestic role is not as subordinate son, but as master of his own household.

New to the Republican *YSPY* is the naturalizing of gender. The Qing text contains a scene in which families and servants marvel at a newly married couple: the two have identical jade-white bodies and vermilion markings. One of the servants notices that the groom's breasts "are like leavened steamed buns, and thinks to herself with pleasure, 'When a man has breasts this large, it is certain he will have high status.'" When the servant reaches inside the bride's undergarments and undoes her breast bindings, she discovers that bride and groom have identical breasts in terms of size and the seven tiny vermilion dots circling their nipples (85.972). Scenes such as this are not unusual in late-imperial fiction; a common trope in scholar-beauty romances is the complementarity and even interchangeability of lovers.[32] All details referring to the couple's androgyny are eliminated from the abridged text.

Although woman warriors continue to be part of the human landscape in the abridged version, gender differences between Zhu Ming and his wives are heightened. Early in the novel, Zhu Ming rescues a young woman from a man who had saved her from drowning but then refuses to release her. The abridged version first amplifies Zhu Ming's anger and aggression. After punching and knocking the other man down, Zhu Ming muses in an interpolated line, "If I ever find him again, I'll give him 'a white blade going in and a red blade coming out' in order to rid society of a menace" (3:29). The young woman is so exhausted that Suchen / Zhu Ming is forced to carry her to the temple. In the original text, the woman explains the reasons for her exhaustion in detail: she had struggled for a long time in the water, her clothing is soaked and heavy, she is deeply chilled, and her bound feet were bruised in the struggle and are starting to swell inside her bindings (3.33). The abridgement highlights the contrast between Zhu Ming's strength and the woman's frailty by focalizing the scene through Zhu Ming's eyes:

> [Zhu Ming] saw that Hongyu's entire body was dripping wet, making her resemble a narcissus. Her shoes were tight and her feet were swollen; when she walked she couldn't express her pain. (3:30)

Not only does this revision eroticize Hongyu's frailty, it makes her physical weakness seem a general state rather than specific to the moment. In the original text, the fact that Suchen and the woman spend a night together alone in a temple acts as a catalyst for an enactment of the classical debate about female chastity and expediency and the question of whether a man may touch his sister-in-law in order to save her life[33] — this philosophical discussion is cut from the abridged text. Substituted for the traditional concept of male-female relations based on complementarity and ethical sexual restraint is a relationship based on female dependence on superior male strength.

Sexual and Editorial Politics and the Good Youth Press

The question of how the abridged *YSPY* fit into the publishing world of late 1920s Shanghai is somewhat puzzling. Although the original novel was traditionally categorized as a scholar novel due to its frequent and lengthy erudite discussions of topics ranging from mathematics and medicine to Cheng-Zhu Neo-Confucian philosophy and metaphysics, the excision of all these passages makes the abridged novel conform much more neatly to the conventions of popular "knight-errant" fiction, a genre that reached new levels of popularity between 1927 and 1930.[34] While fitting the stylistic norms of popular urban "mandarin duck and butterfly" fiction, the abridged *YSPY* at over 1300 pages and priced at six dollars seems to have been targeted at a wealthier readership than typical knight-errant fiction.[35] The edition was handsomely though sloppily prepared.[36] Spacious margins and stock illustrations of plum blossoms and herd boys as well as blond Dutch children (immediately identifiable by their clogs and peaked hats) and modern Chinese girls with their telltale short hair were likely designed to attract the simultaneously nostalgic yet international and modern tastes of the middle-class Shanghai reading public.[37] Moreover, in comparison to other examples of knight-errant fiction discussed by David Der-wei Wang, the revised *YSPY* seems less interested in voicing society's yearning for radical political and judicial changes than in presenting a modern sexual politics.[38]

Significantly, the only other title listed in catalogues as published by the Good Youth Press is a 1929 reprint of the *Collected Discussions on the Rules of Love (Aiqing dingze taolun ji)* by Zhang Jingsheng, the infamous "Dr. Sex," the best known of the May Fourth sexual reformers. *Collected Discussions* was a republication of Zhang's short article first published in 1923 in the *Chenbao fukan* (Morning News Literary Supplement) on "the rules of love" and heated letters that readers sent in to the paper. In his original article, Zhang argued for the right of a female student, a certain Miss B, to break off the engagement arranged by her family to marry one of her professors. The majority of those who wrote in were critical of the ethics of Miss B's behavior. The letters were first published as a collection in 1927 by Zhang's *Meide,* "Beauty," publishing house in Shanghai.[39] Zhang continued to push the boundaries of public discussions on love, sexuality, gender, and individual autonomy through the 1920s with his

1926 publication of *Sex Histories (Xingshi),* a series of explicit autobiographical narratives. Zhang's publications sold extremely well, some going through several printings in one year. Zhang's name had such market cachet that someone else published a false sequel to the *Sex Histories* by 1927.[40] One report claimed that over three thousand copies of *Sex Histories* were found in the dormitory rooms of four thousand students; although the number is undoubtedly inflated, it points to the market interest in publications linked to "Dr. Sex."[41]

Zhang's vision of a modern and "healthy" sexuality was particularly influenced by the writings of Havelock Ellis. Zhang sought to promote a sexuality based on pleasure and emotional intimacy in place of traditional attitudes, which valued reproductive and hygienic sex and viewed all other forms of sexuality as dangerous. Even though Zhang's notion of socially beneficial sexuality was not tied to marriage and reproduction, it was limited to heterosexual couples. Moreover, similar to Ellis and other western sexologists, Zhang Jingsheng naturalized and normalized specific gender traits, particularly aggression in men and passivity in women, as appropriate and proper.[42] One area in which Zhang promoted a more active role for women, however, was in their right to choose sexual and marital partners.[43] Zhang also saw it as part of his mission to eliminate degenerate sexual behaviors such as masturbation, homosexuality and bestiality.[44] Although no evidence links Zhang Jingsheng to the Good Youth Publishing House or to the redacting of the abridged *YSPY,* many of the changes made to the text are consistent with his agenda of modernizing sexual attitudes. It seems likely that the publishers of the abridgment were among those commercial presses hoping to cash in on the market appeal of Zhang's name.

The Republican revision of the *YSPY* fits into the broad modernizing debate on the questions of what constituted healthy sexuality and proper gender roles and relations between the sexes.[45] Nonetheless, during this period, even though imported western sexological discussions about proper gender and sexual identities began to shape and sometimes displace native beliefs and practices, anxieties about male potency and self-containment—themes elaborated in traditional medical and philosophical texts and reflected in fictional texts as varied as *Journey to the West, Golden Lotus,* and *Yesou puyan*—continued to be central to Chinese discussions of male health.[46] Fears that excessive sperm loss could weaken a man's constitution can be traced back to the earliest Daoist sex manuals and seem to explain the fictional trope of male protagonists being kidnapped for the sake of harvesting their sperm. Discussions of pathological sperm loss, known as spermatorrhea, dominated medical discussions of sex during the Republican period;[47] the disease was listed as the cause of death for the Guangxu Emperor in 1907. Even while May Fourth reformists introduced a modern western understanding of sexuality, public discussion of spermatorrhea continued unabated; from the late 1920s to the late 1940s, fears about the disease drove a market for products that claimed to bolster men's vitality.[48]

Traditional philosophical anxieties about sexual desire combined with fears about pathological sperm loss to make male sexual vulnerability an important theme running through late-imperial fiction.[49] Suchen's hypermasculinity, particularly in the arena of sexual control, is a fantastic inversion of the fear of male victimization. The redactor(s) of the Republican version of the *YSPY* were no doubt drawn to Suchen as a model for a modern masculinity. In their revising of the sexual politics of the original novel, they erased the traditional male fears of falling victim of the dangers of heterosexual sex. Instead, they endowed Zhu Ming with a modern masculine superiority over women in terms of physical strength and emotional self-control. The redactors displaced traditional anxieties about the dangers of sexuality—which are almost always associated with male vulnerability in the face of limitless female sexual potential—onto male homosexuality.

Conclusions

Although the curious publication of the abridged *Original, Old-style Yesou puyan* is a minor event in Chinese literary history, it exposes the limits of one of the dominant metanarratives of modern Chinese literature: namely, that issues of Chinese identity for the last century have been predominantly, if not exclusively, engaged with the intertwined projects of nationalism and modernization. The production of the 100-chapter abridgement of *YSPY* should be read as part of the tumultuous history of evolving attitudes toward the bodily practices of sex and gender identity that stretches back well before twentieth-century China. This suggests that literary historians should resist the disciplinary pressures to separate discussions of twentieth-century China from its premodern roots in order to emphasize nationalist narratives. Histories of embodied and affective selves as part of mundane events and systems of beliefs and practices unfold according to rhythms and timeframes quite distinct from that of the state.

Comparing the two versions of *YSPY* we can see the increasing importance of the body to masculine identity. In Xia Jingqu's Confucian vision, an ideal masculinity is anchored not in physical and sexual domination over others but in a moral order actualized through physical and sexual self-control. Suchen achieves moral authority expressly through his willingness to accept a ritually subordinate role to his mother and the emperor. In the Republican edition, Zhu Ming demonstrates leadership through his superior strength. Gone are all those scenes in which he falls victim to female aggressors.

Equally important to Zhu Ming's masculine stance is his mastery of his own home. The Mother, the source of moral authority in the original text, has almost no presence in the abridgment, perhaps because it would diminish the son's autonomy. Although Zhu Ming continues to have an affective attachment to his mother, Lady Wang is never shown having any lasting power over him. Ultimately, the meaning of Zhu Ming's masculinity is framed in the private, sexual, and corporeal terms of the nuclear family. Although Zhu Ming wins his battles against the rebellious and heterodox forces, the Manchu emperor recognizes him as a threat in chapter 100 and rewards him with an empty show of honor. Zhu Ming leaves the imperial court consoling himself that even though he has failed, others will complete the overthrow of the Manchu oppressors. Despite his political failure, Zhu Ming is rewarded with the intimate pleasures of the wedding chamber with which the novel concludes.

Another important shift in the Republican text is the tightened identification of gender with biological sex, rather than being a function of yin-yang correlative thinking. The exuberant performance of yang-associated domestic order in which the women in Suchen's household adopt the masculinist practices of textual study and martial training are cut entirely from the 100-chapter abridgment. Significantly, the symbolic capital associated with masculine yang values is no longer available to those women who align themselves with orthodoxy. Moreover, as the meanings associated with sex have shifted from the moral and hygienic to the bodily practices of male domination and pleasure, the female characters in the novel are no longer depicted as threatening sexual aggressors. Instead, women become objects of male-centered action, to be rescued and desired, but not to be feared, obeyed, or made into agents of orthodoxy.

Sometimes representations of sex are more about its private embodied meanings than national allegory. Reading the two versions of *YSPY*, traditional and Republican, points to the deep native roots of the ongoing "crisis" of masculinity that has gained so much attention in recent scholarship. Anxiety about male vulnerability and sexual performance in the modern period should not be attributed solely to the dual shocks of modernization and the forced recognition of China as the "sick man of Asia." Gender and sex have long been part of the symbolic vocabulary employed in writing about power relations in China.[50] Although Suchen and his modern descendent Zhu Ming are rare models of empowered masculinity in Chinese literature, we can see in their depictions inverted reflections of the weak, flawed, and impotent male characters so prevalent elsewhere in both traditional and modern Chinese fiction.

Notes

1. Xia, *Yuanzhe guben Yesou puyan*. Although print runs could be quite small, Leo Lee has estimated that a typical run during this period was one to two thousand copies. See Lee, *Romantic Generation*, 30.

2. Xia, *Yesou puyan*, 152 chapters (1881; repr., Taipei: Tianyi chubanshe, 1985); Xia, *Yesou puyan*, 154 chapters (1882; repr., Beijing: Renmin Zhongguo chubanshe, 1993). The prolific writer of sequels Lu Shi'e also published a *New Yesou puyan (Xin Yesou puyan)* in 1909. For more on editions, see Wang Qiongling, *Qingdai sida caixue xiaoshuo*, 81–115. The title of the novel refers to a proverb in the *Liezi* about a poor farmer who offers home-spun advice to the ruler. See McMahon, *Misers*, 155.

Text references to the 154-chapter *Yesou puyan* follow the format "chapter.page number" (e.g., 87.1001); references to the abridged version (100 chapters) are based on the 1933 edition (see previous note) and follow the format "chapter:page number" (e.g., 3:29).

3. One scholar has estimated that descriptions of sexual encounters constitute approximately five percent of the novel. Wang Qiongling, "*Yesou puyan*," 17.

4. Han, "Tan *Yesou puyan*."

5. Hou, "*Yesou puyan*," 97–112.

6. McMahon, *Misers*, 157.

7. For more on male urine and semen as pure yang substances, see Epstein, "Inscribing," 19–22.

8. I borrow this phrase from Xueping Zhong's study of representations of masculinity in twentieth-century China, *Masculinity Besieged?* A similar phenomenon is discussed in Epstein, *Competing Discourses*.

9. Louie, *Chinese Masculinity*, 10, 12.

10. Ibid., 2, 8, 23, 36, 49.

11. See Epstein, "Inscribing."

12. Furth, "Androgynous Males."

13. Stone makes a similar argument in *Chinese Erotica*.

14. I make this argument more fully in *Competing Discourses*, 215–238.

15. Zito, "Silk and Skin," 106.

16. Cao, *Honglou meng*, 348.

17. Louie, *Chinese Masculinity*, 23, 36, 49.

18. For early examples of this trope, see Wai-yee Li, *Enchantment*, 4–33.

19. For more on romantic *fengliu* heroes, see McMahon, *Causality*, 132–135.

20. See McMahon, *Misers*, 173.

21. For more on negative yin imagery, see Epstein, *Competing Discourses*, 215–222, 227.

22. For a more detailed discussion of this scene, see McMahon, *Misers*, 162–165.

23. For more on the feminizing qualities of scholar-beauty fiction, see Epstein, *Competing Discourses*, 150–162.

24. See Zhang Zhupo's prefatory essay "Ku xiao shuo" [On Frustrated Filial Piety] in Wang, Li, and Yu, *Jin ping mei*, 19.

25. The monk is an anthropomorphic representation of a phallus. See Roy, "Introduction to *Plum*," xxxiii.

26. See Xia, *Yuanzhe guben Yesou puyan*, 1:1, 40:89, 62:162, 63:177, 100:213.

27. Szonyi discusses this episode in relation to the historical cult of Hu Tianbao, "Cult," 3–4.

28. Traditional coins have a square hole in the center so that they can be bound together in strings of cash.

29. The traditional "southern mode" is used to refer to male-male sex in the original *YSPY*; the Republican text uses the homophone "male mode" exclusively. No variants of the neologism meaning homosexuality, *tongxing lian'ai*, appear in the abridged *YSPY*. For other references to male-male sex, see 11:145, 78:147 and 79:167.

30. See Volpp, "Male Marriage"; Volpp, "Literary Circulation"; and Vitiello, "Exemplary Sodomites."

31. Changes in obscenity standards can be observed from the fact that the 1985 Taiwan Tushuguan gongsi edition expurgates all references to male-male sexuality.

32. Hessney, "Beautiful," 5; McMahon, "Beauty-Scholar," 234.

33. This ethical dilemma was first articulated in the *Mencius* 4A.17.

34. See Hsia, "Scholar-Novelist," 269–270; Link, *Mandarin Ducks*, 22.

35. Most popular novels in the 1920s were priced at about a half dollar (average weekly income was about one dollar). See Link, *Mandarin Ducks*, 12.

36. The publication of *The Original, Old-Style Yesou puyan* used printing plates prepared for an earlier abridged version of *YSPY* called *Jiangu qinxin* [Bones of Sword, Heart of Zither] that is not listed in any major library catalogue. Appearing on the very last page of the abridgement is a table that compares the names used in the original *YSPY* to those used in *Jiangu qinxin*. The names used in the abridgement are the same as those listed for *Jiangu qinxin*. Moreover, the last chapter of the abridgement ends with the formulaic line: "And here concludes my telling of the novel *Jiangu qinxin*" (100:223). Most likely, the publishers had followed the long-standing commercial practice of purchasing preexisting plates and republishing them under a different name. Until an extant copy of that text is found, it is impossible to determine when the various interpolated passages were added. Further evidence of sloppy editing is that characters are printed sideways in 61:131 and 85:4.

37. For more on the contradictory tastes of Shanghai residents, see Schaefer, "Relics," 3–23.

38. David Der-wei Wang, *Fin-de-siècle Splendor*, 121.

39. See Leary, "Sexual Modernism," 138–166.

40. Peng, "Sex Histories," 160.

41. Leary, "Sexual Modernism," 254.

42. Ibid., 228–230.

43. Ibid., 228, 230–231.

44. Ibid., 228.

45. See Dikötter, *Sex*; Sang, *Emerging Lesbian*, 99–126.

46. For a discussion of how fears about limited male sexual potency informs late imperial fiction, see McMahon, *Causality*, 63–64, 78–81.

47. Dikötter, *Sex*, 166–167.

48. Shapiro, "Puzzle of Spermatorrhea," 563.

49. Fox spirits, ghosts and the figuratively linked image of the shrew, all of whom attempt to seduce unwary men, represent direct threats to male health and life.

50. For recent studies on the symbolic meanings of sexuality in early China see Goldin, *Culture of Sex;* and Rouzer, *Articulated Ladies.*

CHAPTER 5

Cross-Dressed Nation
Mei Lanfang and the Clothing
of Modern Chinese Men

JOHN ZOU

ON DECEMBER 27, 1994, former Chinese president Jiang Zemin delivered the opening address at a symposium commemorating the late Peking opera actors Mei Lanfang (1894–1961) and Zhou Xinfang (1895–1975). "As our country's traditional theater communities and literary and artistic groups are celebrating the birthday centennials of Mei Lanfang and Zhou Xinfang," the president proclaimed, "the purpose of the symposium is to address the grand vision of reviving Peking opera, the traditional theater, and the national arts."[1] Between Mei and Zhou, the emphasis lay clearly with the former, however, for since the early days of Communist China (1949–), it was always Mei, in combination with various other actors, who represented the glories of Chinese folk opera.[2] By the mid-1990s, one could even say that the terms "Mei Lanfang," "Peking opera," "traditional theater," and "national arts" had elided to form a highly predictable continuum. The political endorsement of this semantic slide from individual actor to nation in Jiang's speech bespeaks the presence of an important strategy linking culture and politics in the neonationalism of post-1989 China: the revival of certain aspects of the personality cult of high communist times in the regulation of popular culture. On one end of the spectrum was orthodox entertainment such as "epic" cinema about founding fathers of the People's Republic like Chairman Mao (1893–1976), while on the other end were more commercial forms of entertainment such as those epitomized by Hong Kong superstars Jacky Cheung and Andy Lau. The folk theater of Mei Lanfang and his colleagues, in this context, represented a style of artistic amusement in line with more conservative tastes. Mei, Mao, Cheung, and Lau each put an alternative face on the blank and ever-renewable idea of "Chineseness" as the best-selling commodity of a recently formed cultural market, their publicly displayed bodies designated as sites for the production of both entertainment value and vast historical meaning. According to the popular cultural rhetoric of the mid-1990s, if the founding revolution defined the order of China's unique present and Hong Kong in the final days of colonial rule represented the nation's reintegrated future, then it was the celebrated traditional arts like folk opera that exemplified the country's worthy past.[3]

Initial Questions

In contemplating the post-Mao rebirth of the cult of Mei Lanfang that projected Peking opera as China's national theater, however, we must consider certain apparent ironies. Trained as an opera singer in the female roles, Mei developed his career by playing an extensive catalogue of glamorous Chinese women, mostly of past ages. His stage presence, so often the rallying point of passionate nationalist rhetoric and iconography, consisted of a man dressed in fantastically "female" costumes (Fig. 5.1). In a career that extended from the late Qing empire (1644–1911) to the early years of Communist government, not only the excellence of Mei's work but also the support he rendered to the state—for example in his espousal of patriotic messages—rested on his ability to perform as a beautiful woman. A challenge in the study of traditional arts in modern China therefore lies in reconciling the great power of folk operas to invoke Chinese nationhood with the cross-dressed performance, especially as championed by Mei, that routinely left Chinese audiences spellbound.

My questions may be formulated in three related steps. First, if we consider the aspects of Peking opera particularly relevant to Chinese nationalism, it is quite clear that the performance of female roles by male actors is key. In the traditionally all-male folk convention of Chinese performance, male roles dominated the theater until the end of 1900s. But it was only when female roles assumed an overwhelming importance starting in the 1910s that Peking opera took on national significance. While current scholarship attributes this new popularity in part to the presence of women in theater audiences following the founding of the new Republic, nonetheless female actors, when they eventually inherited the theatrical legacy of Mei and his generation of cross-dressed performers, never came close to Mei in terms of the impact and influence in their performances. What then, we must ask, are the specific attributes of male-to-female theatrical performance that put Mei in the service of Chinese nationalism? And how can we critically come to terms with a nationalism configured through the cross-dressed male body?

Second, historical hindsight reveals that male-to-female cross-dressing did not assume a constant form over its long history in Chinese theater.[4] As can also be seen in Wu and Stevenson's essay in this volume, many aspects of theatrical performance, including styles of costume and makeup, the visual ac-

FIGURE 5.1. Mei Lanfang as Imperial Consort Yang coming out of a bath, a clothed exoneration from memories of a half-naked grandfather? Used with permission of the Mei Lanfang Commemorative Society, Beijing.

cessibility of the performing body, male same-sex provocations, and the social prestige of the actor were all greatly transformed in the political upheaval of the early decades of the twentieth century. Mei's own life story to some degree exemplifies these changes. First released in 1911 from a bonded apprenticeship (a system in which older men patronized youthful entertainers) by a senior military officer of the Qing government named Feng Gengguang for the sum of 3000 silver dollars, by 1929 the actor was rubbing shoulders with the gangster Du Yuesheng and the doyen of the Chinese academy Hu Shi at the farewell party preceding Mei's US tour. What took place in China over those eighteen years that gave Mei such influence? What did Mei do that allowed the metamorphosis of a body of such "despicable" origin into such an exemplary and charismatic conveyor of Chinese culture? In what ways did changes that Mei facilitated in theatrical practice become catalysts for nationalist desires? What particular types of male-to-female cross-dressing were adopted to give Mei's seemingly impossible transformation credibility?

Third, how might we explain the long-term viability of theatrically cross-dressed men as icons of Chinese nationalism? At a time when formerly hallowed legacies of China's nationalist rhetoric such as the May Fourth movement or the populist Boxer's uprising have become subject to anxious reflection, how do we come to terms with the ongoing relevance of Mei Lanfang and cross-dressed theater to nationalist rhetoric? No doubt the rediscovery of Mei and his theatrical legacy in post-Mao China has much to do with government policies, but it also registers a discursive point where political and social interests converge. In sartorial terms, if cinematic Mao, the politically sustained box-office winner, advocates a martial, nation-founding spirit in his "uniformed" appearances, and Andy Lau, the Hong Kong superstar, exploits consumer fantasies through his ever-changing attire, how do we account for the artistic importance of Mei's cross-dressed personae in contemporary China?

Toward the Bare Body: The Politics of *Yiguan* and a Theory of Men's Clothing

In contemporary discussions of Mei Lanfang's contribution to nationalist aspirations, the historically important relationship between male clothing and Chinese politics often escapes scholarly attention. For quite some time, indeed as a legacy of the self-mystification by great performers such as Mei himself, the "female" makeup, stage routine and costume in Chinese folk theater have been read one-dimensionally as instruments for representing women and womanhood. Keeping in mind recent work in gender studies, I propose to look at men's theatrical cross-dressing primarily as a figurative mode of the male body and thus intrinsically related to other sartorial practices that assign cultural and political inscriptions to that body.[5] A brief discussion is then in order with reference to changes in Chinese men's clothing styles between the late-nineteenth and early-twentieth centuries, during which time Peking opera, especially its cross-dressed performances, gradually gained national prominence.

If we agree with certain historical accounts, it seems that the imperial decline in the last decades of the nineteenth century and the first of the twentieth was coupled with an increasing confusion concerning male dress codes.[6] After the 1911 Revolution that toppled the Qing empire, the quest for "Chinese" styles beyond Manchu forms coexisted with clear western and Japanese influences upon the male wardrobe. The Japanese style military uniform, the western suit, the Manchu *magua* (a short, stiff-collared jacket), and even the ancient Chinese *shenyi* (a robelike garment whose authentic style was the subject of heated debates among classical scholars) were simultaneously current in different social sectors.[7]

In a political context where Confucian orthodoxy had assigned enormous consequence to the correspondence between male habit and effective political rule, the haphazard clothing of Chinese men bore the patent inscriptions of China's recent history of nearly nonstop political and military turmoil. In this regard the Nationalist government's retightening of the dress code, first in the stipulation of the *Zhongshan zhuang* (the style of suit adopted by Sun Yat-sen, founder of the Republic) as the official outerwear for all civil servants, then during the New Life Movement (1934–1937) with the demand for conformist clothing styles, should be taken as a significant policy choice. It represented not only a conservative, quasi-Confucian attempt to restore political stability by stabilizing male clothing, but also a symbolic closure of political wounds inflicted on the national (male) body in recent times.[8]

Historically, the traditional Confucian insistence upon political continuity between the male body and its attire goes back to the Classics. *The Book of Rites (Liji),* for instance, documents a long-established recognition of the male body that paid tribute in clothing terms to the paternal family and state, thus acquiring political viability within the elaborate system of metaphysical and occasional articulations. In *The Analects,* the Master personally defended Guan Zhong, a grand statesman of the marquisate of Qi, for keeping men of his chaotic time compliant with the headdress and clothing style of the declining Zhou royal house.[9] Over the Qin–Han transition, when Confucianism was transformed from a prominent school of learning to the paramount political doctrine of empire making, the institution of a universal and hierarchical code for male dress became further integrated in the Chinese state's political processes. The generic writings of the *yufuzhi,* or "records of carriages and garments," in dynastic histories that covered nearly two millennia from the Later Han to the Qing, bear testimony to the role a somewhat exaggerated concern with male dress played in the political institutions of China's past.[10] Sumptuary specifications regarding the color, kind, quality, patterns, cut, and combination of materials are the subject of detailed consideration in these texts and point to their grave relevance to political designations and presentations of the male body within the Confucian imperial order. The related doctrine of *yiguan* (literally, clothing and headdress), which celebrated a unique style of male attire as an expression of the Celestial Empire's political magnificence, became a discourse of increasing significance in the Southern Song and the Ming dynasties. The circulation of the doctrine, often attributed to the political strife caused by northern nomadic invaders in China's middle centuries, acquired radical new aspects during the Qing conquest, when the enforcement of the Manchu tonsure and habit upon Han Chinese men by heavy-handed early Qing authorities led to astounding bloodbaths. Such historical memory fueled the calls for nationalist revolution with great excitement and energy in the dynasty's waning years.[11] However, as colonialism and the quest for national survival quickly turned Chinese men toward the west for cultural, including sartorial, models, the historically entrenched equation of empire with the authentically clothed male body was among first casualties of the Qing's collapse.

Within this largely political framework, cross-dressing should be registered not simply as a matter of theatrical performance, but a practice extensively embedded in the ritualistic aspect of everyday life. Also, the question of male attire was not limited to the issue of female impersonation, but seemed in a broader sense to constitute an ever-present cause of anxiety for Chinese men as conditioned by past ethnic conquest and recent colonial onslaught. By the 1910s and 1920s, the failure of *yiguan* politics was writ large in the clothing of the average urban Chinese man. If the anti-Manchu revolution was partially fanned by the passion to erase the painful signs of conquest, neither did the postcolonial early Republican China provide conditions under which Chinese men could systematically return to the authentic "Chinese" clothing of Confucian description. Whether by intention, custom, or necessity, Chinese men again found themselves haplessly dressed in someone else's clothes. In clothing terms, they were effectively homeless.

With regard to Mei Lanfang's rise to superstardom in the so-called warlord period, then, I argue that a generation of professional actors managed to mediate the Republican discourse that uncoupled the male body from its sartorial consequences by means of an unprecedented cross-dressing practice. Contrary to institutions of the Confucian empire and the Nationalist party state that endorsed certain male clothing as symbolic of men's political worth, the relatively underregulated early Republican social imaginary (1911–1927) projected an ahistorical male body isolated from China's recent record of political failure as represented through male clothing. In the cultural discourses of modern China, this momentous severance had a twofold impact. On the one hand, the male body's authenticity was seen to inhere in its imagined *bareness* rather than its clothed expression. This means that the political significance of such a body was determined not in relation to its outer trappings, but in relation to itself as a sartorially uninscribed body. *Bareness* became a privileged condition of the male body, to the extent that it created the discursive space to negotiate a new beginning for politics at the demise of the *yiguan* system; here, men's bodily identification with the state was mediated by its unclothed rather than its clothed condition. On the other hand, male clothing, or clothing per se, was generally evacuated of values traditionally indispensable to the representation of manhood. A direct correspondence between the male body and its national value made irrelevant clothing's time-honored function as a political signifier. Upon the male body independent of its sartorial history, clothing appeared to be a categorical misinterpretation. That is to say, since no clothing captured men's "own," authentic form, all historical negotiations of male attire became merely programmatic or random borrowings and trespass. Mei Lanfang, the ultimate Republican borrower of female clothing, a decided "other" in the politics of *yiguan* who aggressively denied the male body any proper, given, or primary articulation in clothed terms, thus became a prototype for the modern Chinese man, a compelling icon for the modern, cross-dressed, Chinese nation.

Figuring Bareness

To suggest that Mei Lanfang and his colleagues constructed a nationalist male body unattached to its sartorial history is not to assert that they made a concerted effort to arrive at this discursive construct. Rather, as we shall see in Mei's development as a professional actor, the historically isolated and metaphorically divested bare male body came about as the figurative rejection of a very different divestiture: the obscene exposure of the male cross-dressed body on the stage. Only when Mei transfigured this semi-unclothed male body into a fully clothed, concealed one did the male body regain respectability and a *symbolically* bare male body, paradoxically, begin to emerge. It was in the historical context of modernizing the performing system and eliminating traces of its "dishonorable" past that the bare male body was seized upon, as if by accident, for its political significance.

Contrary to the currently popular conceptions of Peking opera as an undisputed national treasure, its canonic position in the theater was not always taken for granted in China. After it achieved national prominence in the early twentieth century, attacks abounded regarding its stage practice and social influence. The May Fourth intellectuals, given their passion for reform and knowledge of western theater, were particularly harsh. The early Republican state also applied pressure for change to some of its core practices. Among attributes that prompted outrage and polemic, Peking opera's obscenities and its participation in the late Qing sex trade were often invoked as a scandal. Zhou Zuoren, one of the major literary authorities of May Fourth, alleged to have been a first-hand witness during his early sojourn in the capital city. Since in the study of modern Chinese literature and folk theater, common wisdom has been that the May Fourth and Peking opera represented institutions of general mutual exclusion, Zhou's poignant early experience and Mei's address of the issues raised therein may help us see the relevant discursive system at work. Zhou commented:

Now what is the so-called scum [of Peking opera]? What I mean is the lurid performance on the stage. In fiction and theater, erotic descriptions are inevitable, but when such matters are being displayed openly, I believe one has to use his judgment. In Peking opera, especially for what I saw at the time, the scenes were really hard to take *(tai nan le)*. I do not remember whether it was Zhongheyuan or Guangdelou, nor do I remember the title of the play. But maybe it was an adulterous episode from *Marshes of Mount Liang*. A mosquito net appeared on the stage. It shook vigorously. And from the net extended a white leg. In another scene, a young Maid accompanied her mistress to meet with the latter's lover. She eavesdropped on them at the window and engaged in self-comforting (i.e., masturbation, *ziwei*) at the same time. As I am describing such occurrences in words, I have to weigh different possibilities and consider the appropriateness of phrasing. It was really remarkable that actors could show everything on the stage. This may be related to the popular male courtesan *(xianggu)* system at the time. As a result, there might not even be much difficulty in finding talents for those tasks.[12]

In Mei Lanfang's family history, it is important to note that his grandfather, Mei Qiaoling (1842–1882), one of the most celebrated performers of female roles in the 1870s, made a name for himself by performing half-naked female characters, such as the spider demon, a sexual predator, in a play taken from the popular narrative *Journey to the West,* as well as the bewitching Imperial Consort Yang Yuhuan in the latter's famous bathing scene.[13] Indeed, his performances were so successful and his ample, fair flesh so convincing that the theater-loving Emperor Guangxu once bestowed upon him the jocular nickname of "Pang Qiaoling," Qiaoling the Plump.[14] Furthermore, besides his acting career, Mei Qiaoling also ran the Jinghe House, one of the most renowned entertainment establishments featuring cross-dressed male performers in the Hanjiatan neighborhood where old Beijing's sex trade was concentrated. It was under the tutelage of Zhu Xiafeng, one of Qiaoling's most successful students and a character made notorious in the contemporary political novel *Niehai hua* (Flower in the Sea of Sin), that Mei Lanfang received his schooling in theater.[15]

If we measure the popularity of such indecent exposure in the 1870s by the unease it caused an educated young man such as Zhou Zuoren, it is apparent that its terms of reception were radically changed at the turn of the twentieth century. To the "enlightened" eye, such performance was a kind of torture for the audience. In Zhou's words, "the scenes were really hard to take." And in a parallel sense, the participant in modern cultural discourses could only speak of them with great difficulty; he had to "weigh different possibilities and consider the appropriateness of phrasing." More specifically, Zhou Zuoren noted the connection between cross-dressed performance and Beijing's prosperous sex trade, where the actors were trained as male courtesans. Insofar as they provided artistic, erotic, and sometimes sexual entertainment to a male clientele, such "scenes" were staged as part of their sexually provocative engagement with the typically male audience. If we relate such comments to Zhou's later works during the May Fourth period, the famous formulation of traditional theater as antihuman and unnatural may be traced back to such youthful experiences.[16] What stood out as perverse may be reconstructed as a three-fold factor. First, there was explicit representation of sex. The stage in Zhou's description bore no sense of shame given its unclothed male body parts and loosened female clothing. Second, the male body did not come across in its "natural" form, but in a marked fashion, that is, as one theatrically scandalous because of its sexual exposure in the context of female clothing. Men were thus exposed as "women"; the male body was perversely combined with female sexuality. Third, since the female clothes were in dreadful disarray and represented together with exposed male body parts, one might say the female persona was incoherent. In Zhou's demand for theatrical naturalism, Peking opera's perversity seemed to culminate in the fact that such figures represented neither men nor women.

Parallel to the discursive registration of perversities resulting from the sexual exploitation of the male body and the violation of sexual distinctions, institutional processes also began to undo some of the established cross-dressing practices in Peking operas. By the time the grandson of "Qiaoling the Plump" ended his professional training thanks to Feng Gengguang's largesse, male prostitution, a trade the grandfather successfully managed, had become an enemy of the newly founded Republican state. On April 15, 1912, the General Police Headquarters of Outer Peking issued a circular banning theater-based male prostitution in the capital that declared:

> It comes to our attention that owners of private homes in the neighborhood of Hanjiatan and Wailangying have engaged in the temptation of children from decent families in the name of theater. The youngsters are dressed for their looks and trained to be expert in singing. Such homes started as occasional venues of literati gatherings, but over time have evolved into asylums of filth and smut. As habits accumulate, they form a unique phenomenon of the capital city, which not only becomes the shame of the entire country, but also makes a scene in front of foreign nations. Such boys are named "false women," and indeed act in ways contrary to human decency. It must be said that theater's propaganda work has made a great contribution to the reform of society, and members of the profession are not damaged in their identity as citizens of the country. However, should one insist on making a living through servile femininity and assuming the ways of

illegal prostitutes, the baseness of his personality indeed reaches extremity. Now with the recent founding of the Republic, the old habits and immoral customs should particularly be amended. Since this office has the responsibility to oversee proprieties and protect human rights, we will certainly not allow such degenerate vogues to continue in the exemplary city of the Capital. This is the notice to announce absolute prohibition, so that the concerned parties may immediately alter their improper ways, pursue suitable careers, give full respect to human dignity and join the ranks of noble citizenry.[17]

Whereas Zhou Zuoren's intellectual discourse focused on the experience of personal shock, the police circular emphasizes the political consequence of such performances. The sexual practices of cross-dressed performers are condemned not because they made the plays uncomfortable for decent members of the audience to watch and speak about, but because they represent the "shame of the entire country," and "make a scene in front of foreign nations." What is specified as punishable here are not the random perversities committed in the past, but the deliberate continuation of perversities into the future, that is, the "insistence" upon perversities. At the same time, the document also makes note of theater's propaganda work immediately before the founding of the Republic. The restoration of actors' "proprieties and human rights" is presented as a realistic and convincing incentive for encouraging service to the state.

If we place Mei Lanfang's fashioning of theatrical styles in relation to such discursive and political permutations, we can appreciate his efforts to tackle the crisis of Peking opera, or more specifically, that of its cross-dressed performance system. First, he needed to act in a theater that conformed to the new rules of decency. Second, he had no choice but to participate in efforts to restore the theater's reputation in a wider social context. Many writers attribute the canonization of Peking opera in Republican China to Mei's courageous international tours and shrewd response to political crises, such as his early retirement during the Japanese occupation. But as I shall argue below, his achievement also lay in less perceptible, and thus less discussed, processes such as the techniques he developed to cover the male body in theatrical performance. Although a seemingly mundane effort, reclothing the male body was in fact an intricate enterprise and had far-reaching consequences for Mei Lanfang, his theater, and the discourse of Chinese nationalism: it generated a sartorially neutral, historically abstract, and politically uncompromised male body. As Mei's elaborate costume made the male body increasingly disappear behind the actor's female persona, the performative copresence of the scandalized male body and incoherent female persona was rendered obsolete. In its place emerged a stylistically intensified female persona and a sartorially independent male body. This new "bare" body was not exposed but hidden. It was bare not because it was "half-clothed" in female garments, but because it was *completely* clothed in such garments, not because it depended on what covered it for articulation, but because fundamentally it had nothing to do with its covering. In more explicitly political rhetoric, such a body provided a discursive reason and theatrical experience through which Republican men could participate in the national universality of "human dignity" and "noble citizenry," particularly by extending such qualities to those who were traditionally excluded from sociopolitical norms.

To analyze the techniques that helped configure the bare body, I provide a close reading, below, of three moments in Mei's career where he employed techniques that effectively made possible radical changes in the relationship of the male body to its clothing. Compared to larger sociopolitical influences upon Peking opera, such as the Orientalist fascination from the west and the Japanese invasion, such techniques represent minor but crucial details that may facilitate our inquiry into more patent performative processes and theatrical events. I begin by looking at one of Mei's attempts to cover the male body in the introduction of an elaborate female persona, with the effect of banishing the former into invisibility. Next, I examine Mei's promotion of virtuous female characters in his performance as a way of turning Peking opera into exemplary theater. Finally, I analyze the articulation of the male body as a performative blank, beginning with Mei's so-called *guzhuang xi,* or "classical costume plays." I argue that it was in such stylistically invisible, morally eloquent, and metaphorically blank modes that the new "bare" male body facilitated, with varying degrees of efficacy, a nationalist imaginary at the very moment of demise for *yiguan* politics.

Clothing Men

Throughout his career Mei Lanfang paid a degree of attention to the female costumes being prepared for his acting—particularly details of the fabric, embroidery, color, and tailoring—that can only be described as compulsive. At one level, such compulsion might have represented a reaction to his notorious family and professional history. But on another more technical level, it reflected the recentering of the female persona in the theatrical experience at the expense of the male body, such that the projected surface of the illusory female character—rather than the male body hidden beneath this surface, always ready to tear it asunder—now occupied the center of the performance. The following is an excerpt from Mei's recollection about his friendship with a group of prominent literati-painters in the early Republic:

> In those years I was aware that the designs had rather little variance, and therefore when I befriended the painters, I often would set them tasks and ask them to turn the [stock figures of Chinese painting] flowers, birds, grasses, and insects into patterns [of embroidery]. . . . As a result, our research [on the plays] often began with these figures. Which play, or which actor's costume, would adopt what design? Which flower or bird would work? What is the best combination of colors? When does a character wear strong, flamboyant colors, and when does he wear quiet, elegant ones instead? How does a pattern look up close? What is the effect when one looks from afar? And then from these considerations, we also thought about ways to best present the costume with the [coloring and material of the] stage curtains. With such work, the costumes we made were of much more appeal than the kind designed by professional tailors.[18]

The reconstruction of this early experience, with its attention to the details of stage effects, the business of costume making, and the actor's personal friendship with the painters, may at first glance seem unremarkable. But when read against accounts such as those penned by Zhou and Mei Qiaoling's contemporaries, four things stand out. First, there was absolutely no mention of body parts. The coordinated display of male limbs with female clothing seems to be transformed, here, into a different system in which the former was hidden behind the latter, so much as that the male body became almost not worthy of mention when female clothing was discussed, and invisible when female clothing was displayed. Female clothing now afforded not an instrument to stage the male body, but a surface that *concealed* such a body. Second, the male body did not disappear *in toto*. It still occupied the center stage of music making, and of dramatic action. But it disappeared as a *directly* visible presence. Instead, it was turned into a matter of tacit understanding. Its presence was interrupted by the visible screen or threshold of female camouflage. It was quite literally displaced by female clothing in terms of visibility and became accessible increasingly as an ideological rather than material construct. Third, the connection made between costume and stage curtains neutralized the gendered consequences of costume. By identifying an aspect of female impersonation with a new technology to separate theater from the mundane world, Mei conferred upon his theatrical clothing a new function. Just as stage curtains registered a neutral separation between dramatic action and mundane reality, so the fabulous clothing that distanced the actor's body from the audience had no substantial impact upon the constitution of either. And fourth, whereas in Zhou Zuoren's description it was the female clothing rather than the male body that was foregrounded in theatrical performance, the opposite is true in Mei's account. For Zhou, the costume was designated as "female" particularly because it was borne by a male body; indeed, in addition to certain conventional references, its designation as "female" was realized through its paradoxical co-appearance with the male body parts. But in Mei's account, the definition of the costume's femaleness went through a radical change. Minus the provocative male limbs and gestures, the traditional "female" clothing became boring, that is, theatrically not "female" enough, and had to be enlivened with new designs. Mei's choices are therefore revealing: If one may divide classical Chinese painting in late imperial China into the major, masculine genre of landscape painting and the minor, feminine genre of birds and flowers, then Mei, with the help of his literati friends, constructed a modern myth of theatrical cross-dressing with reference to high art by adopting the latter generic style. Such classically feminine motifs seem to have been installed to fulfill a function represented by the "white leg" or exposed sexuality in Zhou Zuoren's narrative, that is, they provided definition of the costume's "femaleness." But in terms of formal stylistics, they varied greatly, for if the three-dimensional play between female clothing and male flesh sustained a theater of male same-sex provocation, then birds, flowers, and other feminine designs on the costume registered by contrast a far milder suggestion of mediated female sexuality.

Sexual Erasures

Throughout Mei's career, his tremendous professional success seems intrinsically tied to two projects: his management of the bewitchingly glamorous female personae that secured sales at the box office, and his persistent purge of the "lurid" theatrical elements that once turned away the new literati who espoused what they believed to be enlightened, western artistic ideals.[19] Of all the plays he performed, Mei once confessed that *Yuzhoufeng* was his all-time favorite. The play is about the righteous daughter of a wicked prime minister, who vents her anger at her father's and the emperor's evil by feigning madness. The extraordinary breadth of the character's emotional range allows the actor to develop a complexity and intensity in his acting seldom seen in other Peking opera performances. In its traditional form, however, the play was tainted by traces of obscenity. At the height of the lead female character's pretended insanity, for instance, she deliberately challenges her father by mistaking him for her executed husband and suggesting that they retire together to the back chamber for lovemaking. At this point, the aristocratic lady's mute maid made a hand gesture indicating sexual intercourse just as the lead character sings the phrase "My husband, please proceed with me to . . ." In a conversation that happened long afterwards with the amanuensis of his memoir, Mei ruminated upon a fortuitous innovation that he felt helped to mitigate this disagreeably vulgar detail:

> Before I sang the phrase, the mute maid as a rule would make a hand gesture. So far as the play goes, this indication had to be there. After Lady Zhao started to feign madness, all her interactions with people followed the lead of the mute maid. So if there were no indication from her when we got to this particular phrase, it would look like it was Lady Zhao who suggested the idea of lovemaking. For someone of her station, that does not seem plausible. I had always meant to change the segment for the better, but never quite knew how. Then one time, just as the mute maid was about to begin with her gesturing, I happened to cast my *shuixiu* (long sleeve) across her hands, completely covering the gesture. That is to show that Lady Zhao has understood what the maid tries to convey and does not allow her to continue. Your brother Yuanlai was in the audience that day, and after the performance was over, he came backstage and said to me with great satisfaction, "Your *shuixiu* was dropped in truly the right place today. The mute maid had her say, and you kept Lady Zhao's dignity. But we in the audience did not have to experience goose bumps."[20]

The *shuixiu* was opportune in that when covering the obscene gesture, it repeated the same process as the introduction of flowers and birds onto the theatrical costume—it served as both censorship and registration of a man's unyielding body by items of female clothing. But neither was it a straightforward case of suppression. In this case, covering the body or its sexual simulations was not a part of rehearsal or offstage preparation, but an episode of distinctive, full dramatization in front of the audience. Compared with the imposition of elaborate clothing onto the male body, this scenario takes on an overtly demonstrative, almost educational overtone. Lady Zhao, in correcting the Maid's behavior, publicly delivered a lesson to the latter on sexual moderation. If the actor assuming a stylistically intensified female persona had to project himself as an invisible body, here the inhibitions properly coded become social through the gesture, in a moral agent addressing the trespasser. The agent and recipient of the force of discipline were represented as two different characters: one knowing where his bodily boundary was, the other not.[21] In contrast to the maid, the demure Lady Zhao appears to be source of moral correction for the male body, not only in admonishing the maid, but also in giving moral force to the actor who assumes the persona of Lady Zhao. It is through Lady

Zhao's resistance to untoward sexual expression that the actor's male body recovers its own decency and respectability. Placed next to an embodiment of obscenity, Lady Zhao becomes a moral agent, an expert in the knowledge and resistance of sexuality, a policing force at home in the business of discipline. In character as Lady Zhao, Mei effectively reiterated the 1912 police ban.

Additionally, in his fortuitous screening of the maid's obscene gesture, Mei as Lady Zhao achieved an end to what I call "bad mimesis" in traditional Peking opera, a practice in which the scandalous male body assumed an obscene sexual attitude supposedly attributable to women. To the extent that the scandalous male body embodied "female" sexuality in the traditional cross-dressed actor such as his grandfather, Mei's choice to perform female virtues rather than vices was significant in that it fundamentally restructured the context of cross-dressing in performance. This tendency alone may explain the fact that where cross-dressed acting in the late Qing often featured women of questionable repute, the majority of Peking opera's female characters in Republican productions became distinctly "good," with increasingly marked moral virtues. Thus *Yuzhoufeng* was particularly significant among Mei's numerous stagings of women because of its dramatized, rather than implicit, rejection of the "bad mimesis" of traditional theater. Moreover, this play was unique in Mei's extensive repertoire because it represented a case in which the force of moral authority addressed itself explicitly to sexuality. Particularly at the moment of screening the maid's gesture, Lady Zhao comes across as a dual character: a sane moral agent admonishing the trespasser and a madwoman proposing sex to her dead husband. To her maid, she represents a disciplinary force; to her husband or, indeed, her father, she is as much a trespasser of moral rules as her maid. Such contradictions escalate to a moment of sexual outrage, when in her feigned madness, Lady Zhao makes the indecent suggestion to the father. But in Mei's masterful performance, the play acquired a moral coherence whereby incestuous sex was deployed as an extreme punishment for political evil and domestic tyranny. Moral and political outrage thus displaced sexual excitement, even when the latter was located within, rather than outside, the moral agent.

Drawing a Blank

Among Mei Lanfang's extensive repertoire of performance material, the *guzhuang xi* (classical costume plays) may further illustrate the sophistication of this moral and political mediation of the sexualized male body. These plays were unique not only because they made claims to represent women in the authentic female clothing of olden times, but also because they were often new plays written specifically for Mei's performance alone. Typically, instead of engaging in serious research on period clothing for these plays, Mei would send his cultured patrons in search of reference and inspiration from ancient paintings. This could present problems. Once, for example, competition from a successful rival acting troupe in 1915 led Qi Rushan, one of Mei's loyal advisors, to suggest the production of a fairytale in answer to the approaching occasion of the Mid-Autumn Festival. A natural choice was the legend of Chang E, who ate her husband's magic pills and ascended to the moon. In the process of rehearsal, however, difficulties abounded. The single most problematic aspect of the performance appeared to be the costume of the leading female character. According to Mei Lanfang, although audience expectation dictated that she be a beautiful woman of ancient times, nobody had any idea how she should look in her hairdo and clothing. The possibility of using conventional operatic costumes, however, was rejected because Mei thought it would compromise the novelty of the brand new play. The hairdo in particular became a source of anxiety:

> Female figures in paintings only expose the front or one side of their heads. Therefore the front part of my hairdo could imitate their style and employ some improvement and variation. But as to what happened to the back of the head, few had any clue. In some works, you may tell that the bun weighs to the side even though you are only looking at the front of the woman. I would try to style my hair in the same way, but when I turned around, it simply did not look the way it should.[22]

With much delay and anticipation on the part of the print media, the finalized hair now looked quite elegant and balanced compared with its initial conception:

> On the top of the head I made two buns, one upon the other. From the right, I put an elongated jade pin through the top bun at an angle. At the head of the pin was a string of pearls. To the left of my head, I wore a flower made of emeralds.[23]

Here, given his articulated agenda of creating a persona resonant with the cherished female figure of classical times, Mei placed himself in a rather unprecedented position. On the one hand, his improvisation in creating a classical woman indicated the impossibility of faithfulness in historical representation. On the other hand, the classical costume had the effect of *compounding* the fictionality of the fictionalized classical woman. As in the case where a costume's "femaleness" was derived not simply from its citational authenticity, but most crucially from its prominent coappearance with the male body, Chang E's persona achieved its classicism not because of a given classical value, but because of its costume's function as the garment for a "classically" dressed woman. Clothing did not define the performing context for the body, in other words; rather it was the body that determined the performing context for its clothing. But where Zhou Zuoren's obscene actor gave the clothing its "femaleness" in a way that also implicated his own body—presented with "female" clothing, the male body was contaminated by it and took on the aspect of scandal—Mei Lanfang as Chang E determined the classicism of his outerwear in a categorically detached manner. To the extent that the classical costume could only highlight the very "modernness" of Mei's body, it pertained to pure fiction and had little consequence in characterizing the truth of such a body. At this juncture of Peking opera's modern history, then, one may observe the invention of female clothing as a form of professional costume rather than a staging tool for the erotic male body of same-sex appeal. The traditional linkage between male body and female clothing in cross-dressed theater was severed.

Untouched

If we may be permitted to indulge for a moment in historical generalities, it might be said that since the early twentieth century, the modern Chinese nation has been repeatedly mediated by the figure of the bare body. Be it the May Fourth fantasy of the culturally unencumbered—hence "bare"—youth, or the Communist passion to inspire the politically and economically deprived—hence "bare"—peasants, one may say that such nationalist projects were invariably informed by an anxiety over a system that institutionally inscribed upon the male body its sociopolitical history. The ideological mandate to redeem a wholesome China from its modern history of endless political and cultural damage was thus continuously haunted by the traditional Confucian man, whose elaborate bodily inscriptions ironically only highlighted that mandate's political failure. Bodily bareness in this context signified not only the imaginative identification and unconditional unity of the new nation, but also a new beginning through the rejection of the past. Mei Lanfang and the cross-dressed actors' contribution to this discourse was the elevation of the fantastically despicable cross-dressed actor to the moral level of the mystically young and the innocently poor. Though demographically of minimal consequence, nonetheless, in discursive terms the once marginalized bodies of cross-dressed actors defined an important aspect of the new nation's inclusiveness.

As the bearer of a miraculous metamorphosis from social disgrace to national grandeur, the cross-dresser's dehistoricized body discloses a marvelously reassuring logic in the discursive formation of China's modern national history. Placed alongside Mao in his default, all-climate "uniform" and the extravagant Lau who wears anything but, Mei the suave cross-dresser bears a no less significant message. It is true that in modern times the Chinese empire is no more and every man has to wear someone else's clothing, but amidst such a commingling of signs of China's political failure, one may still discern that unattached, incorruptible, modern male body, to which nothing has yet happened, to which nothing could have happened.

Notes

1. Jiang Zemin, "Hongyang minzu yishu, zhenfen minzu jingshen," 1.

2. Other than Zhou Xinfang of the Shanghai school of Peking opera, Mei was also accompanied for such honors by prominent male colleagues such as Chen Yanqiu, another representative in the Peking school, Yu Zhenfei of the classical Kun opera, and Yuan Xuefen, a female actor of great fame of the Yue opera, popular in the Yangtze Delta region. His friendship with Ma Shizeng, master of Cantonese opera, was likewise cherished.

3. I thank the editors of the volume for this point. It appears that Cantopop, the Mao films, and the renewed interest in Peking opera all appeared in mainland China in the 1990s as part of a regulated system of popular culture. A formative factor within the system, it was precisely Cantopop's energetic commercial exploitation that institutionally and discursively forced other, politically more "elevated" genres, such as the Mao worship and Mei cult, to adopt an explicit entertainment dimension. Only when placed next to a commercial phenomenon such as Cantopop can government-funded projects on Mao and Mei be seen as not simply propaganda work or artistic theater, but part of a competitive yet controlled cultural market. For an article on the nationalization of Mei Lanfang in the early twentieth century, see Joshua Goldstein, "Mei Lanfang."

4. Because of the enormous prestige that has recently accrued to Peking opera, its transition from a popular, and sometimes debauched, form of entertainment is often not written into standard histories. The following texts may be useful to beginning students of the field for their information on Peking opera's unofficial past between the mid-nineteenth to the early twentieth century: Zhang Cixi, ed., *Qingdai Yandu liyuan shiliao huibian* [Collected Historical Sources on the Pear Garden in Peking during the Qing Dynasty] (Beijing: Zhongguo xiju chubanshe, 1988); Qi Rushan, *Qi Rushan huiyilu* [Memoirs of Qi Rushan] (Taipei: Zhongyang wenwu gongyingshe, 1956); and Ouyang Yuqian, *Ziwo yanxiyilai* [Since I Began Acting] (Taipei: Longwen chubanshe, 1990).

5. For a general introduction to the practice of cross-dressing in Chinese folk theater, see Li Siu Leung, *Cross-dressing*. For the conception of male-to-female cross-dressing as a configurative mode of the male body, I draw inspiration particularly from Kaja Silverman's discussion of Fassbinder in *Male Subjectivities*.

6. For information on changing clothing styles, see recent compilations such as Huang

and Chen, *Zhongguo fuzhuangshi;* Liu Zhiqin, "Fushi bianqian—fei wenbende shehui sichaoshi."

7. The revolutionary intellectual Zhang Taiyan, for instance, was an advocate of the *shenyi*.

8. Wang Dongxia, *Cong changpao magua dao xinzhuang gelu*. See particularly chap. 3, section 4 (on *zhongshan zhuang*) and chap. 4, section 5 (on the New Life Movement).

9. *The Analects*, 14.

10. See *Ershiwu shi* [The Twenty-five Histories].

11. For the impact of the *tifa ling* (tonsure order), see the discussion of the Chen Mingxia case in Wakeman, *Great Enterprise*.

12. Zhou Zuoren, *Zhitang huixiang lu,* 200. The term *ziwei,* or self-comforting, is Zhou's euphemism for masturbation. The author obviously deems the display of such a sexual process on the theatrical stage a highly self-degrading practice, which he could only attribute to male prostitutes subject to the system of sexual exploitation current at a time earlier than the one in which he was writing.

13. Luo, "Jubu congtan," 792.

14. See Yi, "Wanggu chou qu: Wei gelang Mei Lanfang zuo," 745.

15. See Zeng Pu, *Niehai hua*.

16. Zhou Zuoren, "Lun Zhongguo jiuxi zhi yingfei" and "Rende wenxue."

17. Zhang Cixi, *Qingdai Yandu liyuan shiliao huibian,* 1243.

18. Mei, *Wutai shenghuo sishi nian,* 512.

19. The beginning of the self-initiated purge within the operatic communities, however, may not be credited to Mei, since it can be traced to the 1912 founding of the Zhengyue Yuhua Hui [Society of Education and Cultivation in the Sanctified Music] by Tan Xinpei and Tian Jiyun, two prominent Peking opera actors in the late Qing, and in Tan's case, the beginning of the Republic. For a brief description of the opening event, see Mei, *Wutai shenghuo sishi nian,* 593.

20. Ibid., 158.

21. Another such instance may be found in the performance of *Guifei zuijiu,* where Mei as the Imperial Consort censored a eunuch's improper suggestion.

22. Mei, *Wutai shenghuo sishi nian,* 282.

23. Ibid.

CHAPTER 6

The Transgender Body in Wang Dulu's *Crouching Tiger, Hidden Dragon*

TZE-LAN D. SANG

FOR FIFTY YEARS Wang Dulu (1909–1977) was forgotten by readers in mainland China and barely known in Hong Kong and Taiwan. His martial arts and social romance novels, written in northern China in the 1930s and 1940s, would likely have remained obscure to today's readers had Ang Lee not recently made a film adaptation of Wang's *Crouching Tiger, Hidden Dragon* (*Wo hu cang long*; serialized 1941–1942), the fourth volume of a five-part martial arts series.[1] Yu Jiaolong, a morally ambiguous and itinerant female fighter, occupies the center of Wang's novel. Willful and ambitious, she is dissatisfied with the gendered nature of work and mobility. She loathes squandering her life away in the idle activity in which upper-class women typically engage—calligraphy, embroidery, reading *The Four Books for Women (Nü sishu)* and *The Biographies of Women (Lienü zhuan)*, adorning herself with cosmetics and jewelry, and playing with pets. She yearns to venture out into the wide, wide world and prove herself an invincible fighter.[2]

Elsewhere, I have argued that the theme of Jiaolong's boundary transgression in *Crouching Tiger* can be read as an allegory about educated new women's entry into the professions in the Republican era. I also suggested that the treatment of this issue in the novel suggests that the author, Wang Dulu, despite being dismissed as a nonserious retrograde writer by leftist literary historians for several decades, was an aspiring cosmopolitan, who was sensitive to the resonance between the so-called progressive new ideas and certain existing elements of China's composite, heterogeneous tradition. Rather than resist the drastic social changes and shifting values occurring in his time, he creatively revised the narrative conventions about chivalrous women in China's long-standing tradition of fantasy literature, thus making tradition relevant for the times. This work also rendered western-imported ideas about female independence, profession, and mobility familiar and palatable to ordinary urban readers. His work instantiates the synthesis of a quintessential national art form—the martial arts fantasy—and transnational ideas of women's liberation.[3]

In this chapter, I intend to take a closer look at one of the most intriguing aspects of Jiaolong's boundary transgression—the way her body defies binary gender categories and lends itself to being deciphered as transgendered. Jiaolong—the daughter of a high-ranking Manchu official who established his name by waging battles in the western province of Xinjiang before being appointed to take charge of the security of the capital Beijing—lives between embodiments and between identities. Unbeknownst to her parents, she is an accomplished martial artist, having studied the art of fighting in secret ever since she was seven years old. When she sneaks out of her bedchamber at night to meet her enemies, or when she travels far away from home to seek adventures, she typically dresses as a man, in tight-fitting tops and pants. Disguised as a man to operate in "the Rivers and Lakes" *(jianghu),* that is, the martial arts underworld, she takes on male-sounding pseudonyms: first, Long Jinchun (literally "Dragon Splendor Spring") and later, in the sequel to *Crouching Tiger,* Chun Da Wangye (literally "Senior Prince Spring"). She has, in other words, a secret martial artist identity separate from her official daytime identity as the young lady of an aristocratic household. How do these two identities cohabit in her? How is one to conceptualize Jiaolong's self? Is there a feminine essence persisting at the core of a masculinized body? Or is there a masculine soul trapped in a feminine body? Intriguingly, both conceptual models seem to be in full play in the novel. Even more provocatively, the author constantly creates dramatic scenes in which Jiaolong in her fighting gear is observed through the eyes of the strangers she encounters, thus constantly playing up the ambiguity of her gender through depictions of the strangers' bewilderment, curiosity, and irresistible urges to uncover the truth of her identity. She strikes her opponents as "neither female nor male" *(bu nü bu nan)* and "half male and half female" *(ban nan ban nü).* Her disruption of gender dimorphism causes discomfort in others, and yet she insists on dressing and behaving as she pleases.

The task of this chapter, then, is to first establish the characteristics of this transgender body, and secondly to venture some hypotheses about the kind of collective desires and aesthetics that may have played a role in producing such a fantastic body and in facilitating its consumption by readers. One of the preliminary conclusions of this analysis, surprisingly, is that the Republican writer Wang Dulu's imagining of the gender-queer body in 1941 is in many ways much more radical than that presented by Ang Lee's 2000 film adaptation, which shortchanges the transgender character, reducing her to a woman who occasionally cross-dresses but is firmly locked in a normative female position in a heterosexual romance. Moreover, by paying attention—a kind of exacting attention that has occurred all too rarely in recent revisionist scholarship on Republican-era popular fiction[4]—to the minutiae of the gender and sexual configurations in Wang's text, I hope to begin to crack the problem of the active negotiation between indigenous popular taste and various modernizing ideologies that went on in nonelite cultural production.

Synopsis: The Life Journey of a Gender Outlaw

Jiaolong's formation as a martial artist and a transgressor of female boundaries begins when she is a child in Xinjiang. Her tutor Gao Langqiu, a middle-aged Confucian scholar, took possession of a set of handwritten manuals on Jiuhua-style swordsmanship and boxing some years earlier and has studied them in secret, but has not had an opportunity to put his martial arts to use. However, being knowledgeable about the kind of raw athletic ability it takes to be a good fighter, he is struck by Jiaolong's natural gift:

> Jiaolong's feet were natural *(tianzu);* her waist was thin; her weight was light; and her hands and feet were quick and flexible. She had fallen in love with horses when she was six or seven *(qi ba sui)*. Whenever her parents were not watching her, she would run out of the house. When she saw a horse belonging to her father's office, she would forthrightly untie the rope and leap on, not caring whose it was. She would let the horse gallop outside the city for half a day and not return home until she was exhausted and soaked in sweat. In the beginning she fell a few times from the horses, but soon her riding techniques had become superb. She dared ride even the most notoriously unruly Yili horses. In fact, she rode them at a lightening speed and had them in total submission and control. Everyone in her father's office and army admired her. (p. 210)

Recognizing Jiaolong's extraordinary athletic talent, an unusual idea comes to Gao Langqiu. He lays out to Jiaolong his grand vision:

> Jiaolong, you are very intelligent, and you have a lively spirit and natural love for the martial arts. Although you are a girl, if you can be well-versed in the classics and histories, acquire expertise in calligraphy and painting, and, in addition, master the art of war, boxing, and swordplay, you can, as much as boys, honor your family and bequeath a miracle to this world *(wei renjian liu yi qiji)*. Since antiquity, Ban Zhao has been revered as the representative of talented women, and Qin Liangyu is the most renowned female general. A female knight-errant *(nüxia)*, however, has never existed. Hongxian and Nie Yinniang are absurd imag-

ined characters in fiction. But if we reason it carefully: A girl can become a female knight-errant if she is willing to study sword fighting and boxing diligently under the tutelage of a competent teacher. Now, I would like to spend ten years teaching you reading and writing, the art of war, and swordplay. I want the capabilities of Ban Zhao, Qin Liangyu, and Hongxian to converge in you. You will be an extraordinary woman *(qi nüzi)* the likes of whom has never before existed—a great rarity in the present world that will seldom appear again in the future. Are you willing? (p. 210)

Jiaolong, then a seven-year-old child, is naturally delighted by the proposal to become the first female knight-errant and immediately commences to study martial arts at nighttime, all the while keeping it a secret from her parents as Gao instructs.

What Gao Langqiu did not expect, however, is that a few years later, when he is away on a trip, Jiaolong clandestinely unlocks a box he has entrusted to her safekeeping and makes a duplicate of the martial arts manuals hidden inside. She then secretly studies the books by herself to master all the techniques in them, including the ones Gao has withheld from her, and her martial arts techniques soon surpass even his. Her superior skills lead her to actions ever more beyond his control. When she is fifteen, a group of desert bandits ambushes the carriage she and her mother are traveling in under the cover of a sandstorm. In the chaotic fight that ensues between the bodyguards and the bandits, Jiaolong kills numerous bandits, unobserved by her mother or the entourage, and even chases the surviving bandits to their mountain base. When Gao Langqiu realizes—without sharing his realization with Jiaolong's mother, the maids, or bodyguards—what a formidable fighter his student has become, partly under her own tutelage, he is filled at first with pride and then with remorse and premonition. He fears that he has nurtured not a female knight-errant but a "venomous dragon" *(du long)* (p. 224). Not long afterward Gao dies of wounds sustained during the ambush.

Jiaolong's superior martial skills have unintended consequences even for herself. As she pursues the bandits halfway across the desert, she meets the bandit leader, Luo Xiaohu, and falls in love with the handsome and tragic hero. After spending several days with Xiaohu, when she returns to her mother's side, she realizes that her heart has become an unharnessed filly, that she can no longer be content spending time with her female relatives in the boudoir; instead, she constantly misses Xiaohu and the unfettered freedom she experienced during her solitary adventure.

Two years later, Jiaolong's father is promoted to a high post in charge of the security of Beijing, so she moves together with her parents to the capital. A few joyous and peaceful months pass in the city before she succumbs to the lure of a marvelously sharp ancient sword in the possession of a Manchu prince, steals it, and unintentionally kills a policeman who is trying to hunt down the female bandit Green-Eyed Fox (Biyan Huli, who coincidentally had pretended to be Gao Langqiu's wife during the last few years of Gao's life and now works as one of Jiaolong's servants). Rumors begin to spread that a thief is hiding in the Yu residence. Jiaolong regrets the worry those rumors cause her parents, is persuaded by a respected female knight-errant Yu Xiulian to return the sword to the prince, and resigns herself to resuming her former constrained life in the boudoir. Soon, an arranged marriage to a man she finds repulsive leads her to run away on the wedding night.

In her chivalric adventures outside the capital, Jiaolong defeats numerous bandits and other strong men of the Rivers and Lakes. However, she rushes back to the capital as soon as she learns that her mother has fallen ill of grief. Moreover, not wanting to hurt her father and brothers' careers in officialdom, she acquiesces to living in her nominal husband's residence. Jiaolong visits her mother daily and tries to console her, but her mother soon dies. Meanwhile, rumors doubting Jiaolong's respectability continue to spread like wildfire in the capital. Consequently, her father also collapses into illness, and it is then that Jiaolong vows that she will make a pilgrimage to the top of the sacred Miaofeng Mountain (Miaofeng shan) west of Beijing and jump off the cliff to repay the Bixia Yuanjun Goddess with gratitude if her father's illness is cured.[5]

These filial and pious sentiments may have endeared Jiaolong to the common Chinese reader of the 1940s, but they certainly would have made anti-traditionalists frown. It is fascinating, then, that the pious girl eventually jumps off the golden summit *(jinding)* not exactly to sacrifice herself in obligation to the merciful goddess but rather to leave her family without causing them shame and harm. It is the fantastic nature of martial arts that saves Jiaolong from her moral quandaries: Unconstrained by gravity, she lands at the foot of the mountains unharmed. She subsequently seeks out her lover Xiaohu and they reunite, which naturally overjoys him. But the lovers' sweet dreams are fleeting; Xiaohu wakes up the next morning to find that Jiaolong has disappeared without explanation. The narrator intrudes at this point and informs the reader, by way of conclusion, that Jiaolong, in order to keep her promise to her mother on her dying bed that she will never marry a bandit, has no choice but to leave (pp. 743–763).

The sequel to *Crouching Tiger—Iron Steed, Silver Vase* (*Tie ji yin ping*, 1942–1943)—opens at night, with Jiaolong, big with child and ready to go into labor, in a Gansu town beset by a heavy snow storm.[6] After she successfully delivers a boy in a tavern, she falls asleep in exhaustion, and another woman who has just given birth to a girl swaps the two babies. After pursuing the thief in vain and failing to recover her child, Jiaolong adopts the abandoned baby girl, Xueping, and raises her as her own. She returns to her beloved Xinjiang where she owns a vast ranch that her Kazakh female friend Meixia helps her manage. For about nineteen years Jiaolong's main career—if we may describe it as such—consists of eliminating bandits from the southern part of the Xinjiang, Shaanxi, and Gansu regions to ensure the safety of travelers and merchants. Her deeds win her the reputation of being prideful and merciless *(jiaoao henla)*; she is both revered and feared. She routinely dresses as a man and is known among the locals as Senior Prince Spring, but occasionally she wears women's dresses or even dresses as a Kazakh when she pleases. She has her adopted daughter call her "aunt" in Manchu, which happens to be a homonym with the word "father" *(diedie)* in Chinese. She forbids people from discussing her gender or speculating about her past, and those who offend her lose either their eyes or their lives.

In the nineteenth year since her return to Xinjiang, Jiaolong is deeply consumptive and decides to travel back east to look for her lost son. However, when she meets her son and discovers his identity by accident, she dares not unveil the truth to him, for she would have to tell him that he is her bastard *(sisheng haizi)*. Afraid of being rejected, Jiaolong chooses to be a male elderly friend *(pengyou)*, rather than a mother, to him. Jiaolong feels ashamed about her illicit love affair *(siqing)* in the past because, after all, she was educated to value chastity. Ironically, her reluctance to restore the mother-son relationship inadvertently disrupts the appropriate gender distinctions and the proper hierarchy of human relationships so fundamental to Confucianism.

Jiaolong convinces her young friend/son, Tiefang, to travel home with her to Weili County in Xinjiang to meet someone who is very dear to her. However, she dies en route in Tiefang's arms before getting a chance to unburden herself of the secret of his birth. Tiefang buries her and continues on to Weili to bring the sad news to his deceased friend's dearest one. There he discovers that the person he is looking for is a prideful young woman named Chun Xueping. He also finds out that his diseased elderly friend, who took offense when he asked whether s/he was Yu Jiaolong and who insisted on being treated like a man, was indeed none other than the legendary female fighter who disappeared two decades ago. After many vicissitudes, Tiefang further discovers that Jiaolong is in fact his biological mother. He also meets his biological father Luo Xiaohu shortly before Xiaohu dies. Tiefang and Xueping fall in love and become husband and wife. The story ends with the two returning to Weili to settle down after many adventures. They will carry on Jiaolong's legacy by studying the martial arts manuals she left behind.

Martial Arts as Body-Altering Technologies

As a child, Jiaolong is chosen by her teacher to receive training in the secret Jiuhua-style martial arts because of a certain natural aptitude of her body. However, the training not only allows her to realize the natural potential of her body, but also drastically alters its gender. After Jiaolong studies martial arts for almost ten years, her body has developed in such an extraordinary fashion that she is equipped to compete and excel in a sphere dominated by men with the strongest physical abilities. Martial arts thus function as a set of technologies for gender change through body alteration. Although these technologies, unlike twenty-first-century sex-reassignment technologies, do not give her a new set of sexual organs, many other aspects of her body and mind that might signify gender socially — strength, speed, explosive power, valor, ambition, and even cruelty — are dramatically enhanced, making her unfeminine, that is, atypical of women in her society, and decidedly in conflict with the frailty, docility, and restraint that others expect of her as a young aristocratic woman.

That martial arts transform Jiaolong's body, rendering her gender-queer, does not contradict the fact that there seems to be a place for women fighters in the Rivers and Lakes underworld Wang creates. There are indeed a few women fighters other than Jiaolong who compete with men. However, those other women as a rule have become members of this underworld only because they are daughters of male fighters and have inherited their professions from their fathers.[7] Even so, women fighters are a minority compared with men who operate in the Rivers and Lakes realm. Even more crucially, they, being of Han ethnicity, can never shed their female identity for the simple fact that their feet are bound. In Wang's fantastic universe set in eighteenth-century China, the cultural practice of footbinding is such a naturalized gender differentiator that a pair of bound feet can authoritatively *fix* or give away the true gender of a fighter as female regardless of the level of her martial skills. The feet supersede other body parts to function as the primary gender-identifying body part.[8]

Jiaolong, born a Manchu, is different from women fighters of Han ethnicity. Her feet never having been bound, her body lends itself to being read as gender-ambiguous, if not outright male, according to one set — the dominant set — of rules of intelligibility in society.[9] In her adventures, she often dresses as a man, in tight-fitting black top and pants. But she has a thin waist and a high-pitched voice, and as a result, fighters she randomly encounters on the road are often baffled by her outer appearance and extremely confused about her gender identity. They constantly curse her for being "neither female nor male." In their confusion, her opponents always look toward her feet as if these were a sure marker of her real gender. Time and again, because her feet are of natural size *(yishuang dajiao),* opponents immediately draw the conclusion that she must in fact be male. In these situations her opponents' blindness to ethnic diversity within China leads them to make reductive and, therefore, mistaken assumptions about the multiple gender systems in China. Wang's sensitivity to the issue of Chinese heterogeneity is arguably attributable to his own Manchu identity.[10] Nevertheless, it is remarkable that his way of affirming Manchu cultural practices is to aggressively exploit ethnic difference to create a new gender that unsettles the dominant binary gender system of the Han majority.

This new gender, or transgender, is the result of mixing and combining bits taken from several divergent ethnic gender codes. On the one hand, Jiaolong has studied the Confucian classics and absorbed certain key Confucian values, such as filial piety, like any daughter of a Han gentry family. On the other, as a child growing up in ethnically diverse Xinjiang, where her father is stationed until she turns seventeen,[11] she also learns horseback riding and hunting as would any Manchu, Kazakh, or Mongol girl in the steppes. Because she retains traces of her nomadic heritage, she can never be fully feminine in the Han sense. Her lack of femininity is moored in her manlike feet, her love for horses, and her love for the open earth and sky in the prairies and deserts.

The developmental course of Jiaolong's transgender body, we thus see, originates in the twilight of childhood: Although her body can achieve an astounding level of masculinity only by means of the powerful body-altering technologies of martial arts study, the seeds of masculinity are nonetheless planted early in her body, when she is a child. That she is drawn to the martial arts is but a logical extension of her love for horseback riding and recreational hunting starting at a young and tender age. What her study of the martial arts has done is not so much force her body to develop in a direction against its natural inclination as allow it to blossom into that female masculine form whose growth would otherwise have been stunted by Confucian-influenced protocols of feminine behavior inculcated as a child matures into a young woman.

The Female Masculine Body and Layered Identities

The story of Jiaolong is, in a fundamental sense, a tale about an intersexual body and layered identities. "The young lady of a renowned household" *(mingmen de xiaojie)* is the social gender role that Jiaolong is inserted into at birth and is expected to perform, but her physical development and psychical identification do not exactly mirror that role. Her anatomical sex is female, and so is her social gender, but her sexed embodiment is masculine with female specificity — constituted differently from the bodies of ordinary women as well as those of men. Hers is a powerful body yearning to break free of the fragile female norm and dominate others in a violent world. Yet it is also a maternal body, one that is able to conceive and give birth, as revealed in the sequel to *Crouching Tiger — Iron Steed, Silver Vase.*

One of the fundamental contributions of late-twentieth-century queer theory is its insistence on "complicat[ing] hegemonic assumptions about the continuities between anatomical sex, social gender, gender identity, sexual identity, sexual object choice, and sexual practice."[12] Recently, transgender theory has further focused on the ways in which transgendered bodily effects "disrupt or denaturalize heteronormatively constructed linkages between an individual's anatomy at birth, a nonconsensually assigned gender category, psychical identifications with sexed body images and/or gendered subject positions, and the performance of specifically gendered social, sexual, or kinship functions."[13] The discontinuities and disruptions examined by queer theorists and transgender theorists are uncannily echoed, or rather, anticipated, by the dissonances and nonnormative relations that Wang Dulu creates among Jiaolong's anatomical sex, social gender, sexed embodiment, psychical gender identification, sexual object choice, and sexual practice. Although Jiaolong is born a biological female and is assigned the social gender role of a daughter of an upper-class household, her sexed embodiment is not purely feminine (in a culturally intelligible way), but rather is an astonishing combination of feminine and masculine traits, such as beauty, agility, strength, the ability to respond violently to challenges, and rashness. Her psychical identification is equally complex. Prior to her pilgrimage to Miaofeng Mountain, she oscillates between identifying as a virtuous, sheltered and well-liked lady and as an invincible masculine fighter who holds social rules in contempt. She switches back and forth between her feminine and masculine roles, inhabits each with almost equal (dis)comfort, and might be understood as a bigendered person with dual psychical identifications. Later, a major turning point — that is, passage to more decidedly masculine psychical and social identities — occurs when she jumps off the cliff of Miaofeng Mountain. At that moment, she forsakes all kinship ties, and her old emotional self undergoes death and rebirth. Also at that moment, her everyday sartorial style shifts from being beguilingly feminine half of the time to being outright masculine, and her performance of social and kinship functions shifts from being a filial daughter and pious believer to being a runaway daughter, a disbeliever, and a merciless prince-like personage of the prairies, steppes, and deserts. Amid the complex gender transformations, her sexual object choice is male during one brief moment, but after that moment elapses, celibacy is her chosen sexual practice, and she relies primarily on networks of female friendship and a mother-daughter bond for intimacy in everyday life.

Jiaolong's transgendered self may therefore seem an aggregate of contradictory elements from a hegemonic point of view. These contradictions often work as façade versus reality in relation to one another. For instance, before Jiaolong permanently leaves her natal family, the exquisite beauty of her facial features and dress works as a glorious façade that masks a masculine body and drive underneath. This gorgeous façade is recounted in the description by Liu Taibao, a clownish character, early in the narrative:

> She was about sixteen. Tall and slender. Covered in a snow-blue cape made of some unknown radiant silk lined with silver mink, she wore a red embroidered Manchu robe underneath. Her feet were natural. She wore thick-soled shoes, the kind that Manchu girls wore, made of golden cloth embroidered in colorful threads and decorated with tiny glass mirrors. Her hair was combed into a braid. The braid, of course, was hidden by the cape, and only the shiny black clouds beside her ears showed. A red velvet phoenix was pinned to her hair, hovering above her ear. A string of dainty lustrous pearls hung from the phoenix's beak. Her face was even more beautiful than her clothes and jewelry: a face shaped like the melon seed, a high nose, big eyes, and handsome eyebrows. If one were to compare her noble and magnificent beauty to flowers, only the peony was comparable, but the peony was not as exquisite as she. (p. 5)

No one suspects that such a flowerlike beauty is anything but a weakling, until the female knight-errant Yu Xiulian meets her and sees right through the façade. With one piercing look, Xiulian discerns right away that Jiaolong is of the same height and has the same thin waist and large feet as the male-looking sword thief she fought with the previous night. Xiulian then proceeds to test Jiaolong's reflex and physical strength by attacking her pressure point and squeezing her wrist (p. 141), against which Jiaolong spontaneously reacts, hence betraying her secret. Her beautiful dress and ornaments can hardly disguise the tough athletic body underneath.

However, this masculinity does not always function as the truth of Jiaolong's body. When she dresses as a man, the opposite dynamic is created—her male clothing becomes the façade veiling a feminine ground. After Jiaolong escapes from her husband's home on the wedding night, she leaves the capital disguised as a man and travels with her maid Xiuxiang as husband and wife. Here is a scene of her morning toiletry in a tavern:

Jiaolong ordered Xiuxiang to take clean underwear [out of their bags] for her to change. She bound her chest very tightly with white gauze. Because she did not prepare many men's clothes, the inner layer she wore was still a red silk short jacket, which she covered with a green silk robe buttoned tightly around the neck, hiding even the collar of the red jacket. . . . That morning, as soon as she had arisen, she had already washed her ears with the water left from the previous day and applied a mixture of powder and oil to her pierced ear holes until they could no longer be seen when she examined herself in the mirror. Only then did she open the door, stiffen her face, and yelled in a deliberately low voice: "Shop clerk! Bring some water for washing over!" (p. 393)

Here, not only is Jiaolong unable to stop behaving as a pampered lady who needs her maid's assistance with even the slightest task, but she is also unable to completely obliterate bodily signs of her femininity: a woman's bosom, a woman's red jacket, a woman's pierced earlobes, and a woman's soft voice. Some of these signs are physical while others originate in cultural practice. Whether they are effects of nature or nurture, however, the signs can only be suppressed and camouflaged rather than eliminated.[14] In other words, even when Jiaolong dresses and behaves in a masculine style, she retains many feminine characteristics, creating an intersexual body, instead of a normative single-sexed one.

The Transgender Imagination

Now that we have traced the contours of Jiaolong's body story, we are left with the question: What enabled Wang Dulu to imagine such a body? And why did readers enjoy his creation?

First of all, late imperial Chinese popular fiction and theater were full of plots and practices involving transgenderism, such as crossing and passing. They undoubtedly created a popular taste for female masculine bodies, as well as transgender male feminine ones, as entertaining spectacles and objects.[15] The popular taste very likely continued to live on throughout the Republican era even after intellectuals of the May Fourth generation, who were active in the New Culture movement of the late 1910s and 1920s, denounced much of traditional popular culture, such as the symbolic and transgender practices in traditional theater, as unrealistic, unnatural, primitive, and harmful to artistic evolution. For instance, Hu Shi criticized traditional Chinese theater as naïve and primitive, containing many vestiges from primordial times such as music, painted faces, stylized singing, stylized movement, and acrobatics. He averred that Chinese theater should abolish singing and remake itself in the image of modern Western spoken drama.[16] In voicing such views, Hu was merely echoing and reinforcing beliefs widely shared by his intellectual cohort writing for the iconoclastic journal *New Youth (Xin qingnian)*. In several issues in 1918, Liu Bannong, Qian Xuantong, Chen Duxiu, Zhou Zuoren, as well as Hu Shi, launched one belligerent attack after another on traditional Chinese theater *(jiuxi)*. Zhou, in particular, claimed that traditional Chinese theater deserved to be extinguished because it was a grotesque vehicle for all the superstitious, licentious, lawless, monstrous, moralistic and frivolous elements of old, "inhumane" literature.[17] His brother Lu Xun's antipathy for Beijing theater and, in particular, the enduring popularity of the famed female impersonator Mei Lanfang is also well known.[18] What the publication and popularity of *Crouching Tiger* in the 1940s suggests is that, in addition to the "modern" aesthetics championed by the westernized elite, there continued to be another set of aesthetic principles and desires that thrived in a stratum of culture deemed middle-brow and unprogressive by the elite.

Ironically, viewed from an early twenty-first-century perspective, the heteronormative alignment of anatomical sex, social gender, sexed embodiment, and sexual object choice advocated by the Republican westernized elite no longer seems unquestionably progressive. The rigidity of the modernizing elite's gender and sexual ideals is precisely what queer theory and transgender theory have taken to task. To further understand how the masses' taste and desires may have resisted the heteronormative vision of the modernizing elite, it is high time that more popular cultural products of the Republican era such as Wang's *Crouching Tiger* be explored.

Secondly, and more specifically, Wang's imagining of the female masculine body may have been inspired by certain elements of the nationalistic discourse in China of the first half of the twentieth century. During the late Qing, the masculine persona of female revolutionaries such as Qiu Jin captured the public's imagination and was often viewed positively by those promoting women's greater participation in efforts to save the nation. Between the 1920s and 1940s it was not unusual for at least some advocates of women's physical education *(tiyu)* and healthy beauty *(jianmei)* to argue that women ought to be subjected to the same kind of rigorous physical discipline and training as men.[19] In other words, even as the May Fourth elite constructed heteronormative gender ideals, there was always another strand of nationalistic discourse that encouraged female masculinity. Wang's creation of the masculine heroine Yu Jiaolong may well have drawn inspiration from such a discourse even when his heroine, individualistic and willful, seems a far cry from the female revolutionary, soldier, or athlete who is fully dedicated to a collective cause.

Wang Dulu refused to give Jiaolong's life journey heteronormative closure. Not only does his heroine choose to live independently without her bandit lover Xiaohu, but in the many years after she exiles herself from the capital to return to the steppes, she also resists recapitulating to any gender norm. She dies, in fact, as a gender-ambiguous person in her son's arms.[20] Simply for this reason alone, reading Jiaolong's story in Wang's *Crouching Tiger* and its sequel is a starkly different experience from watching Ang Lee's 2000 film adaptation. In the film's final scene, Jiaolong's leap from a cliff into the abyss has everything to do with the ambivalent attraction and guilt she feels for Li Mubai, an older knight-errant who tried to discipline her and lost his life saving hers, a plot twist that exists only in the film, not the novel. Lee's heroine, in other words, is firmly locked in a female sacrificial position that bolsters the heterosexual romance, whereas Wang's heroine keeps his readers' enthusiasm for this gender-queer body in the sharpest of focus.

Notes

The author acknowledges generous travel support from the Chiang Ching-kuo Foundation and the American Council of Learned Societies that facilitated the research of this essay.

1. Wang Dulu, *Wo hu cang long*. Text references are to page numbers of the Tiandi tushu gongsi 2000 edition. According to a list of publications compiled by Wang's daughter cited in Xu Sinian, *Wang Dulu pingzhuan*, *Wo hu cang long* was first serialized in *Qingdao xinmin bao* [Qingdao New People's Daily] from March 16, 1941 to March 6, 1942, the accuracy of which my own trip to the Qingdao Municipal Archives in July 2004 confirmed.

2. Wang, *Wo hu cang long*, especially 226, 267, 285, 447. All citations are keyed to this edition authorized by Li Danquan, Wang Dulu's widow. After being serialized, the novel was not published individually until 1948—Shanghai Lili Bookstore put out an edition in five thin volumes.

3. Sang, "Women's Work." Narratives of chivalry and martial prowess constitute a unique indigenous genre, whose roots can be traced as far back as the early historical (and often imaginative) writings of Sima Qian on wandering knights-errant *(youxia)* two millennia ago. Some scholars, such as Xu Sinian and Liu Xiang'an (in Fan ed., *Zhongguo jinxiandai tongsu wenxueshi*, 450–484), have pointed out that the early twentieth-century Chinese martial arts novel represented a partial departure from the chivalric court case novel common in the late Qing period in both form and ideology. However, this by no means detracts from the fact that there are many continuities between the long indigenous tradition of chivalric fiction and the modern Chinese martial arts novel.

4. In the growing number of studies in Chinese and western languages on Republican popular fiction, gender has remained a marginal topic, usually treated in superficial terms if at all. Some exceptions are the provocative close readings of the gender issues in

Mandarin Ducks and Butterflies fiction in David Der-wei Wang's "Impersonating China"; Chow, *Woman and Chinese Modernity;* and Xu Sinian, *Wang Dulu pingzhuan.*

5. Wang Dulu, *Wo hu cang long,* 719. The center of the Bixia Yuanjun cult was Taishan in Shandong; local temples devoted to her were spread throughout North China and Manchuria. It was believed that when jumping off the cliff in repayment to the Goddess, the lives of true believers would be spared. For an analysis of the cult's popularity in late imperial and Republican times and the gender anxieties that may have contributed to the cult's reputation of being *yin* (licentious, supplementary, unnecessary, surplus), see Pomeranz, "Power."

6. My plot summary of *Tie ji yin ping* is based on the Yuanjing edition.

7. Other than Yu Jiaolong, examples of women who can fight in *Crouching Tiger* include Cai Xiangmei, Yu Xiulian, and Biyan Huli (the Green-eyed Fox), who are the daughters, respectively, of a policeman, the male owner of an escort/security service, and a male bandit. Another woman fighter, Yang Lifang, is an orphan and studies martial arts together with her husband with an old friend of her father-in-law's.

8. See also Zito's essay in this volume.

9. On the concept of gender intelligibility, see Butler, "Doing Justice."

10. Unfortunately, although there is almost certainly a significant link between Wang Dulu's own Manchu identity and his creation of Jiaolong, there exists too little biographical information about Wang to tell us just how he felt about his Manchu heritage and the extent of his familiarity with Manchu customs and history. In fact, Wang's widow, Li Danquan, who is herself not of Manchu descent, in her reply to my query (personal email communication, May 4–11, 2004) flatly rejected the idea that the special qualities Wang bestowed on Jiaolong could have been inspired by his own ethnic heritage and even smacked of a certain nostalgia for earlier Manchu culture. Li asserts that some of the Han women fighters Wang created—such as Yu Xiulian—are just as fearlessly deft in combat as Jiaolong is, and that Wang's purpose in creating Jiaolong is to show a woman constricted by Confucianism rebelling against the "feudal system" *(fengjian zhidu)* and "traditional ritual" *(jiu lijiao).* As the present chapter indicates, my interpretation of the significance of the frequent markers of Jiaolong's ethnicity in Wang's text differs from Li's. Jiaolong gains her martial strength mainly through her hybrid, multicultural upbringing being far removed from the center of the Confucian empire. Despite having absorbed some Confucian values, she is ultimately a misfit in the Confucian system. It is only by weighing her sinification over her ethnic otherness that common readers are able to see her as the universal Chinese woman trying to break away from tradition.

11. On page 286, it is mentioned that Jiaolong turns *shiba sui* (18 *sui*) after the New Year, which suggests that Wang is counting her age the traditional Chinese way, which makes her either seventeen or sixteen by western counting.

12. Martin, *Femininity,* 73.

13. Stryker, "Transgender," 149.

14. Interestingly, at the level of narrative construction, Wang is using the white gauze to call into existence Jiaolong's womanly bosom, which the gauze, in the diegetic world, is precisely meant to efface.

15. Studies on gender fluidity and reversals in late imperial literature and theater are many. See, for instance, David Der-wei Wang, *Splendor,* chap. 2; Giovanni Vitiello, "Ex-

emplary Sodomites"; Li Siu Leung, *Cross-Dressing in Chinese Opera,* chaps. 2 and 8; Hua, "Ming Qing funü juzuo zhong zhi 'ninan' biaoxian yu xingbie wenti"; Epstein, *Competing Discourses;* as well as Wu and Stevenson, Zou, and Epstein in this volume.

16. Hu Shi, "Wenxue jinhua guannian," 313–315.

17. Zhou Zuoren, "Rende wenxue" and "Lun Zhongguo jiuxi zhi yingfei." On Zhou Zuoren's dislike for Beijing opera, see also John Zou's article in this volume.

18. See discussions in Wang, "Impersonating China"; Li, *Cross-Dressing in Chinese Opera,* chap. 1.

19. See Yu Chien-ming, "Jindai Zhongguo nüzi tiyu guan chutan"; Yu Chien-ming, "Jindai Zhongguo nüzi jianmei de lunshu (1920–1940 niandai)." On the nationalistic discipline of the body from the late Qing to the 1930s, see Huang Jinlin (Jinlin Hwang), *Lishi, shenti, guojia,* especially chap. 2. For a discussion of urban modern women's appropriation of nationalistic discourses of the body for their own purposes during the New Life Movement (1934–1937), see Hsiao-pei Yen, "Body Politics."

20. It is only after she dies that her son, who has been suspecting that she might be a woman and none other than the legendary Yu Jiaolong, is able to closely examine pierced marks on her ears to determine her gender; he then ascertains her identity as Yu Jiaolong by looking at her natural, unbound feet (Wang, *Tie ji yin ping,* 325). Jiaolong's gender ambiguity is a point that the many illustrations by an artist named Liu Jinghai accompanying the original serialization of *Crouching Tiger* and its sequel in the *Qingdao New People's Daily* in 1941 and 1942 visually struck home. In these pictures she is often depicted as a tall thin figure wearing men's tight fighting gear and a long braid/queue, although the hair above her forehead is not tonsured like men's. (Unfortunately, due to the malfunction of the microfilm reader in the Qingdao Municipal Archives during my visit, I was unable to obtain any prints of the illustrations for reproduction in this volume.) For a brief discussion of the friendship between Wang Dulu and his illustrator Liu, see Xu, *Wang Dulu pingzhuan.*

PART II
Contemporary Embodiments

CHAPTER 7

Introduction to Part II

LARISSA HEINRICH AND FRAN MARTIN

THE ESSAYS IN the first half of this volume explored representations of corporeality amidst the political and social turmoil of Republican-era Chinese modernity. The book's second half shifts our focus to the rapidly transforming corporeal imaginaries of the late modern period, between the 1980s and the present. This section underscores connections between the multiplicity of late-modern Chinese body representations and the multiple and fragmentary character of late-modern Chinese cultures more generally. These essays frame their inquiries against the backdrop of emergent transnationalisms and distinctive forms of late-modern culture found in present-day Taiwan, Hong Kong, mainland China, and Chinese diasporas, as well as the rise of highly developed media and commodity cultures in each of these areas. The specific conditions of late modernity in each of the areas considered lead to distinctive forms of body representation, and the plurality of these representations in turn reflects the multiple, disjunctive character of the contexts from which they emerge.

Studies of Post-1949 Chinese Body Cultures

Just as studies of pre-1949 body cultures in China have employed a wide spectrum of critical methods, studies of the body in post-1949 Chinese cultures have likewise made use of a number of disciplinary and theoretical frameworks to account for the increasingly hybridized discourses and practices around the body today. Research on cultures of corporeality under Mao suggests that, through Party-led regimes of collective action in all fields of social life, from sport and education to work and participation in political campaigns, "the people"/"the masses" *(renmin/dazhong)* were made to represent a collective embodiment of the party-state's revolutionary will, while the individual body within that framework functioned purely as synecdoche. Ann Anagnost's work on "The Politicized Body," for instance, addresses the continuities and discontinuities in conceptions of the social body under Mao, exploring "how the production of docile political subjects . . . undergirds a projection of the party/state as a subject writ large, as the unified voice of the 'people as one' — a projection that conceals the internal fragmentation and diversity not only of 'the people,' but also within the party organization itself."[1] Anthropological and medical studies such as the work by Arthur Kleinman on the collective memory and bodily experience of the Cultural Revolution provide further psychosocial background for cultures of corporeality under Mao.[2]

Alongside the impact of Maoist collectivism on lived body cultures in the People's Republic, another central question that has occupied analysts of modern Chinese body cultures post-1949 is how to account for the complex interrelations between residual, premodern Chinese traditions of body knowledge and new ways of thinking about bodies that entered Chinese societies in this period. In general, the extant scholarship has demonstrated that, rather than simply displacing older Chinese concepts of body, illness, and health, the various western body discourses introduced or developed before and after 1949, such as those concerning health, diet, and exercise, have evolved alongside Chinese concepts to produce syncretic systems of body culture and body knowledge. As Anagnost writes in *National Past-times:*

> Notions such as Society, Nation, Individual, History . . . all belong to the language of colonial modernity, as the categories of a bourgeois ideology that come from elsewhere to operate as signs of what China "lacked" — its inability to access the "real" because of its literary ties to an older metaphysics. And yet, despite their presence as "lack," they offered a powerful source of agency for a modernizing elite intent on the project of constituting a modern nation, a project made compelling by the unequal exchanges of China's semicolonial status.[3]

This argument holds true, too, for the body in contemporary Chinese contexts. Even as Eurocentric discourses of modernity dwelled on what Chinese conceptualizations of the body supposedly lacked, they stimulated Chinese appropriation of elements of western body-thinking to produce hybrid forms marked as both modern *and* Chinese. For example, Susan Brownell's *Training the Body for China* investigates the relationship between sports and morality in the People's Republic and its effect on lived body experiences. Looking at gender, nationalism, and social practice from the point of view of both a former athlete and a present-day anthropologist, Brownell untangles complex webs of social convention, political discourse, and physical practice to demonstrate that the practice of sport in modern China is marked by a partial and uneven rather than a wholesale adoption of western values — those around gender being a particularly clear example.[4] More recently, Judith Farquhar's work takes this focus on lived experience even further, debunking the presumed universality of the body's "appetites" (culinary, sexual, and medicinal) and instead revealing their contingency. As she notes in the introduction to *Appetites: Food and Sex in Post-socialist China,* "The 'problem' of the reality of bodies across temporal and cultural divides is analogous to the problem of translation: to render the history congealed in a text in another language is impossible, yet it is done all the time."[5] Drawing from anthropology and literary criticism as well as personal and institutional histories, Farquhar provides an account of how the most seemingly elemental of human appetites nonetheless are configured contingently, offering at best fleeting glimpses of an always transitioning, always contextual experience. New studies are beginning to emerge that sustain this focus on the complex sources of embodied experience by addressing other phenomena in contemporary Chinese body cultures, including tattooing and body modification, cosmetic surgery, government responses to SARS and HIV transmission, and the like. A number of important discussions on contemporary body representations have also been taking place in art history in recent years; most notably a conference coordinated by Wu Hung and Katherine Tsiang and the subsequent volume, *Body and Face in Chinese Visual Culture.* This project sought "to explain a general Chinese body and face by charting multiple, specific bodies and faces."[6]

Chinese Modernities Post-1949

As we noted in the Introduction to Part I, acknowledging Chinese modernity as a cultural formation historically related to yet also distinct from Western modernity means pluralizing the concept of modernity itself. By insisting on the "coevalness of cultures" and rejecting the construction of Chinese modernity as merely a belated mimicry of a Western original, the work of scholars including Rey Chow, David Der-wei Wang, Aihwa Ong, Lisa Rofel, and others effectively shatters the unity of modernity as it was once conceived—as the sole property of the west.[7] In this section, our treatment of body representations from not just mainland China but also Taiwan, Hong Kong, and diasporic Chinese cultures suggests a further fragmentation: We intend here a self-conscious shift to assessing "Chinese modernit*ies.*"

The distinctive forms of Chinese-language-based cultures found in the contemporary People's Republic, Taiwan, Hong Kong, and the Chinese diaspora have in common a relation of proximity—nearness to and simultaneous distinction from—Euro-American formations of cultural modernity. Within each of these we can identify and track historical linkages with Republican Chinese modernities treated in Part I; still, the precise relations between that early twentieth-century seedbed and the contemporary intellectual, literary, commercial and popular cultures now flourishing in each of these areas are locally specific and often unpredictable. However seductive the dream of a unitary Chinese modernity spanning all geographic areas of Chinese life today, even the most cursory historical consideration reveals unique circumstances that have shaped the regimes of modernity in each. The "Chinese modern" of the contemporary People's Republic is conditioned by three decades of "modernist Marxism" under Mao, followed by the violent shattering of the utopian promise of socialist modernity in the Cultural Revolution (1966–1976). In the wake of that historical trauma, during the New Era of the 1980s under Deng Xiaoping, "culture fever"—an intellectual reengagement with Euro-American modern/ist culture and philosophy—spawned distinctive forms of "modern consciousness" *(xiandai yishi)* as well as literary and cultural postmodernism.[8] The violent repression of reformist intellectuals in the Tian'anmen Square incident in June 1989 led to the wane of the new critical modernism and an unprecedented, rapid saturation of everyday life by commodity logic with the rise of "market fever" during the 1990s.[9]

The central questions and experiences of modernity in Taiwan and Hong Kong, however, are clearly quite different. In the case of Taiwan, Ping-hui Liao has identified four distinct, locally specific modes of modernity. These include: first, the various colonial regimes (the Dutch and Spanish in the seventeenth century, and more recently the Japanese [1895–1945]); second, the Kuomintang (KMT or Nationalist party) military/cultural modernization regime after 1949, which was directed explicitly against the socialist modernity of the People's Republic; third, the internally directed authoritarian KMT regime of 1947 through 1987; and finally, a Taiwanese "alternative modernity" that sees contemporary, democratic Taiwan positioned in between the mainland Chinese and Japanese forms.[10] Other key issues that have occupied theorists of Taiwanese modernity include the role of US military and cultural neocolonialism in the postwar period; these helped shape hybrid forms of popular culture and fueled the far-reaching social impact of the island's breakneck trajectory from agrarian to industrial to unevenly postindustrial commodity culture in less than five decades. Of central importance, too, are the debates since the 1980s between Taiwanese (Hokkien/Holo) nativist intellectuals and the hitherto Mainlander-dominated, Mandarin-speaking cultural elite, with related political arguments over Taiwanese independence versus unification with the Chinese mainland.[11]

Meanwhile, Ackbar Abbas, Rey Chow, Xiaoying Wang, and other theorists of Hong Kong modernity underscore the deep cultural effects brought about by the territory's British colonial history and its tensely ambivalent relation with Beijing both before and since the 1997 handover.[12] Hong Kong, they contend, is distinctively positioned as a postcolonial society with a very strong local Cantonese-language culture that nonetheless seems fated to be passed around between external powers with no prospect of gaining political or cultural autonomy.

Even this very brief, schematic sketch of the basic historical contexts and major contemporary debates is sufficient to make the point that these distinct formations of the Chinese modern cannot be collapsed into any singular whole. These various versions of Chinese-language-based culture not only grow out of different modern histories, they record distinct experiences of colonialism, and they bear differential relations to territorial and political "Chineseness" and to other (Soviet, European, Japanese, American) formations of modernity. Hence our conviction of the necessity to speak to a plurality of "Chinese modern*ies*."

The question of the singularity or plurality of the Chinese modern points to another problem of Chinese cultures in this era of ever-intensifying transnational flows. The center-periphery opposition has provided a structuring dialectic for critical considerations of late modern and diasporic Chinese cultures—the clearest example is perhaps Tu Wei-ming's edited collection, *The Living Tree* (see our discussion above, page 14). Drawing together all four of the geocultural areas known as "Greater China," this dialectic presents a model in which the present work finds itself implicated. But rather than attempting the impossible—determining definitively where the center of Chineseness resides today and where its periphery—we propose a critical rethinking of the center-periphery model itself. Leo Ou-fan Lee argues that "in [the] transnational and cosmopolitan framework [of the present], the old spatial matrix of center and periphery no longer has much validity," and therefore suggests conceptualizing late modern Chinese cultures as "crisscross[ing] each other to form interlocking networks in which there is no single center."[13] This view has something in common with Aihwa Ong and Donald Nonini's view of Chinese transnationalism as an alternative modernity among mobile Chinese entrepreneurs in the Asia Pacific region, who negotiate newly flexible forms of political and cultural citizenship against the backdrop of the "polycentric world of late capitalism."[14] We think the very diversity of the body representations treated by the essays in the second part of this volume strongly supports the centrifugal and pluralizing view of Chinese modernities found in the models proposed by Lee and Ong and Nonini, in distinction to the unifying and paradoxically centripetal pattern suggested by Tu's notion of geographic periphery as new cultural center. Notwithstanding the muscular centrism of the current political culture in the People's Republic, the chapters below on Taiwan, Hong Kong, and Chinese diaspora cultures frame these cultures as sites for the multiplication of modernities, rather than as *either* far-flung peripheries *or* some emergent center of a singular late-modern Chineseness.[15]

The Essays: Part II

If a substantial biological body congealed out of the performative surfaces of imperial-era ritual roles in the early twentieth century, then the early twenty-first century is effecting the fragmentation of that modern body across the various sites of Chinese late modernity. This conceptual fragmentation results from a number of factors, including the increasing scope of medical and scientific intervention; the heightened potential for the commodification of body parts; ongoing transformations in understandings of gender and sexuality; and the arguably decorporealizing effects of expanding image- and techno-cultures. The body representations addressed below are characterized by a notable wane of corporeal presence. These chapters are inhabited by the brutally fragmented bodies of contemporary bioscience; the palimpsestlike, striated bodies of today's techno-cultures; the painfully disintegrating bodies of sexual "others" caught between shifting discourses on gender and sexuality; and the spectral bodies of early twenty-first-century media cultures.

Larissa Heinrich's analysis of body representation in the work of contemporary mainland Chinese author Yu Hua and in the fleshy installations of experimental artists including Zhu Yu, Sun Yuan, and Peng Yu posits the existence of — and practical need to identify — a new trope of organ transplantation and radical surgeries in contemporary literature and art. Noting the impact of developments in science on Chinese literature a century ago, Heinrich asks what we might expect to see in the literature and art of the contemporary period, when rapid development in technologies such as cloning, grafting, transplant, transfusion, stem-cell research, surrogacy, and even adoption, has challenged the limits of ethics, the definition of corporeality, and indeed the boundaries of selfhood in a globalizing economy. She suggests that the recent work of experimental and "uncooperative" artists in mainland China, as well as the philosophical explorations of the writer Yu Hua, provide good entry points for future examinations of the relationship between biotechnology and literature and art.

Addressing the late-modern de-composition of the organic modern body from a different angle, Teri Silvio considers its remake in the informational techno-culture of twenty-first-century Taiwan. Silvio's essay is based on a detailed ethnography of the young fans of digital video knight-errant puppetry serials. She proposes that the largely female fans who dress up as the puppets starring in the popular serials — a practice known as COSplay — are engaged in modeling what she calls an "informational self." Silvio's discussion of the informational self suggests a fascinating loop back to premodern conceptualizations of the self and performance. The parallel drawn in this chapter between traditional Chinese performance aesthetics and the concept of information in contemporary techno-culture links the "striated subject" and "postorganic body" of late-modern pop culture back to the ritual, surface-modeled subjects of imperial-era theater and culture, a linkage that effectively bypasses the solidly corporeal subject of twentieth-century Chinese modernity.

If Heinrich's and Silvio's chapters underline far-reaching challenges to the modern organic body in contemporary cultural production, Jami Proctor-Xu reminds us that corporeality has not made a definitive exit from today's cultural scene. Proctor-Xu observes the resurgence of a modern biological model of the body in Zhang Yang's 1994 film *Shower*, where the violence of urban development in contemporary Beijing is disavowed through a naturalist allegory that parallels the decay and destruction of old neighborhoods with the "natural" lifecycle of biological human and animal bodies. Proctor-Xu's discussion of the subtext in Zhang's film, which champions urban development as a means of advancing the Chinese nation, also recalls the nation-building theme prominent in the book's first section. The spirited resurgence, in this recent film, of both a "natural" human body and a utopian, developmentalist Chinese nationalism is a timely reminder that modern preoccupations are more likely to be unpredictably transfigured than entirely vanquished.

A central theme in the second part of this volume, as in the first, is the problematic of gendered embodiment today. The gendered body emerges as a hotly contested ideological battleground in several of the essays in this section. Silvio, for example, proposes that COSplay may attract young Taiwanese women to the traditionally masculine cultural form of Taiwanese puppet theater because it enables them to negotiate the gap between the immateriality of the techno-culture in which they are immersed and the embodied character of the "affect work" they are expected to perform, as feminine subjects, in their everyday working and personal lives. In playing with codes and treating their bodies as pure surface, Silvio proposes, COSplayers may find a pleasurable respite from the compulsory work of affect production. Louise Edwards' chapter, meanwhile, focuses on the complex symbolic negotiations required for state political culture in the People's Republic to countenance a high-ranking female politician. Through close analysis of both domestic and international media coverage of China's highest-ranking woman politician, Wu Yi, Edwards draws attention to Wu's careful negotiations with hegemonic gender ideologies. She shows how Wu's carefully outfitted public body is skillfully distanced both from the masculinized official femininities of the Cultural Revolution era, and also from oversexualization, with its dangerous implication that Wu's power as a politician arises from sexual favors granted to some male mentor. Wu's closely self-managed public performance implicitly appeals to an ideology of gender as both essential and natural that, as Lisa Rofel has argued in detail, has become dominant in the People's Republic in the post-Cultural Revolution era.[16] As well as Wu's strategic use of displays of "safely" feminine fashion and beauty, Edwards also underlines Wu's public performance of sportiness: her healthy vigor associates her with a long-standing nationalist discourse on sport, health, and patriotism that, as Chris Berry shows in his discussion of the films *Queen of Sports* (1936) and *Woman Basketball Player Number 5* (1957) in this volume, stretches back to the Republican period and has continued through the Maoist era and beyond.[17]

Fran Martin's essay, too, focuses on the gendered body as an ideological war zone. Martin argues that the "stigmatic bodies" of Taiwanese lesbian author Qiu Miaojin's early stories register a clash between residual and emergent regimes of gender and sexuality in late-twentieth-century Taiwan. As has been proposed by recent critical work in Taiwanese feminist and queer studies, Qiu's stories foreground the beleaguered figure of the "mannish lesbian," and show "T" (lesbian tomboy) secondary gender in conflict with both dominant (heterosexist-homophobic) and emergent-resistant (lesbian-feminist) conceptualizations of gender.[18] By juxtaposing Qiu's painful representations of the abject, doubly besieged body of T female masculinity at the start of the 1990s with Yu Dafu's violently phobic 1930s description of a "mannish lesbian," this chapter also underscores the far-reaching cultural shadow of the indigenized Republican-era sexological theory of homosexuality as gender inversion.[19]

Martin's chapter raises a theme that is also taken up by Chris Berry: that of abject bodies — subjects who have suffered violent cultural ostracism via the transforming discourses of gender and sexuality in the late twentieth century. Focusing on the casual degradation of the effeminate homosexual man in Bruce Lee's films, Berry's discussion recalls not only the T body in Martin's essay but also Wu and Stevenson's account of the gradual delegitimation of the *xianggong* in the early twentieth century. Interestingly, all these abject bodies contravene normative modern gender categories: they are masculine women and effeminate men. The violence of dominant cultural responses to these figures in the late twentieth century presents a marked contrast to the popular adulation of Republican-era gender-crossing figures like Mei Lanfang and Yu Jiaolong discussed by Zou and Sang, respectively, in the first part of the volume. The persistent, if marginalized, presence of such figures in contemporary cultural production, as much as the violent desires arrayed against that presence, implies that they haunt late-modern Chinese gender thinking as necessary others against which—and at the expense of which—the normatively gendered feminine-female and masculine-male bodies defensively define themselves.

Through their shared focus on the transnational reach of Hong Kong cinema, both Berry's essay and Olivia Khoo's draw attention to the ways transnational flows trouble the myth of Chineseness as an originary or singular cultural identity. Berry's take on the globally extensive fame of Bruce Lee's star body positions Lee as a neo-*wu* hero negotiating Chinese masculinity, hardbodied eroticism, and postcolonial resistance. Berry observes that Lee's spectacular displays of a bared and heavily muscled male body break with pre-1970s martial arts film tradition. This suggests that Lee's spectacular, neo-*wu* performances can be interpreted as a further stage in the gradual, uneven, but ongoing formation of the corporeally based modern masculinity proposed by Epstein and Zou in this book's first section. While Lee's star image presents a cinematic martial-arts body that is newly marked by clearly visible muscular solidity, Berry also demonstrates that the transnational hypermobility of this same image renders Lee's body multiple and fragmentary, yielding an extensive array of variant meanings when approached by commentators positioned across the worldwide Chinese diaspora and beyond.

Olivia Khoo approaches *In the Mood for Love* from "the margins of Chineseness"—from the perspective of the diasporic Chinese audience of Hong Kong art cinema.[20] Further extending the antifoundationalist approach taken by many of the contributors here, Khoo's discussion of Wong Kar-wai's film foregrounds two different bodies that she argues encode a nonessential or "spectral" Chineseness. These are, first, the ethnically Chinese film spectator who inhabits a body marked as "Chinese" yet rejects the culturally essentialist claims made upon subjects so marked. Second, Khoo focuses on the "lost body" of Maggie Cheung, whose corporeality in the film is visually effaced by the insistent patterning of her tightly enfolding 1960s-style *qipao* dresses. Just as Cheung's presence is rendered ghostly as a result of this effacement of her flesh, Khoo argues that Cheung's Chineseness, too, can be seen as spectral, paralleling the relation between Hong Kong film and the Chinese mainland that haunts this cinema as its "lost origin." Thus, the book closes with a doubly ghostly image of Chineseness—a free-floating, disembodied presence and yet one that continues, insistently and uncannily, to produce effects for bodies, both fleshly and cinematic.

Although Wong's film is a nostalgic take on a very specific time and place—Hong Kong of the 1960s—Khoo's discussion provides a fitting conclusion to the volume, returning us to our central historical concerns through the apt metaphor of the ghost. The figure of the ghost is suggestive of the alchemical transformations wrought by historical change upon entities that once seemed solidly substantial—the body, Chinese identity, modernity itself. As Xiaobing Tang observes,

> a . . . dialectical and historically sensitive approach [to conceptualising the passage from the modern to the postmodern] derives from the notion of spectrality, by which we see the present as continually haunted and disturbed by ghosts of the past. . . . If modernity was famously haunted by the nightmare of history from which the modern subject desperately tried to awaken, postmodernity becomes conceivable when a once self-reassured modern vision metamorphoses into a ghostly, even shameful, afterimage.[21]

The idea of modernity as ghostly afterimage is an apt reminder that traces of the body's multiple histories linger on in Chinese cultures today, and that even the most resolutely contemporary representations are haunted by the phantoms of modernities past.

Notes

1. Barlow, "Theorizing Woman," 131. One considers, for example, the disjuncture pointed out as early as 1960 by C. T. Hsia in his essay on "Residual Femininity," which addressed aspects of femininity that fell outside the boundaries prescribed by Party priorities and agendas.
2. Kleinman, "How Bodies Remember."
3. Anagnost, *National Past-times*, 20.
4. Brownell, *Training the Body*.
5. Farquhar, *Appetites*, 290.
6. On tattooing, for example, see Dutton, *Streetlife China;* on SARS and the "body politic" see Min'an Wang, "Body Politics in the SARS Crisis"; on art, see Hay, *Boundaries* (particularly contributions by Robin D. S. Yates and Jonathan Hay); Gao, *Inside/Out;* Wu Hung, *Transience;* Wu Hung, *Exhibiting Experimental Art;* and the work by contributors to Wu Hung and Katherine Tsiang's important conference volume *Body and Face in Chinese Art*.
7. See Chow, *Primitive Passions*, 175–202; David Der-wei Wang, *Splendor* 7–8 and 16–17; Rofel, *Other Modernities*, 3–37; and Ong, *Flexible Citizenship*, chaps. 1 and 2.
8. Rofel, *Other Modernities*, 25. See also Tang, *Chinese Modern;* Jing Wang, *High Culture Fever,* chaps. 4 and 6; Zhang, *Chinese Modernism,* chaps. 1 and 2; Yang, *Chinese Postmodern;* and Ning Wang, "Mapping Chinese Postmodernity."
9. Zhang, *Chinese Modernism*, 18; Dirlik and Zhang, "Introduction."
10. Liao, "Theorizing the 90s," 8. On the "Japanization" thesis of Taiwanese modernity, see also Ching, *Becoming Japanese;* Iwabuchi, *Recentering Globalization*, 121–157; and Yu-fen Ko, "Desired Form."

11. For a more detailed summary of some of these debates in relation to theorizing Taiwanese modernity, see Martin, *Situating Sexualities,* 8–14.

12. See Chow, *Ethics After Idealism,* 149–167; Abbas, *Hong Kong;* and Xiaoying Wang, "Hong Kong, China."

13. Lee, "On the Margins," 238.

14. Nonini and Ong, "Chinese Transnationalism," 15. See also Ong, *Flexible Citizenship.*

15. In referring to cultural reflections of PRC territorial expansionism and political centrism, we are thinking particularly of the unabashedly aggressive vision of Chinese unification offered up in Zhang Yimou's recent film, *Hero.*

16. Rofel, *Other Modernities,* 217–256.

17. See also Brownell, *Training the Body;* Palumbo, "Evangelism"; and Morris, "I Believe You Can Fly."

18. We refer here especially to Ding and Liu, "Crocodile Skin."

19. Halberstam, *Female Masculinity.*

20. "The margins of Chineseness" is Shih's phrase, though she uses it in a different context. See Shih, "Mainland China," 179.

21. Tang, *Chinese Modern,* 342.

Post-Mao People's Republic of China

CHAPTER 8

Souvenirs of the Organ Trade
The Diasporic Body in Contemporary Chinese Literature and Art

LARISSA HEINRICH

> In realist metaphysics it is always the body that is accorded substantiality, and . . . it is above all those features of the natural world that invasively trespass the imagined autonomy of the body that achieve status as emblems of the Real.
> —Marston Anderson, *The Limits of Realism*

TIMES HAVE CHANGED since Lu Xun first dissected a corpse in Japan at the turn of the twentieth century. At that time, dissection practice in China was limited to a small number of missionary-run hospital schools, and the fact that Lu Xun had such extensive training set him apart from the vast majority of his Chinese peers. One might argue, in fact, that Lu Xun's education in anatomical understandings of the body had a profound impact on his experiments in literary realism, his visions of the self, and his understanding of what constituted human (and Chinese) identity.[1] Today, however, dramatic advances in technologies of the body as well as in global circulations of technology and bodies across national boundaries have replaced the understandings of physicality and selfhood that so transformed literature of Lu Xun's time with new challenges to conceptions of corporeality, identity, and individuality. As the cultural historian John Frow has observed, developments in body technologies like organ transplant practice have created new ethical dilemmas about the practical application of property law to the sale of body parts, or more generally to questions of propriety over the self (individual "ownership" of one's body) as arbitrated through legal and commercial channels. Furthermore, the problem is a uniquely international one, Frow notes, "since the growing trade in body parts crosses national boundaries and the hierarchies of interdependency that they represent." This growing trade in human organs across global boundaries in turn illustrates a new "complexity of the relation between the category of the person and the commodity form that it both opposes and subtends."[2] How then might we expect this to manifest in art and literature in China? If advancements in turn-of-the-century dissection and anatomical practice contributed conceptual vocabulary to Lu Xun's literary innovations and by extension to his emergence as the "Father of Modern Chinese Literature," then what might we expect to see in literature and art of the new millennium, in the age of stem-cell research, cloning, grafting, transplant, and surrogacy? If, as Marston Anderson argues of realism, realist metaphysics are determined by "those features of the natural world that invasively trespass the imagined autonomy of the body," what happens when the body itself becomes the means of trespass?

This essay identifies several examples of contemporary Chinese art and literature that employ images of the organ trade or commerce in bioproducts to explore questions of identity, humanity, and selfhood, and hypothesizes certain changing trajectories in literary and artistic representations of the self based on analyses of these works. In late 1980s and early 1990s fiction by Yu Hua, for example, I argue that the imagery of organ transplant and blood donorship provides an inherently powerful means of questioning categories of selfhood and (human) identity against the backdrop of post-Deng market reform. In these works, Yu Hua does not question his characters' Chineseness so much as their humanity and individual identity in a society transformed by changing market values and practices. As a result, many of the characters Yu Hua creates function as literary universals; the works themselves take an inward, reflective, and ironic turn. Recent experimental art, by contrast, takes this question of identity and corporeal embodiment from the domestic to the transnational arena by using representations of organ exchange and commerce in human bioproducts to explore, among other things, the fraught relationship between the production of Chinese counterculture and the demand for it in the Western marketplace. Consequently the identity at stake in these works—an identity that is always already lost or compromised at the outset—is *precisely* "Chineseness," with its problematic, emblematic identification as "Chinese" by western consumers, as well as by the artists themselves, in an increasingly transnational ideological as well as material economy. A premise of this essay is therefore that evolving trends in representation of the organ trade and related practices in contemporary Chinese art and literature—changing as they do alongside developments in technology itself—may reflect the emergence of an increasingly diasporic view of self and identity, a view according to which Chinese identity itself is subject to "harvesting," transplant, and sale in the global marketplace.

Yu Hua—Resurrection and Alienation

> Transplantation constructs a culturally very powerful myth of the social body—that is, of the limits and the wholeness and of the integrity of the body: a myth of resurrection. Yet this wholeness can be achieved only by the incorporation of the other. The restored body is prostheticized: no longer an organic unity but constructed out of a supplement, an alien part which is the condition of that originary wholeness.
>
> John Frow, *Time and Commodity Culture*[3]

China today is often portrayed in western media not only as a nation-scale "market [in human organs] run or sponsored or at least tolerated by the state, and more importantly supplied by the state from its prisons," but as a moral "grey zone" from which human organs for transplant may be procured by non-Chinese with relative ease and with minimal state regulation/intervention—a place where dissection and its product have, if anything, gone out of control.[4] A cartoon from the January 7, 2002 edition of *The New Yorker* (Fig. 8.1), for example, plays on the idea that the western (White, male, upper middle-class) tourist, having returned home to his comfortable living room, might boast not of the trinkets and photos of famous sites he brought back from China but—drawing more on the safari model of tourism—of the enviable trophy of a new stomach; the organ, or human body, as both trophy and souvenir, as much a part of the westerner's experience of China as the pagodas and Great Wall that he also "took in." While the subject of satire is the western consumer, the structure upon which it is based situates China as the "supplier" or producer of this new commodity, a commodity that can be obtained only in China and which is rendered the rhetorical equivalent of the most famous of metonymic symbols of Chinese identity (i.e., the Great Wall). Where western doctors in China of Lu Xun's day routinely complained of the difficulty of gaining access to Chinese bodies for medical research, this image portrays by contrast the extreme *availability* of Chinese bodies for western consumption—the ironic suggestion that what is forbidden or difficult to obtain in the United States may be obtained in the grey market of China where, it seems, moral and bureaucratic codes do not obstruct the functioning of a "free market" in human

SOUVENIRS OF THE ORGAN TRADE   129

FIGURE 8.1. © *The New Yorker* collection 2002. J. B. Handelsman from cartoonbank.com. Used by permission.

"We saw the Great Wall and lots of pagodas, and I have a transplanted stomach."

organs as they do in the west (the fraternal twin of this subtext, of course, being the critical discourse that situates China as a repeat violator of human rights through unregulated organ "harvesting").

In Yu Hua's fiction of the late 1980s and early 1990s, however, representations of organ transplant and the blood trade do not illustrate exchange and exploitation in a transnational context, but rather function as literary foils for the exploration of self, identity, and humanity in a domestic context. The circulation of blood in the domestic marketplace in the 1995 novel *Chronicle of a Blood Merchant,* for example, lends rhythm and punctuation to the plot.[5] The novel follows the life of the protagonist Xu Sanguan from early days when he sells his blood to earn the money to start a family, to the days of the Great Leap Forward when he sells his blood to feed the family in times of famine, to the Cultural Revolution when money earned from selling his blood allows Xu to help his sent-down sons and then to finance medical care when one of the sons (ironically) contracts hepatitis. The novel concludes with a scene that is strongly reminiscent of a short story from the 1930's by Shen Congwen called "New and Old" *(Xin yu jiu),* in which an old-style executioner is rendered obsolete by the forces of new technology and a new antitraditionalist government: the old man performs the execution as required and then, according to custom of his early career, takes his still-bloody sword to the nearby temple to act out ritual atonement, which involves the confession and "punishment" of the executioner before the city god. Shen's story reaches an emotional climax when the old man's behavior in the temple is misinterpreted as insanity, and youthful modern soldiers, armed with guns, are sent to roust him.[6] Likewise at the end of *Blood Merchant,* the elderly Xu is so distraught when he discovers that the purveyor will no longer accept his blood that he wanders about town, unsure how he will provide for his family in times of need; his sons, uncomprehending, urge him to go home. In both cases, obsolescence generates pathos as the men are separated from their typical means of livelihood; in the latter case, such means (and therefore the story's pathos) involve the ideologically complex question of selling blood for profit. Deirdre Knight's insightful analysis of this novel demonstrates convincingly how the work "offers a strong case of ambivalence toward capitalist values" including issues of "self-ownership, autonomy and selfhood" that bear upon "legal and social debates concerning the distribution and commerce in corporeal commodities."[7] Such debates have turned largely inward, questioning the effects of policy primarily in the domestic context.

Moving backward in time, an even clearer example is Yu Hua's seminal earlier novella called "One Kind of Reality," published in 1988 and subsequently analyzed in a number of critical contexts. Like *Blood Merchant,* "One Kind of Reality" similarly "offers a strong case of ambivalence toward capitalist values" — even as it pioneers the formal instability and self-referentiality of avant-garde literary experimentalism of this period. But where the later novel uses the representation of selling blood for profit (the assignment of commercial value to the body's own product) to allegorize this ambivalence, in the earlier piece it is the specter of the organ trade that haunts any attempts to interpret it symbolically. In "One Kind of Reality" the organ trade and the subsequent failure of subjectivity to cohere in the course of this trade anticipate the problem of "self-ownership, autonomy and selfhood" in China of the mid-1990s under a transitional economy.

"One Kind of Reality" is a gruesome inversion of a family romance, in which a dispassionate narrative voice relates the story of the brothers Shanfeng and Shangang, who live together in a house with their mother, their respective wives (who remain nameless) and their children (Shangang's four-year-old son Pipi and Shanfeng's baby). Early on in the story, Pipi, moved by a kind of apathetic curiosity, kills the baby, setting in motion a spiral of violence and revenge in which both Shanfeng and Pipi are eventually killed, and Shangang, grossly mutilated from an encounter with anonymous executioners, winds up on a makeshift dissection table in the middle of an abstract urban landscape.

In the middle of these soon-to-be-demolished buildings hangs a thousand-watt electric bulb. . . . Below it are two Ping-Pong tables, both of them old and decrepit. . . . Nearby is a pond with water lilies floating on the surface and weeping willows all around, and next to it is a vegetable garden radiant with gold and yellow flowers.[8]

Shanfeng's wife, it turns out, has found a way to complete the cycle of revenge: posing as Shangang's wife, she has decided to "donate Shangang's body to the state, to be used for the benefit of society."

Structurally, a unique aspect of the story is the extended concluding description of Shangang's dissection in the place where one might otherwise expect a moral or a denouement — or as Anne Wedell-Wedellsborg notes, "where one will normally expect the final revelation of 'meaning,' the clue, so to speak, to the preceding narrative."[9] In this scene, even as the structural imperatives set up by the cyclical murders has been satisfied by Shanfeng's wife's "revenge" — and indeed by the absence of remaining central characters — we read through a lengthy narrative description of the systematic demolition of Shangang's body, each incision rendered in excruciating detail. The doctors performing this lengthy dismemberment treat it as an everyday affair, making jokes or handling the body casually:

> The chest surgeon has already removed the lungs and is now merrily cutting through Shangang's pulmonary artery and pulmonary vein, followed by the aorta, and finally all the other blood vessels and nerves coming out of the heart. He is really getting a kick out of all this. Ordinarily, when he is operating on a live human being, he must painstakingly avoid all these blood vessels and nerves, which always makes him feel confined and inhibited. Now he can be as careless as he pleases, and he is going at his job with gusto. Turning to the doctor standing next to him, he quips, "I feel reckless." The other doctors can't stop laughing.[10]

The narrative flow of this blow-by-blow depiction of the dissection is interrupted only by self-reflexive postscripts about the fate of the recycled body parts in question:

> The oral surgeon and the urologist leave the building together, carrying the lower jawbone and the testicles, respectively. After this, each of them will perform a transplant. The oral surgeon will remove the lower jawbone from one of his patients and replace it with the one from Shangang. He has the utmost confidence about the success of this type of operation. But the greatest triumph belongs to Shangang's testes. The urologist will transplant them onto a young man whose

own testicles were crushed in a car accident. Soon after the operation, not only will the young man get married, but his wife will also become pregnant almost immediately. Ten months later she will give birth to a healthy, robust little boy. Not even in her wildest dreams could Shanfeng's wife have imagined such a turn of events—that in the end it was she of all people who had enabled Shangang to achieve his fondest ambition: a male heir to carry on the line.[11]

The story ends when there is no more of Shangang's body left to dissect. The doctor who has come for his skeleton waits for all the other doctors to leave and then begins his task of clearing away the remaining muscle tissue from the bones on the table, beginning with the feet. Upon reaching the thighs, the doctor delivers the line that concludes the story. He "gives the burly muscles there a good pinch and says, 'I don't care how solid and sturdy you are—by the time I bring your skeleton into our classroom you will be the very picture of a weakling.'"[12]

As in many of Yu Hua's works—and in marked contrast to the more sentimental overtones of *Blood Merchant*—one of the most striking features of this story is the contrast not only between the clean prose and the mess it describes, but also between the violent activities of the characters and their diffusely matter-of-fact responses to it. The casual demeanor of the doctors contrasts with the grim task in which they are engaged; the indifferent tone in which the brothers' vengeful impulses are articulated contrasts sharply with the ferocity of their execution (after Shangang declares he wants to tie Shanfeng's wife to a tree as retribution, for instance, Shanfeng offers, "Why don't you tie me up instead?" In response, Shangang smiles "softly to himself. He had known all along this was how it would turn out. 'Should we have breakfast first?' he asked Shanfeng"[13]). This type of contrast even inheres at the imagistic level, where the delicate pastoral landscape ("a vegetable garden radiant with gold and yellow flowers" etc.) is juxtaposed with the stereotypically dark image of the single light bulb and decrepit Ping-Pong tables set among "soon-to-be-demolished" buildings. More importantly, even the narrative voice itself has been pared down to its absolute essentials, as if the author has deliberately tried to remove all language that carries moral or emotional overtones. The result, completely absent of interiority, is elegant, descriptive, and perfectly consistent with the themes and images it describes, so that the "reality" of the title, enacted through language and theme, and ultimately played out in the measured dissection of Shangang's body, turns out to be what Wedell-Wedellsborg calls "an allegorical image of a self reduced to pure physicality." It is thus "by the conscious efforts to remove moralizing and explanation from a tale which cries out precisely for that, [that] Yu Hua . . . activates an allegorical reading to supply the absent 'meaning.' " The text, she concludes, therefore "comes forth as a modern heterogenous allegory of the predicament of the individual self in contemporary Chinese culture and of the problem of its representation in the reality of the literary text."[14]

Just as the sale of blood in *Blood Merchant* highlights the commodification of the human body in contemporary life, then, the organ trade in "One Kind of Reality" enables the plot by allowing for the transfer of, and commerce in, human body parts. In "One Kind of Reality," however, the embodied self—fragile as it already is—disappears entirely in the context of transplant. While the regenerative capacity of blood means that blood donation does not necessarily deplete the subjectivity of the donor, when the self that has been "reduced to pure physicality" is harvested for organs a substantial loss occurs: organs are transferable, memory and identity are not. The predicament of the "individual self in contemporary Chinese culture" thus is a very specific one: that of an illusion of what Frow calls "the wholeness and integrity of the body," and the body as the seat of identity; this identity is subject to dismemberment and distribution based on a combination of vengeful whim and market forces.

Is this then a "Chinese" self, a particularly "Chinese" predicament? In an international context (including the context of the work's translation), this is precisely the question that the text problematizes. There is no absolute self, and the body is as easily distributed among strangers—including its capacity to bring them sons—as it is preserved for use in an anatomy class. In the reference to the organ trade to set up the metaphoric dissection of Shangang, then, we might see less a picture of an eviscerated society (Chinese society in particular) than a portrait of what happens when an identity is fragmented, decentralized, and redistributed, a structural narrative device that challenges the assumption of a unified modern "self" by portraying its dismantling. In this way we might say that Yu Hua's piece is, as a literary work, a kind of anti-Frankenstein. In the Frankenstein myth, the body parts of the many are joined in one functioning yet sad "monster" of human universalism and resurrection; in "One Kind of Reality" the opposite is true. Here the body parts of one are distributed to the many by doctors who are apathetic, and to patients who more often than not turn out to be indifferent or unappreciative ("The kidney transplant . . . will be very successful. . . . But the patient himself will be querulous and resentful, complaining bitterly that [it] cost him thirty thousand yuan, [which] was much too expensive"[15]).

In both of Yu Hua's works, then, the representation of commerce in blood and organs therefore seems best read as a kind of allegory for diaspora, not of Chinese identity, necessarily, but of the self. It is also a meditation on identity and literature amidst the promises of a transitioning economy and the related de/valuation of the things that make us human. Written on the eve of events at Tiananmen, the identity Yu Hua considers in "One Kind of Reality" (and later in *Chronicle of a Blood Merchant*) is therefore not yet the opportunistic, market-driven, and quintessentially transnational model portrayed in the *New Yorker* cartoon. Rather it is the philosophical embodiment—the un-Frankenstein—of anxiety at the looming threat of becoming truly disenfranchised in the most profound sense of the word—of losing ownership over one's body, of becoming alienated from oneself.

Transplant, Transfusion, and Exchange in Contemporary Chinese Experimental Art

> Since its development in the 1960s transplant surgery has constituted, amongst other things, a problem in gift theory: should my body accept or reject the transplanted organ, and on what terms? Who is my stranger, and why should they give me a part of their body? Should their giving receive a return payment, or should it be its own reward? These are problems in national medical policy, but they are also, now, an international problem, since the growing trade in body parts crosses national boundaries and the hierarchies of interdependency that they represent.
> John Frow, *Time and Commodity Culture*[16]

Where Yu Hua's writing from the late 1980s and mid-1990s treats the human body as a source of commercial goods that may be harvested and traded just like any other commodity (a diaspora that occurs within the closed circuit of China's "reality," even as it aims for a more universal valence), recent Chinese experimental art featuring representations of organ transplant, blood transfusion, and exchange in body parts more closely approaches the cartoon I discussed earlier in its satirical or critical treatment of the (Chinese) body in a transnational context. This new artwork portrays a corporeal self that has been compromised by a new transnationalism at the levels both of production and, at times, of exhibition and marketing. In such works, the figure of the harvestable or dis/integrated body—and, increasingly, of the corpse itself—has begun to act as a medium for questioning not only conceptual assumptions about corporeal authenticity and the possibility of resurrection (or "restoration") of the body, but also the perceived superficiality of a "corpus" of Chinese contemporary art that plays to the taste and agenda of a wealthy international market.[17] The curators of the highly controversial 1999 exhibit "Post-Sense Sensibility: Distorted Bodies and Delusion," for instance, noted that their inspiration for the show's concept came partly from the realization that a "dangerous tendency had begun to control the creative activities of experimental Chinese artists. This was the popularization and standardization of so-called conceptual art, which had degenerated into a stereotypical taste for minimalist formulas and a penchant for petty cleverness. The results were manifold: ideas overpowered real feeling for art; verbal explanations became indispensable; and a work was often created to impress the audience with the artist's mind, not to move people with its visual presentation."[18] Likewise curators of the 2000 "Uncooperative Approach" exhibit (*Bu hezuo fangshi*, rendered by the curators simply as "Fuck Off"), timed to coincide with the Shanghai Biennale, mounted the show as a self-consciously "uncooperative" event. They introduce the exhibition catalogue by noting that "In today's art, the 'alternative' is playing the role of revising and criticizing the power discourse and mass convention. In an uncooperative and uncompromising way, it self-consciously resists the threat of assimilation and vulgarization."[19] (Indeed, when I was there on day four, the smell generated by Huang Yan's decaying landscapes on meat was almost unbearable, making the exhibition space decidedly "uncooperative" in marked contrast to the lush internationalism and welcome of the Shanghai theater during these few weeks.) One can read this hypermaterialization of the body combined with self-conscious alterity as the curators' successful capture of the implicit equation between the idea of absolute form — the body as a prime number of visual art — and the "so-called conceptual art" that fails to question this absolutism.

Significantly, then, in these exhibits (and in catalogues like the one self-published in conjunction with "Uncooperative Approach," which contains a number of works that were not in the exhibit itself) it is once again through the tropes of the organ trade — images of transplant, dissection, dismemberment, transfusion, grafting, surgery, and extraction — that many of the artworks attempt to destabilize (literally) the idea of corporeal integrity while simultaneously challenging the "superficial rationalism" of contemporary Chinese art in the context of global market politics. Even when taking an "uncooperative approach," works need not be shock art to communicate this formal instability. For example, Peng Donghui's photomontage, translated in the catalogue as "Group photo No. 1-3" (*Hezong de liunian* No. 1-3, which could also be translated as "Group Souvenir No. 1-3"), on one hand seems to reinforce the idea of corporeal integrity through the vertical organization of images head to toe, the use of uniform dimensions and backdrop among individual frames, and even through basic corporeal similarities such as general height, weight, and age range of the models involved (Fig. 8.2). At the same time, however, the work subverts it: by shuffling these various parts around in a visual slot machine of incomplete faces, torsos, arms, and legs, the piece forces the viewer

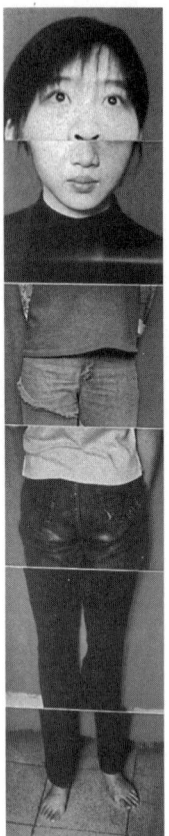 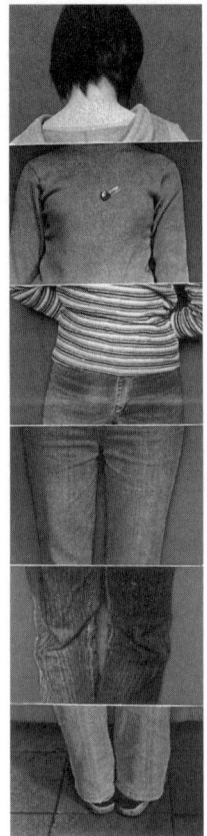 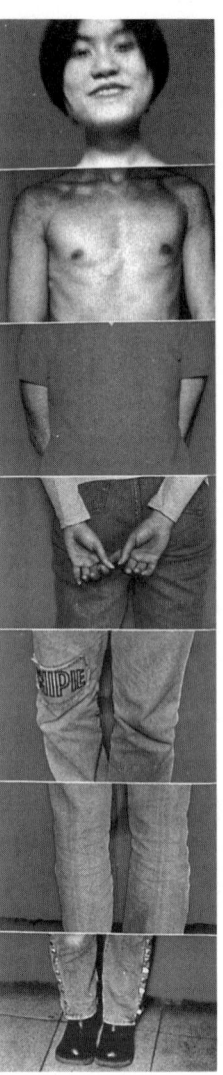

FIGURE 8.2. Peng Donghui, "Group photo No. 1–3," 1999. Used by permission.

to rely on superficial markers such as clothes, expressions, physical orientation, traces of gender, and even representational technique itself (color, exposure, dimension of parts, and so forth) to restore coherence among individual assemblages.[20] The "souvenir" of the title thus refers both to the individual parts "donated" by the members of the group who participated in the photoshoot and to the role of memory in attempting to "re-shuffle" or transplant an always already incomplete corporeal identity. Xu Zhen's installation of black and white photos of body parts printed on hundreds of post-it notes and attached to pillars in the exhibition space works similarly, invoking (short-term) memory and corporeal fragmentation. Notes that normally function as reminders to oneself are multiplied here such that memory, and the reintegration of the body that would go with it, becomes impossible.

Finally, while Li Zhiwang's painting of a "female nude" (Fig. 8.3) on one hand suggests the substantiality of the body through the receding horizon, thick defining lines, and dark background, at the same time the inconsistent wavelike fluctuations of these lines and the flatness of the figure's profile (a reference to Zhang Dali's signature graffiti profiles at demolition sites?) ultimately call this dimensionality into question.

Among experimental artists whose work employs more extreme representational modes, however, perhaps the most infamous is Zhu Yu, whose highly controversial works include a photographed performance of himself eating a human fetus; an installation involving the suspension of a human arm above a room full of rope; and a kind of diary of the artist's own surgery using videos and photography, in which doctors remove skin from his abdomen and Zhu Yu then grafts the skin onto the partial corpse of a pig. In the case of Zhu Yu's notorious act of "cannibalism," the controversy generated by appropriations and recontextualizations of this performance in the media across international boundaries led to an interesting complication of the understanding of the medium itself, of what counts as the body and what does not. "Even after it was revealed that the controversial photographs were actually derived from Zhu Yu's performance in Shanghai," notes one writer, "questions still remained for some viewers over what precisely that performance consisted of. Was it actual cannibalism, or not? Was it a cannibalistic act that was being presented as a work of art, or was it instead an elaborate mock-up intended to mimic an act of consuming actual human flesh?"[21] Notes another: "Despite the fact that during an interview on November 28, 2001, the artist told me that he did eat the fetus, I have strong doubts about the veracity of this statement. In particular, it is my view that the artist intended only for his viewers to *believe* that he was eating the fetus."[22]

Zhu Yu further exploits the problematic nature of flesh as medium in "Skin Graft," his representation of the trans-species skin graft, originally presented as part of the "Infatuated with Injury: Open Studio Exhibition No. 2" on April 22, 2000, in Beijing, and again at the "Uncooperative Approach" exhibit several months later in Shanghai (Fig. 8.4). A photograph-within-a-photograph, this piece shows Zhu Yu transplanting his own skin onto the partial body of a pig against the backdrop of a photo of himself, unconscious, on the operating table, a flap of fatty tissue carefully exposed by two sets of hands wearing surgi-

FIGURE 8.3. Li Zhiwang. "Female nude." Used by permission.

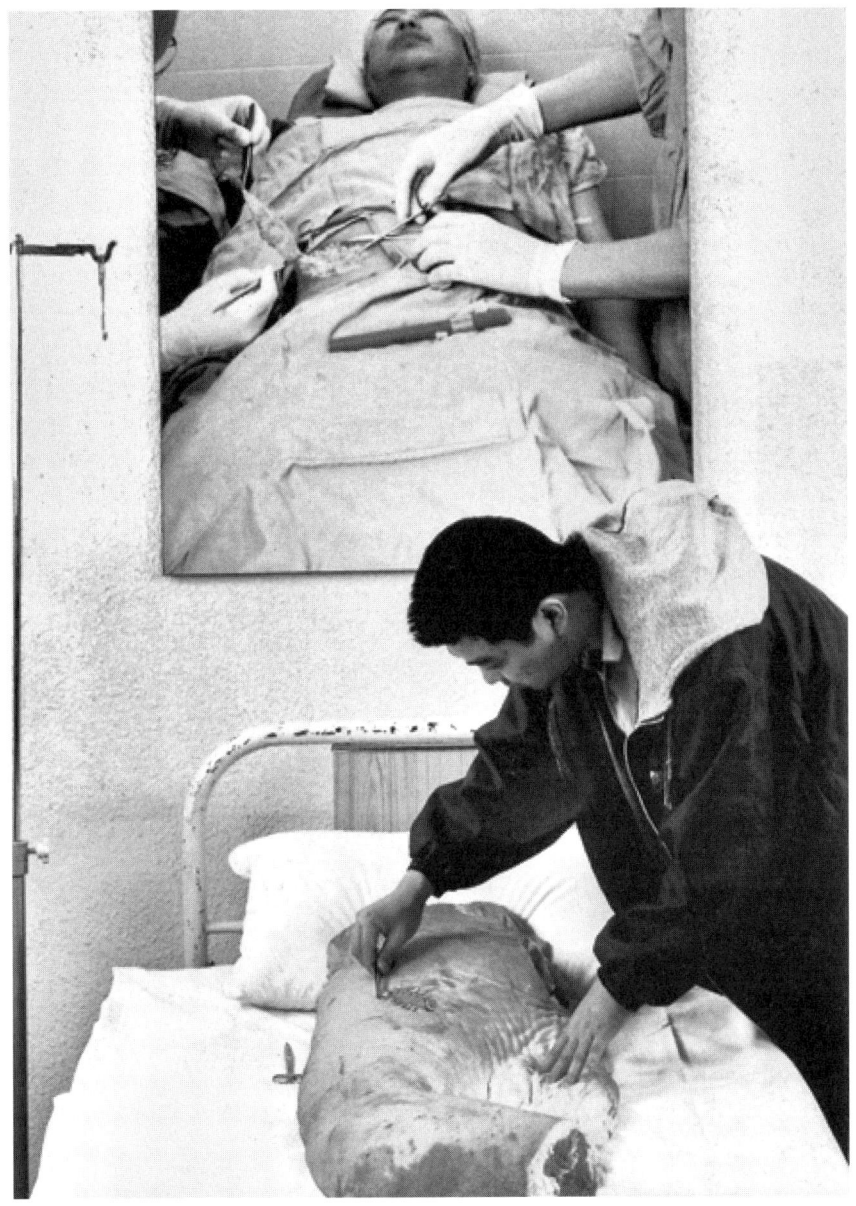

FIGURE 8.4. Zhu Yu, "Skin graft." Skin and pig. Beijing, 2000. Used by permission.

cal gloves; a video playing on a television screen nearby documents the procedure. When this work was displayed in Shanghai, at least (and in its exhibition catalogue), the usual list of materials included neither video nor photography, but rather the explicit mention of "the artist's own skin" *(zuozhe ziji de pifu)* alongside "pork" *(zhurou)*, accentuating the form of the medium as part of the art itself. The use of "grafting" or transplant *(zhipi)*, meanwhile, rendered a conceptual equivalency into a material/physical one: the body of the artist is linked to, or equated with, the body of the pig, the former a physical resource for the latter; here the concept of "graft" or "transplant" brings with it as well the ideological and discursive associations of compatibility of donor and recipient, as well as the possibility of "rejection" by the recipient of the transplant. The suggestion of congruence between artist's body and animal flesh is driven home by the layout of the piece: the embedded image with its surgical markers (gloves, gowns, forceps) and the viewpoint from the foot of the bed parallel the layout of the framing photograph, in which the pig's flesh is laid out on a freshly made hospital bed, resting on a pillow, as the artist leans over it.

What is interesting about Zhu Yu's work here—and what might sometimes be obscured by attention to the "shock" value of the work, or indeed by the coarseness of the artist's own developing expression—is not only that it calls into question the nature of the human body as material for art (as the cannibalism piece does) as well as the "transplantability" of identity in fragments (as Peng Donghui's piece does, or even Yu Hua's in literature), but that it also calls into question the humanity of the body itself—what distinguishes it from the flesh of any other. To borrow the words of one of the curators on the topic of hybrid sculptures, the work expresses "a profound mistrust of the notion of a natural body."[23] Interpreting the piece via the idiom of the organ trade, in other words, one sees here an unmistakable portrait of exchange, of transgressive mutuality. As Frow notes,

> This paradox of an originary state which comes into being only retrospectively and by virtue of a prosthetic addition is foregrounded in some of the key ethical issues that have been raised by transplantation: by, for example, the ban in South Africa under apartheid on the transplantation of black organs into a white body; and by the furore raised by religious groups, and many others, at the prospect of the transplantation of pigs' or baboons' hearts into human bodies. These issues of course are "problems" only within the framework of that myth of organic integrity and self-presence.[24]

For better or worse, then, Zhu Yu's work uses representation of the process of transplant and exchange to play with this "myth of organic integrity" by questioning the ideal of the human body as a point of origin and the irreducible seat of "self-presence."

A focus on transplant and exchange in work like Zhu Yu's also provides a useful framework for interpreting another work that has attracted attention for shock value but little formal analysis: a performance piece and documenting photograph by Sun Yuan and Peng Yu, in which the artists transfuse their own blood into a medical specimen of conjoined fetal twins (Fig. 8.5). Like Zhu Yu's performance of skin graft, this work—translated in the catalogue as "Link of the Body" and described by Peng Yu as "a special kind of coming together" *(yizhong teshu de jihe)*—was originally performed at the "Infatuated with Injury" show; a photograph of this performance was later exhibited on its own as a contribution to "Uncooperative Approach." Like Yu Hua's *One Kind of Reality*, the photograph depicts a distorted family romance: Sun Yuan and Peng Yu sit on either side of a table at the extreme left and right of the photograph, vertically "divided" by the edges of the frame so that only half of each artist's body is visible; depth of field renders the images of the artists slightly indistinct. Thin tubes darkened by blood wind downward from the artists' arms to just below the center of the frame, where they have been inserted into the mouths of the conjoined twins. The twins, meanwhile, occupy most of the full third of the bottom of the photograph, and—unlike the artists—are fully in focus and not limited (or interrupted) by the boundaries of the photograph itself. Joined abdominally, the twins seem to further the overall impression of "linkage" or "connectedness" by (improbably) holding hands. While the visual presence of the blood in the tubes and the traces of blood that have spilled onto one of the twins to some degree preserve the action of the original performance, the photograph manipulates the focus of the viewer and guides it inexorably to the specimen at its center.

The artists' choice of this particular specimen highlights not only the "connectedness" of the twins that completes the closed circuit of bodies in the photograph, but also the idea of twinning, or doubling, of identity and corporeality that such a specimen by nature calls into question: that is, are conjoined twins one body or two? Do they have one set of experiences or two? Further, the use of "Siamese twins"—especially by Chinese performance artists working in a community whose audience can be counted upon to include "quite a few foreigners"—brings with it the historical and ideological legacy of the nineteenth-century freak show and its implications for portrayals of Chinese identity in the west.[25] One thinks most immediately, of course, of the "Siamese" twins Chang and Eng, whose commercial success enabled them to live comfortably in America just before the Civil War, and of the western tendency to conflate East Asian identities and societies with deformity that their particular

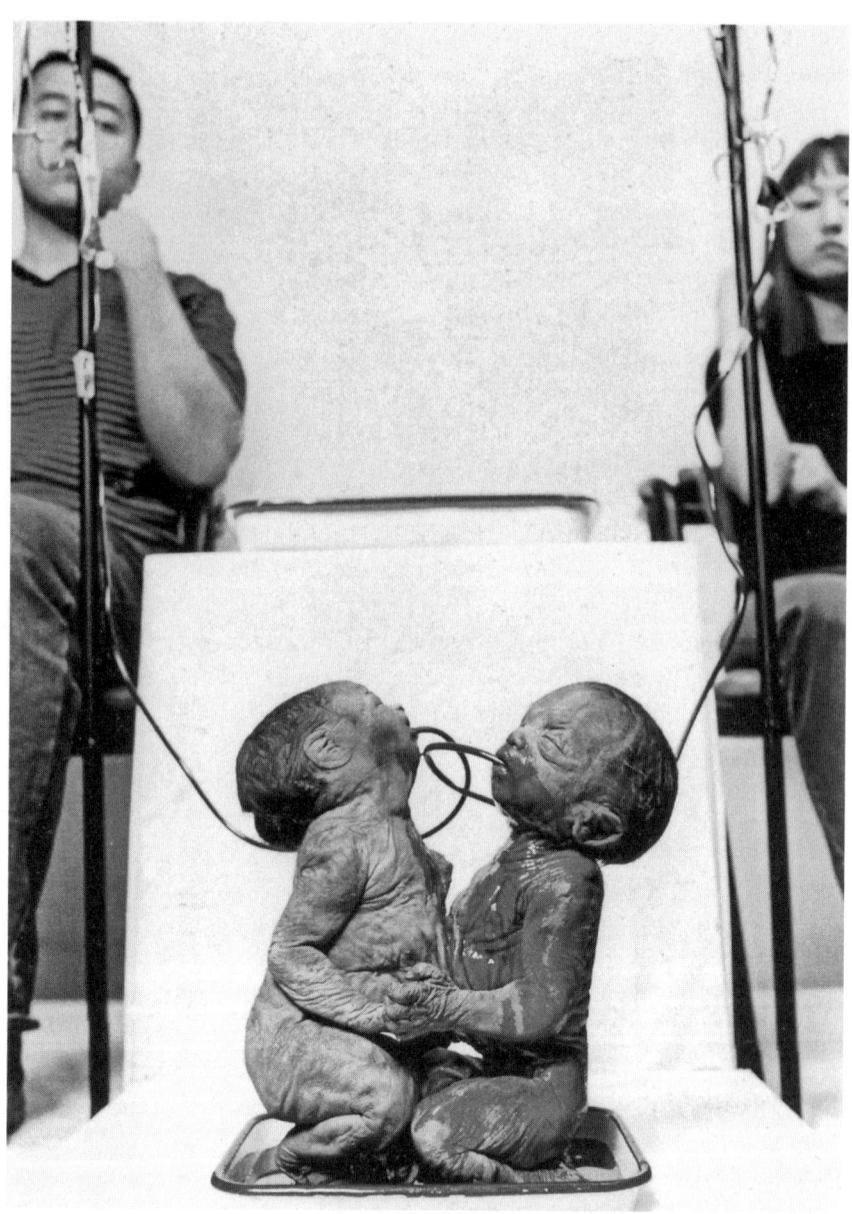

FIGURE 8.5. Sun Yuan and Peng Yu, "Link of the Body" (referred to here as "Connected Bodies"), Beijing, 2000. Used by permission.

case exemplifies so well (the twins were Chinese, but grew up in Siam).[26] The use of transfusion as a means of illustrating the "connectedness" of (Chinese) bodies likewise calls upon the same cultural referents that inform Yu Hua's *Blood Merchant:* not only the widespread practice of blood selling among rural peasants but, since 1998, the Chinese government's inconsistent attempts to stem the spread of diseases like HIV and hepatitis by outlawing the sale of blood, encouraging registration and pre-donation testing, and running public awareness campaigns. At the level of folklore, meanwhile, blood also connotes these days the compatibility of lovers and spouses: blood types are often a factor in determining a good match. Finally (and thus relatedly), through the use of transfusion and the artists' own blood, "Connected Bodies" also asserts an uncomfortable (hetero)sexuality, according to the myth of which "connectedness" between genders has been externalized, or made literal, in the form of the Siamese twins. Here the union of the various bodies creates a self-contained universe of parents and children, self and other, consumer and consumed that, like *Blood Merchant,* succeeds in expressing a certain "ambivalence toward capitalist values," but one that is significantly complicated by sexuality, east-west stereotypes, and the myth of the family.

Conclusions

Though in different mediums, Yu Hua's novella "One Kind of Reality" and the works of artists like Zhu Yu, Sun Yuan, and Peng Yu provide a sort of overview of shifting conceptions of self and physicality since 1988. In the former work, written only a few years after the introduction of organ transplant practice into wider use in China and just before the events of 1989 led to an explosion in foreign critical discourse, the organ trade functions allegorically as a means of problematizing individual identity. The body is still a literary playground in this story, addressing more philosophical questions about individuality and identity and authorship, while issues of globalization have not yet been introduced at the symbolic level. Thus we can read this story not necessarily as a problematizing of Chinese identity *per se,* but as a meditation on the diffusibility of identity itself and the question of where individual identity lives (that is, in the organs or in some random reconfiguration of these). The "Chineseness" of this identity, in other words, is not yet the central question (and arguably never is for Yu Hua), but rather the integrity or dis/integration of self and identity.

By the time of the experimental exhibits, however, the body had become globalized, commodified. The body may now be assigned a market value, and the implications of that new exchange value in the globalizing economy post-

Deng have found their way into art such that the body itself becomes a medium for expressing anxiety about everything from the boundaries of individual selfhood to government policy and health care to the uncomfortable paradoxes of the market for contemporary Chinese art in the west. In the context of these examples of experimental art, boundaries of selfhood and control over power relations are continually being thrown into question, destabilizing the very idea of the body as the seat of self as in the problem of individual identity in Sun Yuan and Peng Yu's "transfusion" scheme. At the same time, however, the framing of the works—the context of their production and exhibition as counter to or "uncooperative" with the Biennale, their international symbolic value, and their self-conscious contrast with existing commercially oriented art—ironically brings attention to, and then proceeds to undermine, the ideas of "Chineseness" in relation to global forces that drive the parallel markets of contemporary art and the organ trade.

Notes

1. Heinrich, "The Afterlife of Images." See also Liu, *Translingual Practice*, 50.
2. Frow, *Time and Commodity Culture*, 162.
3. Frow, *Time and Commodity Culture*, 177.
4. Ibid., 162–165.
5. Yu Hua, *Chronicle*.
6. See Shen Congwen, "*Xin yu jiu*," 250–260. See also Kinkley, *Odyssey*, 208–209.
7. Knight, "Capitalist," 565–566.
8. Yu Hua, "One Kind of Reality," 63.
9. Wedell-Wedellsborg, "One Kind."
10. Yu Hua, "One Kind of Reality," 66.
11. Ibid., 68.
12. Ibid., 68.
13. Ibid., 48.
14. Wedell-Wedellsborg, "One Kind.", 135–143 passim.
15. Yu Hua, "One Kind of Reality," 67.
16. Frow, *Time and Commodity Culture*, 162.
17. For a nuanced and informative discussion of the discourse of the "official" *(guanfang)* and "unofficial" *(fei guanfang)* and contemporary Chinese experimental art (including of the "Uncooperative Approach" exhibition and associated catalogue discussed in this essay), see Berghuis, "Considering *Huanjing*." In his discussion of contributions by Chinese artists to the 48th Venice Biennale in 1999, for example, Berghuis remarks that "[i]n the West, that binary has been most often described in terms of a narrative of liberation in which artists were presented as having broken free from the political mainstream of 'official' art production operating under the control of an oppressive Chinese state and Com-

munist Party apparatus." Such framing was ironic in this case, he notes, because "all of the participating artists had already become part of the 'mainstream,' or at least had gained a measure of recognition at 'home' as well as in terms of reception from abroad prior to the Biennale" (p. 714).

18. As quoted in Wu Hung, *Exhibiting,* 167.

19. Ai, "Fuck Off," 7.

20. Note the applicability of Susan Stewart's critique of the grotesque: "[The] scattering and redistribution of bodily parts is the antithesis of the body as a functional tool and of the body as still life, the classical nude. In medieval rhetoric, for example, we find the convention of description specifying that the body should be viewed from head to foot. But the grotesque presents a jumbling of this order, a dismantling and re-presentation of the body according to criteria of production rather than verticality." Stewart, *On Longing,* 105.

21. Rojas, "Cannibalism," 12.

22. Berghuis, "Considering *Huanjing,*" 730 n. 28 (my italics).

23. Wu Meichun, as quoted in Wu, *Exhibiting,* 166. "Xiao Yu has constructed a fictional creature by sewing together parts of human and bird skeletons; Zhang Hanzi has used pigskin to construct a human form. What these two works express is a profound mistrust of the notion of a natural body."

24. Frow, *Time and Commodity Culture,* 177.

25. Wu, *Exhibiting,* 205.

26. See Fiedler, *Freaks.*

CHAPTER 9

Sport, Fashion, and Beauty
New Incarnations of the Female Politician in Contemporary China

LOUISE EDWARDS

She [Wu Yi] can play bowls, tennis, and golf and is the captain of the Heroines Soft Tennis team. She likes to sing and enjoys Karaoke, both foreign and Chinese music, and likes to fish. Once she was asked "Where did you get that beautiful outfit?" She replied, "This outfit was one that I requested from a designer, these styles were designed by me. When I am in China I am not particularly fussy, but when I am abroad or have matters to do with foreigners, then I follow foreign customs. It is a question of representing Chinese women and not just a personal matter."

Wu Yi's natural and unrestrained nature is also manifest in her clothes. Whenever she is in public her clothing is always refined and elegant and exquisite . . . from inside to outside she gives people a feeling of "beauty."
—Pan Xianchen, *Zhongguo zhengtan nüxing da xunzong*

SPORTING PROWESS, FASHION sense, and bodily beauty are the new tools of twenty-first century politics in the People's Republic of China (PRC). Their presence has introduced a new physicality to the interpellation of female politicians in a liberalizing China. For decades the incarnation of political power in the PRC has connoted masculinity. Yet aspiring PRC politicians also exist in female bodies with feminine attributes. The masculinist tradition of governance has its origins in centuries of Confucian orthodoxy and deeply rooted understandings of which individuals have the legitimate right to rule. An educated body, not an aesthetic, sporty, or stylish one, signified potential for public politics. Class and gender divisions naturalized an educated male as the political body for Chinese culture.[1] Accordingly, men have ruled the PRC since its establishment and female participation in government has been corralled within the narrow scope of "women's work" or discredited by the ideological machinery of a resilient patriarchal tradition.[2] But in recent years within other Chinese polities—on Taiwan and in Hong Kong—politicians in women's bodies have assumed key positions in formal government structures and have exercised real political power. Taiwanese Vice-President Annette Lü and Hong Kong's Anson Chan and Emily Lau are prime examples. The emergence of a legitimate space for a female political incarnation in these small but significant Chinese polities suggests the potential for denaturalizing masculinist traditions of politics in China and for legitimizing the female exercise of political power. A Chinese national identity in the twenty-first century may include space for this in distinctly Chinese ways—that uniqueness generated by and defined against increasing contact with other global and diasporic cultural influences. Indeed, the ready interchange of information between Chinese polities outside the mainland and their internationally savvy diasporas present a new discourse of women and power for the PRC. This chapter reveals how the creation of a new narrative of legitimate women's power in the PRC is being written through fashion, beauty, and sport.

Longstanding beliefs still circulating today present women's power as destabilizing within a male-coded realm such as formal politics—the female's ascendance signifies the demise of men and masculinity. However, in the last two years a subtle change has taken place in the public discourse on women in politics. This chapter explores the print media narratives surrounding China's highest-ranking female politician, Wu Yi (1938-)—known and respected in China and abroad for her competence, openness, and efficiency. In March 2002 she was nominated at the top of *Women of China*'s "Personages of the Epoch" ranking and in August 2004 *Forbes* magazine called her the second most powerful woman in the world.[3] Christina Gilmartin noted that Wu has helped dismantle the negative image of women in politics among Chinese.[4] Accordingly, this chapter examines how media discussions of Wu Yi's persona facilitate a "safe" yet effective female politician for the PRC, dissecting her media image and the unique discourse creating her public persona to explain her unprecedented success as a female political body.

In December 2002, the sixty-five-year-old Wu Yi was elected to the second highest level in the Chinese Communist Party (CCP)—the twenty-two-member Political Bureau. This was the first time in twenty years that a woman had reached this level of political power. The appointment of this engineering-trained politician was uncontroversial—she already commanded the respect of her peers in the upper echelons of party politics. She had performed well as Deputy Mayor of Beijing (1988–1991) and as Minister of Foreign Trade and Economic Cooperation (1993–1998). In 2002 then-Premier Zhu Rongji appointed Wu to oversee China's World Trade Organization obligations—a high-profile, prestigious position. In March 2003, her position strengthened with her appointment as vice-premier within the State Council—the executive cabinet of the National People's Congress (NPC).⁵

Since becoming vice-premier Wu has achieved greater international recognition in her role as Acting Health Minister during the 2003 Severe Acute Respiratory Syndrome (SARS) crisis. *The Straits Times* described her replacement of the dismissed incumbent as indicating the CCP's seriousness of purpose and its "get-tough approach" to SARS. A photo by-line declared, "New Health Minister Wu has the clout to back any moves to fight the bug."⁶ *China Daily* described her appointment as resulting from qualities she displayed in the Trade Ministry, where Wu had "acquired a reputation for a 'swift and resolute' way of working."⁷ It is a significant indication of her domestic and international credibility that Wu Yi was given the task of damage control in the SARS episode. This crisis was described as "the first serious test of China's new leadership," and Wu Yi captained the match before a global media audience of millions.⁸ For her comparatively honest and open political style in dealing with SARS, *Time* magazine dubbed her the "Goddess of Transparency" and reported that many ordinary Chinese regarded her as a reincarnation of the "Goddess of Mercy."⁹ Wu Yi's media persona embodies the strength, fortitude, and the transcendent influence of a credible, fair politician. The raft of media discussion about China's most high-profile political woman reveals a minor but identifiable shift in narratives about women in power. Sport, fashion, and beauty have emerged as fresh and effective tools for achieving this change.

Despite her international influence Wu remains outside the very top level of the CCP's Political Bureau—its nine-member, male-only Standing Committee. Nonetheless, her admittance to the Political Bureau is novel for two reasons. First, she is the only woman Political Bureau member since 1949 to have no marital connections to top men in the CCP. Other women who reached the same level of official political status were Jiang Qing, Ye Qun, Deng Yingchao—wives to Mao Zedong, Lin Biao, and Zhou Enlai, respectively. Second, Wu Yi is not married; she is unique in the PRC political world as a well-respected, independent female leader.

News reports on her appointment both inside and outside China suggest that Wu Yi's ascension is perceived as remarkable within the CCP's half-century rule. China-based Phoenix TV reported an American academic declaring that this was a progressive step in an atmosphere of relative gloom for women's careers in politics.¹⁰ A PRC professor of politics declared in a Singaporean news outlet:

> Wu Yi is the representative of Chinese women within the upper levels of the Chinese Communist Party. After China's liberation, the implementation of the Mar-

riage Law and the policy of "equal pay for equal work," women's status greatly improved. But Wu Yi's entrance to the Political Bureau really is a qualitative leap forward.[11]

Others remain skeptical of her significance. Coauthor of a recent book on the Sixteenth Party Congress, Bruce Gilley, wrote, "The Communist Party will be thrown out of office before there is a woman on the Standing Committee." He argued, "Authoritarian regimes are historically very patriarchal. They thrive on egoism, aggression and intolerance. There's a fundamental disconnect between authoritarian regimes and women's rights."[12] However, as this chapter reveals, a new narrative legitimizing women's exercise of political power within the elite Chinese political scene is emerging in the mainstream Chinese media and both English and Chinese language papers around the Greater China region. It is a narrative that appears only to fit the rather unique Wu Yi, but it has the potential to loosen "the invisible shackles" that have prevented women from reaching the top echelons.[13]

It is difficult to ascertain the extent to which Wu Yi is an agent in the creation of her media persona—it is possible that she has participated in strategically developing the public realm's superwoman politician "Wu Yi." This probability has been strengthened by the deregulation and diversification of the PRC's media sector. The new comparative freedom enables the manufacture of more complex and subtle images of the nation's political figures by apparently seamless interaction between global and regional media and individual political or factional interests. How has Wu Yi been created as a legitimately powerful woman within a culture that has for centuries mistrusted women in formal political power? What gymnastics must take place in the media descriptions of the female political body to create a legitimate persona?

Patronage or Sexual *Guanxi*?

The assumption that the female political body must have illegitimately gained power has a crippling effect on women's exercise of that power. The All-China Women's Federation's Ding Juan explained the problem of "reputation" for female politicians: "If a woman becomes a top official, the first question in people's minds is not how you would operate in the future, but what you have done in the past."[14] The female political body is inscribed with a sexualized history of patronage, and fear of women's potential sexuality tainting formal politics is the central block to creating a credible female political body in China.

In 1991 Wu Yi made a pointed comment about her "independent" political ascendancy. On her appointment as Deputy Minister for Foreign Trade she declared to fellow cadres,

> I am all alone in this world, I have no background, and neither do I have backstage supporters. I was only marginally voted in as Deputy Mayor for Beijing City. I was posted to this position in the Department of Foreign Trade by the organization. No matter what post I have assumed, I have relied on my own abilities, and I struggle with my work on my own.[15]

Wu Yi clearly felt the need to assert her "un-entangled" status. Such public statements suggest that she is an agent in the creation of her own media persona and that she has strategically confronted one of the key blocks for women politicians. She made a similar declaration on her appointment as Deputy Mayor of Beijing. In response to gossip that she was President Yang Shangkun's lover she snapped, "Why is it in China that any time a woman reaches a high position, people start to speculate about who her [male] mentor is? No one can believe you have come to office on your own merits."[16] Nathan and Gilley answer, "The explanation, of course, is that with the brilliant exceptions of women like Wu, male patronage has typically been the only way to the top in Communist China."[17]

In fact, Nathan and Gilley have identified only part of the problem. As their book aptly reveals, patronage is the key not only to female ascension, but also *male* ascension in Communist China. They routinely discuss male politicians in the context of "pedigrees" and "patrons." The fundamental difference between patronage among men and patronage of women lies in assumptions about the *nature* of that patronage. Although Wu Yi used the term "mentor" in her speech as the new Deputy Mayor, this could be understood as a modest allusion to "lover." Few male politicians would be similarly suspected of using sexual favors or romantic attachment for personal political advancement.

The female politician's body is sexualized and perceived as a fundamental tool in her success. Chinese women are categorically denied the naturalized, unproblematized status of a male political body—they are always appraised in a sexual light. The suspicion that sexual *guanxi* (connections) may have given an individual political advantage is more damaging to a reputation than any other form of *guanxi*—and sexual *guanxi* is regarded as being a specifically female tool. Thus Wu Yi's proclaimed independence from patrons or lovers is crucial to her continued personal and public success as a politician. Whether or not her assertions are true, the local and global media generally accept her "independence." Preexisting narratives circulating about the female political body in the public arena demonstrate the importance of establishing legitimacy for it. Whereas the male political body has achieved the status of sexual invisibility, becoming effectively *the* political body, female politicians have not become "naturalized" in contemporary political discourse.

The reduction of the female political body to a tool for mobilizing sexual *guanxi* derives from an apparently contradictory narrative where the sexualized and aestheticized female body, though superficially weak, is imbued with immense social power. An extreme example of the manner in which this body is perceived to disrupt social order can be seen in the post-Cultural Revolution discourse around Jiang Qing. Jiang, who exercised enormous political influence during the Cultural Revolution, was afterwards derided as "the White Boned Demon" invoked from a segment in the sixteenth-century novel *Journey to the West*, where a demon assumes the form of a beautiful woman. The metaphor alluded to Mao's powerlessness in the face of Jiang's beauty and the illegitimacy of her exercise of power through him. For centuries stories of fox fairies and demons have told how they assume the form of beautiful women in their pursuit of power, money, and status—the demons' corporealizations are always most effective when they take female form.[18] The twinning of the powerfully sexualized aesthetic fantasy of the female body with the powerless, modest female body of Chinese social life left little room for the development of legitimate female social and political influence. Wu Yi's persona has found the single path through the mire—staunch and repeated assertions of sexual independence.

Wu Yi spoke frankly about her single-status in a 1999 biography of women political leaders. She explained that her unmarried, nonsexual status was a result of limited opportunities, high standards, and her devotion to hard work rather than distaste for marriage, sex, and men.

> I don't believe in celibacy. That I am single is related to the one-sidedness of my youth. The first is that I was influenced by fiction and in my heart I had an ideal of a "real man" and in the real world there are no such men. Second, I always planned to establish my career and afterwards build a family. Only after I had built my career would I have a family and for a long time I didn't feel that this career was properly established. Then afterwards I lived in remote mountainous regions for over twenty years with a limited social circle, so I had to wait until I left the mountains and by then I was already old, work was busy, and so I thought I'd just forget it.[19]

Rumors of Wu's homosexuality have yet to appear in print and remain street gossip. Her public persona is one of a heterosexually chaste body. Thus, the space Wu Yi's persona creates for women politicians is restrictive and narrow—it requires the denial of contact with "corporeal masculinity" (but with aspiration for it) and a clear respect for "virtual masculinity."

Punishment for the Illegitimate Favorite

The danger for elite women politicians unable to achieve this "virtual male-oriented sexual purity" is evident in the career of Chen Zhili. Throughout 2002 she was predicted to assume the posts Wu Yi has been granted—vice-premier and Political Bureau member.[20] The *South China Morning Post* described her ascent:

> Chen Zhili's meteoric rise to the top echelons of the Chinese bureaucracy attests as much to the backing of a powerful mentor as it does her accomplishments as a scientist. Ms. Chen worked under Jiang Zemin in Shanghai in the late 1980s, and it was he who plucked her out of relative obscurity to head the Education Ministry in 1998.[21]

Although there has been no explicit mention of a sexual relationship between the two, their friendship was public knowledge according to the US-based Chinese-language news bulletin *Da jiyuan*. Alfred Chan describes Jiang's "dalliance with several women" including Chen Zhili.[22] She is also listed among his "four favorite women,"[23] and Jiang supposedly waited eagerly for her with a boyish enthusiasm. Her managerial abilities are regarded as being no more remarkable than those of many other women. "Luck" is seen as her outstanding accomplishment—the luck that Jiang "liked" her.[24] While many other ministers achieved their nominations through patronage, Chen Zhili's peers regarded her gendered patron-client relationship as less than legitimate.

Although a recognized member of Jiang's "Shanghai clique," Chen's gendered position within the clique made the "patron-client" relationship disempowering rather than empowering. Nathan and Gilley note that on her 1998 nomination to the position of Minister of Education Chen received "the worst showing [votes] of any new minister."[25] Chen's objective position was consolidated in March 2003 when she was promoted to state councilor during the Tenth National People's Congress.[26] But she again received an "embarrassingly low vote" of confirmation.[27] Chen's apparently indelible links to Jiang prevent her achieving legitimate political status, undermine her authority, and diminish respect for her as a politician in the eyes of her colleagues. She remains trapped within a female-gendered political body, tainted with the perception of sexual *guanxi*.

Balancing Femininity and Masculinity

Part of the lengthy historical resistance to women's exercise of power derives from notions of essential gender differences and fears for the consequences of blurring these distinctions.[28] The public realm has traditionally been perceived as masculinizing and the domestic realm feminizing.[29] Feminized male bodies or masculinized female bodies are believed to generate social instability. As noted above, publicly powerful women symbolize the decline of the empire or family in part because they imply the weakness of men in male-coded space. Women with public political lives are regarded as becoming like men to the detriment of their essential femininity. Thus, one significant challenge for China's female political body is to ensure that in their exercise of power they do not suggest a critique of Chinese men's governance skills and do not imply a usurpation of Chinese masculinity. Fears of female arrogation of masculine domains remain strong and yet, with political power firmly located within the masculine domain, successful women political leaders like Wu Yi must strike a balance of perceived gender essences within their public persona.

Wu Yi's presentation of physicality is an excellent example of an emerging new narrative for women in power — one that challenges old anxieties about women's misuse of "male" power while simultaneously invoking gender codes sufficiently bounded to be acceptable to a broad public and to her political peers. Sport, fashion, and aesthetic sense play crucial roles in mediating these tensions.

In a 2002 article on "women in society" PRC readers were presented with a succinct enunciation of the contradictions inherent in their unease about women's exercise of political power. Fang Min, a popular female fiction writer, presented the view that women's role in society was to "make the world more beautiful and lovable" whereas men's role was to "make the world more powerful, mighty, and prosperous." She explained that if women compete for leadership positions with men they "completely lose those qualities of gentleness, softness, kind-heartedness and graceful refinement that a woman ought to possess. Actually, from the perspective of society this is damaging and destructive."[30] Yet, in direct contrast to her espoused enthusiasm for separate spheres, she notes that China's global ranking of women in parliament had fallen from twelfth in 1994 to twenty-fourth in 2002. She laments that these results demonstrate continued prejudice against women in China. The article encapsulates the dilemma for contemporary Chinese politicians with a female body: If they are successful in competing with men, they risk being perceived as losing vital feminine qualities necessary for social stability. If they are not competing for political power then it demonstrates continued sexual discrimination and reflects poorly on China in international rankings.³¹

A prominent U.S.-based historian of Chinese women, Wang Zheng, expressed a similar view about women ceasing to be women on entering elite politics. During a 2002 interview about the forthcoming PRC leadership changes, Wang advised a Reuters' reporter, John Ruwitch, "They don't want women in the number one position. It's structural. It's a male-centered culture." Ruwitch reported that Wang believed "the only women who rise to power are those who play by men's rules, and they tend to play more conservatively."³² Wang said, "There's a shared understanding around here that just because there's a woman, that doesn't mean she will represent women's interests. The appearance may be that of a woman, but everything she does is like a man."³³

Both Fang and Wang believe that women are corrupted by formal political power—either through the loss of their femininity or through the betrayal of their (expected) political allegiance to the mass of women. Such views reflect a modernization of ancient prejudices about gender boundaries that have curtailed women's formal political participation. When women enter the public political arena they become unsettlingly masculinized. Yet women politicians are inescapably "embodied" *as* women, as maybe be read from Fang and Wang's assertions about their loss of femininity. But in Wu Yi's public persona a delicate balance of masculinization and essential femininity is achieved. This particular "female high official" has negotiated gendered borders with remarkable dexterity by deploying the female corporeal form in ways that are new to the PRC.

The Patriotic Body Beautiful

The tensions of this "balancing act" are manifest in media discussions of Wu Yi's person. Wu Yi is no epicene woman. Her reputation as a "tough" negotiator is presented alongside her refined elegance and natural beauty. She is credited with a superior sense of style and, as noted in the quotation at the head of this chapter, designs her own clothes. She regards dressing well an important part of her public profile and makes a particular effort when engaged in international visits. Readers are told that she regards stylish dressing as national duty—she represents all of China's women. The body of this powerful woman is attractively adorned—not through vanity but rather as a patriotic duty and to emphasize her continued essential femininity *despite* her exercise of male power. In 2003 she was described as standing out on the stiff political stage with her "pretty, bright, radiant, and enchanting exterior giving full flourish to her humanity."[34] Unlike her male peers, Wu Yi does not dye her hair and she is unique for her head of thick gray locks in any political lineup. In this she comes across as a mature woman and her self-presentation neatly resists any link between adornment and sexualized corporality long associated with top women.

Wu Yi has set the trend for the physical beautification of other women leaders. In July 2004 the All-China Women's Federation employed a prominent image consultant, Yu Ximan, to teach eighty senior women how to dress, wear makeup and style their hair. This plan was explicitly given a patriotic rationale. "Our top female officials should be aware that their appearance is significant and directly related to the nation's image."[35] By adorning their bodies appropriately, Chinese will avoid being "viewed as unpolished, second-class citizens."[36] Female leadership duties now carry responsibility for projecting national status through sartorial display. Their unsettling forays into the male political realm are thus deftly moderated by public displays of perceived "essential" feminine concerns with patriotic decorative corporeality.

The authorized aestheticization of women in top-level political life stands as a significant deviation from the pre-reform period when beautification was bourgeois vanity. Even today, it is a common perception that "if female politicians dressed well and in bright colors, people would think they spent too much time preening themselves and not enough time focusing on their jobs."[37] During the Cultural Revolution, prominent women found that dressing up was a political crime. Liu Shaoqi's third wife, Wang Guangmei, a recognized beauty, was famed for dressing in western-style "feminine" clothing in the 1950s during her international travels with Liu. In 1966, when Liu was purged, Wang was forced to wear a dress split to the hip during her denunciation sessions to remind her of this folly. Jiang Qing was presented after her purge in 1976 as an indulgent traitor. The West German ambassador at the time noted, "Jiang Qing was depicted on the posters living in the lap of luxury, wearing glasses from Japan, false teeth from Hong Kong, a wig from the United States, and—almost invariably—an imperial crown on her head."[38] Her excessive adornment was taken to be styleless and unpatriotic vanity.

Jiang Qing had attempted in the early 1970s to promote a particular style of skirt for women, later dubbed "the Jiang Qing skirt." Subsequent media reports have declared that this style was not acceptable to the majority of people because of its "design flaws."[39] A full skirt, it clearly required amounts of cloth in excess of a family's cloth ration. Moreover, the workplace directives for women to make the "Jiang Qing skirt" caused much anxiety—no doubt contributing to its perceived "faults."⁴⁰ In the climate of the aestheticized woman politician, a critique of her fashion sensibilities—whether accurate or not—connoted someone who was not sufficiently "female."

The portrayal of Jiang Qing contrasts strikingly with the elegant, tasteful style of Wu Yi's persona. The promotion of women's political rights during the Cultural Revolution has left a difficult legacy for women politicians in the reform period.⁴¹ The cause of political power for women was advanced in this reviled period when women "forgot" how to behave as women. Images of styleless Mao-suited women leaders in that era now signal the illegitimacy of those female politicians of the recent past. They were masculinized in an apparent rejection of "bourgeois female vanity," yet their attempts to beautify their bodies continue to be depicted as incompetent or illicit. The present assertion of the aesthetic qualities of the female political body is an important statement of the current female politician's break with this previous era, and by Wu Yi's insistence on dressing beautifully and asserting her femininity through a demonstrated skill in design and superior fashion taste she succeeds in distancing herself from the previous generation of Political Bureau sisters.

Unlike Jiang Qing, Wu Yi's perceived aesthetic expertise is effectively mobilized as a patriotic act and this complements the media portrayal of her as a tough defender of Chinese interests in the international arena. Her patriotic dedication dovetails with her self-sacrificing celibacy, invoking a long tradition of Chinese "woman warriors" who temporarily assume male roles when the family or nation faces a crisis. Patriotism has long been a justification for women seeking political power. Early twentieth-century women's suffrage activists routinely declared patriotic motives.⁴² One of Wu's "tough" assignments in Foreign Trade was the PRC–US intellectual property negotiations. A 1999 biography describes Wu Yi's hard-nosed approach as evidence of her staunch defense of China's reputation. A US delegate reportedly declared, "We are negotiating with thieves." Wu Yi retorted, "Then we are negotiating with bandits. Please have a look at your museums and see how many items were stolen from China."⁴³ News of her retort won Wu fame and respect among ordinary Chinese.

Taming through Naming

A similar balancing of the political masculine and essential "safe" feminine codes is evident in the names granted Wu Yi's persona. These nicknames minimize the threat her power and influence present to overarching male authority. Her image is one of competent, feminine power—and not a dangerous, masculinized woman. A common phrase used to describe Wu Yi since her strong performance in China's WTO bid is "The Iron Lady" *(tie niangzi)*,[44] an invocation of Margaret Thatcher.[45] This gender-specific term connotes familial relationships. Unlike the English "lady"—which invokes class and prestige—the Chinese term *"niangzi"* connotes a stern and competent wife working alongside men. Wu Yi's clear loyalty to her family (the Chinese nation) as an uncompromisingly devoted "spinster" helps to consolidate the legitimacy of her power.

While "the Iron Lady" could present a challenge to Chinese masculine power, the equally common term "China's Iron Lady" provides an additional layer of reassurance to the gender order.[46] The international flavor of "China's Iron Lady" suggests China's "coming of age" in the international arena. Britain had an Iron Lady and now China has one too. The perceived benefits accrued by the presence of a female Chinese political body in the global arena mitigate the threat female leadership might pose to the masculine narrative of domestic governance. The Iron Lady nomenclature provides a linguistic bridge that simultaneously diminishes her Chinese femininity and emphasizes her international femininity.

Still, certain anxieties about her fraught femininity have been publicly aired. A 1999 article referred to her as "a strong and handsome 'man' " *(wei zhangfu)*.[47] The apostrophes around "man" feminize to a degree this appellation, yet in response, Wu Yi nimbly reminded readers that she refers to herself as "the little girl" *(xiao nüzi)*.[48] Wu Yi sometimes uses this expression in public speaking to express self-deprecation and humility, yet here she deploys it to directly rebut the "strong and handsome man" moniker. As a "girl" she is feminine but not tainted by the dangerous power of female sexuality. She is reported to often recite the phrase "the little girl receives her mission in the midst of calamities."[49] Other classic phrases Wu Yi deploys in shaping her media persona include "the little girl goes for broke!"; "the little girl is concerned about this"; and "the little girl has tears but doesn't display them."[50] Wu Yi's political body absorbs the "strong and handsome man" within its "little girl" and so dexterously avoids the taint of excessive masculinization. The self-infantilized Wu Yi is clearly not worried that her peers or the general population will fear that a child is running the country—rather, the prepubescent Wu Yi persona functions simultaneously as an adorable and effective national leader.

Wu Yi has been called "an astonishing and strange woman" *(qi nüzi)* for her talents, this description emphasizing her uniqueness among women. Her strangeness ultimately limits the threat Wu Yi presents to male power—as an outstanding woman, her power cannot be generalized to the rest of the female population. Yet the same article claims that she is "exactly what's required for governing the nation."[51]

Exercising the Female Political Body in Male Arenas

A final startling indicator of how Wu Yi has sought to balance male-coded power and personal femininity is her invocation of the female sporting body. Wu Yi's sporting prowess is a notable and oft-repeated feature of her public persona. The elite female political body in China is not only adorned in refined and elegant clothing but also it is fit, healthy, and sporty. Media reports evoke the physicality of the female politician's sporting form.

> With red faces and shining eyes, they are laughing and sweating in the freezing winter. Like many other sports lovers in Beijing, they met every week at the stadium attached to the Capital Sports Institute to play tennis. "I know who they are," said the guard at the stadium, smiling. Almost all Chinese know who they are: they are the women ministers of the country. "We love sports. Sports keep us fresh and give us great energy, which is necessary for us to do a good job," said Wu Yi, a member of the Political Bureau of the Central Committee of the Communist Party of China. "Sports are also a test of willpower."[52]

Wu Yi is known for her diverse sporting interests (tennis, ten-pin bowling, golf, and fishing) but also for her leadership of other women ministers in their participation in sport. The current persona of the female political body is active and mobile; its engagement in recreational athletics demonstrates physical strength and a competitive spirit. These qualities are masculinizing but not irredeemably so. The women ministers' tennis team Wu Yi captains is the "Heroines" Soft Tennis team. The name aestheticizes their physical activities while simultaneously giving them patriotic polish by invoking centuries of women warriors.[53]

Significantly, Wu Yi notes the health benefits of physical exercise as important to good national administration. A leader's body must be able to cope, in a feminine way, with the physical rigors of leadership. Sport keeps a female politician alert and quick-witted. Wu Yi has perhaps achieved the ideal balance between brains and brawn invoked in the classical phrase "the twin powers of the literary and martial" *(wen-wu shuangquan)*. While Kam Louie argues this concept is uniquely masculine in the Chinese worldview, he also suggests that gender stereotypes in China are being dismantled such that men no longer have sole ownership of traditional male preserves such as *wen-wu*. Wu Yi's promotion of a fit, beautiful body and an alert mind for effective governance suggest that this paradigm may also apply to women leaders in the future.[54] Wu Yi presents participation in sport as a national duty for women politicians and, as the "Heroines" Soft Tennis team demonstrates, the desired health benefits accrue without loss of femininity. The high media profile Wu Yi's sporting body has achieved provides a new and credible space for a limited conceptualization of female competitiveness, aggression, and strength.

Wu Yi's rise to the top echelons of Chinese politics has been achieved with a simultaneous assertion of the femininity of her media persona. Sport, fashion, and beauty have played central roles in establishing the validity of her (female) political status and reducing the sense of threat she might pose to the overarching male political order. The Wu Yi media persona creates a credible, legitimate space for a female political body within the masculine world of elite Chinese politics—albeit a small and prescriptive space where the female body's sexuality is contained by celibacy. Moreover, that political world now expects women to exemplify "feminine" traits of style and aesthetic sense—it has become a space for sporty, patriotic petroleum engineers with glamour and grace. The Chinese woman leader can now find new acceptance via the very physicality that was criticized and suppressed in early eras. Wu's persona is a prominent model for other women leaders. In 2003 a woman, Xue Li, was appointed head of China's besieged National Soccer Association. In a *Sport158* interview, Xue was explicitly reminded of Wu's comment, "The little girl receives her mission in the midst of calamities."[55] Will Xue Li lead the rescue of the national soccer scene like a patriotic, strong, beautiful woman warrior from China's past? She should probably first check with her hairstylist.

Notes

Epigraph. Pan, *Zhongguo zhengtan nüxing da xunzong.*
1. Louie, *Chinese Masculinity.*
2. "Women's work" refers to those areas of governance that specifically pertain to the mobilization of women or the dissemination of Party materials among women. For a discussion of the problems this concept has caused for women's political aspirations see Judd, *Chinese Women's Movement;* and Edwards, "Constraining."
3. Zhang, "Nüxing wang zhang zai fazhan."
4. Gilmartin quoted in Ruwitch, "Chinese Women."
5. Wu Yi is the third woman State Council vice-premier. Previous incumbents were Wu Guixian (1975–1978) and Chen Muhua (1978–1982). Neither woman achieved simultaneous appointment to high levels of the Party structure.
6. Leow, "Vice-Premier."
7. "SARS Cases Top 2,900."
8. "SARS Puts New China."
9. Beech, "Wu Yi Goddess."
10. "Wu Yi: Zhiguo qiaxu 'qi nüzi.' "

11. "Panshang zhengtai dianfeng de Wu Yi."
12. Gilley quoted in Ang, "Few Women."
13. "Panshang zhengtai dianfeng de Wu Yi."
14. Ding quoted in Ang, "Women Still Scarce."
15. Pan, *Zhongguo zhengtan nüxing da xunzong*, 341.
16. Wu quoted in Nathan and Gilley, *China's New Rulers*, 137–138.
17. Ibid., 138.
18. See the Qing dynasty stories of Yuan Mei, *Censored*.
19. Pan, *Zhongguo zhengtan nüxing da xunzong*, 335.
20. "Jiang's Gang"; Ang, "Women Still Scarce"; Ruwitch, "Chinese Women."
21. Weist, "Scientist Rises."
22. Chan, "China's Fourth Generation," 114.
23. "Jiang Zemin he ta xihuan de."
24. Ibid.
25. Nathan and Gilley, *China's New Rulers*, 138. See also "Jiang Zemin he ta xihuan de."
26. "China's New State Councilors"; Fong, "Highs and Lows."
27. Cheng, "China's Next Phase," 48–52.
28. Edwards, "Narratives," 619–630.
29. See for example, the feminization of the male protagonist Jia Baoyu within the classic Qing novel, *The Red Chamber Dream*. Moreover, the dominant daughter-in-law, Wang Xifeng, is masculinized through her illegal financial dealings in the public realm. Edwards, *Men and Women*.
30. Xu Zhan, "Nüren rang shijie keai."
31. Ye, *Zhongguo funü lingdao rencai chengzhang he kaifa yanjiu*, 48–49.
32. Ruwitch, "Chinese Women."
33. Wang quoted in Ruwitch, "Chinese Women."
34. "Wu Yi: Zhiguo qiaxu."
35. "Dressing Up."
36. "Style Counsel."
37. Ibid.
38. Tuinistra, "Shanghai."
39. Yan, "Zhongguo fuzhuang."
40. I am grateful to Jon Unger and Anita Chan for alerting me to this feature of the skirt. For further discussion of the controversy surrounding the skirt see Finnane, "Looking for Jiang."
41. Edwards, "Constraining."
42. Edwards, "Gender Equality"; Edwards, "Narratives."
43. Pan, *Zhongguo zhengtan nüxing da xunzong*, 339.
44. "Wu Yi linwei shou kang yi ji xianfeng," 13–17. In English-language publications from both China and Hong Kong, the term "Iron Lady" is used. In Chinese-language publications from China, Hong Kong, and the Chinese-reading diaspora, the term *"tie niangzi"* is used.
45. Official Chinese media outlets were coy in their usage of this nickname for Margaret Thatcher until 1990. Prior to 1990 the term *"tie niangzi"* or *"tie furen"* was qualified

with apostrophes or with the phrase "as the Soviets termed her." By the mid-1990s such restraints lifted. See Fang, " 'Tie furen' zan."

46. "Zhongguo de tie niangzi Wu Yi xiao dang'an," 14; "Wu Yi."
47. Pan, *Zhongguo zhengtan nüxing da xunzong*, 334.
48. Ibid.
49. "Wu Yi: Zhiguo qiaxu"; "Wu Yi linwei shou kang."
50. "Wu Yi xiao nüzi huo chuqu le."
51. "Wu Yi: Zhiguo qiaxu."
52. Xiao, "Ministers."
53. The name of the team is derived from the term *jinguo* (women's headdress)—a word ascribed to women warrior patriots. Edwards, "Women Warriors."
54. Louie, *Chinese Masculinity*.
55. "Zuxie xinren nü zhuxi Xue Li."

CHAPTER 10

Sites of Transformation
The Body and Ruins in Zhang Yang's *Shower*

JAMI PROCTOR-XU

An old house is an intimate thing. Its walls, floors, windows, and doors bear the traces of human wear and tear.
—Trinh T. Minh-ha, *Shoot for the Contents*

My memories
Scattered wind   scattered flowers
Scattered streets   defeated people
Objects in the wind   melt away
Scatter in Beijing's sky
—Shen Lihui, "Jiyi sanluo le, meiyou shengyin"

THE FILM *Shower* (Zhang Yang, 1999) is one of several recent films to explore the transformation of everyday urban life through the demolition of old neighborhoods and the construction of high-rise commercial buildings and apartments in their place.[1] The film tells the story of a Shenzhen businessman, Daming, who returns to the Beijing bathhouse where he grew up after having left his past and his family behind. His return home is prompted by a postcard from his mentally handicapped younger brother Erming that leads him to mistakenly believe their father has passed away. After he returns home, he learns that his father's health has deteriorated and that the bathhouse he owns and runs is going to be torn down and replaced by a high-rise shopping mall. As the bathhouse patrons attempt to come to terms with the impending demolition of their neighborhood and their relocation to high-rise apartment complexes in different parts of Beijing, the bathhouse owner becomes ill and passes away. Soon after his death, movers arrive at the bathhouse and nearby buildings to assist the residents in their forced relocation, and Daming realizes he must care for his younger brother. In the final scene, bulldozers and wrecking crews descend upon the neighborhood, and two of the bathhouse patrons ride through the alleyways on a bicycle filming their neighborhood in an attempt to capture it before it disappears. The demolition is the culmination of a generalized process of transformation that involves decline, death, adaptation, and the production of traces by those experiencing these changes.

Although *Shower* focuses specifically on the transformation of one community in Beijing, it also reflects the dramatic transformation of urban space that is reshaping everyday life in cities all over China. *Shower*'s self-conscious engagement with a disappearing space situates it in the body of works Wu Hung terms "demolition ruins." These works "do not focus on human tragedies from a retrospective view. Instead they respond to a dramatic change in the environment caused by an ongoing process of destruction and construction."[2] In his analysis of ruins in contemporary Chinese art, Wu remarks that "although large-scale demolition is a regular feature of any metropolis in the world, the enormity of the demolition China has experienced in recent years has had a profound psychological impact on city residents. Such demolition has been continuing for more than a decade and has kept major cities like Beijing in a state of perpetual destruction and disruption."[3] In fact, Beijing is changing so rapidly, the city map has to be revised every other month.[4] As old neighborhoods and their ways of life melt away, a number of filmmakers have attempted to record and comment upon this rapid and ongoing transformation. Images of architectural ruins in these films signify the destruction and disruption of both the visual landscape and lived experience of the city, while bodies become the site where the meaning and effects of this transformation are explored and contested.

Through a close reading of *Shower,* this essay explores the relationship between the body and the architectural structures it inhabits, as well as how the body functions as the focus for reflections on dramatic changes in lived space. The narrative of the film is organized around two impending deaths—that of Old Liu, as the result of illness, and that of the bathhouse, which will follow the neighborhood's demolition. I will examine the relationship between these deaths and then look at how the individual life cycles of Old Liu and his bathhouse are placed within the larger context of developments necessary to the modernization of the Chinese nation. More specifically, these "lives" mark a small but telling transition between China's past and its future. I suggest that this film is important because it marks a moment in Chinese ruins discourse in which ruins have become a locus for looking to the future, and perhaps more importantly, the body becomes a positive presence from which the violence implied by ruins is disavowed.[5] Through its attention to bodies and the production of traces, the film also provides a lens through which to examine the way bodies enliven structures and define them as lived spaces at particular moments in time, as well as the way individual bodies adapt to changes in lived space.

An anticipation of death is set up early in the film when the viewer learns that Daming has returned home for the first time in several years because he misinterpreted a drawing on a postcard his brother Erming sent him. The drawing, which has no caption explaining it, depicts Old Liu lying in bed with Erming sitting next to him. After Daming sees his father is still alive, he tells Erming the drawing scared him because it made him think their father had passed away. Daming's misreading of the postcard foreshadows Old Liu's death and sets up a series of scenes that culminates with the demolition of the bathhouse.

In the first of these scenes, Daming has a conversation with his father in which he discovers that how badly both his father and the bathhouse have declined. The night before their conversation takes place, the roof of the bathhouse starts to leak during a storm. After being awakened by thunder, Daming hears his father on the roof and goes up to help him cover the roof with plastic. Sunrise finds them looking out over the rooftops of the *hutong* where the bathhouse is located. Daming comments that their house has not changed a bit since he was young. Old Liu responds, "It's a lot older. It starts leaking as soon as it rains." When Daming suggests he can fix it, Old Liu responds, "Houses are the same as people. Once they get old, they're still old no matter how much you fix them. But, no matter what, this is where I've spent my whole life" (Fig. 10.1).

The rooftop scene precedes the viewer's knowledge that the bathhouse is going to be demolished, but it suggests the possibility that it should be torn down. Old Liu's comments introduce the notion that buildings and human bodies are subject to the same aging process, and mark his body and his bathhouse as being too old to be repaired. The rooftop scene, shot from a disembodied third person's point of view—that of the omniscient narrator—provides the framework within which the two images of physical decline are to be read. It becomes evident that the film is portraying both the bathhouse and its way of life as part of a dying space, just as Old Liu and the older bathhouse patrons are part of a dying generation.

Subsequent scenes link the physical decline of Old Liu and his bathhouse to an increased vulnerability and to the inevitability of their deaths. Following Old Liu's collapse, a bathhouse patron remarks that a man of his age has to be careful not to get sick, echoing Old Liu's remark that old bodies cannot be healed. Soon afterward, a woman delivers a notice and informs the old man that the bathhouse and its surrounding neighborhood are going to be torn down. But Old Liu does not live to witness the demolition; he dies while bath-

FIGURE 10.1. Daming and his father on the roof of the bathhouse in Zhang Yang's *Shower*.

ing before preparations for the neighborhood demolition actually begin. His peaceful death is juxtaposed with the violent death of the bathhouse, thereby implicitly justifying the latter. The film seems to be suggesting that demolition brings an end to an architectural structure that is too old to be repaired, just as death brings an end to a body that is too old to be healed. Demolition becomes the way in which the bathhouse arrives at a timely completion of its life cycle, whereas repairing it would interrupt this "natural" process of decline and death.

The connection between Old Liu's death, the bathhouse demolition, and the larger context of "natural" development becomes evident in the scenes following Old Liu's death. In the first of these, bathhouse patrons face a portrait of Old Liu while somber music plays in the background. Their backs face the camera, making Old Liu's portrait the focal point of the scene. The film then cuts to Daming turning off the light to the bathhouse, and the somber music is replaced first by the sound of the light switch and then by the audio of a documentary about beetles Erming is watching on television. Since the documentary immediately follows the shot of the bathhouse patrons gazing at Old Liu's portrait, its narrative functions as a sort of eulogy, providing the context in which to read the meaning of his life and death. The narrator states:

> For a period of five months, this specially constructed shell will protect the life of the larva, allowing it to live in the appropriate temperature and humidity. The

egg is hatching. After four months pass, the young insect will have grown up. The ugly larva will eventually turn into a beautiful beetle. The insect's mother finally dies. She has fulfilled her maternal responsibilities. She has labored strenuously and left behind a new life. She will forever lie in an underground cave. The young insect leaves his fate in the hands of the seasons and the climate. . . . The small beetle faces the same dangers as the giant elephant. In this dark and empty grave, he exists accompanied only by decay and the passage of time. One night rains pour down, refreshing the dried out plain. The source of new life emerges from the depths of the earth. The beetle is developing its new life.

While the voice of the narrator and the music of the documentary run uninterrupted throughout the scene, the camera shifts between close-up shots of Erming and Daming's facial expressions, shots of Daming's movement from the doorway to the bed to sit next to Erming, and shots of the television screen where images of the documentary appear. These images include a long close-up of the deceased mother beetle's carcass reminiscent of the shot of Old Liu's portrait, as well as shots of the mother beetle lying next to the young beetle's cocoon, a line of old and young elephants marching forward, and the young beetle's emergence from its cocoon. Just before the scene fades to black, there is a close-up of Daming and Erming sitting side by side as the narrator says, "The young beetle is developing its new life."

The documentary presents a biological argument to explicate Old Liu's death and its connection to the demolition of the bathhouse, identifying both deaths as part of a natural process of survival and development. More specifically, it functions as meta-narrative, framing the film as a story of transition between cycles of development and locating the meaning of this development within a Social Darwinian framework. Old Liu is likened to the mother beetle, who, having fulfilled her life's work, dies to allow the next generation to develop a new life. The *hutong* in which the bathhouse is located is thus defined as a space of death and decay from which the next generation must emerge. Within this framework, the modernization of the urban landscape and the population as a whole is privileged over the preservation of any particular structure or the interests of any given individual. Old Liu's death and the bathhouse demolition are thus necessary parts of a larger process that involves the replacement of traditional neighborhoods and lifestyles with high-rises and modern lifestyles. The dead body of the beetle lying next to the cocoon marks the moment of transition, just as Old Liu's death signals the shift from his way of life to the "new life" that will emerge once the neighborhood is demolished. Daming's career as a businessman in Shenzhen represents this new life.

The inclusion of beetles and elephants in the documentary is significant because it presents a way of generalizing arguments about survival and development across species and provides the framework within which to read two separate comments made about crickets when the older bathhouse patrons are discussing the changes occurring around them. During their final bath before the neighborhood demolition, the old patrons are discussing where they have been relocated and what life will be like in their new high-rise apartments. Old Lin announces that he is no longer going to raise crickets. When his opponent, Old Wu, asks why, he explains that crickets cannot survive in multistory buildings. This comment is particularly poignant since it suggests both the inability of certain aspects of traditional urban culture to survive the city's physical changes and the need to adapt to a new lifestyle once the built environment has changed. Later in the conversation, the patrons imagine what bathing will be like in their new apartments and lament the loss of a communal bathhouse where they can talk and laugh together. In an earlier scene Old Wu had temporarily stopped going to the bathhouse because his crickets were crushed when movers knocked down his neighbor's wall and he became ill from sadness. Old Wu's reaction is another indication of the difficulty of coping with the losses resulting from urban transformation. However, the beetle documentary sets up a way of arguing that these losses are part of the natural course of human history and the evolution of lived space, in which everything faces death and possible extinction. The castings of the human body and the city are the same. Like the insect body, they can and must be shed.

    The biological argument presented in the beetle documentary has a long history in China (linked to the prevalence of Spencerian/Social Darwinian thought among Chinese intellectuals since the late nineteenth century and Yan Fu's translation of T. H. Huxley's work), and its use here signals the film's self-positioning vis-à-vis contemporary discourse concerning what is known as the *chaiqian* (demolition) phenomenon.[6] In contrast to other recent films such as *Xiaowu* (Jia Zhangke, 1997), which ironically includes official slogans regarding the modernization and "cleaning up" of society to challenge the idea of progress through demolition,[7] *Shower* takes a position that echoes both official and popular thinking concerning urban reform. These arguments claim that large-scale demolition is a necessary step in China's modernization since traditional buildings and neighborhoods do not conform to the aesthetic standards of the modern city, nor do they suit modern lifestyles. Like the biological argument, which defines traditional housing structures as decayed and dying spaces, official and popular sentiment defines them as part of China's past, contrasting them to new structures that are linked to China's future. In his essay, "Just Talking about Buildings," the poet Yang Mian remarks that in the contemporary urban climate, development is used to justify the ongoing transformation of urban culture and the urban landscape: "We continually demolish old houses and, either actively or passively, repeatedly move to our new houses filled with hope."[8] Images of high-rises are everywhere — on billboards, commercials, and popular publications that portray the "new Beijing," the "new Shanghai," or the "new China" — while images of traditional houses and buildings are linked to the urban past.

Just as the bathhouse in *Shower* is defined as a space of death and decay before the wrecking crew arrives, it is also established as of a piece with China's urban past or the disappearing present. The time-spaces introduced through the stories and lives of the individuals connected to the bathhouse offer a teleological narrative of China's modernization through urbanization and capitalist development. Each time-space is portrayed in terms of bathing, and the changing relationship between the individual (body) and bathing illustrates the shift from China's rural past to its urban future. Within this narrative, the female body is linked to the rural past as a site of nostalgia for what is being lost through modernization, while the image of the male body alone in space is linked to a technologically advanced future. This invented tradition that evokes nostalgia for an obsolete rural past is part of the Social Darwinian framework. Both a real and an imagined future interact with the past and present of the bathhouse and build momentum for the demolition that concludes the film.

The film's opening scene shows a man (who the viewer later learns is one of the bathhouse patrons, Hezheng) getting cleaned up in an automated shower station that operates something like a car wash.[9] The station is Hezheng's idea for a new kind of shower that will make millions for whoever sells it; it is situated in a distinctly modern urban space, surrounded by high-rises and paved walkways filled with people rushing past each other in different directions and submerged in the roar of traffic rather than sounds of nature. The rapid percussive beat of the techno music in the background sets a tempo that indicates an accelerated pace of life. As Hezheng steps onto the platform outside the automated shower, a panel at the side gives a readout of his height, weight, and skin type, and then allows him to select a three-, five-, or seven-minute shower. Time is broken into smaller units during his five-minute shower with a bell that rings at the beginning of each phase (soaping, rinsing, and drying). When the shower begins, the techno music in the background changes to another percussive beat that mirrors the rhythm of the spray washing Hezheng's body. When the shower ends, the scene cuts immediately to the title of the film and then to the bathhouse in Beijing, thereby highlighting the contrast between the two spaces.

FIGURE 10.2. The bathhouse in Zhang Yang's *Shower*.

With Hezheng's voice commenting that the pace of life is getting faster all the time, the camera pans across the bathhouse interior, showing a space seemingly unaffected by the changes being described (Fig. 10.2). The image of Hezheng's solitary body surrounded by mechanized scrubbing brushes is replaced with images of men standing naked outside the baths, men soaking in the baths, and finally, Old Liu giving Hezheng a massage. In contrast to the metallic silver sign on the shower station, that in the bathhouse is hand-painted and covered with mildew. The nondiegetic techno music from the opening scene is replaced by sounds both inside and outside the bathhouse. Inside, we can hear the percussive beat of the masseuses' hands on their patrons' bodies, Peking opera blaring from one old man's transistor radio, another old man snoring asleep on a bed, the splash of tea being poured, the chirps of a cricket fight, and the voices of men conversing. Outside, the buzzing of cicadas replaces the cars heard in the first scene.

Likewise, a leisurely pace distinguishes this space from the rapid-paced scene described above. Men spend their days in the bathhouse chatting, playing games, conducting cricket fights, and soaking in the baths. Many of them come in the morning and leave after dark. Although time is marked — through the exercise broadcasts that play each morning and through the activities conducted before and after the bathhouse closes — it is not broken into small units that dictate exactly how long each activity lasts. Because the pace of life is leisurely, the patrons have a chance to connect with each other and establish a sense of community. The bathhouse is depicted as a close-knit, distinctly male space, and the surrounding neighborhood is also presented as close-knit. But this place is clearly marked to disappear as the viewer learns the neighborhood is going to be replaced by a shopping mall and a space similar to that in Hezheng's imagination.

If the bathhouse is labeled as anachronistic by juxtaposition with images of modernized urban spaces, bathing is relegated to the past through references to rural scenes. The film marks countryside as a space of the past through its inclusion of Shanbei and Tibet only in the context of Old Liu's stories and Erming's photographs and recollections of his father's stories. In these stories the female body is a figure of nostalgia. As Old Liu tells one of his patrons, Zhang Jinhao, the story of his wife's family trading millet for water so she could take a bath before her wedding, the visual image shifts from the bathwater to the barren hills of Shanbei. Once Shanbei replaces the bathhouse, a folksong replaces Old Liu's voice, and after the song ends, the background music is slow and longing. The sounds of dogs barking, a donkey's bell, bowls of water being poured into the tub, and the wind blowing separate this place from the urban; here, too, the function of bathing distinguishes this place from the urban spaces in the film.

The shower in the opening scene serves a purely hygienic purpose, but the bath in Shanbei is connected to ritual. It is a local custom that sexualizes the female body in preparation for marriage. Old Liu begins the story by saying people in Shanbei do not bathe due to the scarcity of water, but local custom dictates that girls must bathe before they get married. The depiction of the bath focuses on the female body as a sexual object, putting the viewer in the position of voyeur. Unlike the naked male bodies in the bathhouse, which are an unmarked part of the larger scene, Old Liu's wife's body is the focal point. The camera zooms in on her as she undresses for her bath facing the camera. Once she is in the tub, she is shown slowly combing her hair as the evocative music continues in the background. The bathing scene is immediately followed by images of her wedding day. This story, which Old Liu tells shortly before his death, helps create a narrative of the Liu family past and the past of the Chinese nation. Both in this story and in the family story that follows, "woman stands as metaphor for . . . what has been lost (left behind)."[10]

The second family story enters the film through the photos of Tibet Old Liu has given Erming and a story about an old woman and little girl in one of them. Erming recalls the story while he is underwater with Daming standing next to the baths saying that he has to face the fact that the bathhouse is going to be demolished. Erming comments, "Dad said they had to go to a lake that was far away to take a bath," his voice is replaced by Old Liu's saying that it was believed bathing could cleanse the spirit as well as the body. He tells the story of a grandmother and granddaughter walking to the distant Holy Lake to bathe in its soul-nourishing waters. The grandmother explains that they have to go that year because the lake only has these spiritual powers once every twelve years, and she is afraid she will die before another twelve years have passed.[11]

These stories simultaneously create nostalgia for bathing prior to the bathhouse demolition and situate that demolition within the larger context of modernization and mechanization. The film's use of similar images and sounds across the various time-spaces creates the sense of continuous development and highlights the way in which people adapt from one environment to the next. The techno music in the modern urban space, the rhythm of the masseuses' hands, the music to which the neighborhood women do fan dances in the traditional urban space of Beijing, the wedding music in Shanbei, and the rattle of the wooden talisman the elderly woman shakes on her journey in Tibet all have the same percussive beat, but the tempo is different for each. Just like the paces at which individuals walk in each frame, the beat marks the acceleration of time. The availability of baths and the frequency of bathing correspond to the level of modernization and mechanization, shifting the functions of bathing from ritual to hygiene.[12] The bathhouse demolition is thus part of a many-stranded narrative of the development toward modern urban spaces, to which (individual) bodies have already adapted. It is the physical manifestation of a transformation shown to have already occurred.

If the film's defining the bathhouse as a dead space of the past allows it to back away from the violence of the demolition, the actual destruction scenes at the end of the film offer a second disavowal of that violence. The closing scenes enact both the destruction and the production of traces, all choreographed to "O Solo Mio," a song one of the bathhouse patrons sings every day while showering and later performs at the Neighborhood Demolition Party. As the song plays uninterrupted, shots of the demolition run one after another: a migrant worker knocks down a wall, a bulldozer sits surrounded by demolished buildings, then half-completed steel frames and a construction crane in the background signal the transition that is taking place. As the neighborhood structures are torn down, Old Lin and Old Wu ride through the neighborhood on a bicycle. Old Wu pedals as Old Lin films the destruction with a camcorder (Fig. 10.3). Once inside the bathhouse, he continues filming as the others remove wall hangings in preparation for demolition. As Old Lin is filming, Old Wu walks over to the camcorder and looks directly into the lens, revealing that the lens through which the viewer is looking is the same one through which Old Lin is filming. The scene shifts back to include Old Lin's filming in the

FIGURE 10.3. Old Wu and Old Lin filming the demolition of their neighborhood in Zhang Yang's *Shower*.

frame, but the final shot of the film is again viewed through his camcorder. It is Erming standing between the empty baths in front of the hand-painted sign we saw in the very first shot of the bathhouse at the beginning of the film. His eyes are closed, and he is singing "O Solo Mio."[13] His voice has replaced the recorded version of the song from earlier in the scene. The picture momentarily goes out of focus as Old Lin zooms in on him, but regains clarity as Erming hits the final note of the song.

The poem, "Spring," by the Beijing poet Zhou Zan offers an interesting point of comparison with the way violence is glossed over in the demolition scene of *Shower*.[14] The poem is similar to the film in its meditation on the destruction that urban modernization wreaks on the link between the life cycles of a living organism and the architectural structure to which it is most closely connected. The poem focuses on the changes and losses that result from chopping down old trees and replacing them with so-called modernized landscapes, another aspect of the destruction associated with the process of urban modernization. The poem begins with a description of a migrant worker chopping down trees in front of the speaker's house and ends with the speaker asking her cat, to whom the narrative is addressed, whether her agility as a cat enables her to "clearly hear the sound of the ax, and the cry coming from the heart of the tree." Whereas *Shower* links the "natural" passing of Old Liu and the bathhouse to disavow the violence of demolition, "Spring" connects the plight of the trees to that of her house to emphasize the violence of their deaths. After imagining the roots of the tree intertwined with the foundation of her house, the speaker remarks, "It's difficult to imagine how difficult the process of dying is," and describes the tree's resistance during this process.

The resistance and the difficulties of the process of dying are strikingly absent from the demolition scene in *Shower*. Like the beetle documentary, the final scene emphasizes the connection between death and new life, focusing on the context of transformation and on the production of traces rather than on the demolition itself. The image of the steel frames of the new high-rises and the construction crane rising behind the demolished neighborhood lays out the spectacle of transformation and adaptation. The tone of the scene contrasts with the tone of a similar scene that appears in one of the photographs by the Beijing artist Zhang Dali.[15] His "Demolition Beijing 1998 (1:1)" is a black and white photograph showing the frames of two high-rises in the background and ruins in the foreground. There are six hollowed-out heads in the ruins. A tree with no leaves stands between the ruins and the steel frames of the high-rises, giving the photograph a still, almost death-like tone. The steel frames take on the character of skeletons amid the stillness and timelessness of the image. In contrast, the steel frames in *Shower* signify the future of the space that is being demolished, and the bathhouse patrons' actions represent attempts to maintain a connection between the past and the future through the preservation and production of traces. The focus is not on the actual architectural ruins themselves but on the possibility of continuity and adaptation.

As the "walls, floors, windows, and doors" of the old neighborhood, which "bear the traces of human wear and tear" are destroyed through demolition, its residents gather and produce by filming a sort of tangible artifact of it to carry with them as they begin their new lives. The need for some physical vestige as a means of maintaining continuity and the possibility of producing these are established in two related incidents prior to the demolition. The first occurs when Xiuer attempts to perform "O Solo Mio" at the Neighborhood Demolition Party. Even though he sings this song every day in front of the other bathhouse patrons, when he tries to sing it on stage in rehearsals for the Neighborhood Demolition Party, he falls silent. Old Liu tells Daming that a psychologist diagnosed Xiuer with stage fright, but despite this knowledge, other members of the community yell for him to exit the stage if he is not going to sing. During the actual performance, he again stands on stage unable to sing until Erming realizes that it is this new environment that makes him unable to sing. Unlike the rest of the community, Erming realizes that what he needs is a sense of familiarity. He runs on stage and creates the familiar environment of the bathhouse by holding a running hose over Xiuer's head. As soon as this "shower" begins, Xiuer starts singing and is able to complete his song. In a similar gesture, Xiuer helps Erming maintain a sense of the familiar in a changing environment by giving him a walkman and a cassette tape of "O Solo Mio." This preserves Erming's connection to Xiuer, and allows him as well to carry forward an audio trace of the bathhouse.[16]

The photographs, tapes, and stories in *Shower*, and the film itself, are media through which the characters maintain a sense of continuity even when their lives are disrupted or disconnected from their pasts through death, relocation, or demolition. The ability to record, reproduce, and circulate the sights, sounds, images, and physical experience of the bathhouse enables Erming and the bathhouse patrons to carry its traces into their new lives, and allows their bodies to adapt from one type of space to the next. The camera within a camera (Old Lin's camcorder) in the demolition scene functions as a final meta-moment, revealing the film as an attempt to record both what is being lost in the process of destruction and the destruction itself, and positioning the filmmakers as insiders of the community they are portraying. By placing the camcorder in the hands of Old Lin rather than Daming, the filmmakers frame the film as a recording of a disappearing architectural space and its way of life by those who actually lived in this space.

This positioning is striking, particularly since *Shower* was produced by IMAR Film Company, Ltd.—a joint-venture company—in conjunction with Xian Film Studios. Founded in 1997 by Peter Loehr, the American entrepreneur who still runs it, IMAR is an independent film company whose stated objective is to make urban-themed films for the Chinese audience working with talented young filmmakers, but also spending a great deal of effort marketing their films internationally in hopes of appealing to international film critics.[17] *Shower*, the third film produced by IMAR, enjoyed tremendous success at the box office in China and was sold to over fifty countries.[18] While the film presents itself as a testament to what is lost at the individual level through demolition, it is in fact a fictional work produced by a joint-venture company for the Chinese urban youth and international filmgoers.[19]

This bring us to the necessary conclusion that *Shower* marks a moment in which ruins become a legitimizing site for narratives that naturalize the destruction modernization brings even as it occurs. The film is a product of transnational capital that apologizes for the destruction resulting from the modernization via capitalist development and the erasure of traditional architectural structures and lifestyles from China's urban landscape. Old Liu's weakened body and the dilapidated bathhouse signify a cityscape and way of life that the film in the end dismisses as already part of China's past, while the female body evokes merely nostalgia for what is lost in the process.

Notes

Epigraphs. Trinh T. Minh-ha, *Shoot for the Contents;* Shen Lihui, "Jiyi sanluo le, meiyou shengyin."

1. Other recent films on demolition and contemporary ruins include: *Dingzihu* [Demolition and Rehousing], Zhang Yuan, 1988; *Beijing zazhong* [Beijing Bastards], Zhang Yuan, 1992; *Qingchun wu hui* [No Regrets About Youth], Zhou Xiaowen, 1992; *Xiaowu*, Jia Zhangke, 1997; *Guonian huijia* [Seventeen Years], Zhang Yuan, 1999; *Tiexi qu* [Tiexi District: West of Tracks], Wang Bing, 2003.

2. Wu Hung, *Transience,* 111.

3. Ibid., 112.

4. Chih, "Xiaoshi de hutong." In her article, Chih points out that although "there were over 7,000 *hutong* in Beijing during the Republican Period, and in the 1980s, there were around 3,900 *hutong,* following the transformation of the old city, 600 *hutong* will disappear every few years." Of course, the modernization of Beijing is also part of an ongoing process of transformation and modernization dating back to the early twentieth century. For a detailed study of the history and modernization of Beijing, see Wang Jun, *Cheng ji.*

5. For a discussion of the history of ruins discourse in China, see Wu Hung, "Ruins."

6. For a discussion of Social Darwinism in China, see Dikötter, *Imperfect Conceptions;* Pusey, *China;* Pusey, *Lu Xun;* and Schwartz, *Wealth and Power.*

7. Like *Shower, Xiaowu* is situated in a place that is about to be demolished, but the architectural ruins in the latter film are included to question the idea of progress through demolition. Whereas *Shower* looks toward the modernized space that will replace the dilapidated bathhouse, a shopkeeper in *Xiaowu* remarks that despite the demolition of existing stores and structures, nothing is being done to replace what is being lost.

8. Yang Mian, "Jinjin shi tan jianzhu," 131–132.

9. The automated shower actually does not exist outside the space of the film; it is a product of the filmmaker's imagination. The producer Peter Loehr apparently received several inquiries from companies who were interested in purchasing, manufacturing, or patenting the automated shower. See Kuo, "Bathhouse." This anecdote reveals the ability of the media to share technology, even as it claims to be recording or representing the past.

10. Massey, *Space,* 10. In her discussion of gender in relation to place and time, Massey comments that Woman is often linked to the past while progress and linear time is often coded as male.

11. The scenes in Shanbei and Tibet also offer parodies of the Fifth Generation films, *Yellow Earth* and *The Horse Thief,* both of which include a highly filmic countryside. The parody of this filmic countryside is one way the filmmakers have positioned themselves as urban filmmakers, in contrast to the ponderous rural aesthetic of Fifth Generation films.

12. This also provides a lens through which to examine the effects of time-space compression on the body (in terms of the pace at which it moves, how it moves through urban space, hygiene, and the changes in interactions between bodies).

13. I would like to suggest that Erming's singing can be read as an attempt to block out the demolition, but also as a last effort to leave his traces in the bathhouse. The idea of trying to establish one's presence at the bathhouse also occurs earlier in the film when Hezheng installs a neon sign outside even though it is about to be demolished. When Daming asks why

he installed it, he replies that he had promised Old Liu he would install it, and he wanted to see it light up at least once. In her study of *tibishi* (poems written on walls), Judith Zeitlin makes an observation that is relevant to this reading. She argues, "What *tibishi* share with graffiti is the quality of being the opposite of a souvenir. If a souvenir is something that one *takes away* to preserve one's personal memories of a place, graffiti and *tibishi* are things one *leaves behind* to mark one's presence at a particular place on a particular occasion (hence the locution *liuti*)." Zeitlin, "Disappearing Verses," 77. Unlike *tibishi*, which were "meant to be encountered by a later visitor," the neon light and Erming's singing mark their presence in a particular place when that place is about to disappear. These markers highlight the absence that will soon replace the place in which they acquire materiality. At the same time, since they are recorded on film, they can be encountered by later "visitors," but these visitors encounter the traces only within the space of the film.

14. Zhou Zan, "Chuntian."

15. For a discussion of Zhang's work, see Dal Lago, "Space and Public"; Stuart, "Dialogue"; and Borysevicz, *Zhang Dali*.

16. I would like to suggest that the traces these media capture reveal the way in which bodies shape and enliven architectural spaces (and vice versa). The photographs, stories, audio recordings, and the film itself reveal the way the movement, talking, laughter, and the interactions between bodies within a structure enliven and define that structure as a particular space in time. It is precisely these interactions (the sights and sounds) that film can capture. The echoes of loss in ruins, therefore, become part of the filmic ruins themselves.

17. "Men in Towels."

18. See Xie, "Xizao jiang shangwang paimai," chap. 2, p. 17; chap. 15, p. 31.

19. "Men in Towels."

Contemporary Taiwan

CHAPTER 11

Stigmatic Bodies
The Corporeal Qiu Miaojin

FRAN MARTIN

Introduction

Qiu Miaojin (1969–1995) is Taiwan's best-known lesbian author. In local lesbian *(nütongzhi)* subcultures, Qiu's books are frequently cited as classics, particularly her 1994 novel *The Crocodile's Journal (Eyu shouji),* the first novel in Taiwan's modern literary history to be written by an author commonly known to be a lesbian that takes erotic relationships between women as its central theme. Qiu's fiction is much celebrated, too, in the mainstream literary establishment; *The Crocodile's Journal* won the prestigious *China Times* Honorary Prize for Literature for Qiu posthumously, following her suicide in mid-1995. Qiu's unique literary style—mingling cerebral, experimental language use, psychological realism, biting social critique through allegory, and a surrealist effect deriving from the use of arrestingly unusual metaphors—is strongly influenced by both European and Japanese literary and cinematic modernisms. Although her fiction has been compared, in its principal subject-matter, to Radclyffe Hall's 1920s classic of lesbian alienation, *The Well of Loneliness,* most frequently cited in Qiu's writings are male modernist and postmodernist "masters" (many of whose work shows a strongly homoerotic aesthetic) including Andre Gide, Jean Genet, Kobo Abe, Yukio Mishima, Haruki Murakami, Andrei Tarkovsky, and Derek Jarman—locally, Qiu's work has been critiqued for this apparent masculinist bias.[1] Qiu's early short stories "Zero Degree" ("Linjiedian," 1988) and "Platonic Hair" ("Bolatu zhi fa," 1990), to be discussed in this chapter, appeared in her first collection, *The Revelry of Ghosts (Guide kuanghuan)* in 1991, following their earlier serialization in local daily newspapers. They are Qiu's first works to treat thematically homoerotic desire between women.

While Qiu remains an iconic figure for Taiwan's lesbian readerships, the fact that her writing frequently depicts erotic relationships structured around the dimorphous feminine genders of "T" and *"po"*—comparable though not reducible to the English terms butch and femme—has also made Qiu somewhat controversial among local critics. Some feminist scholars, including Liou Liang-ya, have taken Qiu to task for her narrators' purported "male identification" and the apparent pessimism of her representation of sexual relationships between women.[2] In this essay, however, I want less to chastise her for these tendencies in her work than to explore these two aspects further and consider possible links between them by focusing on what I will call the *stigmatic bodies* of the narrators in her two early homoerotic stories.[3] Elsewhere, I have argued that Qiu's *Crocodile's Journal* is exemplary of a particular mode of representing homosexuality *(tongxinglian)* in 1990s Taiwan that lavishly exhibits a subjective injury that, it suggests, constitutes the foundation of *tongxinglian* subjectivity.[4] The injury posited in Qiu's fiction, I argued, is constituted by shame: a shame that at once catalyzes *tongxinglian* identity and inscribes within that identity the irresolvable problem of this foundational injury. Here, I will further develop that discussion of shame as a foundational injury that both inaugurates and fractures the *tongxinglian* subject by relating it to the concept of stigma. As I hope to demonstrate, consideration of the degraded sexual subject in Qiu's fiction, in particular how shame and subjective degradation are figured in Qiu's representations of stigmatic bodies, allows us to formulate a series of interesting general questions about abjection, stigma, and sexual subjectivity—questions that currently also occupy some theorists of sexual minority cultures in Euro-American contexts.[5] This approach additionally reveals the particularities of the local historical context of Qiu's work in late twentieth-century Taiwan, where popular, academic, and subcultural discourses and gender and sexual practices were undergoing rapid transformation. As I have argued elsewhere, such transformation leads on the one hand to an efflorescence of new and enabling identities under the aegis of the new lesbian and gay—*tongzhi*—politics and culture.[6] But these tectonic shifts in discourse on gender and sexuality also inevitably result in violent epistemic clashes with previously prevalent systems, clashes that have real consequences for actual sexual subjects. The period in which Qiu wrote the two stories analyzed here—between the lifting of martial law in 1987 and the rise of the *tongzhi* movement in the early 1990s—was a time of immense turbulence vis-à-vis the meaning of gendered bodies in Taiwan's public cultures. These stories powerfully register this sometimes calamitous turbulence.[7]

Context 1: Indigenized Sexology

As Tze-lan D. Sang has recently shown, modern Chinese representations of female homosexuality *(nütongxinglian* or *nütongxing'ai)* as marked by stigmatic and masculinized bodies may be traced back to the translation and indigenization of European sexology in the 1920s.[8] At that time literary representations of love between women drew simultaneously upon folk beliefs about feminine sexual deficiency and on the translated sexological theory of Richard von Krafft-Ebing and others to construct locally inflected and markedly phobic versions of the "mannish lesbian."[9]

One notable example of this phobic modern *nütongxinglian* representation is a 1932 story by the male modernist author Yu Dafu (1896–1945), "She Was a Weak Woman" *(Ta shi yige ruo nüzi)*.[10] The first part of Yu's story takes place in a girls' school, where the girl Li Wenqing seduces the pretty protagonist Zheng Xiuyue with expensive gifts and an impressive rubber dildo. Li is a personification of the disgrace of *nütongxinglian* conceived as an offense against proper femininity: the terror and hatred of this imagined condition is inscribed on and as the flesh of Li's frightful body. She is described as "both tall and large," with a "loud and resonant husky voice" and "snub nose," while "her face was covered in red-black freckles, and in size outdid that of a normal, huskily-built middle-aged man";[11] she is also described as emitting "a very strange smell of rotting onions that simply suffocated you to death."[12] The first time Li coerces Zheng into an intimate exchange by forcibly pulling Zheng's hand over her own naked body, she reveals to the other girl's touch "skin like sandpaper; a pair of very broad, very saggy, downward-dangling tits; a few straggly hairs in her armpits; and congealed in those hairs, a mass of sticky sweat."[13]

The influence of Krafft-Ebing's theory of female homosexuality as gender inversion is unmistakable in the horrifying literary personage of Li Wenqing: Yu's description attests to the capacity of the translated discourse of sexology to effect a regulatory and markedly phobic corporealization of *nütongxinglian*. Equally, however, the characterization of the monstrous Li also appears to draw on the folk figure of the *enü*, or malignant woman, whom Keith McMahon notes appears both in sex treatises dating back to at least the tenth century and figuring in much later literature and folk wisdom.[14] Possessing several of the inauspicious traits of the *enü*, including coarse skin, masculine voice, and malodorous armpits, Li Wenqing is legible as an amalgam of the sexological inversion theory of the mannish lesbian and local, premodern folk beliefs about the malignant woman who fails to conform to the cultural and corporeal codes of normative, feminine gender.[15]

I will argue in what follows that in her early stories, Qiu Miaojin takes up the phobically masculinized female homosexual to explore the conditions of cultural abjection "from the inside," as it were: from the position of the stigmatic body and "spoiled identity" of masculine-identified *nütongxinglian* itself. By presenting *nütongxinglian* as a form of gender-troubling inscribed on the bodies of their narrators, Qiu's early short stories indirectly cite the modern figure of *nütongxinglian* as stigmatic body. Yet this citation can be read, in part, as resistance to the corporealization of *nütongxinglian* in the Chinese variant of sexual inversion theory. In Foucauldian terms, Qiu's treatment of *nütongxinglian* as a series of painfully out-of-control body-parts can be interpreted as taking up the terms by which female homosexuality is made abject in society only to turn those terms around to produce a compelling critique of the dominant power structures.[16] Specifically, this critique comes from the perspective of a sexual subject whose cross-gender identification on one hand precariously aligns her body and sexuality with the abject figure of the masculinized lesbian, but on the other hand also bespeaks her powerfully felt yearning for a livable "T" self.[17]

Context 2: Subcultural History

While the broader discursive context for Qiu's representations of stigmatic bodies extends back to the Chinese indigenization of European sexual inversion theory in the early twentieth century, the more immediate context for her work is late twentieth-century Taiwan, and the changes then taking place in subcultural and academic conceptualizations of *nütongxinglian* gender. T (pronounced *ti*) and *po* constitute a system of secondary gender which, up until about the mid-1990s, structured most of Taiwan's female homoerotic subcultures. T is an abbreviation of the English term "tomboy," and the T role in sexual relations between women is frequently, if reductively, described as corresponding to the masculine role in the heterosexual relation. In the subcultural practice of the "T bar" since the mid-1980s, Ts have marked their identity by adopting selected masculine-coded cultural signifiers, including masculine dress (suits, ties, men's shoes), short haircuts, aftershave, and masculine bodily gestures, language use, and drinking style, as well as by modifying feminine attributes, for example by breast-binding. *Po* is a derivative of the colloquial term *laopo*, "wife," and *po* style appropriates signifiers of normative femininity (skirts, heels, jewelry, makeup, long hair, revealing clothing, flirtatious behavior) to produce the hyper-feminine counterpart to the dapper masculinity of the T.

Detailed histories and theorizations of T/*po* cultures have been written by a number of scholars, including Antonia Yengning Chao, Zheng Meili, and Gian Jia-shin.[18] They show that the terms T and *po* were first coined in the mid-1960s by the owner of a gay bar in Taipei, who knew the English term *tomboy* through his acquaintance with American GIs, at that time a constant presence in Taipei as a result of the war in Vietnam.[19] The ethnographic research of both Chao and Zheng suggests that between approximately the 1960s and the mid-1980s, T identification tended to equate quite strongly with transgender masculine identification, with Ts considering themselves men, sometimes undergoing gender reassignment surgery, favoring men's rather than women's public toilets, and frequently passing as men in everyday life.[20] Taiwan's first T bar opened in Taipei in 1985, and others soon followed. As Chao's research demonstrates, the fuller development of T/*po* subcultures around the bar scene seems to have led to a shift in many Ts' gender identification. This shift from identity with male-bodied masculinity to a self-reflexively directed achievement of what Chao calls "T-ness" led to a recognizable subcultural style that equates neither to normative femininity nor, exactly, to normative masculinity. Although it certainly draws on masculine sartorial and behavioral conventions, it is, perhaps, a gendered whole qualitatively different from the sum of its masculine and feminine parts.[21] As Naifei Ding and Jenpeng Liu have argued in detail, and as I will discuss further below, around the end of the 1980s and into the early years of the 1990s—the period when Qiu wrote the stories I will discuss—the existing T/*po* gender system of the bars was challenged by emergent lesbian feminist discourse radiating out from Taiwan's universities and nascent *nütongzhi* activist circles.[22] The lesbian feminist critique took issue with T gender as mimetic of the oppressive power of patriarchal masculinity, and in place of T/*po* gendered identity, lesbian feminists began to elaborate new forms of sexual identity such as *bu fen* (literally "not distinguishing," implying outright rejection of T/*po* classification), *lesbian* (using the English term), and *nütongzhi* (literally "woman comrade").[23] Around the mid-1990s, as both Zheng and Gian show, a generation of younger women whose adherence to T/*po* roles was arguably less strict than that of the women in the bar-based subculture a decade earlier had taken up a renewed appropriation and proliferation of T/*po*-modeled subcultural styles. This spawned a plethora of semi-humorous micro-categories like "sensitive new-age T" *(xin hao T)*, "nellie T" *(niangniang T)*, and "super-*po*" *(nüqiangpo)*.[24]

Context 3: The Emergence of *Nütongzhi*

> Once I went to play cards with them. I was curious what it'd be like to play cards with a bunch of Ts, so I went along. There were six or seven Ts there, and we'd just

arrived and sat down to start playing when another T came in, and straight away she started stripping off. It was summer at the time and really hot. It turned out her chest was all flat, with just two scars on it. I did my best to stay composed. And then she undid her belt—she wasn't taking [her pants] off, only undoing her belt on account of the heat, and she sat leisurely down like that and started playing cards. I didn't know where to look, so I just stared at my cards. When we played, the Ts sat at one table and the *po*s at another; the Ts played their game and the *po*s played theirs, you know, it was that notion of "how can women sit at the same table with men?" We played for a while, then someone said "Hey, you women keep playing, we're going to watch a sex show *(niurouchang).*" I didn't want to go—how could they go to a sex show! How could they exploit women that way? I thought the whole thing was completely vulgar *(diji).* But they were very excited, they did go, and in the end they got beaten up! . . . A bunch of men didn't like the look of them—a bunch of men who'd been watching the sex show, the same as them. These guys trapped them in an alley and said to them (in Minnan): "So, you think you look like men, do you?" And some of them got totally beat up.[25]

This story was related to Gian Jia-shin in the mid-1990s by an informant born in 1964, recalling an event in 1989. When Gian spoke to her, the woman was an editor of *Nüpengyou* (Girlfriend) magazine for "Women zhi Jian" (Between Us), one of Taiwan's foremost *nütongzhi* social and political organizations, founded in 1990. The excerpt speaks to my concerns in this chapter in a number of ways. First, the afternoon described illustrates the specificity of the cultural norms of gendered behavior in T/*po* sociality at this time and in this particular social context. It upholds a rigid demarcation between "men" and "women" (Ts and *po*s) such that the two groups socialize separately, a demarcation that privileges those on the masculine side—who may sit shirtless with belt unbuckled and partake in the leisure practice of attending sex shows. The Ts the informant met enact a mode of T/*po* sociality based on a quite specific form of working-class, Hokkien (Minnan-speaking) masculinity.[26] Second, by describing the physical assault on the Ts by male members of the sex show audience, the excerpt illustrates how the hypervisibility of Ts in public space makes them subject to verbal and bodily violence at the hands of a broader heterosexist culture ruthlessly determined to enforce the law that corporeal sex must equate with social gender and, implicitly, must determine the gender of sexual object choice.[27] Third, the excerpt demonstrates particularly clearly the epistemic conflict between older-style T/*po* cultures—figured here in the events of the afternoon the informant describes—and the at-that-time emergent discourse of lesbian feminism. The latter is represented in the informant's own attitude toward the events she describes: she voices disapproval at the rigid gender demarcation between Ts and *po*s, and a feminist but also indicatively middle-class horror at the "exploitative" but also "vulgar" activity of the Ts going to see the sex show. Thus, the excerpt dramatizes the effectively double-abjection of T subjects, *both* by a heterosexist broader culture *and* by the emergent discourse of lesbian feminism.

In an important recent paper, Naifei Ding and Jenpeng Liu make a historicizing argument about Qiu's oft-debated T-like characters. They read Qiu's early works (including *The Crocodile's Journal*) as caught between T/*po* subcultural practice and the then-emergent sexual, political, and academic culture of lesbian feminism. They propose that Qiu's narrators appear always in the process of a painful internal dissolution precisely because Qiu was writing them just when the new, woman-identified lesbian feminism was becoming popularized on university campuses islandwide. This greatly complicated the cross-gender identification required for the forms of (proto-)T subjecthood Qiu's beleaguered protagonists struggle to inhabit. They write:

> By taking into account an emergent . . . lesbian feminist movement in northern Taiwan at the moment of publication of Qiu's two earlier works (1991–1994), we believe that Qiu astutely yet violently represented the fractures within, both constructing and dissolving the representation of unifying and unified lesbian selves and relations.[28]

In this very persuasive reading, Qiu's proto-T characters fall apart and are torn apart as a result of being caught between two historically distinct modes of feminine homoerotic identification. Qiu was engaged in writing into being a "T textuality" at precisely the moment when the cultural conditions for the inhabitation of T subjecthood became doubly problematic. As I will elaborate below, I think this dilemma is revealed particularly clearly in "Platonic Hair."

Gender as Somatic Disorder: "Zero Degree" and "Platonic Hair"

For the reasons I have outlined above, in 1988–1990 when Qiu wrote these first homoerotic stories, the question of gender was at the forefront of local discussions about *nütongxinglian* in at least three interrelated ways. First, due to the lengthy cultural shadow thrown by indigenized sexology's construction of homosexuality as gender inversion, the bearer of lesbianism's stigma, in Taiwan as in Euro-American contexts, was (and is) the "obviously" masculine woman.[29] Second, in the T/*po* subcultures that were then the dominant forms of female homosexual sociality, sexual identification was signaled through the foregrounding of secondary gender in T/*po* style. Third, in the emergent discourse of lesbian feminism, gender was the primary category of analysis by means of which existing social relations—*including* those of T/*po* subcultures—were critiqued. Given all this, it is not surprising that the *nütongxinglian* subjectivity emerges, in Qiu's early works, through painful, internally contradicted gender formations. Although, as many have argued, Qiu's fiction can be seen as centrally concerned with writing into being a particular kind of *sexual subject* (variously interpreted as "lesbian," "T," and "proto-T"), in Qiu's early stories it is *gender,* as much as and arguably even more than sexuality *per se,* that emerges as the locus of subjective and corporeal contradiction, disease, and stigma. In their treatment of *nütongxinglian* as a form of gender-troubling, these stories draw attention to the epistemic clashes around gender that persist at the heart of (post)modern Taiwanese regimes of homosexual definition.

In the stories I discuss below, then, representing sexual desire between women becomes to a large degree a problem of representing complex, dynamic, and internally contradictory formations of gender identification. The protagonists in both stories are ambiguously and difficultly gendered: In "Zero Degree," a "male" narrator provides cover for the subtextual presence of a masculine woman; in "Platonic Hair," the "female" narrator has her hair cut short, wears suits and aftershave, and finally becomes radically unsure of her/his own gender identity. In "Zero Degree," the representation of counter-normative formations of gender and sexuality is relatively covert. The questions of masculine-identified femininity and feminine homosexual desire are not overtly present in the text, but are instead connotatively inscribed in extravagant descriptions of the painful stigmata that erupt eloquently on the narrator's mouth and feet. In "Platonic Hair," written two years later, these questions are closer to the surface. In this case the stigma—unruly and strangely auto-animated hair—overtly refers to the cultural conventions of gender presentation (long versus short hair), and the story concerns a woman who presents herself as a T and sexually desires a *po*-type woman. In each instance, the visibly stigmatized body of the narrator is a staging ground for the ideological and psychic contradictions occasioned by subjectivities whose gendered and sexual identifications run counter to *both* dominant *and* emergent cultural belief systems about what bodies mean. The body becomes dis-integrated into a series of floating signifiers symptomatic of the radical gender displacement entailed in claiming the dangerous identity of *nütongxinglian*.

In my discussion of these stigmatic bodies as expressers of queer shame, I am drawing on Erving Goffman's classic sociological study, *Stigma: Notes on the Management of Spoiled Identity.* For Goffman, writing in the United

States in the early 1960s, "stigma" refers to "the situation of the individual who is disqualified from full social acceptance" due to any of a range of defiling markers, including homosexuality.[30] The identity of the stigmatized individual is "spoiled" as a result of his or her possession of a trait that either visibly and immediately discredits her or his social identity, or potentially does so.[31] Stigma is intimately related to shame; shame arises in the stigmatized person as a response to the internalized value-system of the broader social collectivity that classifies her or his difference as a degrading one.[32] Goffman's theory thus enables a reading of Qiu's narrators' stigmata as the somatic signifiers of the psychic experience of a particular, historically conditioned gendered and sexual shame.

In "Platonic Hair," the ostensibly female narrator's difficult relation to normative gender is played out through her peculiar hair, which is animated with a sinister will of its own and can grow instantaneously longer as if by magic.[33] The narrator is a popular romance writer whose boss pays for a female sex-worker to live with her for six months in order to deepen the narrator's understanding of sex and love from a masculine perspective. After she moves in, the sex-worker, Han-Han, insists on cutting the narrator's hair and makes her don the T-ish accoutrements of hair-gel, men's suits, and aftershave, so that she can better approximate Han-Han's "ideal man." Han-Han herself, meanwhile, favors the distinctly *po* femme-fatale style: long hair, high heels, sequined dresses and handbags, and plunging necklines. As the two live together, a strong emotional bond grows between them until the narrator realizes that she feels an intense physical attraction to Han-Han. They finally have sex one night when Han-Han returns home after being violently raped by two johns. At the end of six months the contract expires and Han-Han leaves, but the narrator remains obsessed with her and stalks her through the city as she works. As the narrator's hair grows longer, it begins to act as an expressive vehicle for her ambivalent yearning for Han-Han. Her long hair behaves as though magnetized by the other woman, straining toward her whenever she is near, as though it wanted to embrace her — or perhaps, to kill her.

Throughout this story the mechanism of gender differentiation is signaled most strongly in the symbol of hair and relative hair length, to which Qiu's text pays sustained, almost obsessive attention. Consider the hair-cutting scene that takes place shortly after Han-Han comes to stay at the narrator's apartment:

> "According to the rules of the contract, you are now my man," [said Han-Han] "and like it or not you've got to look like my kind of man. The first thing we've got to do is cut that pretty hair of yours."

> Picking up some scissors, she ordered me to sit down in front of the big floor-length mirror. First she chopped off the length of my hair in one snip, leaving hair reaching just to the nape of my neck. Then she carefully shaped the remaining hair a pinch at a time. She moved around me, entranced by the pleasure of her activity, examining me from different angles, yet seemingly quite forgetful of my existence.
>
> First she trimmed the ends of my hair at the back into a perfect crescent, and then, after cutting two pointed sideburns in front of my ears, she appeared to wake up again. With a cry of delight she hugged my head and impulsively kissed me on the forehead, shouting "My man has appeared!"³⁴

Here, Han-Han (whose self-assurance and strength of personality lead Liou Liang-ya to classify her in Gian's category of the "super-*po*") takes it into her own hands to construct from the narrator her "ideal man"—who also, uncoincidentally, has much in common with the subcultural image of the T— and the process of transformation begins with the haircut.³⁵ If the narrator's role as ideal man/T is defined primarily by her short gelled hairstyle, correspondingly, the narrator's attraction to Han-Han is catalyzed most readily by the sight of Han-Han's long, soft, wavy hair: it is enough to rob her of her vision and cause her to feel a sensation like an electric shock.³⁶ As Liou persuasively proposes in relation to this story, "hair becomes an important fetish through which T and *po* demarcate their respective positions."³⁷

But as well as staging very clearly the workings of T/*po* secondary gender distinctions, "Platonic Hair" also furnishes an exemplary illustration of Ding and Liu's historicizing argument on the liminal position of Qiu's early fiction vis-à-vis competing models of *nütongxinglian* gender. On the most obvious level, the narrator and Han-Han's erotic identities are animated across *gender difference* (man/woman; T/*po*); still, there also lurks in the text a disruptive countermodel of feminine gender identity and sexual attraction, a model based not on the gender difference of relative hair length but on *gender sameness,* whose symbol is the mirror.³⁸ Indeed, the text as a whole is riven by the tension between these two competing models of sexual relationships between women. The narrator tells of her first sight of Han-Han's body:

> After her shower she emerged wearing a filmy purple negligee. I caught fleeting glimpses of her bra and underpants underneath, and the curves of her body showed up as clean as those of a statue. This was the first time I'd ever been so close to a young woman's body, and though I shouldn't have, I felt slightly excited. *It was just like the feeling I'd had when I'd looked at myself naked in the mirror for the first time.*³⁹

Here, the narrator's desire for Han-Han is sparked not by her *po*-like difference from the narrator's own T-styled body, but instead by its reflection of the familiar mirror image of the narrator's *own* body. But if in this passage gender-sameness produces a generally pleasant sensation of "slight excitement," at the story's conclusion, the doubling effect of mirrors, this time those found in the sex club where the narrator finally locates Han-Han, is far more troubling:

> I follow "her" into the women's washroom, take out my scissors, and before "she" has a chance to scream, *snip snap,* I chop off the hair in great hanks. The fallen hair flies over and winds itself around "her," snatching off "her" longhaired wig. *In the mirrors along both walls I see a bald man, and I can't tell who it is.*[40]

The story's denouement — set, surely not by accident, in that *locus classicus* of gender policing, the "ladies' room" — describes a nightmare vision whose most unsettling aspects are, first, the sudden appearance of a man when both reader and narrator had thought that the bathroom contained two women; and second, the doubling and melding effect of mirroring and the consequent impossibility of differentiating between one gendered body and the other.[41] Is the man in the mirror Han-Han without her wig — enclosed in quotation marks as "her" gendered pronouns have been throughout the sections of the story set in the present — or, is the man the narrator with newly shorn hair? Perhaps most ominously, why is there only *one* figure in the mirror, when, ostensibly, there are two people in the bathroom? What emerges very forcefully from this final confrontation in the ladies' room is not only the monstrosity routinely attributed to gender-deviant T bodies by homophobic and lesbian feminist critics alike; but also and uncoincidentally, the nightmarish vision of a hall-of-mirrors of endless sameness.

Euro-American critics of lesbian feminism's abjection of butch/femme gender have highlighted the limits of the radical lesbian feminist ideal of "egalitarian sex" that celebrates sameness, equality, and the interchangeability of partners and acts and abjures any differentiation of sexual or gendered roles.[42] As I have discussed, related arguments have been going on in Taiwan since the time when Qiu wrote these early stories. As Lü Jinyuan has recently written, this has meant that increasingly, the gendered specificity of the T subject is minimized by the feminist assertion that "Ts are women, too" *(T ye shi nüren),* with the implication that Ts have more to gain from gender identification with the broader category "women" than from gender differentiation from *po*s and heterosexual women and identification with the specific and limited category of Ts.[43] Published in 1990, "Platonic Hair" emerged at a kind of cultural flashpoint for the collision between older, local models of *nütongxinglian* gender differentiation in T/*po*, and the encroaching globalizing discourse of lesbian feminism that emphasized egalitarian comradeship among *all* women. In this light, it is unsurprising that the story should turn on the irresolvable, painfully conflicted definitions of *nütongxinglian* as gender-transitivity versus gender-separatism.[44]

Qiu's story of two years earlier, "Zero Degree," is narrated by a young, ostensibly male narrator who is tortured by two forms of bodily affliction: a crooked mouth, which is a constant source of shame, and feet infected with a severe case of tinea (ringworm) that produces itchiness and painful, pus-filled blisters. The torment of these afflictions is not only physical: The narrator's crooked mouth, in particular, also causes him emotional torment because it prevents him from forming sexual relationships with women. When a relationship does develop between himself and a girl student, his crooked mouth continues to stand in the way of its fulfillment: The woman appears blind to his deformity, but he cannot love her since the feature she overlooks is the one that most defines his own sense of identity. The more the narrator gets involved with the woman, the worse his tinea grows until finally, when she kisses his crooked mouth, he is driven to lock himself up—once again, in a bathroom—and slice at his feet with a kitchen knife.[45] This narrator has been read, by Liou and by Ding and Liu, as a closeted T or proto-T, such that the narrator's physical pathology stands in as a cipher for the "defect" and stigma of the T subject.[46]

Like "Platonic Hair," "Zero Degree" presents an interesting relationship between the narrator's troubled gender identity and his bodily afflictions. The following passage describes the narrator's second meeting with the female student who loves him:

> She was no longer that little sailor wearing khaki shorts, with short hair under a cap. Standing before me was a big girl *(da nühai)* in a long cream skirt and red shoes, with wavy hair down to her shoulders. This new image of her opened up a gulf—a voice saying "she is a girl" pealed out like cathedral bells to all but split my head open, while "I am nothing" echoed back in a thin, twittering cry.[47]

While the girl has changed from her previous cute sailor-boy look to a more feminine—or *po*-like—attire, what torments the narrator is precisely his own seeming lack of *any* gender identity: "she is a girl" *(ta shi nühai)* is answered by "I am nothing" *(wo shenme ye bu shi)*. But the narrator's agonizing lack of an inhabitable gender position is addressed again, differently, at story's conclusion:

> Suddenly, she gently lifted my head, and sucked deeply down on my mouth—I saw the image of this adhesion in slow motion. "Aaaahh—" Just at the moment she sucked down I pushed her away and began to wail, the consciousness that "I am a crooked-mouth" instantaneously flooding my mind.[48]

The girl's kiss precipitates the revelation that answers the narrator's internal voice in the previous passage: no longer "nothing," the narrator now finds that he "is a crooked-mouth" *(wo shi wai zui)*. Reading this alongside the previous passage, "crooked-mouth" emerges, precisely, *as a gender position*: the narrator is neither a "girl" nor a "boy." The affliction of the narrator's mouth, then, signifies his troubled relation to normative dimorphous gender.

A related interpretation can be made of the narrator's infected feet. When the topic of his feet is first raised, the narrator explains:

> They began to get infected from the moment [the girl student] reappeared. I was able to get great pleasure from rubbing them: by means of rubbing faster and faster, hotter and hotter, I was able to relieve myself of many a trivial irritation. But this compulsive rubbing led my feet on the path toward inflammation.[49]

The coincidence of the foot infection with the reappearance of the girl and the highly suggestive imagery of frenzied rubbing leading to satisfying release suggest that the narrator's diseased feet stand metaphorically for his sexual desire—a desire characterized both by its apparently feminine cast, with the evocation of clitoral rubbing, and by its experience by the narrator as pathological. A clue about why this desire may be represented as pathological can be found in the following passage:

> When I was moving house I ran about everywhere in slippers, and some fine dust settled on my feet, making me cry out hoarsely in pain. The blisters, originally confined to one place, had by now crept into all of the spaces between my toes, and most of the blisters had broken from the constant rubbing, so that the skin between my toes was as scarred as the bark of an old tree. . . . After moving house, as though driven to compensate for something, I not only bought all kinds of different medicinal ointments and potions, but discovered an ingenious method by which, as if possessed, I could now bandage [my feet]. Each day I checked the progress of their recovery, as if this were a matter of grave consequence—and yet they seemed not at all appreciative of my efforts, and, showing no fear of all the various obstacles in its path, [the infection] advanced ferociously in its territorial takeover, establishing a steadfast occupation. In the end I surrendered, removed the bandages, and threw away the various medications: let them return to their essential state *(bense)*.[50]

As well as its exemplary illustration of the excessive, almost salacious manner in which the story lingers on the gory details of the narrator's putrefying feet, this passage is also quite suggestive in its revelation of the narrator's attempts to *bandage* his feet. In the context of Chinese fiction, any discussion of foot bandaging inevitably reminds one that the foot—particularly the painful, diseased, bandaged foot—is a body part strongly overdetermined in relation to gender. The history of footbinding and representations of footbinding means that such imagery inevitably brings with it connotations of femininity—in particular, with femininity understood as a cultural state, a state achieved with difficulty by cultivating a set of culturally prescribed (and sometimes actually pathogenic) behaviors.[51] Following this interpretation, the ostensibly male narrator's festering bandaged feet indicate the subtextual presence of a feminine subject. Such a presence begins to account for the fact that the narrator experiences his sexual desire for the female student as pathological: if the apparently male narrator is, in a sense, an undercover woman, then his desire for the other woman is a homosexual one. In the image that then comes into focus—that of a masculine woman who both loves another woman and is presented as pathological and physically repellant (at least to him/herself)—we discern, perhaps, a vestigial shadow of the abjected "mannish lesbian" of Yu Dafu's era.

If this analysis of the symbol of the infected feet supports the common reading of "Zero Degree" as a closeted "T text" in which the apparently male narrator is legible as a masculine-identified woman pursuing another woman, then the painful, bandaged feet suggest a further association. In light of such a reading, the imagery of bandaged body parts brings to mind the subcultural T practice of breast binding. Antonia Yengning Chao has analyzed this widespread practice in detail in her ethnographic study of early 1990s T/*po* bar cultures in Taiwan.[52] As Chao's research shows, the physical modification among Ts of their breast shape in order to have it signify "T-ness" rather than normative femininity is an often excruciating practice. Chao quotes one T informant's description:

> I started to use scotch tape to bind my breasts at fourteen. In summertime when I tore the tape off, there would pour a basinful of sweat. I was waitressing at a restaurant back then and was required to hold plates above my head while catering to patrons. After a while, my armpits hurt like hell. It sometimes bled after I tore off the tape. Next morning before it was healed up I bound my breasts again. As a result, it was never healed over.[53]

The entangled chains of association in Qiu's story that link feet, infection, bandages, and sexual desire between women find another point of reference in this subcultural practice, whose description above recognizably echoes Qiu's narrator's descriptions of his agonizing struggles in bandaging his infected feet. Following this associative chain to its conclusion, the "male" narrator's feet also connote the bound and painful T breast as subcultural signifier of T gender. Once again, the pathological body is symptomatic of the stigma of the ambiguously gendered, same-sex-attracted woman. In Goffman's terms, the T's "spoiled identity" is etched painfully into the very flesh of Qiu's narrator's feet and mouth.

Conclusion

As Qiu's critics have argued, her literary project of representing sexual subjects constituted through spoiled identity does undeniably raise troublesome questions. But as Qiu's fiction itself so powerfully attests, what is required is not the suppression of these questions, relating as they do to what remain among the central experiences of queer life (stigmatization, shame, subjective injury, psychic abjection). Rather, such troublesome questions require further elaboration in order to arrive at more sensitive understandings of the lived experience of variously abjected sexual and gendered subjects, and, through such an understanding, to work toward the transformation, rather than the disavowal, of such negative experience. The strange, violently uneasy bodies that inhabit these early stories by Qiu—painful, stigmatic, out-of-control bodies—can be read as expressive vehicles for the particular cultural contradictions besetting feminine subjects engaged in elaborating counternormative forms of gender and sexuality in Taiwan at the beginning of the 1990s. These contradictions arise not only between dominant and subordinated forms of sexual culture, but also between the various and sharply discontinuous forms of minority sexual culture. In this case, the subjects of local sexual subcultures produced through the secondary genders of T and *po,* may become targets of homophobic abjection by the globalizing rhetoric of lesbian feminism with its emphasis on "woman-identification."[54] Thus the textual bodies of Qiu's early narrators, bodies both tormented and defined by their alarming supernatural tendencies and pathological symptoms, are themselves symptomatic of a wider cultural crisis over the relations between gender and sexuality in late twentieth-century Taiwan. Haunted hair, infected feet, a stigmatic mouth—all can be seen not so much as symptoms of the T body's inherent pathology and deficiency, but, on the contrary, as a prescription directed at those multifarious forms of cultural regulation that collude to render some selves, some bodies, effectively uninhabitable.

Notes

My grateful thanks to Larissa Heinrich, for her wonderfully smart and helpful comments on an earlier draft of this chapter. An Australian Research Council Discovery Grant supported this research.

1. Liou Liang-ya compares Qiu with Hall in *Yuwang gengyishi* (p. 112). Ta-wei Chi criticizes Qiu's reliance on a masculine homoerotic imaginary in *Wan'an* (pp. 137-154). For a discussion of the cultural context in late-1980s Taipei that spawned such a passionate interest in European intellectual and particularly film culture, see the article by Qiu's friend Lai Hsiang-yin, "Youyu Beidi" (thanks to Chen "Deadcat" Yushin and Wang Ying for drawing this article to my attention). To speculate on one possible transnational influence from a less masculinist source: There is a really striking resonance between Qiu's story "Platonic Hair," discussed here, and a painting by Frida Kahlo entitled "Self-Portrait with Cropped Hair" (1940). The painting is of a newly shorn Kahlo dressed in a man's suit, surrounded by the eerily alive-looking fallen ends of her own cropped hair, and the image incorporates the Spanish text of a Mexican song that translates, "You see, if I loved you, it was for your hair, now that you are without hair, I love you no longer"—a theme that is taken up very directly in the opening scene of Qiu's story. The apparent transcultural conversation between Qiu's story and Kahlo's painting is intriguing, but unfortunately unverifiable.

2. Liou, *Yuwang gengyishi,* 83-152.

3. In the remainder of this essay I refrain from calling the sexual subject that begins to surface in Qiu's early stories a "lesbian" one. Although the sexological neologisms *nütongxing'ai* and *nütongxinglian* ("female homosexuality") have been in circulation in Mandarin since early in the twentieth century (Sang, *Emerging Lesbian*, 99-126), nevertheless, in late 1980s and early 1990s Taiwan when Qiu wrote these stories, the politicized discourse of lesbian sexual identity, referenced in the newer term *nütongzhi,* was only just beginning to produce a subculture capable of effectively challenging existing, local, female homoerotic cultures based on T and *po* gender roles. See discussion below.

4. Martin, *Situating Sexualities,* 215-251.

5. See for example Halberstam, *Female Masculinity,* 111-139.

6. Martin, *Situating Sexualities.*

7. This historicizing argument was initially proposed in Ding and Liu's essay, "Crocodile Skin." Ding and Liu's essay provides a primary inspiration for this chapter.

8. Sang, *Emerging Lesbian,* 99-160.

9. However, as Sang underlines, the "homoerotic school romance" genre constituted another, very different Republican-period tendency and portrayed love between women in a highly idealized manner.

10. Sang mentions this story very briefly in *Emerging Lesbian* (pp. 153-154).

11. Yu, "Ta shi yige ruo nüzi," 281-282.

12. Ibid., 308.

13. Ibid., 310.

14. McMahon, *Misers,* 44.

15. See also Ding, *Obscene Things,* 241; and Martin, *Situating Sexualities,* 119-140, on Taiwanese author Chen Xue's queer redeployment of the *enü.*

16. Foucault, *History of Sexuality*, 101.

17. Thanks to Wang Ying and Chen Yushin for their timely reminder on the significance of this latter point.

18. Chao, "Embodying the Invisible"; Zheng, *Nü'er quan,* 130–151; Gian, "Huanchu nütongzhi," 79–99. See also Lü, "Taiwan nütongzhi jiubazhi yanjiu."

19. Zheng, *Nü'er quan,* 130–131; Chao, "Embodying the Invisible," 17; Lü, "Taiwan nütongzhi jiubazhi yanjiu."

20. Chao, "Embodying the Invisible," 17; Zheng, *Nü'er quan,* 132.

21. Chao, "Embodying the Invisible," 30, 37–38, 155.

22. Ding and Liu, "Crocodile Skin." See also Chao, "US Space Shuttles."

23. See also Zheng, *Nü'er quan,* 136; Gian, "Huanchu nütongzhi," 99–107; and Chao, "Embodying the Invisible," 137–141.

24. Gian includes a table with twenty-four such microclassifications in "Huanchu nütongzhi," 94–95.

25. Ibid., 80–81.

26. See also Zheng, *Nü'er quan,* 145.

27. Put another way, these T subjects are unintelligible in terms of what Butler calls the "heterosexual matrix." *Gender Trouble*, 16ff.

28. Ding and Liu, "Crocodile Skin," 4.

29. Newton, *Margaret Mead*, 176–88; Newton, *Mother Camp,* xii; and Edelman, *Homographesis*, 3–23.

30. Goffman, *Stigma,* 9.

31. Ibid., 14–15, 57–128.

32. Ibid., 18.

33. See my translation of Qiu's "Platonic Hair," in Martin (trans.), *Angelwings,* 51–73.

34. Qiu, "Platonic Hair," 60.

35. Liou, *Yuwang gengyishi,* 126.

36. Qiu, "Platonic Hair," 55.

37. Liou, *Yuwang gengyishi,* 125.

38. "Erotic identity" is Newton and Walton's term. "Misunderstanding," 167–175. Like the hair symbol, the mirror symbol recurs throughout the story.

39. Qiu, "Platonic Hair," 60 (emphasis added).

40. Ibid., 72 (emphasis added).

41. See Halberstam, *Female Masculinity*, 20–29.

42. Newton and Walton, "Misunderstanding," 168; Halberstam, *Female Masculinity,* 129–138.

43. Lü, *"Taiwan nütongzhi jiubazhi yanjiu,"* 6–7.

44. Sedgwick, *Epistemology,* 87–88.

45. See note 32 above.

46. Liou, *Yuwang gengyishi,* 119; Ding and Liu, "Crocodile Skin," 7–8.

47. Qiu, "Linjiedian," 8.

48. Ibid., 15.

49. Ibid., 5.

50. Ibid., 13.

51. See, for example, Heinrich, "Handmaids," 267–269.
52. Chao, "Embodying the Invisible," 137–185.
53. Ibid., 151–152.
54. On localizing and globalizing rhetorics in relation to the debate between T/*po* and *bu fen* discourses, see Chao, "US Space Shuttles."

CHAPTER 12

Informationalized Affect
The Body in Taiwanese Digital
Video Puppetry and COSplay

TERI SILVIO

WHEN THE TRADITIONAL southern Chinese hand-puppet theater, *po-te-hi*,[1] was adapted for Taiwanese television in 1970, then to digital video in the 1990s, the genre underwent a revolution, not only in its style, but in the composition of its audience. Traditional *po-te-hi*, which has been performed at Taiwanese temple festivals since the nineteenth century, attracted a mostly male and rural audience, and by the 1960s, this audience tended to be elderly as well. Television *po-te-hi*, however, attracted audiences that had never been interested in traditional puppetry—urbanites, young people, and women. The introduction of digital technology in the mid-1990s saw a further increase in the young female audience.

Today, the most popular of several digital video *po-te-hi* serials are those produced by the Pili International Multimedia Company. According to the Pili Company's publicity, their DVDs reach an audience of over one million, and their official fan club has between 20,000 and 40,000 members.[2] The Pili serials combine traditional puppeteering skills, Hong Kong action cinema's frenetic editing style, and computer-generated graphics and special effects. The stories are in the *wuxia*, or knight-errant genre, with added elements of science fiction and mythology (Fig. 12.1). The Pili world is currently inhabited by flying Daoist swordsmen, Buddhist monks who can cause earthquakes with a flick of the wrist, spider-women and fox-men, elf-eared magicians, Japanese demons, vampires who dress like eighteenth-century French courtiers, clowns, gods, talking dragons, and cyborgs from another dimension.

COSplay (short for "costume play") is one of the most popular activities with the Pili serials' female fans. Today, on any sunny weekend in the parks of Taiwan's cities or at large media fan conventions, one can find groups of (mostly) women in their twenties dressed in the elaborate and fantastic costumes of their puppet "idols," taking photos of each other. In this essay, I will

FIGURE 12.1. Pili poster image. Used by permission of Pili International Multimedia Company.

address the following questions: What does it mean to dress up as a puppet? Why has puppetry become popular with young women at this particular time? Why does COSplay appeal primarily to young women? What can the Pili serials and Pili COSplay tell us about how the body and the self are being reconceptualized by Taiwan's "e-generation"?[3]

According to the Pili Company's statistics, 65 percent of the fan club is between the ages of 18 and 25.[4] I have found the average age of Pili COSplayers to be 24 and around 90 percent of the fans to be female. The fans who do COSplay are thus mostly young women in the process of "entering society" — in the period between graduation from school and settling down in a career and possibly marriage. They are members of the first generation to grow up surrounded by computer technology and to be facing a postindustrial job market. I see Pili COSplay as a uniquely Taiwanese response to the gender effects of globalization.

As in other parts of the "developed" world, Taiwan has seen a shrinking of the agricultural and manufacturing sectors accompanied by a rise in the service and the high-tech/information sectors in the past thirty years.[5] Hardt and Negri have argued that these trends have led to an increasing "immaterialization" of labor and the products of labor. They note two different types of labor driving the current economy: "the immaterial labor of analytic and symbolic tasks" and the "production and manipulation of affect [that] requires (virtual or actual) human contact, labor in the bodily mode."[6] In terms of who does what work, these types of labor tend to be gendered. That is, analytic and symbolic tasks such as software design are dominated by men, while jobs that require bodily production of affect (what Arlie Hochschild called the "emotional work" of monitoring one's own and others' moods or "the presentation of self," in Erving Goffman's terms) are (still) dominated by women.[7]

What I am most interested in here is the way these two modes of immaterial labor are bleeding into each other, at both the levels of ideology and practice. Hardt and Negri note that on the one hand, the ideology of "information" is spreading out from the high-tech sector proper, as factories, schools, government bureaus, and business offices are all becoming computerized. At the same time, areas of work formerly distinct from the service sector, including manufacturing, are being redefined as providing a "service."

Based on my interviews with fans participating in Pili events, I found the majority of these women had clerical jobs (26 percent), followed closely by sales (21 percent).[8] Eighteen percent of the women were teachers (mostly elementary school and kindergarten). There were also several copy editors and a number of women trying to break into the fashion and entertainment industries. There were roughly equal, very small, numbers in factory labor and in the fields of science and engineering. Thus, most of these women are in, or training for, traditional "pink collar" or culture industry jobs that are in the process of being informationalized. They therefore face increasing pressure to be competent in *both* the bodily production of affect *and* in immaterial analytic and symbolic tasks.[9]

In many ways, Pili fandom parallels global processes of boundary blurring between bodily-affective and analytic-symbolic, masculine and feminine, labor. While women fans have reframed a traditionally masculine genre within a fan culture dominated by performance, writing, and visual genres marked as feminine, fan productions are also deeply structured by the digital techno-culture that has transformed *po-te-hi*. I argue that COSplay is a site where this generation of Taiwanese women negotiates the gap between the immateriality of the techno-culture that surrounds them and the embodied nature of the work they are actually expected to do, both in the workplace and at home. But COSplay does not simply "bring the body back" into an increasingly virtual world. Rather, it models the bodily production of affect in a specifically informational way.

After a brief introduction to the Pili serials and Pili fan culture, I will first look at how character is constructed within the Pili serials, and then how Pili characters are re-constructed in COSplay. I argue that digital-video *po-te-hi* and COSplay construct characters in a way that draws out similarities between traditional Chinese performance aesthetics and the binary logic of computer language. Three aspects of character construction are key: first, the striation of character into distinct modalities—voice, movement, physical form, costume, etc.—each of which is conceived as a medium for a distinct Saussurian code; second, the construction of affect through a combination of theatrical and cinematic codes; and third, the necessary passage of the character between a variety of media, a constant back and forth between two- and three-dimensionality, animation, and performance.

Background: The Pili Serials and Pili Fandom

Po-te-hi, a genre of southern Chinese hand-puppet theater, originated in Fujian Province, and legend traces it back to the Ming dynasty (roughly to the mid-sixteenth century). It was probably brought to Taiwan by settlers in the early eighteenth century and has been a popular entertainment at Taiwanese temple festivals ever since. The narratives for traditional *po-te-hi* performances are taken from classic vernacular fiction, particularly the *Romance of the Three*

Kingdoms and *Journey to the West*. The genre is performed in the Holo (Hokkien) language, the mother tongue of around 80 percent of the Taiwanese population. In the 1950s and 1960s, *po-te-hi* began to be performed as a commercial theater genre as well as at temple festivals. At this time, puppeteers began to adapt narratives from *wuxia* (martial arts) novels, to use more popular musical forms, and to use special effects such as dry ice, special lighting, and mechanical sets. One of the most influential puppeteers in developing this style of *po-te-hi* was Huang Haidai.[10]

The first Taiwanese television station, the Taiwan Television Company (TTV) began broadcasting in 1962. Although *po-te-hi* was televised in the 1960s, television *po-te-hi* did not really become its own genre until March 1970, when Huang Haidai's son, Huang Junxiong, produced his first series for TTV, *Yunzhou Da Ru Xia—Shi Yanwen (Shi Yanwen, the Confucian Swordsman of Yunzhou)*. Previously, televised *po-te-hi* had captured around 70 percent ratings, but Huang's serial achieved an unprecedented 97 percent.[11] Even though the Government Information Office severely restricted Taiwanese dialect programming between 1974 and 1982, the series kept going on VHS video.

Between 1984 and 1990, Huang Junxiong began to work with his sons Huang Wenzi and Huang Qianghua, and under their influence the *Shi Yanwen* series gradually segued into the Pili series, in which the brothers began to develop their own unique style.[12] In 1994 Huang Junxiong completely handed over the troupe to his sons, who established the Pili International Multimedia Company. Huang Qianghua is the company's CEO *(dongshizhang)* and the director of the script-writing group. Huang Wenze is the company's general manager *(zongjingli)*, and the artist who records all the voices of the Pili puppet characters.

In a studio built by their father in the Huang family's rural hometown of Hu Wei, the company began releasing the Pili serials on VHS. The Pili Company produced a feature film in 1991 based on the serials, *Sheng Shi Chuanshuo (Legend of the Sacred Stone)*. The film led to a distinct change in the style of the serials, since the digital cameras, editing equipment and software, and many technicians, brought in for the film were subsequently retained by the company. In 2000 the company switched the serials' weekly releases from VHS to DVD.

Each Pili serial consists of thirty to sixty one-hour episodes. Each episode continues the story from the previous one, and continuity is maintained by the presence of a few longstanding characters and themes, and by the practice of ending each episode and each serial with a cliff-hanger. Currently, the company has four production teams working around the clock, and releases approximately two one-hour episodes every week. Pili DVDs are distributed through over 1800 rental stores across Taiwan (approximately 90 percent of all DVD rental stores stock the Pili serials) and reach an audience of at least one million.[13]

Cable television was legalized in 1994, and the Pili Company also established their own satellite station in 1995, with reruns of earlier series as the primary offering. The company also produces, in cooperation with other companies, a wide range of tie-in products, including music CDs, video games, books, and toys.

Pili Fandom and COSplay

Fans of the Pili series began to contact each other and organize, mostly via the Internet and university BBS (Bulletin Board Service) web sites, around 1994. The company has taken great pains to maintain contact with them. Around 1995 fans began to organize themselves into clubs. At their request, the company founded the official Pili Fan Club. Aside from its glossy monthly magazine, the company also maintains a web site and publishes an electronic newsletter for its members. Once the club was established, fans began to organize booster clubs for individual puppet "stars," and again the company helped them set up formal organizations with elected officers. Aside from the official fan club, there are dozens of unofficial ones, including school organizations and smaller private clubs organized via the Internet or friendship networks. There are Internet Pili fan clubs in mainland China and Japan as well.[14]

The practice of COSplay is closely linked to the youth subculture of *tongrenzhi*, or fan fiction and art, which was adopted from Japan (the Japanese term is *dojin*). Japanese manga and anime conventions became extremely popular in the 1990s, and in 1997 the first such Taiwanese conventions were organized. Taiwanese animation fans started doing COSplay of Japanese manga and anime characters at this time, and Pili fans began to COSplay Pili characters shortly after.[15] (Figs. 12.2 and 12.3)

Pili fans currently engage in a wide range of activities, including drawing manga (cartoons), creating animated cartoons using programs such as FLASH, writing short stories about the characters, collecting and photographing puppets, making original music videos starring the puppets, and participating in COSplay. These activities tend to be gender-specific. Women fans prefer writing short stories, drawing cartoons, and COSplay, while male fans are more interested in digital editing and amateur puppetry and vocal imitations, although there are many exceptions. Collecting and photographing puppets seems to be a shared passion.

FIGURE 12.2. COSplayers. Photograph by Huang Lingyi. Used by permission.

Part I: The Ontology of the Pili Character

The Pili diegesis is created through the blending of three different media—puppetry, video, and digital animation—each with its own very different way of conceptualizing character. In this section, I want to discuss various ways in which Pili negotiates the tensions created by this blending.

Traditional Theater Codes and Computer Codes

Traditional *po-te-hi*, like virtually all genres of Chinese folk performance, divides individual characters into a limited set of role types. The primary division is between the male *(sheng)* and female *(dan)* roles. The characters are

FIGURE 12.3. COSplayers. Photograph by Huang Lingyi. Used by permission.

then classified through further binary choices between literary and military, good and evil, young and old, aristocratic and commoner, comic and heroic. In the Pili serials, further distinctions are made between human and non-human; Confucian, Buddhist, or Daoist; Chinese, Japanese, or Western, et cetera.

Each of these paradigmatic choices necessitates the selection of specific sets of codes in different modalities—language, voice, movement, costume, facial features, music—each of which is the responsibility of a different unit within the Pili production team. The Pili production process starts with a script. Once the script is written, it is sent to Huang Wenze, who starts working on the voices, and to the "appearance bureau" *(zaoxing zu)*, which starts to construct the puppets. Independently contracted carvers see the script and sometimes sketches drawn by the script group, then present a set of heads for selection. The costume bureau and props bureau then create costumes, wigs, and weapons for the characters. The script is also sent to the music group, which composes a signature tune for each character as well as theme music for the credits and background music for various types of scenes. Once the dialogue and music have been recorded and the puppets are completed, filming begins. Puppeteers manipulate the puppets while listening to the voice-track, and the director *(daobo)* directs them and the cameraman from a booth. The *daobo* simultaneously edits and commands a set of digital special effects that can be inserted during this preliminary editing. Once a scene is shot, it is sent to postproduction, where background music and more elaborate special effects, such as digital animation, are added.

The sense of a character's coherence is dependent on all these codes "fitting" together. In other words, a character who spoke in the deep voice characteristic of the military male role, but who used the fluid, continuous gestures of the female role would be considered "mismatched" or "incoherent" *(bu xietiao)*. The Pili artists, of course, often use such mismatches to create more complex or unusual characters, but the mismatches must still "fit" at a higher level.

This system is highly compatible with that used by software designers to create various computer "agents." In *Computers as Theatre*, Brenda Laurel argues that human-computer interactions are "theatrical," using Aristotelian aesthetics. She writes that characters in drama and human and computer agents are structurally similar.

> In drama, character may be defined as bundles of traits, predispositions, and choices that, when taken together, form coherent entities. . . . Traits circumscribe the actions (or kinds of actions) that an agent has the capability to perform, thereby defining the agent's potential. There are two kinds of traits: traits that determine how an agent can act (internal traits) and traits that represent those internal predispositions (external traits). . . . Traits function as a kind of cognitive shorthand that allows people to predict and comprehend agents' actions.[16]

The conceptualization of character as a bundle of traits determined by choices among different Saussurian paradigmatic sets is evident not only in the organization of the production company, but in the character "résumés" that appear in both books published by the company and in the fans' web sites and posters. These résumés resemble character descriptions featured in many role-playing games or on Pokemon cards. They usually include a photo of the character and a list of characteristics: place of origin, place of residence, organization, teachers, students, kin relations, weapons, skills, the poem or mantra the character recites when he or she enters *(chu chang shi, kou chan)*, and often a list of personality traits (e.g., "hot-tempered," "gentle," "loyal"). In other words, the résumés make explicit the interior traits symbolized by the exterior traits of appearance, vocal quality, and so forth.

Striation vs. Organicity

Where is the body in this proliferation of Saussurian codes? In his influential essays on Japanese *bunraku* puppetry, Roland Barthes distinguished *bunraku* from Western theater in terms of the ontology of character and the place of the body in creating that ontology. He writes:

> The basis of our [western] theatrical art is indeed much less the illusion of reality than the illusion of totality . . . we conceive lyric art as the simultaneity of several expressions (acted, sung, mimed), whose origin is unique, indivisible. This origin is the body, and the totality insisted on has for its model the body's organic unity.[17]

Bunraku, on the other hand, dispenses with the organic trope. In this tradition the puppet, the puppeteers who manipulate it, and the reciter of the dialogue are simultaneously visible on the stage.

> Bunraku thus practices three separate writings, which it offers to be read simultaneously in three sites of the spectacle. . . . By the discontinuity of the codes, by this caesura imposed on the various features of representation, . . . the copy elaborated on the stage is not destroyed but somehow broken, striated, withdrawn from that metonymic contagion of voice and gesture, body and soul, which entraps our actors.[18]

I believe it is no coincidence that Barthes wrote these essays in the early 1970s, at the dawn of the information age. For *bunraku* provides a "meta" perspective on the body as a semiotic medium that is very similar to that provided by electronic media, particularly when they are new. Although Barthes' fascination with *bunraku* is often read as Orientalism, we could also see it as an early harbinger of the more idealist readings of the potential of the digital media for deconstructing the Western concept of the individual, and of our current fascination with postorganic bodies of various sorts, from cyborgs to "synthespians."

In traditional *po-te-hi*, unlike *bunraku*, the puppeteers are partially hidden behind the stage, and they are completely hidden in the video version. However, the fans' fascination with the backstage workings of the Pili Company, their interest in amateur puppetry, trips to the studio, and so on, indicate that they are quite conscious of the way that aspects of the character are separated in production. Following Barthes' argument, we might hypothesize that the striation of codes in *po-te-hi* creates a certain alienation effect, that it refuses any illusions of a necessary unity to the body, or organic wholeness to the personality. I should note that I am not claiming that the Chinese theater presents the same sort of illusion of psychic "reality" as the Western ("our") theater does. However, the Chinese theater does ground the character's ontology in the organic body—particularly the disciplined body, as I shall discuss later. The modality-striation of *po-te-hi* provides an alternative model of the self that is equally Chinese. Chris Bolton has elegantly argued that the philosophical cyborgs of Japanese anime are best read through the metaphysics of *bunraku*.[19] I would like to make a similar argument here. In combining traditional puppetry with digital technology and playing on the resonances between the aesthetics of Chinese theater and the logics of computer language, Pili both maintains (one set of) culturally specific conceptions of the self *and* provides a resource for negotiating metaphysical challenges posed by the introduction of new globalized technologies.

I will now discuss some of the separate aspects of Pili and how they mediate between puppetry and the digital media.

Puppet Bodies

Changes in the Pili style have had the effect of endowing its characters with an increasing sense of corporeality, if not organic unity. This is most obvious in changes to features of the puppets. One of the primary changes reflects the direction of developments in digital animation—the puppets have become increasingly three-dimensional. The carved faces, especially since production of the feature film, have more planes and wrinkles than the earlier puppet heads. Japanese animation has greatly influenced the Pili artists, and the new puppet cast features abundant spiky hair, long noses, cleft chins, and pointy elf-ears. The demon or cyborg characters have even more protrusions—tentacles, mandibles, and spikes of all sorts (Fig. 12.4). Main characters who have been part of the series since the 1980s, such as Su Huanzhen and Ye Xiaochai, change

FIGURE 12.4. Pili insect-monster puppet. Used by permission of Pili International Multimedia Company.

their look regularly (e.g., old puppets are replaced with new ones), but they must retain their original features. Fans now refer to the older puppets, with their comparatively flat features, as having "cookie faces."

The puppet bodies have also become more visible, more three-dimensional. Traditional puppet costumes are robes that hang from a line across the shoulders; large, stiff epaulets are distinctive of the puppets of the 1970s and 80s. The new Pili costumes soften or remove these epaulets. In the late 1990s characters who wore trousers rather than the traditional robe were introduced, and now most male and some female characters have visible legs. Pili has also introduced both male and female characters with three-dimensional breastplates. Pili *po-te-hi* also heightens the corporeal effect of the puppets by indexing the existence of internal organs beneath the wooden "skin." The puppets can weep, bleed, and spit, and indeed, tears, blood, and poison flow in profusion.

Another trend in the development of Pili style is the increased articulation and mobility of the puppets. One of Huang Junxiong's major changes in adapting *po-te-hi* to television was making the puppets twice the traditional size and giving them movable elbows, wrists, knees, eyelids and lips. The Pili Company has continued to increase the puppets' articulated parts. They have hands made of rubber over wire (rather than wood), and the fingers can be bent individually. Characters can now realistically imitate Huang Feihong's "no-shadow kick," make distinct gestures (slow, angry closings of the fist; Buddhist "lotus fingers"; writing magical Daoist characters in the air) and wink. The greater size and number of articulated parts in the puppets has also necessitated the development of a new style of puppeteering, which brings the puppeteer's entire body into play. When seen in live performance or working in the studio, Pili puppeteers often seem to be dancing. Ironically perhaps, the more invisible the human body becomes, the more "organically" it moves.

Voice: Anchoring Pili in the Local

Tension between organic unity and the distance created by striation is most vivid in the video *po-te-hi*'s voice track. One unique feature of the Pili serials, which separates them from other video *po-te-hi* serials, is the fact that all the voices, young and old, male and female, human and other, are recorded by one man, Huang Wenze, the "Eight-Tone Genius." Every attempt by the company to vary this—for instance, having a group of actors record different characters' voices—has been rejected by the fans. As one member of the production staff put it, "It's like a superstition. If it isn't Huang Wenze's voice, the fans won't accept it." This may be the only aspect of the Pili videos that emphasizes, rather than occludes, the modality-striation of traditional *po-te-hi*. In most traditional *po-te-hi* troupes, the leader of the troupe is the artist who does the voices, while apprentices manipulate the puppets.

One of the effects of Huang Wenze's recording, I believe, is that it makes the corporeal voice the center from which a sense of organic unity extends into all the other codes. Another effect is that it ties this organic unity to the nation. The association of Huang Wenze's voice with national identity is partly related to the fact that contemporary Taiwanese ethno-nationalism posits the Taiwanese dialect as the sign of indigenousness. But there is more to it than that. The melding of the voice, the organic body, and the nation was made clear to me during a dinner with a group of young women fans. They told me that the Pili Company was trying to train the youngest Huang brother to do voice recording. But, they told me, he was raised in the US. As one woman parodied his "American" voice—saying typical Pili lines in a rap rhythm, adding the occasional "Yo!"—she brought her whole body into the performance, punctuating lines with the diagonal, downward pointing hand-thrust and nodding head of an African-American hip-hop singer. When I have seen fans imitating Huang Wenze's voice, on the other hand, their gestures are those of local opera or the circular head-motion of Confucian recitation. Vocalization leads naturally to gesture, and gesture expresses a distinctly, and consciously, local habitus.

Movement and Stillness: Opera and Cinema

The sense that the Pili characters are moving, and thus "alive," comes from two very different sources—the puppeteers' manipulation of the puppets and the movement of the video camera. In traditional *po-te-hi,* puppet movements imitate the highly stylized gestures of Chinese opera. Each role type has a specific repertoire of movements, each of which indexes the character's sex, age, and social position. The still pose, or *liang xiang,* is critical to this nonrealist opera style. The *liang xiang* is usually performed at the end of a sequence of movements, and encapsulates the essence of a character's qualities and state of mind.

According to Gilles Deleuze, the cinematic reproduction of movement is fundamentally opposed to any media which reconstitutes motion through a series of immobile images, with each image representing a "privileged instant," a transcendental ideal form. In contrast, the cinema, by presenting a series of equidistant "any-instant-whatevers," abstracts motion itself.[20] When Pili characters make a dramatic entrance, these two modes of reconstituting movement are combined. The puppet performs a *liang xiang*. Yet this "ideal form" image is placed into the real time of cinema by the movement of the camera, which often presents a series of moving, but fragmented shots of different parts of the character's body from a variety of angles, or pans around the puppet.

The fight scenes, for which Pili is famous, combine the stylized movements and flight of traditional puppeteering with the cinematic editing style of Hong Kong action films. Over the years, the shots in the Pili fight sequences have gotten increasingly shorter and more varied in terms of angle, increasing the effect of a sense of speed, mobility, and fragmented point of view.[21] The simultaneous, constant motion of both puppets and camera creates an impression of pure kinesis. This often hinders following the narrative and identifying with the characters, and this is one reason that the Pili serials retain the stage convention that all fight scenes are accompanied by a voice-over describing the action and the protagonists' feelings.

Affect: The Puppet Close-Up

If the striation of aspects in Pili de-naturalizes the relationship between the body's coherence and that of the character, this is only one element of a tension that is crucial to both puppetry and the digital media generally—that between intellectual distance and emotional identification. As one Pili fan succinctly put it to me: "It's obviously completely fake, but when your favorite character dies you still feel really sad." Fans know perfectly well that the puppets are mere constructions of wood, cloth, and audiotape; nevertheless, the characters are very real to them, and Pili fans are famous for their extreme emotional attachment to their favorite characters.[22] Where does this emotional investment come from?

The "cinematization" (*dianyinghua*) of Pili's aesthetics both creates and alienates emotion. The cinematic codes of framing and distance in the Pili videos do not individuate characters, but rather create affect. This is particularly true of the close-up, which Deleuze identifies as the "affection-image." Intense emotion is indicated by the close-up of the puppet face, and all of the micro-gestures that indicate emotion—the eyes closing, the fist curling up, the placement of a hand on a sword hilt—are shot in close-up.

Deleuze notes that the close-up has the ability to turn the human face into a pure object, and likewise to "facify" objects.[23] The puppet face is both a human face and piece of wood, and there is something both highly redundant and absolutely overdetermined in the close-up of the puppet face—an object objectified, a face "facified." The close-up of the puppet, then, allows for the viewer's projection of emotion, but at the same time makes her aware that she is projecting onto a thing, a nonorganic palimpsest of codes, that this affect comes always simultaneously from inside and outside the self. The puppet close-up embodies the idea that affect is cultural, that the codes by which we communicate emotion are always exterior to us, even when we are experiencing that emotion most intensely and personally.

Part II: COSplay

Between Puppetry and Opera

I divide the current practice of COSplay into two main types: posing for photographs and performance. Fans dress as the Pili characters and pose for photographs in two venues. They attend large *tongrenzhi* (fan) conventions with thousands of others and also organize their own smaller COS-photography sessions. COS performances are done at fan club events and take the form of skits and dances. The skits are almost always comic, and their dominant themes are display and gender reversal. Many narratives involve the male characters competing in some sort of fashion show *(zuo xiu)*, which is judged or commented on by female characters. In dance performances, female characters tend to follow the "national dance" style based on Chinese opera movements, while male characters either do choreographed sword-fighting routines to Pili theme music, or Japanese *para-para* line dances to popular music.

In Taiwan, as in many Asian societies, puppetry developed in tandem with opera *(xiqu)*, drawing on the same set of semiotic codes and presenting narratives derived from the same mythical and historical sources. In terms of its simultaneous embodiment and regendering of the Pili characters, COSplay might be seen as a continuation of this historical relationship. In many ways, COSplay draws on and resembles *koa-a-hi*,[24] the most popular genre of Taiwanese dialect opera. Like *koa-a-hi*, COSplay is performed primarily by and for women, with women playing both the male and female roles, setting up men-embodied-by-women as spectacular objects for female enjoyment. I have argued that *koa-a-hi* and its fan culture provide a space where Taiwanese women can "rehearse" gender roles necessary under a specific regime of modernity based on women's historical movement from domestic to public space.[25] To a certain extent, COSplay can be seen as continuing this function.

Yet there are also significant differences, and COSplay is by no means a traditional transfer of content from puppetry to theater. While *koa-a-hi* flourished in the broadcast media of radio, cinema, and television, in the digital age it is increasingly confined to the stage. I believe the differences between *koa-a-hi* and COSplay are instructive in showing how the nature of women's production of affect has transformed along with Taiwan's technoculture.

The most striking difference between COSplay and *koa-a-hi* lies in what is seen to authorize the ontology of the characters. In *koa-a-hi*, it is the disciplined body that does this. The character is seen as an extension of the actress's persona, a corporeal presence created through the mutual influence of innate characteristics and physical training, which extends into her offstage comportment. An experienced actress operates the codes of movement and vocalization unconsciously. Simply putting on a costume is not enough to "enter into" a character; the role must penetrate the actress's muscles.[26]

In Pili COSplay, the embodied performance is remodeled after the construction of the character in the Pili serials. The COSed character is striated by the separation of corporeal form/surface, movement, and voice. While in the Pili videos the puppets have become increasingly humanized (i.e., more organic), in COSplay, the humans become puppetized. Affect is created by combining *liang xiang* and the codes of glamour photography.

The Voice in COSplay

One of the most striking aspects of COSplay performances is the disconnect between voice and body, even the virtual disappearance of the voice, as a feature of most COSplay. It is rare for COSers at conventions or photo outings to speak in character. They say they try to maintain the character's dignity through an absence of incoherent speech or laughter, rather than through any positive vocal performance style.

In most COS skits at fan club events, the script is prerecorded (either by a group of fans or by one [male] fan), and the COSers lip-synch to the tape. According to a former fan club officer who has been COSing Pili characters since 2000, in the first Pili COS skits the performers did recite their own lines. "But," she told me, "when the COSers picked up the microphone, well, they felt very happy, but the people in the audience didn't understand anything they were saying. Most of the players were women and they didn't have any voice training and couldn't speak clearly."[27] For the next COS performance, she found a male high school student who was particularly good at imitating Huang Wenze and had him do the dialogue recording in the studio. Vocalizing the Pili characters is an activity popular among male fans. As one put it, "Most boys will do the voices a little. Women's voices always sound like women's voices, but since the female characters' voices are done by men in *po-te-hi* anyway, it's easier for men." What I find somewhat disturbing about this is that the voice has become masculinized at the same time that it has become the center of the organic, localized self.

COSplay: Corporeality, Movement, and the Pose

When asked how important a person's figure is for COSplay, most fans agreed that what was most important was the "fit" between the body and the character being COSed. Fans frequently criticized COSers they thought were "too fat" to be playing hardened swordsmen, or, as one COSer told me, "There are some characters that are very cute, and round. If someone who's too skinny COSes them, it doesn't look right." They also said that skin color was important— a dark-skinned fan should not try to COS one of the pale elfin characters. This sense of "fit" is brought up most frequently in decisions about whether to COS male or female characters. Many of the women who COS female characters told me they did so because they were "too short" to play the male roles. Here, the discussion sometimes extends to questions of habitus; athleticism or a vague sense of being "unable to catch the flavor" of a role type may influence decisions on what characters to COS. This discourse of "fit" resembles very closely that of *koa-a-hi* actresses when they discuss why they specialize in a given role type, yet unlike the *koa-a-hi* actresses, COSers never speak of their COSplaying influencing their "offstage" habitus. I believe this is an effect of COSplay's puppetry-like striation of the body, particularly its restriction of the body to a mostly still surface.

At conventions, the majority of fans do not make any special effort to hold their bodies "in character" except when they are in front of a camera. As one fan put it, "The most important thing's the POSE."[28] Most COSers say that they have not studied any movement discipline; they learn the appropriate poses by watching the Pili videos and ancient-costume serial dramas, practicing in front of the mirror, and looking at photos of themselves and others posing in costume. When COSers do say they want to move "in character," they speak of it in terms of an absence of incoherent movement, rather than constructing a coherent movement style. Thus, some fans say that if they are in costume, particularly that of a swordsman, they will try to avoid "horsing around" as a matter of "respect for the character." The privileging of the pose is evident even in COSplay skits, in which the performers tend to pantomime their lines in a jerky series of poses, and subside into a sort of nervous nonaffect or emotional blankness when their character is not the focus of the action.

The main forms of physical movement with flow in COS performance are the dance and the sword routine. These performances are characterized by repetition—the movement sequences "loop." In marked contrast, at one large fan event the organizers hired a pair of modern dancers to do an interpretive piece based on the characters. The dancers, who were clearly influenced by the American school of modern dance, enacted a story of developing passion between two characters, frequently changing speed and mood. Some fans I spoke to afterwards found this dance "boring" and claimed not to "understand" it. I think this was because the modern dance was incongruous—neither its narrativity nor its movement style fit with their idea of what "playing the character" means. In general, COSplayers at conventions want to present, not inhabit, the characters.[29] COSplayers seem to be rejecting both organic unity in the form of disciplined habitus and the cinematic reconstruction of motion that places the human body within real, continuous time. They do not inhabit the character's bodies, nor allow those bodies any progression toward death and decay. Hillel Schwartz has argued that the aesthetics of American modern dance, with its emphasis on graceful flow of energy from a center of gravity out through the whole body, arose in tandem with industrialization and its fantasies of mechanization.[30] The aesthetics of modern dance, then, partake of a body-technology formation sandwiched between the pre-Fordist period, during which the aesthetics of traditional *po-te-hi* developed, and the post-Fordist present. Modern dance's organicism, then, appears doubly anachronistic vis-à-vis digital video *po-te-hi*.

If the Pili videos tend to cinematize puppetry in Deleuze's sense of abstracting motion, COSplay is photographic; it is all about capturing privileged instants of the immobile, transcendental Form of the character. Significantly, although there are thousands of cameras at *tongrenzhi* conventions, I have never seen a video camera there (except my own). COS photos almost always combine the pose, the lighting, and the framing codes of glamour photography. Virtually every COSer I interviewed claimed that COSplay would be meaningless without photography and that their greatest sense of achievement came from having many people photographing them, thus acknowledging that they had captured the essence of the character. This is perhaps the greatest indication that the transition from the stage to television to digital video—with the addition of a qualitatively new code, that of cinematic framing, to the traditional semiotics of puppetry—is having an impact on the experience of the body and self in the culture at large. The production of affect is increasingly dependent on codes exterior to, rather than absorbed into, the body.[31]

Remediation

Bolter and Grusin have noted that all new technologies of representation "remediate" older technologies and genres. They also note that digital technology is particularly intense in the scope and overlaying of its remediation. In order to fully understand the conception of the body emerging in the Pili serials and COSplay, we must put both in the context of contemporary Taiwanese media networks. Pili characters' ontology is ironically simultaneously solidified and diffused by their passage through a wide variety of media. Within the Pili videos, especially in the opening sequences, the characters appear not only as puppets but also as paintings and outline drawings. They also appear as digital animation in video games, and as tie-in figurines or stuffed toys. The passage of the characters between media is expanded within fan culture. At conventions one can see Pili characters not only as puppets and embodied by COSplayers but also as cartoons in a variety of styles, as kewpie dolls, and in photos of puppets and photos of dolls. Within the context of Pili culture as a whole, then, the body is one medium among many, and as such is inadequate in itself to create a whole self.

If intensive remediation is characteristic of digital technologies, it is also characteristic of Chinese cultural discourse. Thus, the Pili characters move through contemporary media in a way that closely resembles how characters from the *Sanguo yanyi* or the *Xiyou ji* have moved across the media of the novel, opera, puppetry, oral recitation, comics, and cinema since the late imperial era. Again, in the way that *po-te-hi* remediates, we can find a "traditional" model for addressing questions of representation and ontology that have (re)surfaced in the postmodern world.

Conclusion: The Body as Interface

Because interaction with the technologies of everyday life is one of the ways in which bodies become gendered, feminist scholars have argued that the introduction of new technologies always holds possibilities, both utopian and dystopian, for the transformation of cultural concepts of masculinity and femininity. Western feminist scholarship on the body in the information age has tended to focus on two fantasies that permeate cyberpunk fiction, academic cybernetic theory, and other speculative discourses around digital technology that are (sometimes) made manifest in the way people actually interact with computers. The first fantasy is of disembodiment, of the transcendence of mind over flesh by "downloading" human consciousness into a computer network, or simply of living one's life primarily in an on-line virtual world.[32] The second is the fantasy of transcending illness, weakness, and mortality itself through the merging of the human body with machine parts—what Alluquere Rosanne Stone calls "cyborg envy."[33] In the Western context of Christian ideology and Descartian scientism, these fantasies of transcendence take on misogynist undertones when the female body is denigrated as excessive, dumb, weak, and more resistantly thing-like than the male body.[34] Yet these fantasies of transcendence also have their feminist utopian side, holding the possibilities for the creation of ungendered, or serially gendered creatures and personas, and for the breakdown of Christian and Cartesian dichotomies.[35]

The fantasies of what the body could become emerging in Pili culture seem to be more about making the body a life-sized puppet, turning it into a material medium, than making it disappear or making it invulnerable. Perhaps the interface, a surface constructed of code that facilitates affective human communication via objects (machines) provides a more appropriate metaphor than the cyborg for the relationship between the body and technology in Taiwan. In Pili videos and fan culture, the body functions not as an organic totality, but as both a palimpsest of modalities in itself and as part of the palimpsest of the total network of available media. Depth of affect and personality become quantitative, measured in the density of the media they move through, rather than qualitative.

Katherine Hayles writes of the American cybernetic and sci-fi construction of the posthuman, "As though we had learned nothing from Derrida about supplementarity, embodiment continues to be discussed as if it were a supplement to be purged from the dominant term of information."[36] Both Pili and

COSplay are Saussurian, both in their "traditional folk art" aspect and in their "digital culture" aspect. Yet Derridean supplement is evident in the intensity of emotion attached to Pili characters. The body is not supplemental to the codes, existing prior to and outside them, it is one (inadequate) set of media through which the codes operate. And affect, supplement, and emotional intensity arise precisely in the interface of all of these proliferating modalities.

The pleasure in COSplay is not the *jouissance* of fragmenting identity described by frequent users of MUDs (multi-user domains), nor is it the pleasure of physical control and the sense of the body as an organic, expressive whole experienced by trained performers. Rather, it is the cool *plaisir* of playing with code. Given the gap between Taiwanese "e-generation" women's knowledge and skill in information technology and the ongoing expectation that they will be responsible for the vast majority of embodied, affective labor, there may be something quite restful in treating their bodies as a communicative interface through which emotion is transmitted, rather than experiencing them as the organic source of emotion subject to discipline. COSplay provides a model of and for how Taiwanese women can embody affect while still displaying their command of abstract information-processing skills.

Notes

Research for this project from July 2003 to July 2005 was funded by a grant from the National Science Council of Taiwan [Project # NSC93-2412-H-001-002]. I would like to thank all the fans and the workers at the Pili International Multimedia Company who allowed me to interview them. I am also deeply grateful to my research assistants, Huang Ling-yi, Hsu Tzu-yi, and Huang Wen-yi, and to the patient and generous people who read or listened to early drafts of this essay, particularly Ilana Gershon, Sara Friedman, Helen Gremillion, and the editors.

In keeping with anthropological ethics, I do not use the names of my interviewees (usually I only ask for their "fan names" anyway). Rather than use false names, I identify them by their position, e.g., "a former fan club officer."

For terms related to the traditional Taiwanese folk arts, I give the Holo pronunciation, using the romanization system developed by the Taipei Language Institute. For other terms, I use pinyin, except in the cases of proper names that have established spellings, such as Taipei.

1. In Mandarin, *budaixi*. For terms related to the traditional Taiwanese folk arts, I give the Holo pronunciation, using the romanization system developed by the Taipei Language Institute. For other terms, I use pinyin.

2. Pili, publicity pamphlet, 2002; head of the Pili Company fan club division, in an interview with the author.

3. This essay is based on fieldwork over the past three years, including interviews with

the staff of the Pili Company and with fans and participant-observation at a wide variety of fan club events.

4. Pili, publicity pamphlet, 2000.

5. See Huang, "Taiwan diqu de laodong zhuanxing"; Tseng, You, and Ho, "New Economy," on the transformation of the labor market. For statistics and more information on the historical development and structure of the Taiwanese economy, see the Government Information Office website ("Story of Taiwan").

6. Hardt and Negri, *Empire*, 293.

7. Hochschild, *Managed Heart;* Goffman, *Stigma.*

8. The most commonly cited occupation, *kuaiji,* refers to a broad range of actual jobs, ranging from secretary/receptionist to accountant.

9. Significantly, I found the majority of the men involved in Pili fan events and COSplay to be in, or training in, the fields of fashion design, advertising, and entertainment—largely "feminized" areas of symbolic labor that are particularly focused on the production of affect.

10. For an overview of the history of *po-te-hi* in Taiwan and Huang Haidai's place in it, see Jiang, "Budaixi"; Tsai, *Xian ge bu chuo.*

11. Wang, "Televised Puppetry"; Pili, "Pili guoji duo meiti qiye jie." Since there were only three television stations operating at the time, the 70 and 90 percent statistics are not as shocking as they may seem.

12. For a detailed account of Huang Junxiong's development of television *po-te-hi,* see Chen Longting, "Huang Junxiong."

13. Pili, publicity pamphlet. A project manager at Group Power, the company that has bought distribution rights for the Pili videos for 2004–2005, estimated that the Pili DVDs constitute 10 percent of a total market of approximately four billion NT. Telephone interview by author, September 29, 2003.

14. This history is compiled from interviews in 2002 and 2003 with fans and with the director of the official fan club.

15. See Su, "Tongren wenhua," for detailed history of *tongrenzhi* and COSplay in Japan and Taiwan.

16. Laurel, *Computers,* 60–61.

17. Barthes, *Empire,* 59.

18. Barthes, *Empire,* 49, 54–55.

19. Bolton, "Wooden Cyborgs."

20. Deleuze, *Cinema 1.*

21. In a comparison of two randomly selected fight scenes (one minute each), one from a 1994 serial, *Xin Yunzhou Da Ruxia,* produced by Huang Junxiong, and one from a 1999 Pili serial, *Pili Lei Ting,* I found that the average length of shots had been reduced from approximately 2.5 seconds to 1.06 seconds, with the longest shot in the sequence whittled down from nine seconds to three. Almost every frame in the 1994 clip was motion-blurred. In the 1994 clip the camera moves only along two axes, left to right and backwards and forwards, maintaining the sense of the set as a proscenium stage. In the 1999 clip the camera most often moves on the left-right axis, but in an arch rather than along a straight line, giving the impression of a more three-dimensional stage space. It zooms in and out and

also tilts left and right, up and down. The camera also moves back and forth between a proscenium view of the action, as in the earlier clip, and a point of view that is in the middle of the action, either from the point of view of different characters, or in a central position around which the characters move.

22. See, for example, the article on "Wood-Be Idols" in Tsai, *Xian ge bu chuo*.

23. Deleuze, *Cinema 1*.

24. In Mandarin, *gezaixi*.

25. Silvio, "Drag Melodrama."

26. For a discussion of how this organic model of the role relates to actress's conceptions of gender and sexuality, see Silvio, "Reflexivity."

27. Interview by author, August 9, 2003. I did not have a tape recorder with me for this interview, so this quote is reconstructed from memory.

28. The word "pose" was said in English, a common practice.

29. I do not want to overstate my case, however. COSers adopt a range of relationships, both physical and mental, to the characters they are dressing as. The majority of COSers I interviewed chose the characters they were playing because the character was "gorgeous" and/or because the costume was available. Most did not do anything, mentally or physically, to get into character and even seemed puzzled by the question. Yet a large number did say that they felt that they took on some of the character's qualities when they were in costume, and a few said they had chosen the character because it allowed them to express an aspect of their own personality.

30. Schwartz, "Torque."

31. For a discussion of the relationship between photography and self-identity in Taiwan, see Adrian, *Framing the Bride*, on how wedding salon photo albums simultaneously create and memorialize the self-as-bride.

32. See Morse, "Cyborgs"; Hayles, *Posthuman*; Turkle, *Life*.

33. Stone, *War*.

34. See Grosz, *Volatile Bodies*, for a thorough critique.

35. Haraway's 1985 essay, "Manifesto for Cyborgs," is the classic articulation of this position. Also see Stone, *War*. These fantasies are just as prominent, if not more so, in the Japanese popular culture that heavily influences Taiwan, although here they seem both more ambivalent and less gendered. See Bolton, "Wooden Cyborgs"; Napier, *Anime;* and Orbach, "Sex."

36. Hayles, *Posthuman*, 12.

Transnational Incorporations in Hong Kong Cinema

CHAPTER 13

Stellar Transit
Bruce Lee's Body or Chinese Masculinity in a Transnational Frame

CHRIS BERRY

BRUCE LEE'S STELLAR transit across the world's screens was all the more spectacular for its shocking brevity. His untimely death at the age of thirty-one, at the height of his success and after only four martial arts features, transformed him from new star to shooting star. Born in the United States, appearing suddenly out of Hong Kong, and flashing across the world's screens, he no sooner became the first global Chinese film star than he disappeared. In the years to follow, numerous Bruce Lee look-alikes tried and failed to fill the gap. They only succeeded in confirming his unique charisma, central to which is the body he delights in displaying in his films. Stripped to the waist, lean muscles taught with fury, and poised to pounce (Fig. 13.1), iconic images of Bruce Lee continue to appear on book covers, DVD covers, and fan web pages.

Everybody loves Bruce Lee's body, or so it seems. But they may not all love it for the same reasons. Bruce Lee's body is a transnational frame, shaped by his own experiences in the United States and Hong Kong and by perceptions of the various transnational markets his films were aimed at. If all mass cultural products are open to interpretation in the quest for maximum sales, this polysemic potential must be even truer for transnational cultural products.[1] Lee's deployment of his body as a weapon to win international and interracial competitions has been variously celebrated as the triumph of the Chinese, Asian, or third-world underdog. It has also been understood within different models of masculinity and different body ideals, each with its own history. Finally,

FIGURE 13.1. Bruce poised to pounce in *Fist of Fury* (1972).

Lee's display of his body has elicited queer readings. These queer readings have intersected with the other ways of understanding Lee's body, sometimes provoking anger, sometimes being appropriated for pro-feminist or queer-friendly purposes.

The different interpretations of Bruce Lee have developed in different times in different places according to local circumstances; they are situated. Some commentators are clearly aware of other discussions that have preceded them. However, overall, each discourse has proceeded relatively autonomously. The underdog interpretations rarely incorporate issues of masculinity, and although the discussions of masculinity may acknowledge Lee's underdog triumphs, they rarely relate this to the type of masculinity he developed. This essay aims to understand not only Bruce Lee's body as a transnational frame, but also the interpretations of it as such. In a transnational framework, it becomes significant that the vehicle for the "triumph of the underdog" narrative is also a Chinese man and that the particular masculinity he embodies foregrounds the eroticized male body.

Focusing on this framework enables me to make a further leap. In the past, I have noticed in passing that, while everybody else loves Bruce Lee's body, I feel more ambivalent. After focusing on the transit of Lee's star body more carefully, another altogether less spectacular asteroid comes in to view. Trailing Lee, it haunts his reworking of Chinese masculinity, revealing the price of success for his model of Chinese masculinity. I therefore argue that Lee's body is an agonized one — caught in the double-bind of a compulsion to respond to the challenge of modern American masculinity on one hand, and a homophobic and racially marked self-hatred that is a precondition for that ability to respond on the other.

Triumph of the Underdog

Bruce Lee's breakthrough as the first Chinese global star was based on only four features he made as an adult before his death. In the Lee legend, this achievement is a triumph of the underdog and a struggle against racism.[2] Born in the United States in 1940, Lee grew up in Hong Kong, where he was as a 1950s child star. Returning to the United States and graduating from the University of Washington in Seattle with a BA in Philosophy, he had some success on American television before losing the role of Caine in the *Kung Fu* series to Caucasian actor David Carradine.[3] American martial arts star Chuck Norris is reported as commenting, "Carradine's as good at martial arts as I am at acting."[4] Returning to Hong Kong, Lee debuted as an adult in 1971 with *The Big Boss*.[5] It broke box office records in Hong Kong. He followed this in 1972 with *Fist of Fury*. It also set new box office records and enabled Lee to establish his own production company, for which he wrote and directed *The Way of the Dragon*. In 1973 he made the James Bond-style film *Enter the Dragon* for Warner Brothers. At this high point, he died of a mysterious brain seizure. A fifth film, *The Game of Death,* was completed later by splicing scenes he had completed with new footage using stand-ins.

Each film is a variation on the triumph of the underdog theme. In *The Big Boss,* Lee is a migrant working at a factory run by a Chinese boss in Thailand. His mother has warned him not to get into fights, but he gets drawn into protests after two workers die. Impressed by his martial arts skills, the boss promotes him to foreman. But when Lee discovers he is being used and the company is in fact a front for drug smuggling and prostitution, he goes on a furious rampage. The film ends with him being taken away by police after killing the boss.

The Big Boss takes place almost entirely in the Chinese community in Thailand, and so it seems more about class than nationality or ethnicity. *Fist of Fury* is his most evidently nationalistic work. Set in semi-colonized Shanghai in 1908, it is based on a true event—the death of the founder of the Jingwu martial arts school. Lee plays a student. Discovering that a rival Japanese karate school killed his master, he breaks his school's ban on deploying its fighting skills with a series of retaliatory killings. The Japanese taunt him with a sign bearing the "sick man of Asia" slogan used to denigrate China. Lee destroys it and also the notorious "No Dogs or Chinese" sign at a park gate. The film culminates in a contest with a Russian champion brought in by the Japanese school. When the police come to arrest Lee, he runs at them and the camera. The film ends with a freeze frame of Lee in mid-leap as we hear his characteristic angry shriek and the hail of police gunfire.

As Tony Rayns points out, *The Way of the Dragon* combines the migrant worker theme from *The Big Boss* with the contest or tournament theme from *Fist of Fury*.[6] A bumpkin from Hong Kong's New Territories, Lee flies to Rome to help his female cousin, whose restaurant is threatened by local gangsters. Lee trains the waiters to fight back, against his uncle's advice that they should not fight. The gangsters bring in an American martial artist, played by Chuck Norris. The film culminates in the iconic Coliseum fight scene, followed by a twist when it transpires that his uncle was conspiring with the gangsters.

The box office success of these films led to *Enter the Dragon*, directed by Robert Clouse and guaranteed international distribution by Warner Brothers. Playing off the popularity of the Bond series, Lee takes on the familiar role of an international police agent combating a wealthy evildoer. He is a highly trained Shaolin martial artist, and his opponent is a Shaolin-disciple-gone-wrong called Han. He travels to Han's fortress with a Caucasian American and an African American. The latter is killed, but together with his Caucasian colleague, he destroys the fortress and takes down Han.

The wide range of ethnic and national affiliations in this small body of work hardly constitutes what critics think of as an artist's oeuvre that inscribes a consistent signature. The possible exception is the fight scene choreography, which Lee was intensively involved with. Most commentators note his commitment to realistic fighting without the aid of trampolines, wirework, or editing tricks, as well as his development of his own unique Jeet Kune Do style.[7] But even here, there are significant variations in the direction. Lee was only involved in writing and directing one film, *The Way of the Dragon*. Cheng Yu notes that director of *The Big Boss* and *Fist of Fury* "Luo Wei depended on editing and close-ups to convey the impact of the fight. Luo also often used subjective point-of-view shots such as Lee kicking or punching directly into the camera. In the Coliseum scene, Lee adopts a markedly different approach, using a medium or long shot to show the fighters on opposite sides of the (wide) screen or in two-shots. As such the style is closer to capturing the *fight-performance* or representing a reportage of a fight from the ring-side."[8] As for *Enter the Dragon*, Tony Rayns is not the only one to disparage Robert Clouse, pointing out that he "fails to comprehend the most basic rule for filming the martial arts—that it is imperative to show protagonists full-length if their movements are to constitute the dynamics of the drama."[9]

This variety extends to the narratives as well as the directing styles, forcing audiences to decode selectively if they want to "make sense" of what Bruce Lee stands for. Four main and often overlapping possibilities for understanding Lee's underdog triumphs circulate; they either represent a triumph for Hong Kong, for diasporic Chinese in general, for the third world, or for Asian

Americans. Not all commentators try to assign meaning to Lee's kung fu, and a formalist appreciation of the fighting style is also common. However, noting Lee's Caucasian opponents in *Fist of Fury* and *The Way of the Dragon*, Stephen Teo is rightly suspicious of this approach.[10]

Most who see Lee as representing Hong Kong base this on his childhood there and his participation in the Hong Kong cinema. However, Kwai-Cheung Lo acknowledges that Lee does not connote a clear Hong Kong identity to most people from Hong Kong. Not only did Lee spend much of his life in the United States and hold a US passport, but he also appeared as generically Chinese rather than specifically from Hong Kong in all his films except *The Way of the Dragon*. Furthermore, his films were in Mandarin, rather than the local Cantonese language of Hong Kong.[11] This lack of Hong Kong specificity leads other authors to see Lee's triumph as a metaphor for diasporic Chinese pride. Ying-chi Chu states, "No other Hong Kong star can more clearly express diasporic consciousness than Bruce Lee. His three best-known films ... present stories of Chinese who live in places dominated and controlled by non-Chinese."[12] Stephen Teo takes a similar view, seeing Lee's "cause" as "cultural nationalism," an ethnically based form implicitly distinct from the state-based nationalism of either the People's Republic with its capital in Beijing or the Republic with its temporary capital in Taiwan after 1949.[13] However, Lo reads the same characteristics differently, believing that Hong Kong inhabitants identify with the imaginary China of Lee's films. Precisely because "Lee's body is unable to offer a solid ground for locating a specific entity, 'Hong Kong,' " Lo sees a homology between this slippery identity-in-non-identity with Hong Kong's own ghostly presence fading out of British colonial status and into mainland China.[14]

The same lack of nation-state specificity grounds the third-world reading of Lee. Hsiung-Ping Chiao notes that Lee's anti-western aggression "was congenial not only to Chinese, but literally to all people who felt that they had been degraded by western Imperialism (South Americans, Arabs, and Orientals)."[15] Vijay Prashad not only remembers seeing *Enter the Dragon* on its release in India, but also contrasts the film with the Bond series as follows: "Bond was the agent of international corruption manifest in the British MI-5, while Lee stood his ground against corruption of all forms.... With his bare fists and his *nunchaku*s, Lee provided young people with the sense that we could be victorious, like the Vietnamese guerillas, against the virulence of international capitalism." In order to make this interpretation that Lee is fighting in solidarity with what he elsewhere calls "the army in black pajamas," Prashad has to overlook the inconvenient fact that in *Enter the Dragon* Lee is himself an MI-5 agent.[16] Furthermore, the horror many diasporic Chinese audiences had of communism constrained Lee's image from any explicit socialism.

At the time of the original release of Lee's features, the kind of third-world internationalism Prashad remembers fondly was, as he details, closely interwoven with ethnic minority politics in the United States. For example, David Desser has traced the popularity of Lee's films with African American audiences,[17] and the importance of non-Caucasian audiences for later crossover actors such as Jackie Chan and Jet Li is both well known and also manifest in the ethnicity of many of their American co-stars.[18] However, as Jachinson Chan has pointed out, if there was ambivalence in Hong Kong about whether Lee counted as a genuine local, the same is true in the United States for his status as an Asian American.[19] Perhaps in these circumstances it is not so surprising that much of the literature on Asian American culture makes only passing reference to Lee. Apart from Chan's work, the only other major exception is that of Sheng-mei Ma, who places Lee's nationalism as part of a broad Chinese and Asian phenomenon, including Asian American culture.[20] Chan, however, places Lee as a breakthrough in the representation of Asian American men, who appear feminized in figures such as Fu Manchu and Charlie Chan.

Competing Masculinities

As part of a monograph about Asian American masculinity, Jachinson Chan's discussion of Bruce Lee analyzes both the triumph of the underdog narrative and Lee's masculinity. It is exceptional in this regard, since most commentators make no connection between Lee's underdog triumphs and the type of masculinity he deploys. Even for Chan, masculinity exists only in the singular and there is no discussion of different ways of being masculine. Maybe this is also why other authors do not discuss Lee's embodied masculinity; maybe it seems "natural" that only a masculine man could symbolize the communal reempowerment they see in his narratives, and "masculine" only means one thing.

For example, Kwai-cheung Lo notes Matthew Turner's research on the turn to a "modern western mode of health, posture and physique" in Hong Kong in the 1960s, adding that "a unique combination of western bodybuilding and Chinese kung fu (with an admixture of James Bond karate and mainland flying action) were brought together in the figure of Bruce Lee."[21] This is a telling observation, suggesting a tension between other Chinese masculinities and western muscle culture, but Lo does not pursue this line of enquiry any further. Similarly, in her essay on race and masculinity in martial arts cinema, Yvonne Tasker hints at different masculinities when she comments, "The Chinese hero often fights for and as part of a community, while within the American tradition the hero has become an increasingly isolated figure."[22] Tasker implicitly treats Chinese community and American individualism as fixed cultural characteristics here, rather than as figures in the dynamic contestation of what a real man is in different but increasingly interconnected spaces in the wake of colonialism, imperialism, and global "free trade."

Kam Louie's recent study of Chinese masculinity gives us a better understanding of this. He details two longstanding masculinities, both valorized in Chinese society. *Wen* or refined masculinity is symbolized by Confucius and the gentleman scholar-official, and emphasizes culture-based power rather than physical prowess. Highly attractive to women, the *wen* man may dally with them, but in the end must give up erotic pleasure to fulfill his ethical obligations. *Wu* or martial masculinity is symbolized by the god Guan Yu—shrines to whom figure in many a John Woo film—and the fighters who inhabit the legendary domain of the *jianghu* (rivers and lakes) outside civil society. These heroes emphasize physical strength and skill. Except when drunk, they eschew women completely, and their primary commitments are to their blood brothers. The *wu* fighter's body may be more revealed than the *wen* scholar's, which is almost always lost in billowing robes. But in neither case is the male body eroticized: the fighter's body signifies his martial prowess only.[23] Indeed, the very concept of the "muscle" did not exist until appropriated from western anatomy studies in the nineteenth century.[24] This specific "invisibility" of the male body in earlier Chinese culture is part of a broader absence of the revealed body in Chinese fine art prior to contact with the west.[25]

Louie notes, "The Bruce Lee screen persona has all three characteristics of loyalty, righteousness and mateship to justify him as a *wu* hero." He adds that "like the *wu* heroes in traditional narratives, even when the women around him are concerned about him, the Bruce Lee characters do not romance these beauties like a *wen* scholar would do: he always attends to his social obligations first."[26] Jachinson Chan, apparently unaware of these other masculinities, interprets Lee's behavior within the conventions of American masculinity only, claiming that "the characters he portrays are not typically patriarchal or misogynistic. Lee's characters do not oppress the female characters nor do they exhibit an exaggerated James Bond-like heterosexism."[27] Within the codes of *wu* masculinity, however, Lee's behavior is not about honoring women, but perfectly patriarchal and misogynistic; he either recognizes his duty to protect them because of his relationship to their family, or treats them as a dangerous distraction to be ignored.

This difference of interpretation also points up an underlying tension between Asian American and older Chinese expectations of the *wu* hero. For Jachinson Chan, Lee disappointingly "perpetuates the asexual role that western culture has constructed for Asian men and does not spend the night with the Asian female character—something that would be unthinkable in a James Bond film."²⁸ But behavior that would represent masculine achievement within contemporary American codes—although not earlier English notions of gentlemanly behavior—would signal failure within *wu* masculinity. (Although it falls outside the scope of this essay, these tensions continue to dog Chinese male martial arts stars trying to cross over into the international market. Both Jackie Chan and Jet Li's awkward negotiations of sexuality demonstrate the difficulty of these mutually incompatible expectations.)

Louie does not treat the two Chinese masculinities as static, nor China as a sealed unit unaffected by the rest of the world. International success constitutes the Bruce Lee phenomenon as "a reassertion of a Chinese *wu* masculinity in the international arena," Louie claims. But in line with Kwai-cheung Lo's comments about the cult of bodybuilding in Hong Kong in the 1960s, he also notes that "the world dominance of American media means that the western masculine ideals represented in many of the American images are becoming more and more commonly accepted in China" and acknowledges that Lee's display of his body, along with gossip about his alleged off-screen womanizing, breaks with the old *wu* masculinity because it "exudes much sexuality." Therefore, Lee represents not just a reassertion of *wu* masculinity, but also a modification "to suit the new hybrid culture of the diaspora Chinese."²⁹

However, Louie may understate Lee's departure from the established *wu* model. First, the display of the eroticized body is a startling break with almost all the martial arts stars of the past. Before the late 1960s, the heroes of Hong Kong action films appeared not only clothed but also usually covered from neck to toe in loose outfits that completely de-emphasized the body. This is true not only of swordplay heroes, but also of those associated with the kung fu fist-based martial arts like Lee himself. For example, Kwan Tak-hing, who played Wong Fei-Hong in the popular 1950s and early 1960s series, always dressed in dark traditional clothing.³⁰ Only with Zhang Che's films did this begin to change and open the door for Lee's consistent self-display.³¹

Although Lee's self-display may have been novel in the martial arts genre, the fit body as a mark of modernization has a long history in the Chinese cinema. As early as the 1930s, Li Lili appeared in bathing costumes and gymnastics outfits in *Queen of Sports* (*Tiyu huanghou*, 1934), and male stars appeared stripped to the waist as workers building a highway to help the army get to the front and fight the Japanese in *The Highway* (*Dalu*, 1934). This film also features a notorious male nude scene, but such titillation disappeared after 1949. Bodily display in People's Republic cinema continued, but was confined to healthy and active physical participation in nation building. For example, in superficially de-eroticized sports genre films such as *Woman Basketball Player*

No.5 (Nülan wu hao), playing for the national team was a metaphor for devoting oneself to building the nation.

With this larger history in mind, Bruce Lee's own hybridization of Chinese *wu* masculinity and American masculinity can be read as not separate from but closely tied to the various nationalist and anticolonial interpretations of the underdog narratives in his films. At the same time as Lee asserts Chinese/Asian/third-world reempowerment through his films and persona, he also does so through the assertion of masculinity.

Furthermore, within a dynamic Chinese context, Lee also symbolizes choosing *wu* over *wen* masculinity to carry out this mission. This is a significant shift. As Kam Louie points out, *wu* is not generally as highly valued as the more refined *wen*, which stresses submission to order and rule through ethics over the aggression and force associated with *wu*.[32] Indeed, one of the recurring themes in Lee's films is the need to overturn the conventional *wen* insistence on not using force. In *The Big Boss*, Lee's mother has warned him not to fight, but in the end the quest for justice requires him to. In *Fist of Fury*, the Jingwu School has trained its students to treat their skills as a form of physical exercise, but Lee cannot let his master's death go unrevenged. In *The Way of the Dragon*, Uncle Wang tells the younger waiters to pay the Italian gangsters off rather than get into a fight, but it turns out that he himself is in the villains' pay.

According to Cheng Yu, this narrative pattern conforms to "the Chinese maxim of being able to bear provocation and not having to fight unless absolutely necessary."[33] Indeed, it is the case that in extreme circumstances *wu* aggression may be unleashed. However, *The Way of the Dragon* also marks an important deviation from the usual codes and a point where Lee's modern and transnational neo-*wu* masculinity appropriates from American codes. Usually, the legal and ethical breaches that *wu* violence constitutes must ultimately be eliminated, even if they are used to restore order. This is why Lee is arrested at the end of *The Big Boss* and even shot by the Chinese foreign settlement police at the end of *Fist of Fury*. However, in *The Way of the Dragon*, instead of being arrested Lee bids goodbye to his young female cousin, returning to Hong Kong and leaving her to run her restaurant in peace. This is equivalent to the cliché of the cowboy who rides off into the sunset, regretfully leaving the young widow after saving her life and homestead. By *Enter the Dragon*, Lee has appropriated the American masculinity codes of the gunfighter film even more fully, when he is specially hired by MI-5 to take on the evil Han.

There is another way in which Lee's neo-*wu* masculinity appropriates American masculinity. The moment at which he can no longer turn the other cheek is not only marked by his engaging the enemy with the full force of his fury, in the typical *wu* manner. It is also when the shirt literally comes off and he bares his muscular upper body. Unlike all other Chinese martial arts stars, Lee displays his muscles as the 1950s sword-and-sandal film stars had done and Schwarzenegger and Stallone were to do in the near future. Furthermore, the response of women characters to Lee signals that this is not just a display of weaponry but also an erotic moment. However, continued difference between neo-*wu* and American masculinity can be discerned in *Enter the Dragon*. Both Lee's Caucasian and African American colleagues have no qualms about sleeping with the girls Han provides on the night before the tournament — indeed the African American character's behavior conforms to racist stereotypes about hypersexuality. In contrast, Lee refuses all such temptations, conforming to the core *wu* value of eschewing involvement with women lest they sap his strength or damage his concentration.

Bruce Lee and the Queer Body

Not only women are attracted to Lee's stripped torso. His body is appropriated for queer viewing pleasure in both films and critical literature. In *The Way of the Dragon,* Wei Ping'ao reprises the role of the traitorous translator from *Fist of Fury*. In the first film, he worked for the Japanese karate school that assassinated the Jingwu master. This time he works for the Italian gangsters. In *Fist of Fury,* he already embodied the physically weak and fawning "sick man of Asia," but in *The Way of the Dragon* what was just a certain lack of masculinity becomes fully fledged effeminate homosexuality. Not only does he flounce around in a variety of Elton John-style outfits, but he also makes no effort to hide his attraction to Lee's character. Tony Rayns refers to two occasions when he "is required to fondle Lee's biceps and pectorals." Indeed, during one effort to pressure Lee into working for the gangsters, Wei does find himself running his fingers across Lee's (clothed) chest and mumbling, "What rippling muscles!" However, their very first meeting is even more suggestive. At the end of an earlier attempt to browbeat the restaurant, Wei literally bumps into Lee for the first time on his way out. Annoyed at first, his tone changes when he steps back and gets a better look at Lee. Reaching down between Lee's legs to where Lee's cloth belt is dangling, Wei picks it up and tucks into his waistband. "Watch where you're going," he tells Lee sweetly. The symbolic possibilities of the belt action leave little doubt that Wei hopes Lee might be going his way (Fig. 13.2).

The queer appreciation of Lee's body is also realized in the critical literature. For Stephen Teo, who is fiercely insistent that his Chinese "cultural nationalist" interpretation of Lee is the only correct one, queering Lee interferes with Lee's devotion to his cause: "These critics speak of Lee's 'narcissism',

FIGURE 13.2. A little belt action in *The Way of the Dragon*.

a codeword for homosexual imagery, and only grudgingly acknowledge his nationalistic stance." He notes that "a section of gay critics" describes the scene in which Lee trains in his room in *The Way of the Dragon*, looking at himself in a mirror, as "onanistic," and "One western critic has even gone to the extent of quoting Lee's wife, to point out that 'he had one undescended testicle,' so as to prove that Lee was plagued by an inferiority complex . . . leading to bodybuilding, martial arts, and narcissism in later life."[34]

In fact, all these quotes come from one source, Tony Rayns. Putting aside for a moment the issue of Teo's outrage, there is an interesting slippage in Rayns's discussion of *The Way of the Dragon* that reveals his investment in the film. Rayns does indeed describe the training scene as "narcissistic (it involves a mirror) to the point of being onanistic," and adds that, "The audience observes it voyeuristically, through the eyes of the character's female cousin, who enters the room unknown to him." He then observes that, "In later scenes, the audience surrogate is a homosexual member of the villain's gang, who is required to fondle Lee's biceps and pectorals admiringly on two occasions."[35] In fact, there is an important difference between the female cousin and Wei Ping'ao's character, Mr. Ho. As Rayns describes, Lee's cousin spies on him and the audience is given a point-of-view shot from her perspective. But in the two scenes where Mr. Ho admires Lee, the audience maintains a separate, third person perspective, and there is no point-of-view shot. In other words, to identify with Mr. Ho in this moment of gay pleasure, as Rayns' slippage indicates he does, requires spectatorial projection.

Teo's sarcastic anger at Rayns reveals both incompatibility between the queer appropriation of Lee and various triumph-of-the-underdog readings, and also that the transnational circulation of Lee's neo-*wu* masculinity has positioned him in a world of American masculinity. First, the tension between queer appropriation of Lee and the underdog interpretations pivots on how Lee's bodily display is understood and which scenes are emphasized. In the underdog interpretations, Lee's bodily display at moments of high anger prior to fighting is highlighted as a display of superior physical weaponry. In gay appropriations, staring at himself bare-chested in the mirror is highlighted as the male-to-male narcissistic foundation on which to build a gay appreciation.

In the underdog interpretations, Lee's body is a vehicle for the assertion of power. In the gay appropriations, it is an object of desire. Of course, Lee may be desired as a powerful and masculine man. Indeed, Tan Hoang Nguyen explains that Bruce Lee's star image provides the foundation for that of a gay porn actor named after Lee's son Brandon and noted as the first Asian star top rather than bottom.[36] But this does not change the fundamental shift from subject with which audiences identify to object of desire. Furthermore, if the gay spectator is also imagined to be white, like Tony Rayns, then the pleasure Bruce Lee seemed to reserve for Chinese, third-world, and Asian American audiences appears re-appropriated or "stolen" by their symbolic oppressors. This also explains the discomfort Teo and others have with western "formalist" interpretations of Lee that appreciate the grace of his movements but wipe out the politics of reempowerment.

Second, the anxiety about homosexuality and its meanings further reveals the degree to which Lee's neo-*wu* masculinity is hybridized with and positioned within globalized American masculinity. Homophobia and its attendant anxieties are an integral component of that masculinity. However, according to Louie and others, they were not an important feature of either *wu* or *wen* masculinity prior to contact with the modern west.[37] One can speculate on the reasons for this (see one treatment of the question in chapter 3 above). However, if earlier *wen* and *wu* masculinities provide models for emulation, this emulation is built on different mechanisms from those associated with modern American masculinity. Written and oral narratives preclude possibilities for gazing upon the muscular body. The actors in "traditional" Chinese popular performance modes are clothed. The one exception would be acrobats, but here absence of narrative might limit the possibilities for identification. In contrast, visual media such as the cinema and the printed image are key vehicles encouraging engagement with modern American masculinity, making the display of a strong body more important.

In these visual circumstances, there is always a tension between the male body as agent in action and object on display. Techniques such as photographing the male body displaying bulging armor-like muscles or as though frozen in action are deployed to contain the implicit threat of feminization in objectification and, according to the codes of modern masculinity, homosexualization.[38] However, anxiety about potential homosexuality follows modern American masculinity wherever it goes. For not only is the display of the body destabilizing, but the ultimate goal of this model of masculinity is to win the acknowledgment of other men. This homosocial aim can also tip all too easily into homosexuality if respect and admiration become the foundation for desire, and therefore the boundary line between the two must be rigorously policed.[39]

As Robin Wood has pointed out, the action movie can be understood as a site where these tensions are worked out. Under this symbolic umbrella, violence between men displaces and transforms the threat of desire, expelling it with the same force as the punches landed on an opponent.[40] Bruce Lee's neo-*wu* masculinity carries the full force of this homophobic structure. However, it is further complicated and specified by the politics of imperialism and anti-imperialism. As is often noted, there is usually a racial hierarchy amongst Lee's opponents. Taking on other Chinese or even Japanese is an easy beginning. The ultimate test is often a Caucasian opponent, like the Russian champion employed by the Japanese in *Fist of Fury,* or the Chuck Norris character employed by the gangsters in *The Way of the Dragon.*

Furthermore, there is a marked difference in the way Lee treats his different opponents in some of his films. Whereas other Asian fighters are crushed with contempt, Caucasian opponents are taken seriously and, in the Coliseum scene in which Lee takes on and defeats Norris, even treated with respect. Cheng Yu points out that Lee eschews "his usual tactics of shrieking, grimacing, or sneering at his opponent."[41] For Cheng, this marks a move towards realism, but for Vijay Prashad the fight is "a battle between Chinese civilization and western civilization, between the paper tiger of U.S. imperialism and the rising tide of the Red East."[42] For Sheng-mei Ma, on the other hand, going to Rome and fighting in the Coliseum is a classic manifestation of the double consciousness that submits to colonial values at the same time as it resists.[43] Tony Rayns concludes from this scene (contrary to Teo's claims about his grudging acknowledgment of nationalism) that "*The Way of the Dragon* . . . constitutes an aggressive assertion of identity, both as an individual fulfilled through martial arts and as a Chinese proud of his race." But under the rubric of the "narcissism" that Stephen Teo sees as a code word for homosexuality, he also writes, "the entire sequence is predicated on the fighters' mutual respect for each other's art . . . [Lee] kills him *in a spirit of reverence.* After the killing, he drapes the dead man's tunic and black belt over the body, and kneels beside it in silence."[44] (Fig. 13.3)

The tension between Lee's need to overcome Norris and his respect for him reaffirms Sheng-mei Ma's observations about double consciousness. It

FIGURE 13.3. Reverence for the white man's body in *The Way of the Dragon*.

also underlines how much Lee desires acknowledgment from his American opponent. On a metaphorical level, this reveals a tension at the heart of the anticolonial politics of remasculinization epitomized by Bruce Lee.[45] If Lee's star image affirms the ability of Chinese men to win in the international arena, it also affirms their submission to the values of modern American masculinity. This tension echoes that between homosexuality and homosociality that Sedgwick notes at the core of modern American masculinity.

Furthermore, the loving homosociality of the Coliseum scene contrasts significantly with the fate of the Wei Ping'ao characters. First, these absolutely despised characters do not even have the status of an opponent. As a result, they also do not even make the bottommost rung in the hierarchy of Lee adversaries discussed by other writers. In *Fist of Fury*, Lee's first revenge killings are the two henchmen who assassinated his teacher, one Chinese and one Japanese. They are dispatched in one brief fight scene with a series of furious and unrestrained blows to the stomach and are found hanging from a lamppost the next day. Wei Ping'ao's traitorous translator is next. But where an actual fight scene is used to dispatch the assassins, he does not merit this. Lee disguises himself as a rickshaw driver whom Wei hires one night. Taking him down a blind alley, Lee turns and lifts the rickshaw by the shafts with Wei in it, tossing it to its destruction. His aim is to get Wei to confess who ordered the assassination. Gutless and without loyalty even to his foreign masters, Wei quickly tells Lee it was Suzuki from the Japanese club. Claiming to have been "only following orders," he begs for mercy. But when Lee turns, Wei grabs a brick to bludgeon him. Lee turns back in fury, but the film does not even consider it worth showing us the actual crushing of this insect-like figure, and we cut immediately to the next morning and Wei's body hanging from a lamppost. In *The Way of the Dragon*, Lee does not even deign to lay a finger on Mr. Ho, his homosexual suitor. Rather, after the Coliseum scene, when Ho runs up to Uncle Tang to tell him the bad news, his Italian boss also drives up and shoots him before he can confess. In other words, he is treated as an afterthought.

The contrast between Lee's loving killing of Chuck Norris in the Coliseum and treatment of Wei's characters as vermin is thought provoking. Could it be that in the cosmos of Lee's neo-*wu* masculinity, the slender body that used to signify the refined *wen* scholar now signifies effeminacy and even "the sick man of Asia"? Where *wen* refinement was combined with education to signify wisdom and the superior power of the cerebral over the merely muscular, along with a sure command of ethics, in the neo-*wu* cosmos it is bundled together with spinelessness and disloyalty to signify not only failed Chinese masculinity, but also the "fag" or "pansy." Jachinson Chan is optimistic about Lee's behavior towards Mr. Ho, his homosexual admirer in *The Way of the Dragon*. He reads Lee's stoic response to Ho's come-ons as a tolerant attitude compared to the homophobic violence that might be expected from a macho American hero.[46] But within the neo-*wu*, the overall treatment and fate of Wei Ping'ao's characters in both *Fist of Fury* and *The Way of the Dragon* configures Ho's behavior as being not even worthy of a violent response.

A particular exchange and translation mechanism is at work here. Tan Hoang Nguyen notes that in the economy of gay porn star Brandon Lee's image, his relatively assimilated Americanness contrasts with the migrant and marked Asianness of the bottoms he is often paired up with. This may be a subset of a larger pattern that Lee's neo-*wu* masculinity is the archetype for. Lee reinvigorates *wu* by appropriating elements of modern American masculinity; power is produced in exchange for jettisoning various aspects of earlier Chinese masculinities. In this way, the Lee persona's trajectory resembles the classic production of the Lacanian subject through a process of subjection, whereby one is acknowledged and given status in return for subjecting oneself to the Law of the Father. In the process the "fag" is produced as the hated part of the self that is to be repressed and symbolically expelled. However, in the case of Bruce Lee the intersection of the colonial and masculinity in the production of neo-*wu* masculinity further marks the despised "fag" or "pansy" as Chinese, and the model to be admired and emulated as white. Here an irony emerges in Bruce Lee's otherwise completely unironic persona: while appearing to overcome all odds and defeat the imperialist, this is only achieved by subscribing to his larger value system. Here again we have another manifestation of the "double consciousness" Sheng-mei Ma notes in Lee.

In these complex circumstances, I would like to conclude by returning to Meaghan Morris's discussion of Lee as a teacher. She discusses an episode in a film about Lee, where he and his wife Linda are shown going to the movies together. They watch *Breakfast at Tiffany's*. When Mickey Rooney's supposedly humorous character, Mr. Yunioshi, comes on screen, the audience howls. Linda laughs, too, until she notices Bruce's stony reaction. Morris's point is about how Linda learns across the cultural divide as a result of being with Bruce.[47] The personal dimension of my discomfort when watching Bruce Lee movies is similar. Much as my eye is caught by his spectacular body, it is also drawn to the smaller asteroid trailing in its wake—Wei Ping'ao—and the homophobia produced simultaneously with Lee's neo-*wu* masculinity. And further, I cannot help notice the specific racialized structure of that homophobia. To equate the fag with Chineseness and ideal masculinity with America is not only homophobic, it also inscribes a trace of self-hatred onto Chinese remasculinization.

Notes

1. Fiske, "Television," 392–393.

2. There are numerous books and websites devoted to Bruce Lee. For this essay, I have drawn heavily on Little's biography, *Bruce Lee: A Warrior's Journey*. Made with the cooperation of Lee's widow, this book does not dwell on the rumors that surrounded his death in the bed of a Taiwanese actress, all of which can be found readily in other "unauthorized" accounts. Earlier biographies include Thomas, *Bruce Lee: Fighting Spirit*; Lee, *The Bruce Lee Story*; and Clouse, *Bruce Lee: The Biography*.

3. On the television series, see Hamamoto, *Monitored Peril*, 59–63; Ma, *Deathly Embrace*, 60–61.

4. Meyers et al., *Bruce Lee to the Ninjas*, 221; cited in Morris, "Learning," 183.

5. Lee's first three films had different English titles in the United States. *The Big Boss (Tangshan daxiong)* is known there as *Fists of Fury*. *Fist of Fury (Jingwumen)* is known as *The Chinese Connection*. *The Way of the Dragon (Meng long guo jiang)* is known as *The Return of the Dragon*.

6. Rayns, "Bruce Lee and Other Stories," 28.

7. For example, see Chiao, "Bruce Lee," 33. For Chiao, Lee's choreographic style is understood not only under the rubric of realism but also as simultaneously western in comparison to the Chinese fantasy-style that emphasized wirework and so forth. It is true that this dominated the swordplay martial arts films that Lee's kung fu films replaced. However, many earlier kung fu films from the 1950s such as the famous Wong Fei-hong series also featured relatively "realistic" styles of fighting.

8. Cheng, "Anatomy," 25.

9. Rayns, "Bruce Lee: Narcissism," 112.

10. Teo, "True Way," 70. From formalism to fan worship, self-serving western readings of martial arts films that ignore the colonial and neocolonial dynamics and therefore repeat the colonial dynamic of resource extraction are too numerous to mention.

11. Lo, "Muscles."

12. Chu, *Hong Kong Cinema*, 38.
13. Teo, "Bruce Lee," 110–114.
14. Lo, "Muscles," 111.
15. Chiao, "Bruce Lee," 37.
16. Prashad, "Bruce Lee," 54, 64.
17. Desser, "Kung Fu."
18. See, for example, Marchetti, *"Jackie Chan."*
19. Chan, *Chinese American Masculinities*, 75.
20. Ma, *Deathly Embrace*, 54–55.
21. Lo, "Muscles," 106–107.
22. Tasker, "Fists," 316.
23. Louie, *Chinese Masculinity*, 1–22ff.
24. See Heinrich, *The Afterlife of Images*, especially chapter 4.
25. Hay, "Body Invisible."
26. Louie, *Chinese Masculinity*, 145, 147.
27. Chan, *Chinese American Masculinities*, 77.
28. Ibid., 89.
29. Louie, *Chinese Masculinity*, 13, 147–148.
30. On the Wong Fei-hong (a.k.a. Huang Feihong) series, see Rodriguez, "Hong Kong."
31. Not only did Zhang make his stars display their bodies, but, like Lee, this display has also provoked queer readings, as in Stanley Kwan's 1996 documentary film *Yang + Yin: Gender in Chinese Cinema*.
32. Louie, *Chinese Masculinity*.
33. Cheng, "Anatomy," 24.
34. Teo, "True Way," 70–71, 75, 77.
35. Rayns, "Bruce Lee: Narcissism," 111. The observation about the undescended testicle is on 110.
36. Nguyen, "Resurrection of Brandon Lee."
37. Hinsch, *Passions*. However, this does not mean "homosexuality" was accepted or even exists as a concept in China at this time. Dikötter, *Sex*, 145; Sang, *Emerging Lesbian*, 45–46; and Martin, *Situating Sexualities*, 32.
38. On muscles as armor, see Dyer, "White Man's Muscles." On photographing action poses, see Meyer's comparison of Rock Hudson to other (more mobile) stars in "Rock" (pp. 261–262).
39. Sedgwick, *Between Men*.
40. Robin Wood's discussion of *Raging Bull* is exemplary. Wood, "Two Films."
41. Cheng, "Anatomy," 25.
42. Prashad, "Bruce Lee," 63.
43. Ma, *Deathly Embrace*, 58.
44. Rayns, "Bruce Lee: Narcissism," 112.
45. I am borrowing "remasculinization" from Susan Jeffords, *Remasculinization*.
46. Chan, *Chinese American Masculinities*.
47. Morris, "Learning," 180.

CHAPTER 14

Love in Ruins
Spectral Bodies in Wong Kar-wai's *In the Mood for Love*

OLIVIA KHOO

> He remembers those vanished years
> As though looking through a dusty window pane
> The past is something he could see, but not touch
> And everything he sees is blurred and indistinct.[1]

Recent popular interest in Hong Kong's art cinema has been met by a critical admonition from Western film academics to consider the ethics of cross-cultural spectatorship, in particular in the context of international film festival circulation and reception. While some attempts have been made to consider the place of these films in the lives of diasporic Chinese viewers, far fewer inquiries into an ethics of *ethnic* spectatorship have been engaged; that is, almost no one has challenged the claims for either a self-evident "Chinese gaze" or Chinese identity in existing conceptions of embodied spectatorship.[2]

This essay joins these debates by proposing an inhabitable, ethnically marked, and ethically engaged position from which to view Hong Kong art cinema, specifically from a diasporic Chinese perspective. I use the figure of the specter—something neither simply disappearing nor wholly material—to challenge existing notions of embodied spectatorship so as to consider how we might conceive of the body in recent Hong Kong art cinema. This body can no longer be regarded as a dependable marker of identity, whole and fully present, since Chineseness also appears today in increasingly fragmented forms tied to diasporic experience. In considering the spectatorship for this cinema, what emerges as the most difficult and perhaps the most pressing issue is how to conceive of an ethical diasporic Chinese viewing position out of the impossibility of rooted Chineseness. I will use the film *In the Mood for Love* to describe how a theory of spectatorship might be formed through rehearsals of and for viewing, just as this film, like others in Wong's *oeuvre,* are rehearsals of and for love.

The lines quoted at the beginning of this chapter appear as an epilogue to the film. They speak to the question of how we are to conceive the bodies on the screen in recent Hong Kong art cinema, and whether we can respond, in an embodied sense, to figures that are vanishing, distant, and far from touch.

The epilogue resonates with an article by Laura U. Marks entitled "Loving a Disappearing Image" in which Marks discusses the photographic theory of Roland Barthes in *Camera Lucida,* and in particular his use of the Wintergarden photograph as an affective pivot for the book. Marks suggests that "the very blurriness and illegibility of the photograph . . . may *aid* the process of memory."[3] This is because such an image, a "disappearing" image, invites a look that is haptic, that "uses the eye like an organ of touch."[4]

Marks' argument engages with literally disappearing images, such as when the emulsion on a piece of film starts bleeding or when a videotape begins to decay. The important point that she makes, however, is that love plays an integral part in how we might view these images. According to Marks, we respond to these situations of "loving a disappearing image" with a sense of loss and a premonition of our own disappearance.[5] Love is crucial in understanding how we as spectators fall for certain images on the screen, and this is particularly important in a theory of ethnic spectatorship.

A Phantom Discipline

In a recent article entitled "A Phantom Discipline," Rey Chow argues that the relatively late interest by film scholars in nonwestern cinemas, and a corresponding desire by nonwestern subjects to see themselves mimetically reflected on the screen, has had a paradoxical effect on how the ethnic body has been conceived. The concerns of identity politics have foregrounded the issue of the ethnic body but in doing so have also essentialized or reified it, making the body "disappear." The problem is, therefore, how to make this body function as "visible" without at the same time "trapping" it — in the sense of providing a fixed representation that ethnic spectators cannot escape from.

From a different critical trajectory, Ackbar Abbas has suggested that a politics of identity is expressed *indirectly* in Hong Kong cinema — through new kinds of cinematic images or a rewriting of film genres.[6] Abbas argues that Hong Kong at the time of the handover was a culture of reverse hallucination. If hallucination means seeing what is not there then reverse hallucination means not seeing what *is* there. What is it Abbas wants us to see? He says it is "Hong Kong itself as a subject."[7] Despite his preoccupation with hallucinations and ways of seeing, Abbas does not really attend to the issue of spectatorship or, furthermore, the problems attendant upon spectators identifying with an elusive (or "disappearing") subject.[8] If we read Abbas's comments on a "politics of identification" as part of a strategy of disappearance in tandem with Rey Chow's comments on film studies as a phantom discipline, what are we left with for ethnic spectators? Can ethnic spectators be freed from bodily identification while at the same time continuing to see themselves reflected materially on the screen?

For this theory of ethnic spectatorship, my focus is specifically diasporic Chinese spectators. Although Hong Kong's status as a Special Administrative Region means that it is now officially considered part of China, it is in many respects culturally and economically closer to a Chinese diaspora than it is a part of the mainland. Hong Kong's cinematic engagement with the mainland appears spectral, replaying the wound of loss and potential "recovery" loop that is also characteristic of many diasporic contexts.[9]

In foregrounding the connection between the spectral and the spectatorial, I wonder if spectrality can provide a model for the ethical circulation and reception of recent Hong Kong art cinema. In this model, the spectator would reside not merely as a ghostly figure within a disappearing mass, but as a localized subject within a diasporic community bound by a shared ethics of viewing. My use of a theory of spectrality is not concerned with literal ghosts or phantoms within representation—of which there is an entire, separate history—but with the ethical effects (or traces) of Hong Kong cinema as a traveling culture.

Rehearsals for Love

Taken together, Wong Kar-wai's films constitute a body of love. All his films are about love—unrequited, mistaken, missed, tragic and (in very rare cases) found.[10] In this film, *In the Mood for Love,* we are presented with a love that is "coincident," yet paradoxically one that never meets its object within the frames of the film (Fig. 14.1).

In the Mood for Love is set in Hong Kong in 1962. The two protagonists —newspaper journalist Chow Mo-wan (Tony Leung Chiu-wai) and shipping secretary Su Li-zhen (Maggie Cheung Man-yuk)—move into adjacent rooms in a Hong Kong apartment building on the same day. They join other displaced Shanghainese who left the mainland after the communist takeover in 1949. Each night, the two descend the same staircase to buy noodles for dinner, barely acknowledging each other as they pass. Eventually, they discover that their spouses are having an affair and they resist having one of their own when they begin to fall in love. Their spouses remain, significantly, hidden from view; we hear only their voices, or see the backs of their heads. Mirroring

FIGURE 14.1. Love at a distance in *In the Mood for Love*, dir. Wong Kar-wai.

this unseen romance between their spouses, Chow Mo-wan and Su Li-zhen imagine the beginnings, or the possibility, of an affair by rehearsing it.

At the level of both dialogue and representation, the film engages with issues of intersection and coincidence.[11] This preoccupation is set up in the opening frames of the film when Mrs. Suen, the landlady, exclaims, "What a coincidence! Moving in on the same day!" Later, when Mo-wan and Li-zhen first admit their spouses' infidelity, their conversation is coded through commodities—the handbag that Li-zhen's husband bought both his wife and his mistress; the tie bought on an overseas business trip that both Mo-wan and Li-zhen's husband wear. Li-zhen responds unconvincingly, "What a coincidence!" Coincidence implies a simultaneous and apparent connectedness between two otherwise unconnected events or occurrences. Although love may appear to be a "coincidence" between two otherwise separate beings, theirs is a love never realized, that never meets its object.

Yet love is precisely a *noncoincidence*. According to Lacan, love involves a misrecognition, a noncoincidence between the eye and the gaze. Essential to love is a wishing, a frustration, and a desire stemming from the belief that there is something more behind what we see:

> From the outset, we see, in the dialectic of the eye and the gaze, that there is no coincidence, but, on the contrary, a lure. When, in love, I solicit a look, what is

profoundly unsatisfying and always missing is that— *You never look at me from the place from which I see you.* Conversely, *what I look at is never what I wish to see.*[12]

I suggest that in *In the Mood for Love,* love is similarly a noncoincidence. We do not see the protagonists with their spouses, or the spouses with their lovers. Rather, the contrived "coincidences" and "chance" meetings between Mo-wan and Li-zhen are a rehearsal for some belated reunion or meeting that cannot happen *now,* or indeed within the frames of the film.[13] What we see instead are practices of love manifested in repeated dialogue, images, and situations in the film. Mo-wan and Li-zhen also rehearse how they will react when they confront their spouses about the affair, thus allowing them to play out their own emotions. After a rehearsed confrontation, Mo-wan says to Li-zhen, "That's not the right reaction. Do it again." When Li-zhen begins to cry, Mo-wan says, "Don't cry. This is only a rehearsal. This isn't real."

Scenes from this film also resonate with those in other films by Wong. For example, when Li-zhen breaks into Mo-wan's room in Singapore, she steals his slippers and leaves lipstick on a cigarette, echoing Faye Wong's phantom presence in Officer 663's room in *Chungking Express* (Officer 663 is also played by Tony Leung Chiu-wai). The film also includes a scene whereby Li-zhen and Mo-wan are sitting in the back of a taxi together and Li-zhen rests her head on Mo-wan's shoulder; this is the same composition as the shot of Leslie Cheung resting his head on Tony Leung's shoulder in *Happy Together.* Is love always a cliché, or has it disappeared into a *mise-en-abîme* of scenes from other Wong movies? Can we see in these rehearsals an ethics of viewing and responding to the film, and to the political preoccupations of recent Hong Kong art cinema more generally? With each film, Wong is literally starting again, coaxing us to believe in a love that rarely seems to find its object.

In *In the Mood for Love,* Wong presents an image on the screen that is (lovingly) detailed, dense, and saturated, and yet on the edge of ruin and decay. The specter of an almost ungraspable love is nevertheless made present at the level of film form and style in what I call a spectral aesthetics.

Spectral Aesthetics and the Ethics of Film Spectatorship

In the fall 2001 volume of the journal *positions,* the guest editors Esther Yau and Kyung Kim suggest that films of the Asia/Pacific "turn the filmic space into a spectral surface by which shadows of the past colonial modernity . . . are invented as survival tactics. To envision the spectral surface, the act of looking engages the continuous effort of memory and translation."[14] There are numerous references to the notion of the phantasmic and the spectral in debates relating to film and feminism (among other things), within an Asia/Pacific context.[15] Most of these discussions draw on Jacques Derrida's *Specters of Marx*, despite the fact that in this book Derrida does not explicitly mention film at all. Why this sudden flurry of concern with a vocabulary of spectrality, and what is there in *Specters of Marx* that might be useful to film studies? In particular, how can spectrality inform our reading of a film that represents a precise moment of Hong Kong modernity (Hong Kong of the 1960s)?

On the specter's relationship to visibility, Derrida notes, "The specter, as its name indicates, is the *frequency* of a certain visibility.... The specter is also, among other things, what one imagines, what one thinks one sees and which one projects—on an imaginary screen."[16] The implications of his comments for film studies, and in particular theories of spectatorship, are obvious, but he does not explore them in any detail.[17]

Like the "supplement" in his earlier theorizations, the specter exists as a trace that is forever incomplete, always a promise for the future. Hence my term "spectral bodies" in this chapter indicates something part impossibility, part future promise of a spectator paradigm. Like Rey Chow's imagining of an alternative community for Hong Kong (through her analysis of Stanley Kwan's *Rouge* and nostalgia as a forward-looking operation, a searching rather than a return to a space of the past), it might be possible to conceive of spectators of Hong Kong films as themselves constituting another kind of community, through a shared ethics of film reception based on memory and inheritance.[18]

While I am reluctant to confer upon Derrida any status as an "original," what I will draw from his discussions on Marx is a concern with ethics—in the sense of responsibility within everyday interactions and negotiations, rather than as a grand philosophical project. (In Derrida's case, this is an ethics for the operation of an international political community, which he terms "the New International.") This ethics is also engaged in how we might conceive of the body in recent Hong Kong art cinema.

The specter has a curious relationship to embodiment. For Derrida, the specter is "a paradoxical incorporation" in that it is both phenomenal and material.[19] Although the specter is not corporeal, is not ontology, it has, as Antonio Negri notes, an "ontological pertinence" that acknowledges a connection to the material world.[20] There is a common slippage between the represented body and what is presumed to be an authentic, material existence. Therefore, I would modify Negri's phrase slightly by saying that ethnicity in film also has an "ontological *im*pertinence."

Film is meant to inspire us, but how do we prevent the specter from becoming ontology? How do we refute, or hold at bay, its "ontological *im*pertinence"? And what would be the implications of this for a theory of ethnic spectatorship? I take up the issue of spectral aesthetics again in a later section on the "overripe image," but first, I wish to explore how spectrality might inform an ethics for the global circulation and reception of recent Hong Kong art cinema.

The Ethics of Circulation

In her edited collection *At Full Speed,* Esther Yau describes New Hong Kong cinema as encompassing: "film as art, . . . an ethical concept of authorship, . . . the film auteur's social responsibility regarding Hong Kong, and . . . cinematic realism as a preferred mode of cinematic representation that reflects artistic and ethical commitment to a local community."[21] Yau's mantra of a "New Hong Kong cinema ethics" equates the "art film" with the production of locality as an ethical concern.

Thinking about Hong Kong cinema in the western context of spectatorship, we could start with a particularly striking example by a prominent theorist of spectatorship, Miriam Bratu Hansen. Hansen begins her essay on Walter Benjamin with the following line: "More than any other contemporary film practice, Hong Kong cinema seems to me to resonate with Benjamin's efforts to theorize mass-mediated modernity, with its twin etiologies of technological reproduction and capitalist consumption."[22] After a brief discussion of John Woo's *Face/Off* and Peter Chan's *Comrades: Almost a Love Story,* Hansen dispenses with any further consideration of Hong Kong film per se. Rather, she uses the concepts of speed and violence in the films leading up to the 1997 handover as a segue into a discussion of western theory (in particular the concept of "innervation" in Benjamin's work). It is only in the last line of her essay that Hansen returns to Hong Kong cinema, suggesting that it is "a film practice that engages with technologies of incorporation and embodiment that indeed make the cinema a memory, in more than one sense."[23] Hong Kong cinema has virtually disappeared in Hansen's article, surviving only as a trace or a memory, without a body or object.[24]

In the context of art cinema more specifically, much has already been written on the ethics of art film circulation within the international festival circuit. In his article "Discovering Form, Inferring Meaning," Bill Nichols notes, "Hovering, like a specter, . . . are those deep structures and thick descriptions that might restore a sense of the particular and local to what we have now recruited to the realm of the global."[25] Nichols's use of the language of structural anthropology ("deep structures and thick descriptions") attests to a profoundly mimeticist way of reading (local) culture as it circulates globally through cinema. Although writing with a different agenda, David Bordwell similarly suggests, "Whatever success they find in festivals or foreign markets, Hong Kong's most recent art films remain strongly rooted in the conventions of local entertainment."[26] Implicitly, critics such as Nichols and Bordwell equate the production of the local with the assumption of ethical responsibility on the part of the filmmakers.

Yet the inheritance of this kind of assumption from existing models of (western) criticism can also be productive in working toward a countermodel of ethnic spectatorship. Inheritance, Derrida reminds us elsewhere, "implies decision, responsibility, response, and consequently, critical selection, choice" in the founding of a new political community.[27] Similarly, it might be possible to think through a concept of community modeled on the neighboring protagonists in *In the Mood for Love*. The film reconceptualizes the notion of community within the frame of an aesthetic of ruin. Or more precisely, the film moves from an "overripe" image (one rendered in loving detail) to an image of ruin to conceive of how we might salvage a notion of (a spectral) community.

The Overripe Image

> The film looks and feels overripe, on the edge of decay because no amount of repetition, long fades, or slow motion epiphanies can keep the images—the time, place, characters they inscribe—from wafting into thin air.[28]

So much of this film exists outside the frame. We can regard the film's aesthetic as spectral, in the sense of its functioning like a supplement.[29] What occurs *within* the frame also looks and feels overripe—full of dense, saturated colors and slow-motion shots (of swirling cigarette smoke and fetishized bodies) that are almost suffocating in their beauty. Paul Arthur notes, "Close-ups are reserved for things unnoticed except by the hypersensitive lovers; slow pans build a delicate tracery of looks and spectral retreats; mirrors, foreground obstructions, and frames-within-frames create a thicket of individual isolation amidst human congestion."[30] (Fig. 14.2)

There are specific cinematic practices that I regard as forming the "spectral aesthetics" of this film. One example is the voice-over, which, when used in *film noir*, typically involves the use of a strong male voice to control the narrative and unify the story of the film world. In Wong's films, however, the voice-over fractures the narrative, offering different, often unreliable points of view that are crowded with insignificant details. In an interview with Tony Rayns, Wong notes, "Nowadays, people are more likely to talk to themselves than to others."[31] Wong uses "anachronistic" film techniques while placing them in a

FIGURE 14.2. Looks and traces. *In the Mood for Love,* dir. Wong Kar-wai.

temporal present to signify a modern-day preoccupation. His recurrent use of slow-motion shots and stop-motion photography are other examples whereby spectrality is inscribed into the film's form. In this film, Wong suggests that the slow-motion shots are "not [about] carrying the action, but the environment," that is, about capturing a certain *mood* of Hong Kong modernity in the 1960s.[32]

I would argue that although Wong is meticulous in his detailed rendering of 1960s Hong Kong, the film is only ostensibly about the city of that period. It is what spills outside the (time) frame that provides the possibility of the formation of a modern-day spectatorial community.

As Paul Arthur notes, "The figures upon the screen are at once immediate and absent."[33] This paradox is embodied in the figure of Maggie Cheung. The lighting scheme employed throughout the film appears to make her shimmer, as though she exists only precariously, on the verge of fading away, while at the same time her appearance on-screen is fetishized and over-invested with meaning. The overripe image is also a highly eroticized space filled with desires that cannot fully be expressed either within the mise-en-scène or the narrative.

Much has been made of Cheung's *cheongsam* (or *qipao*) in the film. In particular, critics suggest that the tight-fitting *cheongsam* accentuates Maggie Cheung's body and foregrounds her movements. Shelley Kraicer writes, "Cheung can use her body as an expressive instrument just as effectively as she uses her face. Her posture, the timing of her walk, the way she caresses a

FIGURE 14.3. Spectral body in *In the Mood for Love*, dir. Wong Kar-wai.

door frame all radiate a world of deeply felt, just barely suppressed feeling."[34] (Fig. 14.3)

I argue that rather than being "present," Maggie Cheung operates as a *lost* body and a point of spectral identification in this film. The extravagant patterns and colors of her numerous *cheongsam* play over a site of loss and nostalgia. In fact, the clothes take the place of her body, which becomes merely an outline. Rather than accentuate her physical movements and performance, they dictate and create them. As Cheung herself has pointed out in several interviews, the high-collared *cheongsam* literally altered how she was able to move, instating new gestures in her performance.[35]

Maggie Cheung is a "paradoxical incorporation," a spectral body that makes Hong Kong modernity visible through surface display rather than an embodied depth. Against her representation of a lost or fragmented body, there is a tendency, a "specular failure," to want to recuperate it as a whole. It is precisely through Cheung's fragmented representation that spectators attempt to construct a modernity for Hong Kong out of the loss of China (synechdochically rendered in the film through Shanghai's displaced community in Hong Kong).[36]

The "over-ripeness" of the images also places them on the edge of ruin and decay, and the film ends, literally, in the ruins of Angkor Wat. Ruins are remainders and reminders of things past; they provide evidence of the past, of its authenticity. The fact that ruins are by their nature fragmentary invites viewers to imagine or reconstruct a lost whole from the enduring fragment; they also reflect the ethnic spectator's desire for a whole body, an authentic presence, to be mirrored on the screen—despite this impossibility.[37]

The connection between Cheung's fetishized body and the exterior display of fashion marking a particular moment of Hong Kong's modernity is not exclusive to her role in *In the Mood for Love*. In fact, it builds on her previous roles in films such as Stanley Kwan's *Center Stage* and Olivier Assayas' *Irma Vep*. Carlos Rojas examines the relationship between what he calls "specular failure" and the "spectral returns" of Maggie Cheung in these two films.[38] In both Cheung appears as a figure in the "present" recreating periods and films from the past.[39] Rojas suggests that Cheung functions as a site of "inevitable loss, and potential recovery" for the emergence of Hong Kong modernity across different eras. In both films, she also represents a lost body that is paradoxically made hypervisible by exquisite *cheongsam* or equally tight-fitting latex. In the Wong film and *Center Stage* in particular, the *cheongsam* represents the liberated Chinese woman that emerged with modern Chinese femininity in the 1920s and 1930s.[40] Yet the dresses seem out of place, inappropriate. The neighbors remark, "She dresses up like that to go out for noodles?"

While Su Li-zhen is watched by all her neighbors, she herself escapes to the movie theaters to watch the films she loves (significantly, this activity occurs entirely off-screen). Echoing this cinephilia, Wong Kar-wai made a short film celebrating early Hong Kong film actresses entitled *Huayang de nianhua* (The Age of Flowers), featured on the Criterion Collection special edition DVD of *In the Mood for Love*. The short consists of a montage of shots from early Hong Kong nitrate films that were found in a warehouse in Southern California. The Chinese title of *In the Mood for Love* closely mirrors that of the popular song "Huayang de Nianhua," sung by Zhou Xuan, a famous Shanghainese singer of the 1930s and 1940s, which is playing on the radio in the film. Wong tells us that the term is used to describe women in their prime, but he extends it to 1960s Hong Kong, thus feminizing the city in its modernity. The nitrate films also invoke nostalgia and archive a collective memory of what we as spectators can now inherit. In fact, Wong made this short to raise awareness about these literally disintegrating films he wanted to see preserved. In *In the Mood for Love*, Maggie Cheung represents this confluence of modernity, nostalgia, and a paradoxical "over-ripeness" that blooms from loss. Like the images from the ruined nitrate films, the past also provides a vision of a possible future. Thus, if we read the final sequence at Angkor Wat allegorically, as Gina Marchetti suggests we should, the relationship of ruins to time, and to a Chinese, or more specifically Hong Kong, modernity, is worth elaborating on.[41]

In the context of western modernity, Walter Benjamin made a relevant distinction between symbol and allegory according to "the category of time."[42] Time is "fluid and changing" in symbol; in allegory, it is "mortified," not "in bud and bloom, but in the over-ripeness and decay of her creations."[43]

For Benjamin, the allegorical form in Charles Baudelaire's poetry had been outmoded since the Baroque. In the Baroque, a period of intense social conflict and war, it had been a dominant mode of perception, "when human suffering and material ruin were the stuff and substance of historical experience."[44] Baudelaire, however, was writing in nineteenth-century Paris—an era and realm of material abundance (world expositions, the first department stores, etc.)—the epitome of a mood or environment of "over-ripeness." *In the Mood for Love* invokes a fraught political era—worldwide socialist revolts in the 1960s and the Cultural Revolution in China—yet it is also figured as a time of "over-ripeness," an "age of flowers."

My discussion of Benjamin's observations and early-twentieth-century western discourses on ruins are not out of context here. Indeed, the Chinese encounter with western traditions on ruins is significant. Commenting on the historical antecedents to contemporary Chinese art, Wu Hung notes that while ruins were written about in poetry, they were never painted in Chinese art prior to the twentieth century: "There was indeed a taboo in premodern China against preserving and portraying ruins: although abandoned cities or fallen palaces were lamented in words, their images, if painted, would imply inauspiciousness and danger."[45] Wu suggests, however, that when the Chinese encountered "European 'ruin' culture" through the work of photographers in China at the beginning of the mid-nineteenth century, this had a great impact on modern Chinese visual culture: "What ensued has been a separate history of ruins in China. Ruin images were legitimated; but what made them 'modern' (i.e., what distinguished them from classical Chinese ruin poetry) was their emphasis on the present, their fascination with violence and destruction, their embodiment of a critical gaze, and their mass circulation."[46]

If we apply Wu's comments to representations of ruins in Chinese film, two significant issues are worth exploring. The first is the "modernity" of ruins (or a modern conception of images of ruin), and the second is the development of a critical gaze for regarding these images. This critical gaze does not appear out of nowhere; it is an *embodied* gaze. This final point is crucial because Wu also ethnicizes the gaze. Analyzing an anonymous photograph of ruins from 1911 that captures a devastated street scene and only the back of a person's head within the frame, Wu writes, "Although the photographer is unknown, the intrinsic gaze, embodied by the street onlooker in the scene, is Chinese."[47] The development of a modern Chinese visual culture thus depends upon the attendant development of a "Chinese gaze" that is at once historicized and politicized.

These developments within the pictorial arts can also be contextualized more specifically within the history of Chinese cinema. At least three critics have drawn a parallel between *In the Mood for Love* and Fei Mu's 1948 classic *Spring in a Small City*.[48] Recently remade by Tian Zhuangzhuang as *Springtime in a Small Town,* the film is languorous in its long takes and slow tracking shots. Set in 1946, Tian's film invokes the same sense of claustrophobia as *In the Mood for Love* (Mark Li Ping-bing is the cinematographer for both *In the Mood for Love* and *Springtime in a Small Town*). The film depicts four main characters who remain in the ruins of their bombed-out dwelling after the Japanese occupation. Their lives are interrupted by the sudden appearance of a Shanghainese doctor who seeks out an old school friend after a decade apart. The doctor is surprised to find his first love there, now married to his school friend. They realize they are still in love but that their own reunion is precluded by honor and tradition. The literal and metaphoric representation of ruins effectively preserves the past in memory and reconstructs China's history through a displaced modernity elsewhere: The cosmopolitan space of Shanghai is referred to often in the film but never shown, just as *In the Mood for Love* references many off-screen spaces, including a nostalgia for Shanghai.[49]

I attended the Australian premier of *Springtime in a Small Town,* with the director Tian present and in conversation with writer Geremie Barmé.[50] After the film I was approached by a man from China who asked what I thought of it. When I remarked on the film's slow pace and expressed my frustration and dissatisfaction with it, he looked at me incredulously and asked, "Are you Chinese?" The existence of a naturalized "Chinese gaze" that my fellow viewer implies is inherently linked to the film's project of remaking and reconstructing through ruin imagery. I was questioned as to how I could view a modern-day remake of a classic Chinese film by an acclaimed Fifth Generation director with anything but a sense of cultural nationalism.[51] Far from wanting to subscribe to the possibility of an essentialized "organic" Chinese gaze, what I now aim to theorize is an inhabitable, ethnically marked position from which to view Hong Kong art cinema out of the impossibility of rooted Chineseness.

I began this section by noting that so much of the film exists outside the frame, spilling over into other off-screen spaces. The film is constructed around a series of contrived coincidences, deletions, and additions that can be seen in the wider context of rehearsing, remaking, and attempting to start over again. Ruins suggest the opposite of being able to "start over," a preoccupation in Wong's films *Chungking Express* and more explicitly in *Happy Together,* since they still invoke the endurance of the present. Yet despite this, the film continually attempts to renew itself, to start again, albeit *outside the frame*.

Starting Again: The Deleted Scenes

It may appear to be a sign of desperation when one is forced to analyze the scenes that are taken *out* of a film, but I argue that in this case, the status of what is left out is of almost equal import to what we in fact see on the screen. The deleted scenes featured on the Criterion Collection special edition DVD of *In the Mood for Love* supplement the film's attempts to renew itself, thereby inviting us to view it differently. Moreover, these scenes are almost raised to the status of fetish objects by having the director Wong Kar-wai provide a voice-over commentary for them.

The scene that appears first, "The Secret of Room 2046," shows the omitted love scene between Chow Mo-wan and Su Li-zhen. Wong's voice-over informs us that the setting for the hotel was in fact an old hospital for British soldiers; after the 1997 handover, most of these soldiers left, leaving the building deserted and about to be torn down. Wong said that the hospital reminded him of buildings in Hong Kong in the 1950s so he shot there, redecorating the patients' quarters to look like hotel rooms and hoping that the building would be preserved on film, even if it were to be torn down. Wong tells us further that he wanted the film to begin there, although it ends up towards the close of the film in the final cut. Fearing that the building would be torn down, Wong filmed there as much as he could, but found the shots he took were never right, so in the fifteen months it took to make the film, he and the crew went back five or six times. What is interesting is that he constantly returns to this beginning, which turns out never to have been the beginning at all. This scene, of course, is the one that most viewers are interested in seeing, although the general sentiment has been that Wong, by not including scenes of Chow Mo-wan and Su Li-zhen making love, made the right decision; their affair somehow makes the film purer and more poignant in its "unconsummated" form.

Another deleted scene called "A Lost Encounter" involves a reunion of the two in the ruins at Angkor Wat. Yet the meeting of their bodies in this encounter at the end of the film is likewise "lost." These failed connections and lost reunions speak of bodies that are disconnected, existing only as a trace in the final cut of the film. What we are left with is a concluding scene of a ruin and two bodies that are not reunited *except outside* the main film text, in a form that is spectral. The ending we are offered is two bodies that don't meet again, at least in this film.

Coda

The recent fascination in the west with Hong Kong art cinema perpetuates an impossible search for an authentic Chineseness or "Asianness" behind the images on the screen. Rey Chow asks, "Would it not be more pertinent to see Asianness itself as a reproducible phantom, an exotic yet consumable commodity . . . ?"[52] The corresponding return to an identity politics imperative by ethnic spectators reads realism as mimeticism in order to recuperate an authentic body or full presence. Chow adds, "The attempt to find oneself properly imaged, mirrored, and represented (on the screen as well as off) as the definitive way of anchoring one's identity is . . . a newly fetishistic reading in an ever-expanding phantom field."[53]

My argument has been that if we read the images on the screen as being spectral rather than as disappearing, on the one hand, or as a fully present and authentic "whole," on the other, this may provide us with the beginnings of a model for, and an ethics of, ethnic spectatorship. That is, from what appears "lost" or outside the film's body, the outline of another community can be seen. I have thus sought to construct an ethical diasporic Chinese viewing position out of the impossibility of rooted Chineseness as it is represented by the film's displaced community and its lost bodies.

The formation of such a community of spectators involves a reconfiguration of the notion of the neighborhood, such as the film seems to engage with, between bodies that remain spectral, that never meet, and yet are bound by love (or at least a "mood" for love), that spills outside the frame. The question remains whether this way of viewing is something that can be rehearsed. I think the film gives us a sense that it might be possible.[54] In the film, Su Li-zhen, who is, importantly, a cinephile, says, "You notice things if you pay attention." By examining the spectral aesthetics of *In the Mood for Love,* it is possible to see that the (ethnic) body has not disappeared entirely; it is both on-screen and off, in memories and in archives, building alternative communities outside the film. We might have to wait for *2046,* Wong's next film, to see how we can add to this renewal and rehearsal.[55]

Notes

I am very grateful to Jodi Brooks for her invaluable comments and advice on this essay.

1. The intertitles appearing in the film are adapted from Liu Yichang's novella, *Duidao,* on which the film is based.

2. On existing theories of ethnic spectatorship, see for example Mayne, *Cinema and*

Spectatorship; hooks, *Black Looks;* Gaines, "White Privilege," and Chow, *Woman and Chinese Modernity,* 3–33. Rey Chow's work is uniquely significant in that it addresses cross-cultural spectatorship from a Westernized, diasporic Chinese perspective.

3. Marks, *Touch,* 105 (original emphasis).
4. Ibid.
5. Ibid.
6. Abbas, *Hong Kong,* 28.
7. Ibid., 23.
8. The specter is not a substitution or a replacement as it exists in Abbas's schema (e.g., ghost = cinematic space). Nor is it a misrecognition—of not seeing what is there. Rather, it is an over-investment, of recognizing too much.
9. Until January 1, 2004, Hong Kong films were not considered "local production" in China and so faced China's strict import quotas, among other restrictions. Hong Kong films engaged the Chinese mainland before that time: Co-productions were being made, and some Hong Kong films were screened in China. They were not, however, "wholly present" in the sense that they were not considered "fully Chinese," i.e., local productions. Similarly, diasporic contexts are to some degree "here" and "there" and "neither here nor there." On the "spectrality" of postcolonial nations, see Cheah, "Spectral Nationality."
10. Many critics have compared *In the Mood for Love* to Wong's earlier film *Days of Being Wild.* Both films are set in Hong Kong of the 1960s and feature a character played by Maggie Cheung named Su Li-zhen.
11. The novella *Duidao* is also translated as "Intersection."
12. Lacan, *Four Fundamental Concepts,* 102–103 (original emphasis).
13. Wong's latest film, *2046,* is set fifty years after the Hong Kong handover or "reunion" with China. The room which Mo-wan rents in *In the Mood for Love* to write his martial arts serials in is also numbered 2046.
14. Yau and Kim, "Asia/Pacific Cinemas," 285.
15. For instance, the first issue of *Traces* is entitled "Specters of the West" (Hanawa and Sakai, eds.), and the 13th annual Hong Kong International Film Festival produced a catalogue on "phantoms of Hong Kong cinema."
16. Derrida, *Specters,* 101.
17. The section of *Specters of Marx* that is most pertinent to film studies occurs where Derrida discusses the "visor effect." He writes, however, that he won't discuss this further in any explicit terms (p. 7).
18. See Chow, "Souvenir of Love." Derrida suggests that we must learn to live with specters and that "this being with specters would also be, not only but also, a politics of memory, of inheritance, and of generations." Derrida, *Specters,* xix.
19. Derrida, *Specters,* 6.
20. Negri, "Specter's Smile," 7.
21. Yau, *Full Speed,* 19–20.
22. Hansen, "Benjamin," 306.
23. Ibid., 321.
24. To be fair, Hansen writes that she is "not trying to offer a Benjaminian reading of Hong Kong films" since she does not claim expertise in that area (p. 307).

25. Nichols, "Discovering Form," 27.
26. Bordwell, *Planet*, 265.
27. Derrida, in Derrida and Steigler, *Echographies*, 69.
28. Arthur, review of *In the Mood*, 41.
29. "Adding to, but not adding up." Derrida, *Of Grammatology*, 144.
30. Arthur, review of *In the Mood*, 41.
31. Wong, "Poet of Time," by Rayns, 13.
32. Wong Kar-wai, interview by Ciment and Niogret, in *In the Mood for Love*, DVD special edition (Criterion Collection, 2002).
33. Arthur, review of *In the Mood*, 41.
34. Kraicer, "Time Blossoms."
35. I thank Sean Metzger for bringing this point to my attention. The same is true also in the film *Irma Vep* where the latex catsuit similarly constrains Cheung's movements. I have discussed this in more detail in Khoo, "Anagrammatical Translations."
36. We only ever see the slow-motion brush of Cheung's arm over a railing, a glimpse of her calf above the hemline. The "absent" spouses in the film are similarly hidden from full view and glimpsed only in part, never as whole figures.
37. Wu, "Ruins," 62.
38. Rojas, "Specular Failure."
39. The spectral presences within the films are of Ruan Lingyu and Musidora, respectively.
40. Together with the Sun Yat-sen suit, the *qipao* represented modernity in Chinese clothing during the Republican era. See Roberts, *Evolution*. Thanks to Sean Metzger for initially bringing this point to my attention.
41. Marchetti, "Essay."
42. Benjamin, *Trauerspiel* study, I, 342; quoted in Buck-Morss, *Dialectics*, 168.
43. Ibid. Benjamin is responding to the temporality of the "arrested" image, which he says has a profound impact on how we might regard the historical present (as a past which hasn't past).
44. Ibid., 178.
45. Wu, "Ruins," 60.
46. Ibid.
47. Ibid.
48. See Teo, *"Wong Kar-wai"*; Kraicer, "Time Blossoms"; and Marchetti, "Essay." These critics draw attention to the themes of unrequited love, honor despite an unhappy marriage, and so on.
49. Besides Shanghai, the "elsewheres" referenced in the film (some on-screen, some off-screen) include Cambodia, Singapore, Vietnam and Japan. The film ends with Mrs. Suen, Li-zhen's landlady, about to migrate to the United States.
50. Tian (director, *Springtime in a Small Town*), in discussion with writer Geremie Barmé, Sydney, Australia, July 29, 2003.
51. Ibid. Tian said that he wanted to remake Fei Mu's classic out of a sense of love for the original.
52. Chow, "Phantom," 1393.

53. Ibid., 1392.

54. See also Hou Hsiou-Hsien's *Good Men, Good Women (Hao Nan, Hao Nü)*. This film tells the story of a modern-day actress starring in a film about the White Terror (the Taiwanese government's crackdown on suspected communists during the 1950s). Through her rehearsals for the movie, she visualizes scenes from the script, bringing her personal memories to a "re-visioning" of Taiwanese history. The film explicitly links the practice of "rehearsals" with reimagining history and community in Taiwan.

55. *2046* screened in competition at the 58th Cannes Film Festival on May 20, 2004. Prior to its Hong Kong premiere on September 29, 2004, Wong made further changes to the film: shooting additional scenes, incorporating CGI shots, and revising the beginning and the ending. The screening at Cannes can therefore be regarded as merely another rehearsal. *2046* has been scheduled for release in various cities across Asia and Europe throughout the rest of 2004 and into early 2005. At the time this essay was completed, no North American or Australian release date had yet been set.

Bibliography

Abbas, Ackbar. *Hong Kong: Culture and the Politics of Disappearance.* Minneapolis: University of Minnesota Press, 1997.
Adrian, Bonnie. *Framing the Bride: Globalizing Beauty and Romance in Taiwan's Bridal Industry.* Berkeley: University of California Press, 2003.
Ai Weiwei, Hua Tianxue, and Feng Boyi, eds. "Fuck Off" [*Bu hezuo de fangshi,* "An Uncooperative Approach"]. Limited private publication as catalogue accompanying exhibit. Shanghai: Eastlink Gallery, 2000.
Alsetter, Rob. "Trailer Park." http://www.dynamicforces.com/htmlfiles/trailerpark28.html (accessed March 23, 2004).
Anagnost, Ann. *National Past-times: Narrative, Representation, and Power in Modern China.* Durham, NC: Duke University Press, 1997.
———. "The Politicized Body." In Zito and Barlow, *Body, Subject and Power,* 131–156.
The Analects of Confucius. Translated and annotated by Arthur Waley. London: Allen & Unwin, 1938.
Anderson, Marston. *The Limits of Realism: Chinese Fiction in the Revolutionary Period.* Berkeley: University of California Press, 1990.
Ang, Audrey. "Few Women Lead China. Some Progress, but Men Retain Most Power." *Houston Chronicle,* November 6, 2002.
———. "Women Still Scarce in China's Power Structure." *Desert News,* November 5, 2002.
Ang, Ien. *On Not Speaking Chinese: Living Between Asia and the West.* New York: Routledge, 2001.
Anonymous. *Dumen zhuzhici* [Folk Tunes from the Capital]. 1814. Reprinted in Zhang Cixi, *Qingdai Yandu liyuan shiliao huibian,* 1172–1173.
Anthony, Andrew. "The Long and the Shirt of It." *Observer,* July 6, 2003. http://film.guardian.co.uk/interview/interviewpages/0,6737,992144,00.html (accessed March 24, 2004).
Appadurai, Arjun. *Modernity at Large: Cultural Dimensions of Globalization.* Minneapolis: University of Minnesota Press, 1996.
Apter, Emily. Introduction to *Fetishism as Cultural Discourse,* edited by Emily Apter and Willian Pietz. Ithaca: Cornell University Press, 1993.
Arthur, Paul. Review of *In the Mood for Love,* directed by Wong Kar-wai. *Cineaste* 26, no. 3 (2001): 40–41.

Asad, Talal. *Genealogies of Religion: Discipline and the Reasons of Power in Christianity and Islam.* Baltimore: Johns Hopkins University Press, 1993.

Ba Jin. "He duzhe tan *Jia*" [A Chat with Readers about *Jia*]. In *Ba Jin wenji* [Collected Works of Ba Jin], vol. 4, appendix 3: 478–486. Beijing: Renmin wenxue chubanshe, 1958.

———. *Jia* [The Family]. Vol. 4, *Ba Jin wenji* [Collected Works of Ba Jin]. Beijing: Renmin wenxue chubanshe, 1958.

Barlow, Tani E., ed. *Gender Politics in Modern China: Writing and Feminism.* Durham: Duke University Press, 1993.

———. "Teaching International Feminism in a Global Frame." Drafts presented to Women's Studies Retreat, Duke University, February 5, 1999; and Women's Studies Symposium, Osaka Women's University, March 4, 2001.

———, "Theorizing Woman: *Funü, Guojia* and *Jiating* [Chinese Woman, Chinese State, Chinese Family]." In Zito and Barlow, *Body, Subject and Power,* 253–289.

Barthes, Roland. *Empire of Signs.* Translated by Richard Howard. New York: Hill and Wang, 1982.

———. "The Reality Effect." Translated by Richard Howard. In *The Rustle of Language,* 141–148. Berkeley: University of California Press, 1989.

Beech, Hannah. "Wu Yi Goddess of Transparency." *Time,* April 26, 2004.

Benedict, Carol. *Bubonic Plague in Nineteenth-Century China.* Stanford: Stanford University Press, 1996.

Berger, Patricia. *Empire of Emptiness: Buddhist Art and Political Authority in Qing China.* Honolulu: University of Hawai'i Press, 2003.

Berghuis, Thomas. "Considering *Huanjing*: Positioning Experimental Art in China." *positions: east asia cultures critique,* 12, no. 3 (2004): 711–731.

Bhabha, Homi. "The Other Question: Stereotype and Colonial Discourse." *Screen* 24, no. 6 (1983): 18–36.

Blake, C. Fred. "Footbinding in Neo-Confucian China and the Appropriation of Female Labor." *Signs* 19, no. 31 (1994): 676–713.

Bolter, Jay David and Richard Grusin. *Remediation: Understanding New Media.* Cambridge, MA: MIT Press, 1999.

Bolton, Christopher. "From Wooden Cyborgs to Celluloid Souls: Mechanical Bodies in Anime and Japanese Puppet Theater." *positions: east asia cultures critique* 10, no. 3 (2002): 729–771.

Bordo, Susan. *The Male Body: A New Look at Men in Public and Private.* New York: Farrar Straus and Giroux, 2000.

———. *Unbearable Weight: Feminism, Western Culture, and the Body.* Berkeley: University of California Press, 1995.

Bordwell, David. *Planet Hong Kong: Popular Cinema and the Art of Entertainment.* Cambridge, MA: Harvard University Press, 2000.

Borysevicz, Matthieu. *Zhang Dali: Demolition and Dialogue.* Beijing: The Courtyard Gallery, 1999.

Brownell, Susan. *Training the Body for China: Sports in the Moral Order of the People's Republic.* Chicago: University of Chicago Press, 1995.

Buck-Morss, Susan. *The Dialectics of Seeing: Walter Benjamin and the Arcades Project.* Cambridge, MA: MIT Press, 1997.
Butler, Judith. *Bodies That Matter: On the Discursive Limits of "Sex."* New York: Routledge, 1993.
———. "Doing Justice to Someone: Sex Reassignment and Allegories of Transsexuality." *GLQ* 7, no. 4 (2001): 621–636.
———. *Gender Trouble: Feminism and the Subversion of Identity.* New York: Routledge, 1990.
Callaway, Helen. "Dressing for Dinner in the Bush: Rituals of Self-definition and British Imperial Authority." In *Dress and Gender: Making and Meaning,* edited by Ruth Barnes and J. E. Eicher, 232–247. Oxford: Berg, 1992.
Cao Xueqin, and Gao E. *Honglou meng bashihui jiaoben.* Hong Kong: Zhonghua shuju, 1985.
Central News Agency. "Taiwan's Online Game Market Ranks Second at NT$4.9b." *eTaiwan News.com,* August 8, 2002. http://www.etaiwannews.com/Taiwan2002/08/29/1030583286.htm (accessed August 8, 2002).
Chan, Alfred. "China's Fourth Generation: The New Rulers and the Secret Files." *China Journal,* no. 50 (2003): 107–119.
Chan, Jachinson. *Chinese American Masculinities: From Fu Manchu to Bruce Lee.* New York: Routledge, 2001.
Chao, Antonia Yengning. "Embodying the Invisible: Body Politics in Constructing Contemporary Taiwanese Lesbian Identities." Ph.D. diss., Cornell University, 1996.
———. "US Space Shuttles Going to the Moon: Global Metaphors and Local Strategies in Building Up Taiwan's Lesbian Identities." Paper presented at the Third International Super-Slim Conference on the Politics of Gender and Sexuality, Center for the Study of Sexualities, National Taiwan Central University, November 27, 1999.
Cheah, Pheng. "Spectral Nationality: The Living On *[sur-vie]* of the Postcolonial Nation in Neocolonial Globalization." *Boundary 2* 26, no. 3 (1999): 225–252.
Chen Longting. "Huang Junxiong dianshi budaixi yanjiu." MA thesis, Chinese Culture University, 1991.
Chen Sen. *Pinhua baojian* [The Precious Mirror of Ranked Flowers]. 1836. Reprint, Shanghai: Shanghai guji chubanshe, 1990.
Cheng, Li. "China's Next Phase: Hu's New Deal?" *China Business Review* 30, no. 3 (2003): 48–53.
Cheng, Yu. "Anatomy of a Legend." In *A Study of Hong Kong Cinema in the Seventies,* edited by Li Cheuk-to, 18–25. Hong Kong: The Urban Council, 1984.
Chi, Ta-wei. *Wan'an Babilun—Wanglu Shidaide Xingyu, Yiyi, yu Zhengzhi Yuedu* [Sexually Dissident Notes from Babylon]. Taipei: Tansuo, 1998.
Chiao, Hsiung-Ping. "Bruce Lee: His Influence on the Evolution of the Kung Fu Genre." *Journal of Popular Film and Television* 9, no. 1 (1984): 30–42.
Chih Po-lan. "Xiaoshi de hutong" [Disappearing *hutong*]. http://www.bjdi.pku.edu.cn (accessed November 18, 2002).

"China's New State Councilors Approved." *Xinhua News Agency,* March 16, 2003.
Ching, Leo T. S. *Becoming "Japanese": Colonial Taiwan and the Politics of Identity Formation.* Berkeley and Los Angeles: University of California Press, 2001.
Chou Wah-shan. *Houzhimin tongzhi* [Postcolonial Tongzhi]. Hong Kong: Xianggang tongzhi yanjiushe, 1997.
Chow, Rey. *Ethics After Idealism: Theory-Culture-Ethnicity-Reading.* Bloomington and Indianapolis: University of Indiana Press, 1998.
———. "On Chineseness as a Theoretical Problem." *Boundary 2* 25, no. 3 (1998): 1–24.
———. "A Phantom Discipline." *PMLA* 116, no. 5 (2001): 1386–1395.
———. *Primitive Passions: Visuality, Sexuality, Ethnography, and Contemporary Chinese Cinema.* New York: Columbia University Press, 1995.
———. "A Souvenir of Love." In *Ethics After Idealism: Theory-Culture-Ethnicity-Reading,* 133–148. Bloomington: University of Indiana Press, 1998.
———. *Woman and Chinese Modernity: The Politics of Reading Between East and West.* Minneapolis: University of Minnesota Press, 1991.
Chu, Yingchi. *Hong Kong Cinema: Colonizer, Motherland, and Self.* London: RoutledgeCurzon, 2003.
Chun, Allen. "Fuck Chineseness: On the Ambiguities of Ethnicity as Culture as Identity." *Boundary 2* 23, no. 2 (1996): 111–138.
Clouse, Robert. *Bruce Lee: The Biography.* Burbank: Unique Publications, 1988.
Cole, Alan. *Mothers and Sons in Chinese Buddhism.* Stanford: Stanford University Press, 1998.
Cooper, B. B. *The Chinese Repository* 3, no. 12. 1835.
Croll, Elizabeth. *Wise Daughters from Foreign Lands: European Women Writers in China.* London: Pandora, 1989.
Dal Lago, Francesca, and Song Dong, Zhang Dali, Zhang Wang, and Wang Jianwei. "Space and Public: Site Specificity in Beijing." *Art Journal* 59.1, Spring (2000): 74–87.
Daly, Mary. *Gyn/ecology: The Metaethics of Radical Feminism.* Boston: Beacon Press, 1990.
Darrobers, Roger. *Opéra de Pékin: Théâtre et société à la fin de l'empire sino-manchou.* Paris: Blue de Chine, 1998.
Deleuze, Gilles. *Cinema 1: The Movement-Image.* Translated by Hugh Tomlinson and Barbara Habberjam. Minneapolis: University of Minnesota Press, 1986.
Derrida, Jacques. *Of Grammatology.* Translated by Gayatri Spivak. Baltimore: Johns Hopkins University Press, 1976.
———. *Specters of Marx: The State of the Debt, the Work of Mourning, and the New International.* Translated by Peggy Kamuf. London: Routledge, 1994.
Derrida, Jacques, and Bernard Steigler. *Echographies of Television: Filmed Interviews.* Translated by Jennifer Bajorek. Malden, MA: Polity Press, 2001.
Despeux, Catherine. *Taoïsme et le corps humain: Le Xiuzhen tu.* Paris: Guy Tredaniel Editeur, 1994.
Desser, David. "The Kung Fu Craze: Hong Kong Cinema's First American Reception." In *The Cinema of Hong Kong: History, Arts, Identity,* edited by Poshek Fu and David Desser, 19–43. Cambridge: Cambridge University Press, 2000.

Desuoting. "*Caozhu yichuan*" [A String of Dew Beads]. In Zhang Cixi, *Qingdai Yandu liyuan shiliao huibian,* 1172, 1988.

Dikötter, Frank. *Imperfect Conceptions: Medical Knowledge, Birth Defects, and Eugenics in China.* New York: Columbia University Press, 1998.

———. *Sex, Culture and Modernity in China: Medical Science and the Construction of Sexual Identities in the Early Republican Period.* Hong Kong: Hong Kong University Press, 1995.

Ding, Naifei. *Obscene Things: Sexual Politics in* Jin Ping Mei. Durham: Duke University Press, 2002.

Ding, Naifei, and Jenpeng Liu. "Crocodile Skin, Lesbian Stuffing: Half-man Half-horse Qiu Miaojin." Paper presented at the Third International Super-Slim Conference on the Politics of Gender and Sexuality, Center for the Study of Sexualities, National Taiwan Central University, November 27, 1999.

Dirlik, Arif, and Xudong Zhang. "Introduction: Postmodernism and China." In Dirlik and Zhang, *Postmodernism and China,* 1–17.

———, eds. *Postmodernism and China.* Durham and London: Duke University Press, 2000.

"Dressing Up the Image of China's Women Ministers," *Straits Times,* July 3, 2004.

Drucker, Alison. "The Influence of Western Women on the Anti-Footbinding Movement 1840–1911." In *Women in China: Current Directions in Historical Scholarship,* edited by R. W. L. Guisso and Stanley Johannesen. Youngstown NY: Philo Press, 1981.

Dutton, Michael. *Streetlife China.* Cambridge: Cambridge University Press, 1998.

Dworkin, Andrea. *Woman Hating.* New York: Dutton, 1974.

Dyer, Richard. "The White Man's Muscles." In *Race and the Subject of Masculinities,* edited by Harry Stecopoulos and Michael Uebel, 286–314. Durham: Duke University Press, 1997.

Eastman, Lloyd E. *Family, Fields, and Ancestors: Constancy and Change in China's Social and Economic History, 1550–1949.* New York: Oxford University Press, 1988.

Ebrey, Patricia. *Confucianism and Family Rituals in Imperial China.* Princeton: Princeton University Press, 1990.

Echols, Alice. "The New Feminism of Yin and Yang." In *Powers of Desire: The Politics of Sexuality,* edited by Ann Barr Snitow, Christine Stansell, and Sharon Thompson, 439–459. New York: Monthly Review Press, 1983.

Edelman, Lee. *Homographesis: Essays in Gay Literary and Cultural Theory.* New York: Routledge, 1994.

Edwards, Louise. "Constraining Women's Political Work with 'Women's Work.'" In *Chinese Women: Working and Living,* edited by Anne McLaren, 109–130. London: RoutledgeCurzon, 2004.

———. "From Gender Equality to Gender Difference: Feminist Campaigns for Quotas for Women in Politics." *Twentieth Century China* 24, no. 2 (1999): 69–105.

———. *Men and Women in Qing China: Gender in* The Red Chamber Dream. Leiden: E. J. Brill, 1994. Reprint, Honolulu: University of Hawai'i Press, 2001.

———. "Narratives of Race and Nation in China: Women's Suffrage in the Early Twentieth Century." *Women's Studies International Forum* 25, no. 6 (2002): 619–630.

———. "Women Warriors and Amazons of the Mid Qing Texts *Jinghua yuan* and *Honglou meng.*" *Modern Asian Studies* 29, no. 2 (1995): 225–255.

Elvin, Mark. "Tales of *Shen* and *Xin:* Body-person and Heart-mind in China During the Last 150 Years." In *Fragments for a History of the Human Body, Part 2,* edited by Michael Feher, Ramona Naddaff, and Nadia Tazi, 267–349. New York: Zone Books, 1989.

Epstein, Maram. "Inscribing the Essentials: Culture and the Body in Ming–Qing Fiction." *Ming Studies* 41 (1999): 6–36.

———. *Competing Discourses: Orthodoxy and Authenticity in Late-Imperial Chinese Fiction.* Cambridge, MA: Harvard University Asia Center, 2001.

Erens, Patricia, ed. *Issues in Feminist Film Criticism.* Bloomington: Indiana University Press, 2002.

Ershiwu shi [The Twenty-five Histories]. Shanghai: Shanghai guji chubanshe, 1986.

Fairbank, John K., and Edwin O. Reischauer. *China: Tradition and Transformation.* Boston: Houghton-Mifflin, 1978.

Fan Boqun, ed. *Zhongguo jinxiandai tongsu wenxueshi* [A History of Modern Chinese Popular Literature]. Nanjing: Jiangsu jiaoyu chubanshe, 1999.

Fang Xuan. " 'Tie furen' zan" [In Praise of the "Iron Lady"]. *Renmin ribao,* November 11, 1979.

Farquhar, Judith. *Appetites: Food and Sex in Post-socialist China.* Chapel Hill: Duke, 2002.

———. *Knowing Practice: The Clinical Encounter of Chinese Medicine.* Boulder: Westview Press, 1994.

Fiedler, Leslie. *Freaks: Myths and Images of the Secret Self.* New York: Simon and Schuster, 1978.

Finnane, Antonia. "Looking for the Jiang Qing Dress." *Fashion Theory,* forthcoming.

Fiske, John. "Television: Polysemy and Popularity." *Critical Studies in Mass Communication* 3 (1986): 391–408.

Fong, Tak-ho. "Highs and Lows for Women as Two are Promoted but Men Get All the Ministries." *South China Morning Post,* March 18, 2003.

Foucault, Michel. *Discipline and Punish: The Birth of the Prison.* Translated by Alan Sheridan. Harmondsworth: Penguin, 1977.

———. *The History of Sexuality Volume 1: An Introduction.* 1978. Translated by Robert Hurley. London: Penguin, 1990.

———. "Nietzsche, Genealogy, History." In *The Foucault Reader,* edited by Paul Rabinow, 76–100. Harmondsworth: Penguin, 1986.

Freud, Sigmund. "Fetishism." In *Sexuality and the Psychology of Love,* 107–132. New York: Collier, 1966.

Frow, John. *Time and Commodity Culture: Essays in Cultural Theory and Postmodernity.* Oxford: Clarendon Press, 1997.

Furth, Charlotte. "Androgynous Males and Deficient Females: Biology in Sixteenth and Seventeenth Century China." *Late Imperial China* 9, no. 2 (1988): 1–31.

———. "Blood, Body and Gender: Medical Images of the Female Condition in China." *Chinese Science* 7 (1986): 43–65.

———. "Concepts of Pregnancy, Childbirth and Infancy in Ch'ing Dynasty China." *Journal of Asian Studies* 46 (February 1987): 7–35.

———. *A Flourishing Yin: Gender in China's Medical History, 960–1665.* Berkeley: University of California Press, 1999.

———. "From Birth to Birth: The Growing Body in Traditional Chinese Medicine." In *Chinese Views of Childhood,* edited by Anne Behnke Kinney, 157–192. Honolulu: University of Hawai'i Press, 1995.

Gaines, Jane. "White Privilege and Looking Relations: Race and Gender in Feminist Film Theory." In Erens, *Feminist Film Criticism,* 197–214.

Gao Hongxing. *Chanzu shi* [A History of Footbinding]. Shanghai: Wenyi chubanshe, 1995.

Gao, Minglu, ed. *Inside/Out: New Chinese Art.* Berkeley: University of California Press, 1998.

Gaonkar, Dilip Parameshwar. *Alternative Modernities.* Durham: Duke University Press, 2001.

———. "On Alternative Modernities." In *Alternative Modernities,* 1–23. Durham: Duke University Press, 2001.

Gatens, Moira. *Imaginary Bodies: Ethics, Power, and Corporeality.* London: Routledge, 1996.

Gian Jia-shin. "Huanchu nütongzhi: jiuling niandai Taiwan nütongzhide lunshu xinggou yu yundong jijie" [Bringing Out Taiwan Lesbians: Lesbian Discourses and Movements in Taiwan 1990–1996]. MA thesis, National Taiwan University, 1996.

Goffman, Erving. *Stigma: Notes on the Management of Spoiled Identity.* Middlesex: Penguin, 1968.

Goldin, Paul R. *The Culture of Sex in Ancient China.* Honolulu: University of Hawai'i Press, 2002.

Goldstein, Joshua. "Mei Lanfang and the Nationalization of Peking Opera, 1912–1930." *positions: east asia cultures critique* 7, no. 2 (1999): 377–420.

Government Information Office. "The Republic of China Celebrates Taiwan Film's Success at the Oscars." March 26, 2001. http://www.gio.gov.tw/taiwan-website/7-av/anglee/os_4.htm (accessed January 7, 2003).

———. "The Story of Taiwan." http://www.gio.gov.tw/info/taiwan-story/economy/eframe/frame3.htm (accessed September 30, 2003).

Grosz, Elizabeth A. *Volatile Bodies: Toward a Corporeal Feminism.* Bloomington: Indiana University Press, 1994.

Halberstam, Judith. *Female Masculinity.* Durham: Duke University Press, 1998.

Hall, Catherine. "Missionary Stories: Gender and Ethnicity in England in the 1830s and 1840s." In *Cultural Studies,* edited by Lawrence Grossberg, Cary Nelson, and Paula A. Treichler, 240–276. New York: Routledge, 1992.

Hall, Radclyffe. *The Well of Loneliness.* New York: Anchor Books, 1990.

Hamamoto, Darrell Y. *Monitored Peril: Asian Americans and the Politics of TV Representation.* Minneapolis: University of Minnesota Press, 1994.

Han Lü. "Tan *Yesou puyan*" [On *Yesou puyan*]. *Taibai yuekan* 1, no. 12 (1935): 594–599.

Hanawa, Yukiko, and Naoki Sakai, eds. "Specters of the West and the Politics of Translation." Special issue, *Traces: A Multilingual Journal of Cultural Theory and Translation*, November 2000.

Hansen, Miriam Bratu. "Benjamin and Cinema: Not a One-Way Street." *Critical Inquiry* 25, no. 2 (1999): 306–330.

Haraway, Donna J. "A Manifesto for Cyborgs: Science, Technology, and Socialist Feminism in the 1980s." *Socialist Review* 80 (1985): 65–108.

———. *Modest_Witness@Second_Millenium: FemaleMan_Meets_OncoMouse*. New York: Routledge, 1997.

———. *Simians, Cyborgs, and Women*. New York: Routledge, 1991.

Hardt, Michael, and Antonio Negri. *Empire*. Cambridge, MA: Harvard University Press, 2000.

Hay, John. "The Body Invisible in Chinese Art?" In Zito and Barlow, *Body, Subject and Power*, 42–77.

———, ed. *Boundaries in China*. London: Reaktion Books, 1994.

———. "The Human Body as a Microcosmic Source of Macrocosmic Values in Calligraphy." In *Theories of the Arts in China*, edited by Susan Bush and Christian Murck, 74–102. Princeton: Princeton University Press, 1983.

Hayles, N. Katherine. *How We Became Posthuman: Virtual Bodies in Cybernetics, Literature, and Informatics*. Chicago: University of Chicago Press, 1999.

He Gangde. *Chunming menglu* [Dream Record of the Capital]. Taiyuan: Shanxi guji chubanshe, 1997.

Heinrich, Larissa N. "Handmaids to the Gospel: Lam Qua's Medical Portraiture." In *Tokens of Exchange: The Problem of Translation in Global Circulations*, edited by Lydia Liu, 239–275. Durham: Duke University Press, 2000.

———. *The Afterlife of Images: Translating the Pathological Body between China and the West*. Duke University Press, forthcoming.

Hessney, Richard. "Beautiful, Talented and Brave: Seventeenth-century Scholar-Beauty Romances." Ph.D. diss., Columbia University, 1979.

Hinsch, Bret. *Passions of the Cut Sleeve: The Male Homosexual in China*. Berkeley: University of California Press, 1990.

Hochschild, Arlie. *The Managed Heart: Commercialization of Human Feeling*. Berkeley: University of California Press, 2003.

Hong Mengkai. "Lingjiao buxiya, baihou dan mingxin—hou xiandai guandian zhong de pili budaixi" [Learning from Baudrillard, Visiting Jameson—Pili *Po-te-hi* from the Viewpoint of Postmodernism]. In *Huang haidai yishu yantao hui ziliao ji* [Papers Presented at the Conference on the Art of Huang Haidai], National Taipei Arts University, October 31–November 1, 2002.

hooks, bell. *Black Looks: Race and Representation*. Boston: South End Press, 1992.

Hou Jian. "*Yesou puyan* de biantai xinli" [The Perverse Psychology of the *Yesou puyan*]. In *Zhongguo gudian wenxue luncong* [A Collection of Essays on Classical Chinese Literature], edited by Wang Meng'ou, vol. 3, 97–112. Taipei: Zhongwai wenxue, 1975.

Hsia, C. T. "Residual Femininity: Women in Chinese Communist Fiction." In *C. T. Hsia on Chinese Literature*, 376–397. New York: Columbia University Press, 2004.

———. "The Scholar-Novelist and Chinese Culture: A Reappraisal of *Ching-hua* yuan." In *Chinese Narrative: Critical and Theoretical Essays,* edited by Andrew H Plaks, 266–308. Princeton: Princeton University Press, 1977.

Hsu, Cho-yun. "A Reflection on Marginality." In Tu Weiming, *The Living Tree: The Changing Meaning of Being Chinese Today,* 239–241.

Hu Shi. "Letter to Qian Xuantong." In "Letters Section," *Xin qingnian* 3, no. 4 (1917): 9.

———. "Lun xiaoshuo ji baihua yunwen" [On Fiction and Vernacular Verse]. *Xin qingnian* 4, no. 1 (1918): 75–79.

———. "Wenxue jinhua guannian yu xiju gailiang" [The Concept of Literary Evolution and Theater Reform]. *Xin qingnian* 5, no. 4 (1918): 308–321.

Hua Wei. "Ming Qing funü juzuo zhong zhi 'ninan' biaoxian yu xingbie wenti" [Male Performance and the Issue of Gender in Ming–Qing Women's Dramatic Works] In *Ming Qing xiqu guoji yantaohui lunwenji* [Collected Papers from the International Conference on Ming–Qing Drama], edited by Wei Hua and Wang Ailing, 573–643. Taipei: Academia Sinica, 1998.

Huang Jinlin (Jinlin Hwang). *Lishi, shenti, guojia: Jindai Zhongguo de shenti xingcheng, 1895–1937* [History, Body, Nation: The Modern Chinese Formation of the Body, 1895–1937]. Taipei: Lianjing, 2000.

Huang Minming. "Taiwan diqu de laodong zhuanxing" [Labor Transformation in the Taiwan Region]. *Zixun shehui yanjiu* 1 (July 2001): 257–278.

Huang Nengfu and Chen Juanjuan. *Zhongguo fuzhuangshi* [A History of Clothing in China]. Beijing: Zhongguo luyou chubanshe, 2003.

Huang Nengyang. "Quanqiuhua shidai li de bentu wenhua gongye: Yi dianshi budaixi we lie" [Native Culture Industries in the Era of Globalization: The Example of Televised Puppet Theater]. MA thesis, National Chung Cheng University, 2001.

Hunter, Jane. *The Gospel of Gentility: American Women Missionaries in Turn-of-the-Century China.* New Haven: Yale University Press, 1984.

Iwabuchi, Koichi. *Recentering Globalization: Popular Culture and Japanese Transnationalism.* Durham and London: Duke University Press, 2002.

Jeffords, Susan. *Remasculinization of America: Gender and the Vietnam War.* Bloomington: Indiana University Press, 1989.

Jia Yijun. *Zhongguo funü chanzu kao* [An Investigation of Chinese Women's Footbinding]. Beijing: Beiping wenhua xieshu, 1925.

"Jiang's Gang Poised to Cement His Legacy." *South China Morning Post,* October 26, 2002.

Jiang Wuchang. "Budaixi jianshi" [A Brief History of *Po-te-hi*]. *Min Su Qu Yi* [Journal of Chinese Ritual, Theatre, and Folklore] 67/68 (1990): 66–126.

Jiang Zemin. "Hongyang minzu yishu, zhenfen minzu jingshen" [Encouraging National Arts, Raising National Spirit]. In *Meiyun Qifeng: Commemorative Essays on the Centennial of Mei Lanfang and Zhou Xinfang,* edited by Mei Lanfang and Zhou Xinfang. Beijing: Zhongguo xiju chubanshe, 1996.

"Jiang Zemin he ta xihuan de sige nüren" [Jiang Zemin and the Four Women He Likes]. *Da Ji Yuan,* October 27, 2002. http://www.epochtimes.com (accessed July 3, 2003).

Judd, Ellen R. *The Chinese Women's Movement: Between State and Market.* Stanford: Stanford University Press, 2002.

Kao, Raye. "Fame by Frame: The Lee Ang Story." *Taipei Review* 51, no. 7 (2001): 54–65.

Kaptchuk, Ted J. *The Web That Has no Weaver: Understanding Chinese Medicine.* New York: Congdon and Weed, 1983.

Kasulis, Thomas P., Roger T. Aimes, and Wimal Dissanayake, eds. *Self as Body in Asian Theory and Practice.* Albany: State University of New York Press, 1993.

Khoo, Olivia. "Anagrammatical Translations: Latex Performance and Asian Femininity Unbounded in Olivier Assayas' *Irma Vep*." *Continuum: Journal of Media and Cultural Studies* (1999): 383–393.

Kinkley, Jeffrey. *The Odyssey of Shen Congwen.* Stanford: Stanford University Press, 1987.

Kleinman, Arthur. "How Bodies Remember: Social Memory and Bodily Experience of Criticism, Resistance and Deligitimation Following China's Cultural Revolution." *New Literary History* 25, no 1 (Winter 1994): 27–48.

Knight, Deirdre Sabina. "Capitalist and Enlightenment Values in 1990s Chinese Fiction: The Case of Yu Hua's *Blood Seller*." *Textual Practice* 16, no. 3 (2002): 547–568.

Ko, Dorothy. "The Body as Attire: The Shifting Meanings of Foot-binding in Seventeenth-century China." *Journal of Women's History* 8, no. 4 (1997): 8–27.

———. "Bondage in Time: Footbinding and Fashion Theory." In *Modern Chinese Literary and Cultural Studies in the Age of Theory: Reimagining a Field*, edited by Rey Chow, 199–226. Durham: Duke University Press, 2000.

———. *Teachers of the Inner Chambers: Women and Culture in Seventeenth-century China.* Stanford: Stanford University Press, 1994.

Ko, Yu-fen. "The Desired Form: Japanese Idol Dramas in Taiwan." In *Feeling Asian Modernities: Transnational Consumption of Japanese TV Dramas*, edited by Koichi Iwabuchi, 107–128. Hong Kong: Hong Kong University Press, 2004.

Kraicer, Shelley. "Time Blossoms, Time Fades." *A Chinese Cinema Page.* 2000. http://www.chinesecinemas.org/inthemood.html (accessed March 25, 2004).

Kuo, Kaiser. "From the Bathhouse to the Box Office: ChinaNow.com Talks to Shower Producer Peter Loehr." *Chinanow.com.* See http://www.Chinanow.com/english/shanghai/city/movies/peterloehr (accessed March 6, 2001).

Kuriyama, Shigehisa. *The Expressiveness of the Body and the Divergence of Greek and Chinese Medicine.* New York: Zone Books, 1999.

Lacan, Jacques. *The Four Fundamental Concepts of Psychoanalysis.* Translated by Alan Sheridan. London: Hogarth Press, 1977.

Lai, Hsiang-yin. "Youyu Beidi" [Betty Blue]. *China Times Online,* December 27, 2003. http://ec.chinatimes.com/scripts/chinatimes/iscstext.exe?DB=ChinaTimes&Function=ListDoc&From=1&Single=1 (accessed January 11, 2004).

Laquer, Thomas. *Making Sex: Body and Gender from the Greeks to Freud.* Cambridge, MA: Harvard University Press, 1991.

Latour, Bruno. *War of the Worlds: What about Peace?* Chicago: Prickly Paradigm Press, 2002.

Laurel, Brenda. *Computers as Theatre.* Reading, MA: Addison-Wesley, 1993.

Leary, Charles Leland. "Sexual Modernism in China: Zhang Jingsheng and 1920s Urban Culture." Ph.D. diss., Cornell University, 1994.

Lee, Linda. *The Bruce Lee Story.* Santa Clarita: Ohara Publications, 1989.
Lee, Leo Ou-fan. "On the Margins of the Chinese Discourse: Some Personal Thoughts on the Cultural Meaning of the Periphery." In Tu Weiming, *The Living Tree: The Changing Meaning of Being Chinese Today,* 221–238.
———. *The Romantic Generation of Modern Chinese Writers.* Cambridge, MA: Harvard University Press, 1973.
———. *Shanghai Modern: The Flowering of a New Urban Culture in China 1930–1945.* Cambridge and London: Harvard University Press, 1999.
Leow, Jason. "Vice-Premier is China's New Health Chief." *The Straits Times,* April 27, 2003.
Lévi, Jean. "The Body: The Daoists' Coat of Arms." Translated by Lydia Davis. In *Fragments for a History of the Human Body, Part 1,* edited by Michael Feher, Ramona Naddaff, and Nadia Tazi, 105–126. New York: Zone Books, 1989.
Levy, Howard S. *Chinese Footbinding: The History of a Curious Erotic Custom.* New York: W. Rawls, 1966.
Liji [The Book of Rites]. Taipei: Taiwan Zhonghua shuju (Minguo 54), 1965.
Li, Shang-jen, ed. *Medicine, Imperialism and Modernity [Yixue, diguo zhuyi yu xiandaixing],* special issue of *Taiwan: A Radical Quarterly in Social Studies [Taiwan shehui yanjiu],* no. 54 (June 2004).
Li Siu Leung. *Cross-dressing in Chinese Opera.* Hong Kong: Hong Kong University Press, 2003.
Li, Wai-yee. *Enchantment and Disenchantment: Love and Illusion in Chinese Literature.* Princeton: Princeton University Press, 1993.
———. "The Late Ming Courtesan: Invention of a Cultural Ideal." In *Writing Women in Late Imperial China,* edited by Chang Kang-i Sun and Ellen Widmer, 46–73. Stanford: Stanford University Press, 1997.
Liao, Ping-hui. "Theorizing the 90s: How Not to Talk About Taiwan in Terms of the World System, Global Cultural Economy, etc." Paper presented at "Re-mapping Taiwan," the Fifth Annual Conference on the History and Culture of Taiwan, University of California, Los Angeles, October 12–15, 2000.
Link, Perry. *Mandarin Ducks and Butterflies: Popular Fiction in Early Twentieth-Century Chinese Cities.* Berkeley: University of California Press, 1981.
Liou Liang-ya. *Yuwang gengyishi: Qingse xiaoshuode zhengzhi yu meixue* [Engendering Dissident Desires: The Politics and Aesthetics of Erotic Fictions]. Taipei: Meta Media, 1998.
Little, John R. *Bruce Lee: A Warrior's Journey.* Chicago: Contemporary Books, 2001.
Little, Mrs. Archibald. *In the Land of the Blue Gown.* First edition 1901. Reprint, London: T. Fisher Unwin, 1908.
———. *Intimate China.* First edition 1898. Reprint, London: Hutchinson and Co., 1901.
Liu, Lydia. *The Clash of Empires: The Invention of China in Modern World Making.* Cambridge, MA: Harvard University Press, 2004.
———. "The Female Body and Nationalist Discourse: Manchuria in Xiao Hong's The Field of Life and Death." In Zito and Barlow, *Body, Subject and Power,* 157–177.
———. *Translingual Practice: Literature, National Culture, and Translated Modernity—China, 1900–1937.* Stanford: Stanford University Press, 1995.

Liu Xiuting. " *'Pili' qi shi lu*" ["Pili" Revelations]. *Biaoyan Yishu* 87 (2000): 44–47.
Liu Yichang. *Duidao* [Intersections]. Translated by Nancy Li. *Renditions* 29–30 (1988): 84–101.
Liu Zhiqin. "Fushi bianqian—fei wenbende shehui sichaoshi" [Changes in Clothing: A Non-Textual History of Social Thought]. *Dongfang wenhua* no. 6 (2000): 101–107.
Lo, Kwai-cheung. "Muscles and Subjectivity: A Short History of the Masculine Body in Hong Kong Popular Culture." *Camera Obscura* 39 (1996): 105–126.
Lorde, Audre. *Sister Outsider: Essays and Speeches*. Freedom, CA: Crossing Press, 1984.
Louie, Kam. *Theorising Chinese Masculinity: Society and Gender in China*. Cambridge: Cambridge University Press, 2002.
Lü Jinyuan. "Taiwan nütongzhi jiubazhi yanjiu" [A research note on Taiwan's lesbian bars]. *Cultural Studies Monthly* 23 (2003). http://www.ncu.edu.tw/~eng/csa/journal/journal_park153.htm.
Luo Yinggong. "Jubu congtan" [Miscellaneous Comments on Theater]. In Zhang Cixi, *Qingdai Yandu liyuan shiliao huibian*, 777–798.
Luomo'an Laoren. "Huaifang ji" [Notes Recalling Flowers]. 1876. Reprinted in Zhang Cixi, *Qingdai Yandu liyuan shiliao huibian*, 581–595.
Ma, Sheng-mei. *The Deathly Embrace: Orientalism and Asian American Identity*. Minneapolis: University of Minnesota Press, 2000.
Mackerras, Colin. *The Rise of Peking Opera, 1770–1870: Social Aspects of the Theatre in Manchu China*. Oxford: Clarendon Press, 1972.
Malkki, Liisa. "Citizens of Humanity: Internationalism and the Imagined Community of Nations." *Diaspora: A Journal of Transnational Studies* 3, no. 1 (1994): 41–68.
Marchetti, Gina. "Essay by Gina Marchetti." In Wong Kar-wai, *In the Mood for Love* DVD, Criterion Collection, 2002.
———. "Jackie Chan and the Black Connection." In *Keyframes: Popular Cinema and Cultural Studies*, edited by Matthew Tinkcom and Amy Villarejo, 137–158. New York: Routledge, 2001.
Marks, Laura U. *Touch: Sensuous Media and Multisensory Theory*. Minneapolis: University of Minnesota Press, 2002.
Martin, Biddy. *Femininity Played Straight*. New York: Routledge, 1996.
Martin, Fran. *Situating Sexualities: Queer Representation in Taiwanese Fiction, Film and Public Culture*. Hong Kong: Hong Kong University Press, 2003.
———, trans. *Angelwings: Contemporary Queer Fiction from Taiwan*. Honolulu: University of Hawai'i Press, 2003.
Massey, Doreen. *Space, Place and Gender*. Minneapolis: University of Minnesota Press, 1994.
Mayne, Judith. *Cinema and Spectatorship*. London: Routledge, 1993.
McClintock, Anne. "The Angel of Progress: Pitfalls of the Term Post-Colonial." *Social Text* 31, no. 31 (1992): 84–98.
———. *Imperial Leather: Race, Gender and Sexuality in the Colonial Context*. New York: Routledge, 1995.
McMahon, Keith. *Causality and Containment in Seventeenth-Century Chinese Fiction*. Leiden: E. J. Brill, 1988.

———. "The Classic 'Beauty-Scholar' Romance and the Superiority of Women." In Zito and Barlow, *Body, Subject and Power*, 227–252.

———. *Misers, Shrews and Polygamists: Sexuality and Male-Female Relations in Eighteenth-Century Chinese Fiction*. Durham: Duke University Press, 1995.

———. "Sublime Love and the Ethics of Equality in a Homoerotic Novel of the Nineteenth Century: *Precious Mirror of Boy Actresses*." *Nan Nü* 4, no. 1 (2002): 70–109.

Mei Lanfang. *Wutai shenghuo sishi nian* [Forty Years on the Stage]. Beijing: Zhongguo xiju chubanshe, 1987.

"Men in Towels: American Film Producer Peter Loehr Comes Clean About the International Success of Director Zhang Yang's Bathhouse Tale 'Shower.'" *Beijing Scene* 6, no. 4, 1999. http://www.beijingscene.com/cissue/feature/feature.html (accessed August 4, 2000).

Meyer, Richard. "Rock Hudson's Body." In *Inside/Out: Lesbian Theories, Gay Theories*, edited by Diana Fuss, 259–288. New York: Routledge, 1991.

Meyers, Richard, Amy Harlib, and Karen Palmer. *From Bruce Lee to the Ninjas: Martial Arts Movies*. New York: Carol Publishing Group, 1991.

Mohanty, Chandra Talpade, Ann Russo, and Lourdes Torres, eds. *Third World Women and the Politics of Feminism*. Bloomington: Indiana University Press, 1991.

Morris, Andrew. "'I Believe You Can Fly': Basketball Culture in Postsocialist China." In *Popular China: Unofficial Culture in a Globalizing Society*, edited by Perry Link, Richard Madsen, and Paul G. Pickowicz, 9–38. Lanham, MD: Rowman and Littlefield, 2002.

Morris, Meaghan. "Learning from Bruce Lee: Pedagogy and Political Correctness in Martial Arts Cinema." In *Keyframes: Popular Cinema and Cultural Studies*, edited by Matthew Tinkcom and Amy Villarejo, 171–186. New York: Routledge, 2001.

Morse, Margaret. "What Do Cyborgs Eat? Oral Logic in an Information Society." In *Virtualities: Television, Media Art, and Cyberculture*, 125–151. Bloomington: Indiana University Press, 1998.

Napier, Susan J. *Anime from Akira to Princess Mononoke*. New York: Palgrave, 2000.

Nathan, Andrew, and Bruce Gilley. *China's New Rulers: The Secret Files*. London: Granta, 2002.

Negri, Antonio. "The Specter's Smile." In *Ghostly Demarcations: A Symposium on Jacques Derrida's Specters of Marx*, edited by Michael Sprinkler, 5–16. London: Verso, 1999.

Newton, Esther. *Margaret Mead Made Me Gay: Personal Essays, Public Ideas*. Durham: Duke University Press, 2000.

———. *Mother Camp: Female Impersonators in America*. Chicago: University of Chicago Press, 1979.

Newton, Esther, and Shirley Walton. "The Misunderstanding: Toward a More Precise Sexual Vocabulary." In Newton, *Margaret Mead*, 167–175.

Nguyen, Tan Hoang. "The Resurrection of Brandon Lee: The Making of a Gay Asian American Porn Star." In *Pornographies On/Scene*, edited by Linda Williams. Durham: Duke University Press, forthcoming.

Nichols, Bill. "Discovering Form, Inferring Meaning: New Cinemas and the Film Festival Circuit." *Film Quarterly* 47, no. 3 (1994): 16–28.

Nochlin, Linda. *The Body in Pieces: The Fragment as a Metaphor of Modernity*. London: Thames and Hudson, 1994.
Nonini, Donald M, and Aihwa Ong. "Chinese Transnationalism as an Alternative Modernity." In Nonini and Ong, *Ungrounded Empires: The Cultural Politics of Modern Chinese Transnationalism*.
Nonini, Donald, and Aihwa Ong, eds. *Ungrounded Empires: The Cultural Politics of Modern Chinese Transnationalisms*. New York: Routledge, 1997.
Ong, Aihwa. "Anthropology, China and Modernities." In *The Future of Anthropological Knowledge*, edited by Henrietta L. Moore, 60-92. London: Routledge, 1996.
———. *Flexible Citizenship: The Cultural Logics of Transnationality*. Durham and London: Duke University Press, 1999.
Orbach, Sharalyn. "Sex and the Single Cyborg: Japanese Popular Culture Experiments in Subjectivity." *Science Fiction Studies* 29, no. 3 (2002): 436-452.
Palumbo, Judy. "From Evangelism to Entertainment: The YMCA, the NBA, and the Evolution of Chinese Basketball." *Modern Chinese Literature and Culture* 14, no. 1 (2002): 178-230.
Pan Guangdan. *Zhongguo lingren xueyuan zhi yanjiu* [A Kinship-based Study of Chinese Actors]. Changsha: Shangwu yinshuguan, 1941.
Pan Xiangchen, ed. *Zhongguo zhengtan nüxing da xunzong* [The Grand Search for Traces of Women on China's Political Platform]. Huhehaote: Neimenggu renmin chubanshe, 1999.
"Panshang zhengtai dianfeng de Wu Yi" [Wu Yi Who Has Climbed the Political Peaks]. *Zaobao.com*, November 20, 2002. http://www.zaobao.com/special/china/congress16/pages/congress16201102b.html (accessed July 3, 2003).
Peng, Hsiao-yan. "Sex Histories: Zhang Jingsheng's Sexual Revolution." In "Feminism/Femininity in Chinese Literature," edited by Hsiao-yan Peng and Whitney Crothers Dilley. Special issue, *Critical Studies* 18 (2002): 159-178.
Pietz, William. "The Problem of the Fetish, I." *Res* 9 (1985): 5-17.
Pili International Multimedia Company. "Pili guoji duo meiti qiye jie" [Introduction to Pili International Multimedia Enterprise]. Publicity pamphlet, 2000.
———. Untitled publicity pamphlet, 2002.
Pomeranz, Kenneth. "Power, Gender, and Pluralism in the Cult of the Goddess of Taishan." In *Culture and State in Chinese History: Conventions, Accommodations, and Critiques*, edited by R. Bin Wong, Theodore Huters, and Pauline Yu, 182-204. Stanford: Stanford University Press, 1997.
Porkert, Manfred. *The Theoretical Foundations of Chinese Medicine: Systems of Correspondence*. Cambridge, MA: MIT Press, 1974.
Prashad, Vijay. "Bruce Lee and the Anti-imperialism of Kung Fu: A Polycultural Adventure." *positions: east asia cultures critique* 11, no. 1 (2003): 51-90.
Pusey, James Reeve. *China and Charles Darwin*. Cambridge, MA: Council on East Asian Studies, Harvard University, 1983.
———. *Lu Xun and Evolution*. Albany: State University of New York Press, 1998.
Qi Rushan. *Xiban* [The Troupes]. Vol. 1, *Qi Rushan quanji* [Memoirs of Qi Rushan]. Taipei: Chongguang wenyi chubanshe, 1954.
Qiu Miaojin. *Eyu shouji* [The Crocodile's Journal]. Taipei: Shibao, 1994.

———. "Linjiedian" [Zero Degree]. In *Guide kuanghuan* [The Revelry of Ghosts], 3–15. Taipei: Lianhe wenxue, 1991.

———. "Bolatu zhi Fa" [Platonic Hair]. In *Guide kuanghuan* [The Revelry of Ghosts], 127–148. Taipei: Lianhe wenxue, 1991. Translated by Fran Martin in *Angelwings: Contemporary Queer Fiction from Taiwan,* 51–73.

Rayns, Tony. "Bruce Lee: Narcissism and Nationalism." In *A Study of the Hong Kong Martial Arts Film: The 4th Hong Kong International Film Festival, April 3–18, 1980, City Hall,* edited by Lau Shing-Hong, 110–112. Hong Kong: The Urban Council, 1980.

———. "Bruce Lee and Other Stories." In *A Study of Hong Kong Cinema in the Seventies,* edited by Li Cheuk-to, 26–29. Hong Kong: The Urban Council, 1984.

Records of the General Conference of the Protestant Missionaries of China Held at Shanghai, May 10–24, 1877. 1879.

Records of the General Conference of the Protestant Missionaries of China Held at Shanghai, May 7–20, 1890. 1890.

Roberts, Claire, ed. *Evolution and Revolution: Chinese Dress 1700s–1900s.* Sydney: Museum of Applied Arts and Sciences, 2000.

Roddy, Stephen. *Literati Identity and Its Fictional Representations in Late Imperial China.* Stanford: Stanford University Press, 1998.

Rodriguez, Hector. "Hong Kong Popular Culture as an Interpretive Arena: The Huang Feihong Series." *Screen* 38, no. 1 (1997): 1–24.

Rofel, Lisa. *Other Modernities: Gendered Yearnings in China After Socialism.* Berkeley: University of California Press, 1999.

Rogaski, Ruth. *Hygienic Modernity: Preserving Health and Preventing Disease in Treaty-Port China.* University of California Press, forthcoming 2003.

Rojas, Carlos. "Cannibalism and the Chinese Body Politic: Hermeneutics and Violence in Cross-cultural Perception." *Postmodern Culture* 12, no. 3 (2002). http://muse.jhu.edu/journals/pmc/v012/12.3rojas.html (accessed March 26, 2004).

———. "Specular Failure and Spectral Returns in Two Films With Maggie Cheung (and One Without)." *Senses of Cinema,* no. 12 (2001). http://www.sensesofcinema.com/contents/01/12/cheung.html (accessed March 25, 2004).

Ropp, Paul S. *Dissent in Early Modern China: Ju-lin wai-shih and Ch'ing Social Criticism.* Ann Arbor: University of Michigan Press, 1981.

Rouzer, Paul. *Articulated Ladies: Gender and the Male Community in Early Chinese Texts.* Cambridge, MA: Harvard University Asia Center, 2001.

Roy, David T. "Introduction." *The Plum in the Golden Vase.* Princeton: Princeton University Press, 1993.

Rupp, Leila J. "Toward a Global History of Same-Sex Sexuality." *Journal of the History of Sexuality* 10, no. 2 (2001): 287–302.

Ruwitch, John. "Chinese Women Making Breakthrough in Politics." *Reuters News,* August 16, 2002.

Sakamoto, Hiroko. "The Cult of 'Love and Eugenics' in May Fourth Movement Discourse." In *positions: east asia cultures critique* 12, no. 2 (2004): 329–376.

———. *The Myth of Nationalism in Modern China: Race, Body and Gender.* Tokyo: Iwanami Shoten, 2004.

Sang, Tze-lan D. *The Emerging Lesbian: Female Same-Sex Desire in Modern China.* Chicago: University of Chicago Press, 2003.

———. "Women's Work and Boundary Transgression in Wang Dulu's Popular Novels." In *Gender in Motion,* edited by Bryna Goodman and Wendy Larson. Rowman and Littlefield, forthcoming.

"SARS Cases Top 2,900." *China Daily,* April 28, 2003.

"SARS Puts New China to the Test." *South China Morning Post,* May 8, 2003.

Schaefer, William. "Relics of Iconoclasm: Modernism, Shi Zhecun, and Shanghai's Margins." Ph.D. diss., University of Chicago, 2000.

Scheibinger, Londa. *Nature's Body: Gender in the Making of Modern Science.* Boston: Beacon Books, 1993.

Schipper, Kristofer. *The Taoist Body.* Translated by Karen C. Duval. Taipei: SMC Publishing, 1993.

Schwartz, Benjamin I. *In Search of Wealth and Power: Yen Fu and the West.* Cambridge, MA: Harvard University Press, 1964.

Schwartz, Hillel. "Torque: The New Kinaesthetic of the Twentieth Century." In *Incorporations,* edited by Jonathan Crary and Sanford Kwinter, 71–126. New York: Zone Books, 1992.

Sedgwick, Eve Kosofsky. *Between Men: English Literature and Male Homosocial Desire.* New York: Columbia University Press, 1985.

———. *Epistemology of the Closet.* London: Penguin, 1990.

Shapiro, Hugh. "The Puzzle of Spermatorrhea in Republican China." *positions: east asia cultures critique* 6, no. 3 (1998): 551–596.

Shen Congwen. "Xin yu jiu" [New and Old]. In *Shen Congwen wenji,* vol. 6, 250–260. Hong Kong: Sanlian, 1985.

Shen Lihui. "Jiyi sanluo le, meiyou shengyin" [Memories Have Scattered, Without a Sound]. In *Qingxing, Hao ji Le.* Modeng tiankong youxian gongsi, audio CD, 1997.

Shen Taimou. "Xuannan lingmeng lu" [A Record of Fragmented Dreams from South of Xuanwu Gate]. In Zhang Cixi, *Qingdai Yandu liyuan shiliao huibian,* 801–810.

Shi, Anbin. *A Comparative Approach to Redefining Chinese-ness in the Era of Globalization.* New York: Edwin Mellen Press, 2003.

Shih, Shu-mei. *The Lure of the Modern: Writing Modernism in Semicolonial China, 1917–1937.* Berkeley: University of California Press, 2001.

———. "The Trope of 'Mainland China' in Taiwan's Media." *positions: east asia cultures critique* 3, no. 1 (1995): 149–183.

Silverman, Kaja. "Fragments of a Fashionable Discourse." In *On Fashion,* edited by Shari Benstock and Susan Ferriss. New Brunswick: Rutgers University Press, 1994.

———. *Male Subjectivity at the Margins.* New York: Routledge, 1992.

Silvio, Teri. "Drag Melodrama/Feminine Public Sphere/Folk Television: 'Local Opera' and Identity in Taiwan." Ph.D. diss., University of Chicago, 1998.

———. "Reflexivity, Bodily Praxis, and Identity in Taiwanese Opera." *GLQ* 5, no. 4 (1999): 585–604.

Sivin, Nathan. "State, Cosmos, and Body in the Last Three Centuries B.C." *Harvard Journal of Asiatic Studies* 55 (1995): 5–37.
———. "Studies of the Body: A Selected, Annotated Bibliography in Process." http://ccat.sas.upenn.edu/~nsivin/bib414.html (accessed January 12, 2005).
Sommer, Matthew. "The Penetrated Male in Late Imperial China: Judicial Constructions and Social Stigma." *Modern China* 23, no. 2 (1997): 140–180.
———. *Sex, Law, and Society in Late Imperial China.* Stanford: Stanford University Press, 2000.
Springer, Claudia. *Electronic Eros: Bodies and Desire in the Postindustrial Age.* Austin: University of Texas, 1996.
Starr, Chloe. "Shifting Boundaries: Gender in *Pinhua baojian*." *Nan Nü* 1, no. 2 (1999): 268–302.
Stevenson, Mark, and Cuncun Wu. "Quilts and Quivers: Dis/covering Chinese Male Homoeroticism." *Tamkang Review* 15.1 (2005): 119–167.
Stewart, Susan. *On Longing: Narratives of the Miniature, the Gigantic, the Souvenir, the Collection.* Durham: Duke University Press, 1993.
Stone, Allucquere Roseanne. *The War of Desire and Technology at the Close of the Mechanical Age.* Cambridge, MA: MIT Press, 1995.
Stone, Charles R. *The Fountainhead of Chinese Erotica: The Lord of Perfect Satisfaction (Ruyijun zhuan).* Honolulu: University of Hawai'i Press, 2003.
Stryker, Susan. "The Transgender Issue: An Introduction." *GLQ* 4, no. 2 (1998): 145–158.
Stuart, Lyn. "Dialogue: The Graffiti Art of 18k." *Beijing Scene* 5, no. 4 (1999). http://www.beijingscene.com/V05I004/feature.feature.html.
"Style Counsel." *South China Morning Post,* July 8, 2004.
Su, Weibu. "Tongren wenhua yuanliu yu Taiwan tongren hudong fazhan gaiyo" [The Origins of *Tongren* Culture and the Development of Taiwanese *Tongren* Activities]. Paper presented at the "Internet Culture and Lifestyle Communities" conference, National Chiaotung University, December 2003. http://www.cc.nctu.edu.tw/ʻcpsun/internet-lifestyle-workshop-schedule.htm.
Szonyi, Michael. "The Cult of Hu Tianbao and the Eighteenth-Century Discourse of Homosexuality." *Late Imperial China* 19, no. 1 (1998): 1–25.
Tang, Xiaobing. *Chinese Modern: The Heroic and the Quotidian.* Durham and London: Duke University Press, 2000.
Tasker, Yvonne. "Fists of Fury: Discourses of Race and Masculinity in the Martial Arts Cinema." In *Race and the Subject of Masculinities,* edited by Harry Stecopoulos and Michael Uebel, 315–336. Durham: Duke University Press, 1997.
Teo, Stephen. "Bruce Lee: Narcissus and the Little Dragon." In *Hong Kong Cinema: The Extra Dimensions,* 110–121. London: The British Film Institute, 1997.
———. "True Way of the Dragon: The Films of Bruce Lee." In *Overseas Chinese Figures in Cinema: The 16th Hong Kong International Film Festival,* edited by Law Kar, 70–80. Hong Kong: The Urban Council, 1992.
———. "Wong Kar-wai's *In the Mood for Love:* Like a Ritual in Transfigured Time." *Senses of Cinema,* no. 13 (2001). http://www.sensesofcinema.com.au/contents/01/13/mood.html (accessed March 25, 2004).

Thomas, Bruce. *Bruce Lee: Fighting Spirit.* Berkeley: Frog, 1994.
Trinh T. Minh-ha. *Shoot for the Contents.* Berkeley: Moon Gift Film, 1991.
Tsai, Ventine [Cai Wenting]. *Xian ge bu chuo: Taiwan xiqu gushi* [Hold that Note! Stories from Taiwan's Stage]. Taipei: Guanghua zazhi [Sinorama], 2004.
Tseng Shu-fen, You Yu-Ching, and Ho Chin-Chang. "New Economy, Underemployment, and Inadequate Employment." *Zixun shehui yanjiu* 3 (2002): 215–237.
Tu Wei-ming. "Cultural China: The Periphery as the Center." In Tu Weiming, *The Living Tree: The Changing Meaning of Being Chinese Today,* 1–34.
———, ed. *The Living Tree: The Changing Meaning of Being Chinese Today.* Stanford: Stanford University Press, 1994.
Tuinistra, Fons. "Shanghai: Ruijin Park." http://www.iht.com/IHT/SUP/TRAVAG/0816-nabes.html (accessed July 8, 2003).
Turkle, Sherry. *Life on the Screen: Identity in the Age of the Internet.* New York: Touchstone, 1995.
Turner, Christina L. "Locating Footbinding: Variations Across Class and Space in Nineteenth and Early Twentieth Century China." *Journal of Historical Sociology* 10, no. 4 (1997): 444–479.
Tuttle, A. H. *Mary Porter Gamewell and Her Story of the Siege in Peking.* New York: Eaton and Mains, 1907.
van Gulik, R. H. *Erotic Colour Prints of the Ming Period: With an Essay on Chinese Sex Life from the Han to the Ch'ing Dynasty (BC 206–AD 1644).* Tokyo, 1951.
Vinograd, Richard. *Boundaries of the Self: Chinese Portraits, 1600–1900.* Cambridge: Cambridge University Press, 1992.
Vitiello, Giovanni. "The Dragon's Whim: Ming and Qing Homoerotic Tales from *The Cut Sleeve.*" *T'oung Pao* 78 (1992): 341–373.
———. "Exemplary Sodomites: Chivalry and Love in Late Ming Culture." *Nan Nü* 2, no. 2 (2000): 207–258.
Volpp, Sophie. "Classifying Lust: The Seventeenth-Century Vogue for Male Love." *Harvard Journal of Asiatic Studies* 61, no. 1 (2001): 77–117.
———. "The Discourse on Male Marriage: Li Yu's 'A Male Mencius' Mother.' " *positions: east asia cultures critique* 2, no. 1 (1994): 113–132.
———. "The Literary Circulation of Actors in Seventeenth-Century China." *Journal of Asian Studies* 61, no. 3 (2002): 949–984.
Wakeman, Frederic, Jr. *The Great Enterprise: The Manchu Reconstruction of the Imperial Order in the Seventeenth Century.* Berkeley: University of California Press, 1985.
Wang, David Der-wei. *Fin-de-siècle Splendor: Repressed Modernities of Late Qing Fiction, 1849–1911.* Stanford: Stanford University Press, 1997.
———. "Impersonating China." *Chinese Literature: Essays, Articles, Reviews* 25 (2003): 133–163.
Wang Dongxia, ed. *Cong changpao magua dao xinzhuang gelu* [From Scholar's Gown and the Magua to Western-Style Pants and Leather Shoes]. Chengdu: Sichuan renmin chubanshe, 2003.
Wang Dulu. *Tie ji yin ping* [Iron Steed, Silver Vase]. Taipei: Yuanjing, 2001.

———. *Wo hu cang long* [Crouching Tiger, Hidden Dragon]. 3 vols. Hong Kong: Tiandi tushu gongsi, 2000.
Wang, Georgette. "Televised Puppetry in Taiwan: An Example of the Marriage Between a Modern Medium and a Folk Medium." In *Continuity and Change in Communication Systems: An Asian Perspective*, edited by Georgette Wang and Wimal Dissanayake, 169–179. Norwood: Ablex Publishing, 1984.
Wang, Jing. *High Culture Fever: Politics, Aesthetics, and Ideology in Deng's China*. Berkeley: University of California Press, 1996.
Wang Jun. *Cheng ji* [City Record]. Beijing: Shenghuo, dushu, xinzhi sanlian shudian, 2003.
Wang Mengsheng. *Liyuan jiahua* [Anecdotes from the Theater World]. Shanghai: Shangwu yinshuguan, 1916.
Wang, Min'an. "Body Politics in the SARS Crisis." In *positions: east asia cultures critique* 12, no. 2 (2004): 587–596.
Wang, Ning. "The Mapping of Chinese Postmodernity." In Dirlik and Zhang, *Postmodernism and China*, 21–40.
Wang, Ping. *Aching for Beauty: Footbinding in China*. Minneapolis: University of Minnesota Press, 2000.
Wang Qiongling. *Qingdai sida caixue xiaoshuo*. Taipei: Taiwan shangyin chubanshe, 1997.
———. "*Yesou puyan* yanjiu" [Research on the *Yesou puyan*]. MA thesis, Dongwu University, Taiwan, 1986.
Wang Rumei, Li Zhaoxun, and Yu Fengshu, eds. *Zhang Zhupo piping* Jin Ping Mei. Ji'nan: Qi Lu shushe, 1991.
Wang, Shuo. *Please Don't Call Me Human*. Herts, UK: No Exit Press, 2000.
Wang, Xiaoying. "Hong Kong, China and the Question of Postcoloniality." In Dirlik and Zhang, *Postmodernism and China*, 89–119.
Ware, Vron. *Beyond the Pale: White Women, Racism, and History*. London: Verso, 1992.
Wedell-Wedellsborg, Anne. "One Kind of Chinese Reality: Reading Yu Hua." *Chinese Literature: Essays, Articles, Reviews* 18 (1996): 129–143.
Wei, Hui. *Shanghai Baby*. Washington, DC: Washington Square Press, 2002.
Wiest, Nailene Chou. "Scientist Rises through Ranks to the Top Echelons of Power." *South China Morning Post*, March 19, 2003.
Wong Kar-wai. "Poet of Time: Interview with Wong Kar-wai." By Tony Rayns. *Sight and Sound* 5, no.9 (1995): 12–15.
———. Interview. By Ciment and Niogret. *In the Mood for Love*. DVD special edition. Criterion Collection, 2002.
Wood, Robin. "Two Films by Martin Scorsese." In *Hollywood from Vietnam to Reagan*, 245–269. New York: Columbia University Press, 1986.
Wu, Cuncun. *Homoerotic Sensibilities in Late Imperial China*. London: RoutledgeCurzon, 2004.
———. *Ming–Qing shehui xing'ai fengqi* [Sex and Sensibility in Ming and Qing Society]. Beijing: Renmin wenxue chubanshe, 2000.
Wu Hung. *Exhibiting Experimental Art in China*. Chicago: The David and Alfred Smart Museum of Art, 2000.

———. "Ruins, Fragmentation and the Chinese Modern/Postmodern." In Gao, *Inside/Out*, 59–66.

———. *Transience: Chinese Experimental Art at the End of the Twentieth Century.* Chicago: The David and Alfred Smart Museum of Art, 1999.

Wu Hung, and Katherine T. Tsiang. *Body and Face in Chinese Visual Culture.* Cambridge, MA: Harvard East Asian Monograph Series, 2004.

Wu Jingzi. *Ru lin wai shi/Wu Jingzi zhu; Zhang Huijian jiaozhu; Cheng Shifa cha tu.* Beijing: Renmin wenxue chubanshe, 1958. Reprint 1985.

Wu, Kuang-ming. *On Chinese Body Thinking.* Leiden: Brill, 1997.

"Wu Yi." *Renmin wang, people* 2003. http://www.people.com.cn/GB/paper81/9356/867109.html (accessed July 19, 2003).

"Wu Yi: Zhiguo qiaxu 'qi nüzi' " [Wu Yi: Exactly What the Country's Governance Needs, an Astonishing Woman]. *Phoenix TV.* March 18, 2003. http://www.phoenixtv.com/home/zhuanti/xwshj/lhtbbd/lhtbbdx/200303/18/41641.html (accessed July 3, 2003).

Wu, Yi-Li. "Ghost Fetuses, False Pregnancies, and the Parameters of Medical Uncertainty in Classical Chinese Gynecology." In *Nan Nü* 4, no 2 (October 1, 2002): 170–206.

"Wu Yi linwei shou kang yi ji xianfeng" [Wu Yi Takes the Daring Vanguard Position in Combating a Critical Epidemic]. *Yazhou zhoukan,* April 14–20, 2003, 13–17.

"Wu Yi xiao nüzi huo chuqu le" [The Little Girl Wu Yi Goes for Broke]. *Kan Zhongguo,* May 1, 2003. http://www.secretchina.com/news/articles/3/5/1/41317.html (accessed July 22, 2003).

Xia Jingqu. *Yesou puyan* [A Rustic's Words of Exposure]. 152 chapters. Woodblock Piling Huizhenlou edition, 1881. Reprint, Taipei: Tianyi chubanshe, 1985.

———. *Yesou puyan.* 154 chapters. 1882. Reprint, Beijing: Renmin Zhongguo chubanshe, 1993.

———. *Yuanzhe guben Yesou puyan* [Original, Old-style Rustic's Words of Exposure]. 100 chapters. Shanghai: Hao qingnian shudian, 1933.

Xiafu. "Youchang bu yi xiangti binglun" [It Is Inappropriate to Place Actors and Prostitutes on a Par]. *Beijing zhengzong aiguo bao* [Beijing True Patriotism News], no. 1929, (May 6, 1912).

Xiao, Ping. "Ministers Hold Court in Tennis Team." *China Daily,* February 13, 2003.

Xiaomingxiong. *Zhongguo tongxing'ai shilu, xiuding ben* [History of Homosexuality in China, Revised Edition]. Hong Kong: Fenhong sanjiao chubanshe, 1997.

Xie Yanchen. "Xizao jiang shangwang paimai" [*Shower* Will be Sold on the Internet]. *Remin ribao wangluoban,* February 23, 2000.

Xu Sinian. *Wang Dulu pingzhuan* [The Life and Work of Wang Dulu]. Forthcoming.

Xu Sinian, and Liu Xiang'an. *Wuxia danghui bian* [Book on Martial Arts and Secret Society Fiction). In Fang Boqun, *Zhongguo jinxiandai,* 439–735.

Xu Zhan. "Nüren rang shijie keai" [Women Make the World Lovable]. *Zhongguo guotu ziyuan bao,* March 18, 2002.

Yan Xiaohong. "Zhongguo fuzhuang wushinian bian zouqu" [Fifty Years of Changes in Chinese Clothing]. *Zhongguo xiaofeizhe bao,* July 19, 2002.

Yang Mian. "Jinjin shi tan jianzhu" [Just Talking about Buildings]. *Jinre xianfeng* 12 (2002): 129–132.
Yang, Xiaobin. *The Chinese Postmodern: Trauma and Irony in Chinese Avant-Garde Fiction.* Ann Arbor: The University of Michigan Press, 2002.
Yao Lingxi. *Caifei lu: Zhongguo funü chanzu shiliao* [Picking Radishes: A History of Chinese Women's Footbinding]. Tianjin: Shidai gongsi, 1936.
Yates, Robin. "Body, Space, Time, and Bureaucracy: Boundary Creation and Control Mechanisms in Early China." In Hay, *Boundaries in China,* 56–80.
Yau, Esther, ed. *At Full Speed: Hong Kong Cinema in a Borderless World.* Minneapolis: University of Minnesota Press, 2001.
Yau, Esther, and Kim Hyung Kyung. "Asia/Pacific Cinemas: A Spectral Surface." Special issue, *positions: east asia cultures critique* 9, no. 2 (2001).
Ye Zhongai, ed. *Zhongguo funü lingdao rencai chengzhang he kaifa yanjiu* [Research on the Maturing and Development of Talent Among China's Women Leaders]. Shanghai: Kexue jishu wenxian, 2000.
Yeh, Wen-hsin. "Introduction: Interpreting Chinese Modernity, 1900–1950." In *Becoming Chinese: Passages to Modernity and Beyond,* edited by Wen-hsin Yeh, 1–28. Berkeley: University of California Press, 2000.
Yen, Hsiao-pei. "Body Politics, Modernity and National Salvation: Modern Girls and the New Life Movement." *Asian Studies Review,* forthcoming.
Yi Shifu. "Wanggu chou qu: Wei gelang Mei Lanfang zuo" [Song of Everlasting Sorrows: For Mei Lanfang the Singing Boy]. In Zhang Cixi, *Qingdai Yandu liyuan shiliao huibian,* 744–746.
Yilansheng. "Cemao yutan" [Leisured Conversations with Hat Removed]. 1879. Reprinted in Zhang Cixi, *Qingdai Yandu liyuan shiliao huibian,* 597–626.
Youhuansheng. "Jinghua bai'er zhuzhici" [One Hundred and Twenty Folklore Poems from the Capital]. In *Zhonghua zhuzhici* [Chinese Folklore Poems], edited by Lei Mengshui, vol. 2, 273–297. Beijing: Beijing guji chubanshe, 1997.
Young, Robert. *White Mythologies: Writing History and the West.* London: Routledge, 1990.
Yu Chien-ming. "Jindai Zhongguo nüzi jianmei de lunshu (1920–1940 niandai)" [Modern Chinese Women's Beauty Discourse, 1920–1940]. In *Jindai Zhongguo de funü yu shehui (1600–1950)* [Modern Chinese Women and Society, 1600–1950], edited by Yu Chien-ming, 141–172. Taipei: Academia Sinica, 2003.
———. "Jindai Zhongguo nüzi tiyu guan chutan" [Modern Chinese Women and Sport: A Preliminary Discussion]. *Xin shixue* 7, no. 4 (1996): 119–158.
Yu Dafu. *Ta shi yige ruo nüzi* [She Was a Weak Woman]. In *Yu Dafu Quanji* [The Complete Works of Yu Dafu], vol. 2, 279–375. Zhejiang: Zhejiang wenyi chubanshe, 1992.
Yu, Hua. *Chronicle of a Blood Merchant.* Translated by Andrew F. Jones. New York: Pantheon, 2003.
———. "One Kind of Reality." Translated by Jeanne Tai. In *Running Wild: New Chinese Writers,* edited by David Der-wei Wang and Jeanne Tai, 21–68. New York: Columbia University Press, 1994.

Yuan Mei. *Censored by Confucius: Ghost Stories by Yuan Mei.* Translated by Kam Louie and Louise Edwards. Armonk: M. E. Sharpe, 1996.

Yue, Ming-bao. "Gendering the Origins of Modern Chinese Fiction." In *Gender and Sexuality in Twentieth-Century Chinese Literature and Culture,* edited by Lu Tonglin. Albany: State University of New York Press, 1993.

Zeitlin, Judith. "Disappearing Verses: Writing on Walls and Anxieties of Loss." In *Writing and Materiality in China: Essays In Honor of Patrick Hanan,* edited by Lydia Liu and Judith Zeitlin. Cambridge, MA: Harvard East Asia Center, Harvard-Yenching Institute, 2003.

Zeng Pu. *Niehai hua* [Flower In a Sea of Sin]. Shanghai: Shanghai guji chubanshe/Xinhua shudian Shanghai faxingsuo faxing, 1991.

Zhang Cixi. "*Beiping liyuan zhuzhi ci huibian*" [Collected Folklore Poems from the Theater Circles of Beijing]. In *Qingdai Yandu liyuan shiliao huibian,* 1171–1182.

———, ed. *Qingdai Yandu liyuan shiliao huibian* [Collected Historical Sources on the Pear Garden in Peking during the Qing Dynasty]. Beijing: Renmin wenxue chubanshe, 1988.

———. "Yanguilai yi suibi" [Jottings from the Returning Swallow Studio]. In *Qingdai Yandu liyuan shiliao huibian,* 1215–1253.

Zhang Jiliang. "*Jintai canlei ji*" [Record of the Golden Stage's Unwept Tears]. In Zhang Cixi, *Qingdai Yandu liyuan shiliao huibian,* 225–253.

Zhang Li. "*Nüxing wang zhang zai fazhan*" [Women's Websites Developing]. *Jiangsu jingji bao,* March 5, 2002.

Zhang, Xudong. *Chinese Modernism in the Era of Reforms.* Durham: Duke University Press, 1997.

Zheng Meili. *Nü'er quan: Taiwan nütongzhide xingbie, jiating yu quannei shenghuo* [Girls' Circle: Taiwan's Lesbians' Gender, Home life and Subcultural Practice]. Taipei: Nüshu wenhua, 1997.

Zhong, Xueping. *Masculinity Besieged? Issues of Modernity and Male Subjectivity in Chinese Literature of the Late Twentieth Century.* Durham: Duke University Press, 2000.

"Zhongguo de tie niangzi Wu Yi xiao dang'an" [Brief Dossier on China's Iron Lady, Wu Yi]. *Yazhou zhoukan,* April 14–20, 2003.

Zhou Zan. "Chuntian" [Spring]. *Shichao* 11–12 (2002).

Zhou Zuoren. "Lun Zhongguo jiuxi zhi yingfei" [On the Necessity to Abolish Traditional Chinese Theater]. *Xin qingnian* 5, no. 5 (1918): 526–527.

———. "Rende wenxue" [Literature of Humans]. In *Zhongguo xiandai wenxue guan* [Views on Modern Chinese Literature], edited by Zhou Zuoren, 225–232. Beijing: Huaxia chubanshe, 2000. Originally published in *Xin qingnian* 5, no. 6 (1918): 575–584.

———. *Zhitang huixiang lu* [Memoirs of Zhitang]. Taipei: Longwen chuban gufei youxian gongsi, 1989.

———. "*Zhongguo xijude santiao lu*" [Three Possible Paths of Chinese Theater]. 1924. Reprinted in *Jingju yishu congtan bainian lu* [A Collection of Remarks on Peking Opera in the Past Hundred Years], edited by Wen Sizai. Shijianzhuang: Hebei jiaoyu chubanshe, 1999.

Zito, Angela. "Silk and Skin: Significant Boundaries." In Zito and Barlow, *Body, Subject and Power,* 103–130.

———. *Of Body and Brush: Grand Sacrifice as Text/Performance in Eighteenth-century China.* Chicago: University of Chicago Press, 1997.

———. "Secularizing the Pain of Foot-binding in China: Missionary and Medical Stagings of the Universal Body." In *Secularisms at the Millennium,* edited by Ann Pellegrini and Janet Jakobsen. New York: New York University Press, forthcoming.

Zito, Angela, and Tani E. Barlow, eds. *Body, Subject and Power in China.* Chicago: University of Chicago Press, 1994.

"Zuxie xinren nü zhuxi Xue Li: 'Wo jiang wei xinxin er gongzuo' " [Newly Appointed Football Association Woman Chairperson Xue Li: "I Will Work With Confidence!"]. *Sport158 on-line.* See http://www.sport158.com/news/2003-6-11-103412.html (accessed July 8, 2003).

Filmography

As Tears Go By (Mongkok ka mun), Wong Kar-wai, Hong Kong, 1988.
Ashes of Time (Dong xie xi du), Wong Kar-wai, Hong Kong/China/Taiwan, 1994.
Beijing Bastards (Beijing zazhong), Zhang Yuan, China, 1992.
Big Boss, The (Tangshan daxiong) a.k.a. *Fists of Fury*, Lo Wei [Luo Wei], Hong Kong, 1971.
Breakfast at Tiffany's, Blake Edwards, USA, 1961.
Center Stage (Ruan lingyu) a.k.a. *Actress*, Stanley Kwan, Hong Kong, 1992.
Chungking Express (Chongqing senlin), Wong Kar-wai, Hong Kong, 1994.
Comrades: Almost a Love Story (Tian mimi), Peter Chan, Hong Kong, 1996.
Crouching Tiger, Hidden Dragon (Wo hu cang long), Ang Lee, Taiwan, 2000.
Days of Being Wild (A Fei zheng zhuan), Wong Kar-wai, Hong Kong, 1991.
Dingzihu [Demolition and Rehousing], Zhang Yuan, China, 1988.
Enter the Dragon, Robert Clouse, Hong Kong/USA, 1973.
Face/Off, John Woo, USA, 1997.
Fallen Angels (Duoluo tianshi), Wong Kar-wai, Hong Kong, 1995.
Farewell My Concubine (Bawang bie ji), Chen Kaige, 1993.
Fist of Fury (Jingwumen) a.k.a. *The Chinese Connection,* Lo Wei [Luo Wei], 1972.
Game of Death, The, Robert Clouse, USA/Hong Kong, 1978.
Good Men, Good Women (Hao Nan, Hao Nü), Hou Hsiou-Hsien, Taiwan/Japan, 1995.
Guonian huijia [Seventeen Years], Zhang Yuan, China, 1999.
Happy Together (Chun guang zha xie),Wong Kar-wai, Hong Kong, 1997.
Highway, The (Dalu), Sun Yu, China, 1934.
In the Mood for Love (Huayang nianhua),Wong Kar-wai, Hong Kong/France/Thailand, 2000.
Irma Vep, Olivier Assayas, France, 1996.
Qingchun wu hui [No Regrets About Youth], Zhou Xiaowen, China, 1992.
Queen of Sports (Tiyu huanghou), Sun Yu, China, 1934.

Shower (Xi zao), Zhang Yang, China, 1999.
Spring in a Small City (Xiao cheng zhi chun), Fei Mu, China, 1948.
Springtime in a Small Town (Xiao cheng zhi chun), Tian Zhuangzhuang, China/Hong Kong/France, 2002.
Tiexi qu [Tiexi District: West of Tracks], Wang Bing, China, 2003.
2046, Wong Kar-wai, Hong Kong, 2004.
Way of the Dragon, The (Meng long guo jiang) a.k.a. *The Return of the Dragon*, Bruce Lee, Hong Kong, 1972.
Woman Basketball Player No.5 (Nülan wu hao), Xie Jin, China, 1957.
Xiaowu, Jia Zhangke, China, 1997.
Yang + Yin: Gender in Chinese Cinema, Stanley Kwan, Hong Kong, 1996.
Yingxiong [Hero], Zhang Yimou, China, 2002.

Contributors

Chris Berry is Professor of Film and Television Studies at Goldsmiths College, University of London. His research specialization is screen-based media in East Asia. He is the author of *Postsocialist Cinema in Post-Mao China: The Cultural Revolution after the Cultural Revolution* (Routledge, 2004); coauthor with Mary Farquhar of *Cinema and the National: China on Screen* (forthcoming, Columbia University Press and Hong Kong University Press); editor of *Chinese Films in Focus: 25 New Takes* (British Film Institute, 2003); coeditor with Feii Lu of *Island on the Edge: Taiwan New Cinema and After* (Hong Kong: Hong Kong University Press, 2005); coeditor with Fran Martin and Audrey Yue of *Mobile Cultures: New Media and Queer Asia* (Duke University Press, 2003); and translator of Ni Zhen, *Memoirs from the Beijing Film Academy: The Origins of China's Fifth Generation Filmmakers* (Duke University Press, 2002).

Louise Edwards is Professor of China Studies at the University of Technology in Sydney and is Convener of the Australian Research Council's Asia Pacific Futures Research Network. Her publications include *Men and Women in Qing China* (E. J. Brill, 1994, University of Hawai'i Press, 2001); *Recreating the Literary Canon: Communist Critiques of 'The Red Chamber Dream'* (Projekt Verlag, 1995); *Censored by Confucius* (M. E. Sharpe, 1996) (with Kam Louie); *Women in Asia: Tradition, Modernity and Globalisation* (Allen and Unwin and University of Michigan Press, 2000) (with Mina Roces); and *Women's Suffrage in Asia* (Routledge, 2004) (with Mina Roces). In addition she has published numerous articles on gender in China, including several on the women's suffrage movement in Republican China.

Maram Epstein is Associate Professor of Ming–Qing literature at the University of Oregon. Her research focuses on the ideological and aesthetic constructions of meaning in late imperial Chinese texts. Her first book, *Competing Discourses: Orthodoxy, Authenticity, and Engendered Meanings in Late Imperial Chinese Fiction* (2001) explores symbolic representations of gender and sexual desire, and she is currently researching the representations of filial passions in eighteenth-century fiction, exemplary biographies, and legal discourse.

Larissa Heinrich is Lecturer in Chinese Studies at the University of New South Wales, Sydney, Australia. She works on the intersections of Chinese visual culture, literature, and medical history in the nineteenth and twentieth centuries. In addition to her contribution to Lydia Liu's edited volume *Tokens of Exchange: The Problem of Translation in Global Circulations* (Duke University Press, 2000), Heinrich's work is forthcoming in the journals *History of Photography* and *positions: east asia cultures critique*. Her book *The Afterlife of Images: Translating the Pathological Body Between China and the West, 1726–1926* is forthcoming from Duke University Press.

Olivia Khoo is Lecturer in Film and Media Studies at the University of New South Wales, Sydney, Australia. Her research interests include the cinemas of Hong Kong, China, Taiwan, and Singapore, cultural studies and popular culture in East and Southeast Asia, and Asian-Australian cultural production. She is currently completing a book manuscript on modern exoticism and representations of diasporic Chinese femininity.

Fran Martin is Lecturer in Cultural Studies at the University of Melbourne, Australia. Her research interests include Chinese-language film and mass media and the politics of sexuality in contemporary Chinese societies. She is author of *Situating Sexualities: Queer Representation in Taiwanese Fiction, Film and Public Cultures;* translator of *Angelwings: Contemporary Queer Fiction from Taiwan* (University of Hawai'i Press, 2003); coeditor with Chris Berry and Audrey Yue of *Mobile Cultures: New Media and Queer Asia* (Duke University Press, 2003); and coeditor with Peter Jackson, Mark McLelland, and Audrey Yue of *AsiaPacifiQueer: Rethinking Gender and Sexuality in the Asia-Pacific* (University of Illinois Press, forthcoming). Her current research project investigates lesbian representation in the transnational Chinese popular cultures that circulate between Hong Kong, Taiwan, and the People's Republic of China.

Jami Proctor-Xu is a Ph.D. candidate in the Department of East Asian Languages and Cultures at the University of California, Berkeley. Her research interests include ruins, contemporary Chinese poetry, urban space, Chinese film, and feminist theory.

Tze-lan D. Sang is Associate Professor of Chinese Literature in the Department of East Asian Languages and Literatures at the University of Oregon. Her research interests include gender and sexuality, modern Chinese fiction (elite and popular), urban theory, Chinese cinema, and performance studies. She is author of *The Emerging Lesbian: Female Same-Sex Desire in Modern China* (University of Chicago Press, 2003). She is currently working on a book-length manuscript on Chinese urban culture and popular fiction of the early twentieth century.

Teri Silvio is an Assistant Research Fellow at the Institute of Ethnology, Academia Sinica, Taiwan. She is an anthropologist whose research interests include media technologies and social change, gender and sexuality, and the historical relationship between popular and intellectual culture in Taiwan. Her recent ethnographic projects have focused on transforming local performance genres, including opera and puppetry.

Mark Stevenson received his Ph.D. in Anthropology from the University of Melbourne, Australia, and teaches Asian Studies at Victoria University of Technology, Melbourne. His current research interests include the anthropology of outer-northeastern Tibet (Amdo), late imperial Chinese literature (including the reception and translation of Chinese erotic literature in English), and travel poetry in Chinese history. He is the author of *Many Paths: Searching for Old Tibet in New China*.

Cuncun Wu received her Ph.D. in Chinese Studies from the University of Melbourne, Australia. She is Lecturer in Chinese in the School of Languages, Cultures and Linguistics at the University of New England, Australia. She has published widely on gender and sexuality in premodern China, in both Chinese and English. Her latest book is *Homoerotic Sensibilities in Late Imperial China* (RoutledgeCurzon, 2004).

Angela Zito received her Ph.D. in East Asian Studies from the University of Chicago, after training in both anthropology and history. She is Associate Professor of Anthropology and Director of Religious Studies at New York University and founding co-director of The Center for Religion and Media there. She coedited, with Tani Barlow, *Body, Subject and Power in China* (University of Chicago Press, 1994) and is author of *Of Body and Brush: Grand Sacrifice as Text/Performance in 18th c. China* (University of Chicago Press, 1997). Her current research centers on religion in China under economic reform; documentary film making around issues of social justice in China; and on filial piety and social distinctions in old Huizhou (present-day Huangshan, Anhui). She remains committed to understanding social life through its embodied performances over time.

John Zou is Assistant Professor of Chinese at Bates College in Maine. His research interests include modern and late imperial Chinese literature, and he is currently completing a book manuscript on May Fourth theater, tentatively entitled *Of Crimes and Men: The Legal Imaginary in Chinese Drama, 1919–1942*.

Index

Abbas, Akbar, 118–119, 236–237
Abe, Kobo, 177
Age of Flowers, The. See *Huayang de nianhua*
Aiqing dingze taolun ji [Collected Discussions on the Rules of Love], 72–73
All-China Women's Federation [Fulian], 8, 149, 155
America/American culture, 4, 12, 31, 53, 56–57, 117–119, 128, 155, 181, 183, 208, 212, 217–233. *See also* missionaries
Anagnost, Ann, 19n. 11, 116
Analects, The. See *Lun yu*
Anderson, Marston, 127–128
androgyny, 37, 62–63, 71. *See also* transgender
Anecdotes from the Theater World. See *Liyuan jiahua*
Appadurai, Arjun, 9
Apter, Emily, 25–26
Arthur, Paul, 242–243
Asian-American identity, 223–233
"Asianness"/Asian identity, 232, 249
Assayas, Olivier, 245

Ba Jin, 42–45, 56
Barlow, Tani, 7–8, 31, 35
Barmé, Geremie, 247
Barthes, Roland, 204–205, 236
Baudelaire, Charles, 246
Beijing zhengzong aiguo bao [Beijing True Patriotism News], 52
Benjamin, Walter, 241, 245–246
Berger, Patricia, 7
Berry, Chris, 15, 122, 218–234

Bhabha, Homi, 29, 38
Big Boss, The [*Tangshan daxiong*], 218–233
Biographies of Women, The. See *Lienü zhuan*
"Bolatu zhi fa" ["Platonic Hair"], 177–178, 183–191
Bolter, Jay David, 213
Book of Rites, The. See *Liji*
Bordwell, David, 242
Breakfast at Tiffany's, 233
breast-binding, 71, 180, 190–191
Britain/British culture, 31, 43, 118–119, 157, 222
Brownell, Susan, 116
Buddhism/Buddhists, 7, 30, 60, 195, 202
bunraku [Japanese theatre], 204–205

Carradine, David, 220
Center Stage [*Ruan Lingyu*], 245
Chan, Alfred, 152
Chan, Anson, 147
Chan, Charlie, 223
Chan, Jachinson, 222–224, 232
Chan, Jackie, 223–225
Chan, Peter, 241
Chao, Antonia Yengning, 181, 190–191
Chen Duxiu, 54, 59n. 33, 109
Chen Kaige, 46
Chen Zhili, 152
Chenbao fukan [Morning News Literary Supplement], 72
Cheng Yu, 221, 226, 230
Cheung, Jacky, 79–80
Cheung Man-yuk, Maggie, 9, 123, 235–249
Chiao Hsiung-Ping, 222, 233n. 7

China Daily, 148
China Times, 177
Chinese Communist Party (CCP), 146–149
"Chineseness"/Chinese identity, 4–5, 13–14, 20n. 36, 74–76, 79–80, 119–120, 123–124, 127, 133–134, 143–144, 235, 247, 249
Chow, Rey, 117–119, 236, 240, 249
Christianity, 22, 26–30, 34–35, 62–63, 214. *See also* missionaries
Chronicle of a Blood Merchant, 129–134
Chu Ying-chi, 222
Chungking Express [*Chongqing senlin*], 239, 247–248
Chunming menglu [Dream Record of the Capital], 54–55
clothing/costume, 17, 30–32, 79–96, 107–108, 147, 154–156, 180, 225, 229, 243–245, 251n. 40. *See also* cross-dressing; fashion
Clouse, Robert, 221
Collected Discussions on the Rules of Love. See Aiqing dingze taolun ji
colonialism/coloniality, 9–10, 24, 29, 33–38, 57, 60, 68, 80, 84, 116, 118–119, 123, 220–233, 239. *See also* missionaries; postcolonialism/postcoloniality
Comrades: Almost a Love Story [*Tian mimi*], 241
Confucius/Confucianism, 16–17, 27, 42–43, 45, 52, 60–76, 83–84, 95–96, 103, 105, 111n. 10, 146, 202, 208, 224
Cooper, B. B., 21, 23
COSplay. *See* subcultures
Crocodile's Journal, The. See Eyu shouji
cross-dressing, 4, 12, 17–18, 46, 79–96, 98–110. *See also dan* actors; *xianggong; xianggu*
Crouching Tiger, Hidden Dragon [*Wo hu cang long*], 17–18, 98–112

Da jiyuan news bulletin, 152
Daly, Mary, 33–36, 38
dan actors, 15, 17, 42–57, 58n. 13, 59n. 36, 201. *See also* cross-dressing; prostitution; *siyu*
Daoism, 7, 73, 195, 202, 207
Deleuze, Gilles, 208–209, 213
Deng Xiaoping, 118, 127, 143–144

Deng Yingchao, 148
Derrida, Jacques, 214–215, 240–242, 250n. 18
Despeux, Catherine, 7
Desser, David, 223
diaspora, 4–5, 11–14, 19n. 21, 37, 115, 117, 119, 123, 126–144, 147, 160n. 44, 221–222, 225, 235–237, 249, 250n. 9
Ding Juan, 149
Ding, Naifei, 181, 183, 186, 188
Dong'Ou nühaojie [The Heroine from Eastern Europe], 62
Dream of the Red Chamber. See Hong lou meng
Dream Record of the Capital. See Chunming menglu
Du Yuesheng, 81
Dworkin, Andrea, 33–36, 38

Edwards, Louise, 121–122, 146–161
Ellis, Havelock, 73. *See also* sexology
Elvin, Mark, 7
Ensler, Eve, 37
Enter the Dragon, 220–227
Epstein, Maram, 8, 10, 16–17, 45, 60–78, 123
Eyu shouji [The Crocodile's Journal], 177–178, 183

Face/Off, 241
Family, The. See Jia
fandom, 195–215
Fang Min, 153–154
Farewell My Concubine [*Bawang bie ji*], 46
Farquhar, Judith, 116–117
fashion, 30–32, 37, 146–149, 153, 154–156, 159. *See also* clothing/costume; cross-dressing; footbinding
Fei Mu, 247
feminism, 15, 18n. 10, 24–30, 33–38, 122, 178–181, 183, 187–188, 214–215, 219. *See also* gender; lesbian feminism
Feng Gengguang, 81, 87
fetish/fetishism, 15, 21–38, 186, 242–245, 248
film, 3–4, 98–100, 121–124, 162–176, 218–234, 235–252; spectatorship and, 123, 227–233, 235–252. *See also kung fu* genre; *wuxia* genre

Fist of Fury [*Jingwumen*], 218–233
Flower in a Sea of Sin. See *Niehai hua*
footbinding, 13, 14–15, 21–38, 43, 71, 104, 190
Forbes magazine, 147
Foucault, Michel, 6–9, 15, 18n. 10, 180
Four Books for Women, The. See *Nü sishu*
Frankenstein myth, 133–134
Freud, Sigmund, 4, 24–25. *See also* psychoanalysis
Frow, John, 126–128, 133–134, 140–141
Fu Manchu, 223
Fulian. *See* All-China Women's Federation
Furth, Charlotte, 6, 63
Fuseli, Henry, 22

Game of Death, The, 220
Gamewell, Mary Porter, 21
Gao Hongxing, 30
Gaonkar, Dilip Parameshwar, 9
gender, 7–8, 11–13, 16–18, 31–32, 62–63, 120–124, 146–161, 197–198, 214–215; female masculinity, 12, 17–18, 98–112, 121–122, 153, 156–157, 177–194; femininity, 7–8, 21–41, 146–161, 180–181; male femininity, 12, 46–47, 79–97, 122–123, 153, 227–233; masculinity, 16–17, 60–78, 79–97, 146–147, 151–153, 182–183, 218–234. *See also* feminism; *wen* and *wu* traditions
Genet, Jean, 177
Gian Jia-shin, 181–183, 186
Gide, Andre, 177
Gilley, Bruce, 149–150, 152
Gilmartin, Christine, 147
globalization, 4, 9, 120, 144–145, 197
Goffman, Erving, 184–185, 191, 197
Golden Lotus, The. *See* Jin ping mei
Goldstein, Joshua, 56
Good Youth Publishing House, 60, 72–73
Grusin, Richard, 213
Guanchang xianxingji [Officialdom Unmasked], 53
Guangxu Emperor, 73, 86
guanxi [(sexual) connections], 149–152
Guide kuanghuan [The Revelry of Ghosts], 177–178
guzhuang xi [classical costume plays], 89, 93–95

hairstyle, 42–43, 72, 94, 107, 112n. 20, 155, 184–191, 192n. 1, 205
Hall, Radclyffe, 177
Han Chinese, 18n. 5, 30, 40n. 46, 83–84, 104–105, 111n. 10
Han Lü, 60
Hansen, Miriam Bratu, 241
Hao qingnian shudian [Good Youth Publishing House], 60, 72–74
Happy Together, 239, 247–248
Hardt, Michael, 197
Hayles, Katherine, 214
He Gangde, 54–55
Hegel, G. W. F., 24
Heinrich, Larissa, 3–20, 115–125, 126–145
Heroine from Eastern Europe, The. *See Dong'Ou nühaojie*
Highway, The [*Dalu*], 225
History of Homosexuality in China. *See Zhongguo tongxing'ai shilu*
HIV/AIDS, 117, 143
homophobia, 35, 122, 187, 191, 219, 229–233. *See also* homosexuality
homosexuality, 42–59, 151–152, 177–194, 218–234. *See also* homophobia; lesbianism; *nütongxinglian/ nütongxhing'ai*; *tongxinglian/tongxing'ai*
Hong lou meng [Dream of the Red Chamber], 63
Hou Jian, 60–61
Hu Shi, 53–54, 81, 108–109
Huang Haidai, 199
Huang Junxiong, 199, 207
Huang Qianghua, 199
Huang Wenze, 199, 203, 207–208, 211
Huang Yan, 135
huapu ["flower guides"], 47
Huayang de nianhua [The Age of Flowers], 245
Hulk, 3–4
Huxley, T. H., 167

IMAR Film Company, Ltd., 174
In the Mood for Love [*Huayang nianhua*], 123–124, 235–249
Incredible Hulk, The, 3
Irma Vep, 245, 251n. 35
Iron Steed, Silver Vase. See *Tie ji yin ping*

Japan/Japanese culture, 8–10, 60, 68, 82, 88–89, 118–119, 126, 155, 177, 195, 200, 202, 204–205, 210, 220, 225–227, 230–231, 247
Jarman, Derek, 177
Jia [The Family], 42–45, 56
Jiang Qing, 148, 151, 155–156
Jiang Zemin, 80, 152
jianghu ["rivers and lakes"; the mythical *wuxia* underworld], 99, 102, 104, 224. See also *wuxia* genre
Jiaqing period, 47–48, 53
Jin ping mei [The Golden Lotus], 54, 67, 73
Jinghe House, 86
Jingtai canleiji [Record of the Golden Stage's Unwept Tears], 48
Jiuweigui [The Nine-Tailed Turtle], 53
Journey to the West. See *Xi you ji*

Kazakh Chinese, 103, 105
Khoo, Olivia, 123–124, 235–252
Kim Kyung, 239–240
Kleinman, Arthur, 116
Knight, Deirdre, 130
Ko, Dorothy, 31
koa-a-hi [Taiwanese opera], 210–212
Krafft-Ebing, Richard von, 179
Kraicer, Shelley, 243–244
kung fu genre, 218–234. See also martial arts
Kuriyama Shigehisa, 6
Kwan, Stanley, 240, 245
Kwan Tak-hing, 225

Lacan, Jacques, 232, 238–239. See also psychoanalysis
Lanling Youhuansheng, 50
Lau, Andy, 79–80, 82, 96
Lau, Emily, 147
Laurel, Brenda, 203
Lee Ang, 3–4, 17–18, 98–99, 110
Lee, Brandon, 229, 232
Lee, Bruce, 9, 11, 15, 122–123, 218–233
Lee, Leo Ou-fan, 11–12, 76n. 1, 119
Legend of the Sacred Stone. See *Sheng shi chuanshuo*
lesbian feminism, 122, 177–194. See also feminism

lesbianism, 56, 122, 177–194. See also homosexuality; lesbian feminism; *nütongxinglian/nütongxing'ai*
Leung Chiu-wai, Tony, 235–249
Li, Jet, 223–225
Li Lili, 225
Li Ping-bing, Mark, 247
Li Zhiwang, 137–138
Liao Ping-hui, 118
Lienü zhuan [The Biographies of Women], 98
Liji [The Book of Rites], 83
Lin Biao, 148
"*Linjiedian*" ["Zero Degree"], 177–178, 183–191
Liou Liang-ya, 178, 186, 188
literature, 11–12, 15, 60–78, 85, 98–112, 128–134, 177–194. See also May Fourth cultural and literary movements; modernism
Little, Mrs. Archibald [Alicia Little], 27–32
Liu Bannong, 109
Liu Jenpeng, 181, 183, 186, 188
Liu, Lydia, 9, 19n. 15
Liu Shaoqi, 155
Liyuan jiahua [Anecdotes from the Theater World], 54
Lo, Kwai-cheung, 222–225
Loehr, Peter, 174
Lorde, Audre, 33–34
Louie, Kam, 62–63, 158, 224–229
Lü, Annette, 147
Lü Jinyuan, 187
Lu Xun, 12, 15, 109, 126–129
Lun yu [The Analects], 83

Ma Sheng-mei, 223, 230–232
Mackerras, Colin, 45
Manchu Chinese, 30, 68, 75, 82–84, 99, 102–107
manga, 200
Mao Zedong, 7–8, 79, 96, 115–124, 148, 151
Marks, Laura U., 236
martial arts, 12, 17–18, 25–26, 66–67, 98–110, 123, 199, 218–234
Martin, Fran, 3–20, 115–125, 177–194
Marx, Karl, 24, 240
Marxism, 118
May Fourth cultural and literary move-

ments, 11–12, 19n. 21, 53, 61–62, 72–74, 79–96, 108–109. *See also* literature; modernism; New Culture movement
McMahon, Keith, 61, 179
medicine, 10, 17, 73–74; Chinese, 5–6, 31–32; western, 5–6, 21–24, 30–31
Mei Lanfang, 12, 17–18, 50, 56–57, 79–96, 109, 122
Mei Qiaoling, 86–87, 90–91
Meide [Beauty] publishing house, 72–73
Ming dynasty, 45, 67–68, 83, 198
Mishima, Yukio, 177
missionaries, 15, 21, 26–33
modernism, 10–11, 19n. 21, 20n. 36, 38, 118, 177. *See also* May Fourth cultural and literary movements; postmodernism
modernity, 22–24, 52, 56, 116, 241, 245–246; alternative, 9–13; Hong Kong, 118–119, 240, 243–248; late, 4, 115; post-1949 Chinese, 117–124; Republican era Chinese, 5–18, 42–45, 57; Taiwanese, 118. *See also* colonialism/coloniality; modernism; postcolonialism/postcoloniality; postmodernism/postmodernity
modernization, 8, 11, 15–16, 42–59, 62–63, 74–76, 118, 162–174, 225–227
Mongol Chinese, 105
Morris, Meaghan, 232–233
Murakami, Haruki, 177

Nanye. *See* Shen Taimou
Nathan, Andrew, 150, 152
nationalism, 6, 10, 74–75, 79–89, 116–117, 121, 207–208, 221–223, 230, 247–248; and nation-building, 13, 16, 42–57, 79–97, 225–226
Natural Feet Society, 27–28
Needham, Joseph, 5
Negri, Antonio, 197, 240–241
New Culture movement, 53, 108–109. *See also* May Fourth cultural and literary movements
New Life movement, 83, 112n. 19
New Yorker, The, 128–129, 134
Nichols, Bill, 241–242
Niehai hua [Flower in a Sea of Sin], 53, 86
Nine-Tailed Turtle, The. See Jiuweigui

Nochlin, Linda, 22–23, 25
Nonini, Donald, 119
Norris, Chuck, 220–221, 230–232
nostalgia, 22–23, 56–57, 72, 111n. 10, 123–124, 162–176, 235–252
Noyes, Rev., 27
Nü sishu [The Four Books for Women], 98
Nüpengyou [Girlfriend] magazine, 182
nütongxinglian/nütongxing'ai, 177–194. *See also* lesbianism

Officialdom Unmasked. See Guanchang xianxingji
One Kind of Reality. See Xianshi de yi zhong
Ong, Aihwa, 9, 117, 119
organ trade, 13, 120–121, 126–145
Original, Old-style Rustic's Words of Exposure. See Yuanzhu guben Yesou puyan

Pan Guangdan, 50–51
Pan Xianchen, 146
Peking [Beijing] Opera, 15–16, 46, 50, 56, 79–96, 169
Peng Donghui, 135–136, 140
Peng Yu, 120, 141–144
Perovskaia, Sofia, 62
Phoenix TV, 148
Pietz, William, 24–25, 33, 38
Pili International Multimedia Company, 195–215
Pinhua baojian [The Precious Mirror of Ranked Flowers], 48, 53
"Platonic Hair." See *"Bolatu zhi fa"*
Pokemon, 204
Porkert, Manfred, 5
postcolonialism/postcoloniality, 9, 15, 24, 36–38, 84, 119, 123. *See also* Bhabha, Homi; colonialism/coloniality
postmodernism/postmodernity, 19n. 21, 118, 124, 177. *See also* modernity: late; post-structuralism
post-structuralism, 7–9, 18n. 10, 36. *See also* postmodernism/postmodernity
po-te-hi [Taiwanese puppet theater], 195–215
Prashad, Vijay, 222–223, 230

Precious Mirror of Ranked Flowers, The.
See *Pinhua baojian*
Proctor-Xu, Jami, 121, 162–176
prostitution, 13, 16, 29, 42–59, 87–88, 97n. 12, 220. *See also* cross-dressing; *xianggong/xianggu*
psychoanalysis, 24–25. *See also* Freud, Sigmund; Lacan, Jacques

Qi Rushan, 94
Qian Xuantong, 59nn. 30, 33, 109
Qianlong period, 47, 53, 55
Qiu Miaojin, 15, 122, 178–191
Queen of Sports [*Tiyu huanghou*], 122, 225

race/racism, 4, 31, 33–36, 220–223, 227
Rayns, Tony, 221, 227–230, 242–243
Record of Fragmented Dreams from South of Xuanwu Gate, A. See *Xuannan lingmeng lu*
Record of the Golden Stage's Unwept Tears. See *Jingtai canleiji*
Revelry of Ghosts, The. See *Guide kuanghuan*
Rofel, Lisa, 9, 117, 122
Rogaski, Ruth, 6
Rojas, Carlos, 245
Romance of the Three Kingdoms. See *Sanguo yanyi*
Rouge, 240
Rulin waishi [The Scholars], 53, 57n. 5
Rustic's Words of Exposure, A. See *Yesou puyan*
Ruwitch, John, 154

Sang, Tze-lan D., 8, 12, 17–18, 56, 98–112, 122, 179
Sanguo yanyi [Romance of the Three Kingdoms], 198–199
SARS, 117, 148
Saussure, Ferdinand de, 198, 203–204, 214–215
Schipper, Kristof, 7
Scholars, The. See *Rulin waishi*
Schwartz, Hillel, 212
Sex Histories. See *Xingshi*
sexology, 8, 15, 73, 122, 179–181, 183, 192n. 3. *See also* Ellis, Havelock; *Xingshi*

Shanghai Biennale, 135
"She Was a Weak Woman." See "*Ta shi yige ruo nüzi*"
shen ["body-self"], 7
Shen Congwen, 129–130
Shen Lihui, 163
Shen Taimou [Nanye], 48–49
Sheng shi chuanshuo [Legend of the Sacred Stone], 199
Shi Yanwen, the Confucian Swordsman of Yunzhou. See *Yunzhou Da Ru Xia–Shi Yanwen*
Shih, Shu-mei, 10–11, 125n. 20
Shower [*Xi zao*], 121, 162–176
Shuihuzhuan [The Water Margin], 53
Silvio, Teri, 120–121, 195–217
Sivin, Nathan, 6
siyu [private residences of *dan* actors], 47, 49–56, 58n. 21, 59n. 36. *See also dan* actors
South China Morning Post, 152
sport, 115–116, 121–122, 146–149, 153, 158–159
Spring in a Small City [*Xiao cheng zhi chun*], 247
Springtime in a Small Town [*Xiao cheng zhi chun*], 247
Stevenson, Mark, 8, 10, 12, 15–17, 42–59, 80
Stone, Alluquere Rosanne, 214
Straits Times, The, 148
subcultures: COSplay subculture, 120–121, 195–215; T/*po* subcultures, 177–191; *tongrenzhi* [fan fiction and art] subcultures, 200, 209, 213
"Suifu Appeal," 32–33
Sun Yat-sen, 83, 251n. 40
Sun Yuan, 120, 141–144

T/*po* subcultures. *See* subcultures
"*Ta shi yige ruo nüzi*" ["She Was a Weak Woman"], 179–180
Taiwan Television Company (TTV), 199
Talmadge, Rev. Mr., 26
Tan Hoang Nguyen, 229
Tang Xiaobing, 14, 19n. 21, 20nn. 27, 36, 124
Tarkovsky, Andrei, 177
Tasker, Yvonne, 223–224

techno-culture, 3–4, 120–121, 126–130, 195–215
Teo, Stephen, 222, 227–230
Thatcher, Margaret, 157, 160n. 45
Tian Chunhang, 48
Tian Jiyun, 54, 97n. 19
Tian Zhuangzhuang, 247
Tie ji yin ping [Iron Steed, Silver Vase], 102–103, 106
Time magazine, 148
tongxinglian/tongxing'ai [homosexuality], 8, 15–16, 55–57, 77n. 29, 177–194. See also homosexuality; lesbianism; *nütongxinglian/nütongxing'ai*
transgender, 8, 17–18, 98–110, 181. See also androgyny
Trinh T. Minh-ha, 162
Tsiang, Katherine, 117
Tu Wei-ming, 14, 119
Turner, Matthew, 223
2046, 249, 250n. 13, 252n. 55

Unschuld, Paul, 5
U.S.A. See America/American culture

Vinograd, Richard, 7
Volpp, Sophie, 45

Wang, David Der-wei, 19n. 21, 72, 117
Wang Dulu, 17–18, 98–112
Wang Guangmei, 155
Wang Mensheng, 54–55
Wang Ping, 36–37
Wang Xiaoying, 118–119
Wang Zheng, 154
Warner Brothers, 220–221
Water Margin, The. See *Shuihuzhuan*
Way of the Dragon, The [*Meng long guo jiang*], 218–233
Wedell-Wedellsborg, Anne, 131–133
Well of Loneliness, The, 177
wen and *wu* traditions, 61, 64, 123, 158, 224–230. See also gender
westernization, 16, 20n. 39, 42–45, 51–55, 61–62, 109. See also modernity; modernization
Woman Basketball Player Number 5 [*Nü-lan wu hao*], 122, 225–226

Women of China, 147
Women zhi Jian [Between Us], 182
Wong Kar-wai, 123–124, 235–249
Woo, John, 224, 241
Wood, Robin, 230
Wu Cuncun, 8, 10, 12, 15–17, 42–59, 80
Wu Hung, 117, 163, 246–247
Wu Yi, 121, 146–159
Wu Yi-Li, 6
wuxia genre [knights-errant fiction], 72, 195, 199. See also film; *jianghu*

Xi you ji [Journey to the West], 73, 86, 151, 199
Xia Jingqu, 60–76
Xian Film Studios, 174
xianggong/xianggu [catamite-role male actors/prostitutes], 9, 15–16, 42–59, 86, 122. See also cross-dressing; *dan* actors; prostitution
Xianshi de yi zhong [One Kind of Reality], 130–134
Xiaomingxiong, 55
Xiaowu, 167, 175n. 7
xin ["heart-mind"], 6, 7
Xin qingnian [New Youth], 53, 109
Xingshi [Sex Histories], 72–73
Xu Zhen, 136–137
Xuannan lingmeng lu [A Record of Fragmented Dreams from South of Xuanwu Gate], 48–49
Xue Li, 159

Yan Fu, 167
Yang Mian, 167–168
Yang Shang-kun, 150
Yau, Esther, 239–241
Ye Qun, 148
Yeh Wen-hsin, 10–11, 20n. 28
Yesou puyan [A Rustic's Words of Exposure], 9, 16–17, 60–78, 122–123
yiguan [clothing and headdress doctrine], 82–85, 89
yin/yang, 31, 61–69, 75
youth cultures, 12, 195–215
Yu Dafu, 15, 122, 179, 190
Yu Hua, 120, 124–144
Yu Ximan, 155

Yuanzhu guben Yesou puyan [Original, Old-style Rustic's Words of Exposure], 60–78
Yunzhou Da Ru Xia–Shi Yanwen [Shi Yanwen, the Confucian Swordsman of Yunzhou], 199

"Zero Degree." See "*Linjiedian*"
Zhang Che, 225
Zhang Dali, 137, 173
Zhang Jingsheng, 72–73
Zhang Yang, 121, 162–176
Zheng Meili, 181

Zhongguo tongxing'ai shilu [History of Homosexuality in China], 55
Zhou Enlai, 148
Zhou Xinfang, 79
Zhou Xuan, 245
Zhou Zan, 172–173
Zhou Zouren, 85–91, 95, 109
Zhu Rongji, 147
Zhu Xiafeng, 86
Zhu Yu, 120, 137–144
Zito, Angela, 7, 8, 10, 14–15, 18n. 5, 22–41
Zou, John, 12, 17–18, 79–97

Production Notes for Martin/*Embodied Modernities*

Cover design by Santos Barbasa Jr.

Text Design by University of Hawai'i Press production staff using Minion and Gill Sans

Text composition by Tseng Information Systems, Inc.

Printing and binding by The Maple-Vail Book Manufacturing Group

Printed on 60 lb. Text White Opaque, 426 ppi